MEDIA ETHICS

CONRAD C. FINK

The University of Georgia

ALLYN AND BACON

Boston London Toronto Sydney Tokyo Singapore

❖

This book is for those men and women
who try so very hard and who give so very much,
sometimes even their lives,
to get the news and to get it right.

Senior Editor: Stephen P. Hull
Production Editor: Christine M. Harrington
Cover/Text Designer: Thomas Mack
Production Buyer: Pamela D. Bennett
Electronic Text Management: Marilyn Wilson Phelps, Matthew Williams,
Jane Lopez, Karen L. Bretz
Marketing Manager: Lisa Kimball

A Simon & Schuster Company
Needham Heights, Mass. 02194

Previously published under the title *Media Ethics*, © 1988 by McGraw-Hill, Inc.

LIBRARY OF CONGRESS CATALOGING-IN-PUBLICATION DATA

Fink, Conrad C.
Media ethics / Conrad C. Fink.
p. cm.
Includes bibliographical references and index.
ISBN 0-02-337753-4
1. Mass media—Moral and ethical aspects. 2. Journalistic ethics.
3. Mass media—Social aspects. I. Title.
P94.F47 1995
174—dc20 94-7522
CIP

PRINTED IN THE UNITED STATES OF AMERICA
10 9 8 7 6 5 4 3 2 1 99 98 97 96 95

CONTENTS

Preface

This book is written for all who are interested in the mass media and their profound effect on our individual lives and our society as a whole.

The book should have special appeal to two broad groups of readers:

First, those of you who seek careers in news, information and entertainment, as reporters, writers, editors or media managers, and those who want to work in other communications sectors, perhaps as advocates in public relations or advertising.

Second, the book should appeal to discerning media consumers—readers, viewers and listeners who want to better understand the media and to think critically, yet constructively, about the flow of information and the open marketplace of ideas so crucial to our democracy.

For each of you (and your teachers), I hope this book provokes stimulating study and discussion. Above all, I hope the book inspires your personal development of a rational decision-making process through which you can judge media performance for yourself and arrive independently at answers to crucial questions of ethics and social responsibility confronting the media today.

The study of ethics can be divided into three approaches:

1. Metaethics is inquiry into the meaning of abstract terms such as right and wrong, and what is just or unjust, in an effort to define the characteristics of ethics. Pinpointing ethical values, not making moral judgments, is the goal.
2. Normative ethics has moral behavior as a goal, and study is aimed at developing general principles through which it can be achieved.
3. Applied ethics is the attempt to solve actual real-life ethical problems, using the guidance and understanding derived from study of metaethics and normative ethics.

I have four principal goals in this book:

First, to help you understand, through case studies and examples, complex ethical questions and their many forms in the media. Ethicists call this sensitization or consciousness-raising.

Second, I will illustrate how media professionals handle actual ethical issues. I will describe the decision-making process journalists follow under pressure of deadlines and competition, what factors they consider when facing ethical dilemmas and how they solve them. This is called descriptive ethics.

Third, I want to help you move beyond merely understanding what media professionals do, and into deciding for yourself how the media should act when confronted with ethical questions. This is called prescriptive normative ethics.

Fourth, I hope to help you assemble your own decision-making formula or process, a step-by-step plan you'll need for spotting, evaluating and deciding ethical questions for yourself. You'll find I frequently encourage you to make your own independent call on ethical judgments, which is termed autonomous moral reasoning. Accepting personal responsibility for deciding what is the right thing to do and then doing it is the fiber of ethical journalism and moral conduct.

For those of you seeking media careers, I urge the same methodical approach to studying ethics that you take to learning reporting, writing and editing. A reasoned, well-developed sense of right and wrong—plus the courage to stick to your ethical principles—is as important to your career preparation as are strong reporting and writing skills.

For media consumers, learning ethics is central to effectively using the media. You must learn to select responsible, credible newspapers, magazines and broadcast outlets, then critically judge their performance in news, information and entertainment. But there is more: The day is gone when consumers had to passively accept whatever the media dish out. Readers, viewers and listeners can—and should—bring pressure to bear on the media to ensure they don't go astray ethically or fail in their journalistic mission.

Throughout this book, and with aid from your instructor, you should make special effort to understand the process of decision making in ethics. Don't concentrate so intensely on the outcome of an ethical dilemma or case study that you fail to understand the various methods of moral reasoning used. Learn to identify and understand structures of moral reasoning used by others and you'll advance toward developing your own decision-making structure.

I urge you to view ethical problems through the eyes of others, using their approaches to moral reasoning, even though those approaches may be foreign—or contrary—to your beliefs and principles. It's too easy (and a cop-out) to merely stand firm in a discussion of ethics, repeating, "I believe . . . I believe . . ." Making great effort to truly understand the views of others can lend new sophistication to your own moral reasoning.

The importance of studying ethics is clear. Effective flow of information and a truly open marketplace of ideas are crucial in our democracy. Our mass media are the principal providers of both. But unethical performance by the media can lead to such public distrust that the system breaks down. It is imperative that you of the next generation—media professionals and media consumers alike—don't let it break down.

Overall, media performance today in news and information is better than ever. Newspapers and magazines generally are far superior to those of yesteryear. Some broadcast journalism is outstanding. New, exciting means of electronic communication are just beyond the technological horizon. In the commercial marketplace, many public relations and advertising firms can be lauded for principled handling of ethically sensitive issues.

Yet, everywhere are signs of ethical deterioration. NBC News admits to the worst institutional journalistic fraud in recent memory—staging a pickup truck explosion to illustrate an exposé on vehicle safety. Individual print and broadcast journalists are accused of unreasonable invasion of privacy, insensitive treatment of victims of rape and other crimes, and a host of other ethical lapses.

Opinion polls show much of the public views media performance negatively. Journalists are regarded by many as arrogant, biased, unfair, unethical. Unarguably, there is widespread distrust of what the media do and how they do it.

So, our study of ethics comes at an opportune time. Before we proceed, however, two warnings:

First, although thinking deeply about ethics should add valuable dimensions to your understanding of the media, there are no generally accepted standards for approaching ethical questions or, certainly, no universally accepted answers to those questions. Indeed, as we'll discuss in pages ahead, media professionals cannot even agree on whether there should be written codes of ethics for reporters, editors or the media themselves.

Second, I intend nothing in this book to dampen your enthusiasm for aggressive, probing journalism. Pulling into view and explaining whatever the public needs to know is what good journalism is all about. Certainly, that kind of journalism is essential to ensuring our democracy functions properly. So, we must not get so knee-jerky about ethics that we forget the media's mission is to find and tell in the public's interest. Those of us in the media must not become so concerned about possible public reaction that we lapse into ethical-reactive journalism—considering first how the public will react, rather than deciding first to do what is journalistically necessary and right.

ORGANIZATION OF THIS BOOK

In this, the second edition of this book, first published in 1988, I have made substantive changes in structure and content.

In early chapters I've added new emphasis to the decision-making process in ethics. Discussions of societal values and journalistic principles are expanded.

As in the first edition, content is heavy with case studies and illustrations. I've updated many and, importantly, again used only actual ethical quandaries faced by real-life media professionals. I've tried to avoid the abstract what-if meandering that inevitably results from discussing fictional case studies or made-up ethical quandaries.

Here is how I've structured the book:

PART 1: MEDIA ETHICS: THE BACKGROUND AND PROCESS

The single chapter of Part 1 revolves around a case study illustrating various decision-making processes used by ethicists and journalists. Throughout, we look briefly to history for understanding of societal values and journalistic principles that influence decision making today in media ethics.

There is no rule book for your conduct as a journalist, no widely held code of ethics. So, the instructional thrust of Part 1 is directed at helping you move beyond merely stating passionately (but perhaps without articulated reasoning) your own stance on ethical issues. Your goal in Part 1 should be to develop a rational, methodical structure for your moral reasoning.

PART 2: ETHICS IN THE PURSUIT OF NEWS

Enormously complex ethical issues confront journalists throughout their careers. We examine many of those issues, along with the processes, values and principles used by media professionals in handling them.

Your goal in Part 2 should be to understand the ethical complexities of reporting, writing and editing news, and to begin building your personal approach to resolving them.

PART 3: ETHICS IN THE PURSUIT OF PROFIT

In our marketplace economy, all media (except a few that are nonprofit or publicly supported) are businesses that must yield profit to their owners—or die. Newspapers, magazines, radio, television—all must attract readers, viewers or listeners, then sell them to advertisers, who provide the bulk of financial support for the media.

You will learn in Part 3 that profit, not ethics or a sense of social responsibility, often motivates corporate managers and that therefore what happens in the countinghouse often affects—dramatically—newsroom ethics. Nevertheless, many profit-motivated media corporations take highly principled approaches to the news, and journalists frequently can operate ethically and responsibly in a bottom-line atmosphere.

PART 4: THE MEDIA IN SOCIETY

The media are a major influence in our nation and truly one of our most important societal institutions. Yet, they operate free of many cross-checks and constraints that control other institutions, such as government or business.

In Part 4 we look at how public perceptions of the media institution are changing and whether that threatens media independence. We consider the serious discussions among influential people of whether, in times of peace as well as war, the media should be permitted to barge about in public and private affairs, to operate independently of some legal and societal restraints that govern conduct of other major institutions influencing American life.

PART 5: PUBLIC RELATIONS, THE MEDIA AND SOCIETY

Part 5 is a single-chapter look at the public relations industry and its relationships with the media and society. Public relations in America is a huge, strongly financed effort to influence how you, the media and the public view governments and individuals, companies and products, issues and causes. No study of media ethics is complete without thorough understanding of the impact PR has on media and public attitudes.

ACKNOWLEDGMENTS

No book is the product of its author alone, and that holds true for this one. Many colleagues helped me create *Media Ethics.*

So, thanks to all those professionals I worked with around the world in my many years as a reporter, editor, foreign correspondent and media executive. Those who followed the principled path in journalism had profound effect on me.

Thanks, also, to colleagues in academia—Tom Russell, dean of the University of Georgia's Grady College of Journalism and Mass Communication; Ernie Hynds of the Grady College, and others who have been so helpful in my second career, teaching. Melinda Hawley of the Grady College provided valuable critiques of my manuscript. Hal Buell of The Associated Press and one of the leading photo editors of his time provided for Chapter 3 the excellent illustration of electronic manipulation of photos.

Special thanks to Kevin Davis, an outstanding book editor who was important to the structuring and writing of this book. Thanks also to his cheerful assistant, Susan Wesner. A very low bow to Christine Harrington, an extremely capable production supervisor.

I received tremendously valuable guidance from colleagues in academia who reviewed the manuscript: Ben Burns, Wayne State University; Joe W. Milner, Arizona State University; Jeffrey A. Smith, University of Iowa; Don E. Tomlinson, Texas A & M University; Ruth Walden, University of North Carolina.

PART 1

MEDIA ETHICS: THE BACKGROUND AND THE PROCESS

It's easy to understand what the study of ethics is all about: It's a systematic search for choices in what's good or bad in human conduct—what's right or wrong. It's an effort to identify principles that constitute values and rules of life recognized by us as individuals, a group or culture. Then we can reason out an approach that *should* govern human conduct.

It's not so easy, however, to see how ethics applies to reporters and the print and broadcast media and how they do (and should) act. Complex—and sometimes conflicting—societal values and journalistic principles influence ethical decision making by reporters and editors. The pressures of deadlines and competition complicate matters tremendously.

As a result, many journalists approach moral reasoning and ethical problem solving without a structured framework. Rather, they often decide quickly, almost instinctively, basing their judgments on narrow personal attitudes that stem principally, perhaps, from religious training or the attitudes of colleagues, family and friends.

Unfortunately, that's like attempting a long journey into unfamiliar territory without a map: You risk wasting time wandering aimlessly along backroads and never reaching your destination.

Here in Part 1 you should begin mapping out your own structured approach to decision making in journalism ethics. Keep in mind: If you don't develop your own reasoned method you'll find yourself merely going with the flow when confronted, as a media professional or reader or viewer, by ethical dilemmas. That will force you to scramble to adapt to situations as they arise without making reasoned moral judgments you can articulate clearly and persuasively. This is called situational behavior, and it might get you lost.

CHAPTER 1

Deciding and Acting: Ethics on the Job

Follow reporters on their news beats and you'll see them talking, listening, questioning, reading—*absorbing* enormous quantities of facts, figures and diverse views.

They winnow and sift, discarding irrelevant and secondary material as they search for the right approach to writing or broadcasting their stories. Gradually, a story form emerges in their minds: *This* angle, not that one, is the lead; *these* facts, not those, are most important in the story.[1]

That, of course, is a classic scenario of reporters on the job, but it has one major failing: It doesn't acknowledge that throughout the reporting and writing process, perhaps beneath the surface and probably out of sight and out of mind, there often are enormously complicated ethical issues that can lead reporters badly astray, even invalidating the most sincere and professional journalistic effort.

Let me show you how that can happen, using a case study from my own experience as a young Associated Press correspondent in New Delhi, India. Note the ethical complexities that arise in what appears at first glance to be a simple news story—just another day on the foreign news beat.

ASSEMBLE *ALL* THE FACTS

A ragged mob of about 100 persons marched on the U.S. embassy in the Indian capital, shouting slogans (in Hindi) and waving signs (in English): "Baby Killer Tebbets Go Home!"

The mob's target was Col. Paul Tebbets, U.S. Air Force attaché at the embassy. Anti-American demonstrations in New Delhi weren't new and this one fit into a pattern of protest popular worldwide then, in the 1960s, at the height of the Cold War.

The story initially seemed routine—at best, probably worth only a short cable to The Associated Press foreign desk in New York City. But, as on every story, I began muttering the reporter's mantra: *Who* is involved? *What* is happening? *Why?* I concluded I had only superficial understanding of those three Ws (although *Where?* and *When?* were clear and *How?* looked straightforward).

Then, I noted one demonstrator obviously couldn't read his own English-language sign: He was holding it upside down. Anyway, why wave signs in a language most Indian onlookers couldn't understand?

I wondered, "Who *really* is demonstrating? Who is the *real who* here?" I waded among the protesters with an interpreter and discovered the real who: This was a ragged mob of unemployed, illiterate villagers hired for a few rupees (equivalent to a few U.S. pennies) to demonstrate—as several cheerfully volunteered—against whom and for what cause they had not a clue. I worked my way to the head of the column, to a man shouting directions through a bullhorn. The real who turned out to be an official of the Communist party of India.

Suddenly, this story became a bit more complicated than I thought. My reporter's instinct was beginning to stir:

Should I report what, after all, appeared to be just one more anti-American demonstration in India, and a small one at that?

If so, how should I handle the angle about paid demonstrators? Didn't the English-language signs prove the demonstration was staged solely in hope that foreign correspondents would cover it and thus spread the Communist party's message worldwide?

Then, my reporter's instinct really kicked in: Why were the protesters after Tebbets *by name?* Why not just the usual, "Down With America . . . Yankees Go Home"?

Tebbets, it turned out, wasn't just another U.S. Air Force officer. He was *the* officer who, almost 25 years earlier, flew the Enola Gay, a B-29 that dropped the first atomic bomb on Hiroshima, Japan, killing thousands and helping end World War II.

My reporter's training made my ethical duty clear: To ensure fairness and balance, I obviously had to talk with Tebbets. He told me—rather sadly, I thought—that regardless of where he was stationed, the communists eventually found him and demonstrated with their baby-killer signs. He seemed resigned, tired of being chased.

Lessons learned by this experience:

- If you're a reporter, learn *all* you can about a story. (If you're a reader or viewer—a media consumer—critique coverage carefully on whether it's superficial or probing.) Our society highly regards honesty and truth-telling as basic values. Translated into job-specific journalistic principles, those values require reporters to dig deeply. I would have betrayed those principles if I hadn't probed until I found the real who that day in New Delhi. That probing revealed the what of this story—a ragged demonstration—in fact had a deeper real what: It was a propaganda set-up.

- As you probe for facts, consider your responsibilities—your loyalties—to your reading or viewing public and its right (or need) to know, to your employer, to yourself and to those involved in the story and who thus will be affected by it. Even early in the Tebbets story I could see conflicting loyalties appearing.
- Seek balance in your reporting. I would have violated a fundamental societal value and journalistic principle—be fair—had I not interviewed Tebbets. Clearly, *reporting that's superficial, incomplete and one-sided is, by definition, unethical reporting.*
- Listen to your conscience. It's likely the product of humanity's 2,500 years of philosophical debate, since the time of the ancient Greeks, over what's right and what's wrong. It's not only your journalistic training that must guide you through a story. As I sat in Tebbets' office my conscience was whispering that this officer was more than a Cold War warrior. He really was a Cold War victim—a real, live human being, not merely a news object. He was a man who could be hurt, just like any other, with a family—real people—who could be wounded, as were many innocents caught in the ideological crossfire of that era. (Tebbets had photographs of his family in his office. I remember to this day that they were all smiling.)

I was increasingly troubled by this story. But I couldn't put my finger on exactly what concerned me.

DEFINE THE ETHICAL ISSUE

Assembling facts sometimes leads you to a quick, almost automatic, definition of an ethical issue. Beware. Instantaneous enlightenment may be too good to be true.

Often, multiple ethical issues lie intertwined just beneath the surface. Obviously, trying to untie them in your mind complicates your task, but you would fail in your duty as an ethical decision maker—as a moral agent—if you didn't make the attempt.

As Tebbets talked I wondered:

- How would I feel in Tebbets' shoes? I certainly hadn't dropped an atomic bomb on anybody, but I earlier had spent several years doing exactly as ordered in the U.S. Marine Corps. Would I like to be hassled now—by demonstrators or reporters—for what I did then? It occurred to me only years later: Was I subconsciously assuming Tebbets' identity to better understand how he felt?
- Was I, the product of Methodist upbringing, responsible for acting humanely and compassionately with this man across the desk? I didn't think in terms of "Christian ethic" but I realize now that my professional self was inseparable from my personal upbringing, and I felt a sympathy that surely flowed from

humanity's 2,500-year-old debate over how civilized human beings should treat each other.

- Was this, I wondered, really a story of consequence? Measured against other news breaking worldwide that day, what journalistic mission would be served by filing it? Was this story, which could harm Tebbets and his family, really a two-bit story that would be tucked away deep in a few American newspapers, if published at all? My readers had a *right* to know this story; did they *need* to know about one more mob of ragged marchers in a far-off land?

Now, don't let me create a myth in your mind. Those heavy thoughts indeed were flitting through my head but I wasn't agonizing over what God's will might be.

In reality, I was a tremendously aggressive young correspondent determined to build a successful career in AP, one of the world's most competitive news organizations. On this story—as on each of thousands I covered—I was considering whether my actions were good or bad for my career. Anyone who defines selfishness as a prime motivator of human conduct would have pegged me as extremely self-centered in my career drive. It's that way with every outstanding reporter I know.[2]

No, I was reacting instinctively that day in New Delhi, making judgment calls swiftly and based on my training and experiences in journalism (not ethics). It would have been good to seek "diverse viewpoints"—to talk over the story with AP colleagues, but the nearest was thousands of miles away. However, I wasn't concerned. I had made tougher judgment calls independently on other stories in, literally, seconds as I ran breathlessly to a telephone so I could dictate urgent copy.

Leaving the embassy and driving back to my bureau, I defined the issues:

1. Did this story, basically, have news value? Did I have a journalistic obligation to my readers to file it? I saw no obvious ethical question in this. I was making just another workday decision: Was this news or wasn't it?
2. If the story warranted coverage, how would I handle the reality that I was being "set up" by a paid-for demonstration orchestrated purely for international propaganda purposes? Here, there *was* an ethical issue: Could I write cleverly enough to make clear the real what of this story? Could I do so and still maintain my stance as a dispassionate reporter? (Yes, at that stage in my career I thought it possible to be a truly "objective" reporter and, further, that I was one.)
3. What would AP (the hand that fed me) expect of me? And, frankly, what were my news-service competitors—United Press International and Reuters—doing on this story?

CONSIDER ALTERNATIVE SOLUTIONS

You may think ethical problems get reasoned and full consideration by reporters and that diverse viewpoints are considered before decisions are made.

That's a myth. In reality, on the news beat and in most newspaper and broadcast newsrooms, judgments frequently are made quickly and instinctively, often by a single individual, under pressure of deadlines and what can only be called the controlled pandemonium of covering the news.

I won't pretend I understood I was a "moral agent" that day in New Delhi or that I knowingly proceeded logically and methodically through a structured process of moral reasoning. What emerged were decisions that, in retrospect, were based on a confusing (and, now I see, embarrassing) mixture of self*less* and self*ish* motives.

I decided the story had only secondary value. There was no front-page byline—no journalistic glory—in this one. Nobody back home would miss it. So, why inflict agony on Col. Tebbets?

Why take the communist bait of a paid-for demonstration? Besides, I hadn't seen other correspondents at the scene, so I probably wasn't under competitive pressure—and that made my decision easy: I wouldn't file a story.

Very soon came what all correspondents dread: A "rocket"—an angry cable—from my New York desk. United Press International was transmitting a story on the anti-Tebbets demonstration.

New York added: "Need ours soonest." I was beaten on a story, a disgrace in the news service business—and something that better not happen too often or I would be back on AP's night rewrite desk in Chicago.

What to do?

A confession: I seized on a thought that has occurred to more reporters than the few who will admit to also having it: As long as I already was beaten on the story, couldn't I, first, belittle its news value? Denigrating the story would cast doubt on UPI's news judgment. And then, second, couldn't I take the moral high ground? Couldn't I tell New York I didn't file originally on this "second-rate" story because I didn't want to inflict agony on Col. Tebbets?

And that was the substance of my cabled response to New York. Ah, youth! Careerism, ego, faulty reasoning, an ill-developed personal sense of ethics—all were my sins that day.

Immediately, AP's foreign desk editor responded: Understand and sympathize your position. File soonest.

Now I really was in the ethical soup. I had taken a stand on a shaky matter of principle, and the hand that fed me was demanding first call on my loyalty.

Was there a legitimate (and, face-saving) way out of my dilemma?

DECIDE AND ACT

It became clear to me that day in New Delhi that you shouldn't lightly make ethical decisions in the media.

First, as a reporter in the field, unlike a student role playing in the forgiving classroom, you must act on your decisions, often right now, and you must live with the consequences.

Second, stakeholders in your decisions—those with vested interest in their outcome—can get hurt. People in the news can get hurt; innocents on the sidelines (the smiling woman and children in Tebbets' photos) can get hurt; you, your career, all you've worked for can get hurt.

Third, it became clear that if you don't thoroughly, logically and honestly reason out an ethical problem, you dramatically increase the odds that you'll make a bad call. Indeed, you can worsen your ethical dilemma.

I certainly worsened mine. I had blundered my way into one of the worst positions any journalist can face: I had to file a story despite my stated ethical objections or face the ire of my AP superiors.

Refusing orders wasn't smart in the AP of those days, and I needed an out. Again I blundered, this time into luck. It occurred to me that I could take a position somewhere between the two extremes of (1) flirting with corporate punishment or (2) knuckling under (my egocentric term was *groveling*) and being forced to file despite my protest that doing so would harm Tebbets.

I went to Tebbets again, explained my dilemma, and to my relief, he gave me an out: He said he was proud of having served his country in World War II and wasn't ashamed of having flown the Enola Gay. And, although he was sick of being hassled over it, one more story wouldn't hurt—so I should go ahead and write my story.

And that gave me an idea. I put a reverse spin on this story: Once again the communists have found Paul Tebbets and once again he is a victim of the Cold War.

That angle enabled me to get the paid-for demonstration up high in the story and thus explain the real who and real what. And, importantly, although I wasn't seeking Tebbets' permission to do the story, I felt better—my conscience felt better—because I had talked it over with him.[3]

Actually, after my bumbling—and agonizing—start, I rather liked the story I wrote. So did my editors. They cabled congratulations: My story was better than UPI's!

THE STRUCTURE OF DECISION MAKING

Let's examine the New Delhi case study for clues on how you can establish a structured approach to ethical decision making.

As the case illustrates, when you sniff an ethical problem on the wind you can break your approach into five separate steps.

A FIVE-STEP PROCESS

Visualize decision making as a continuum:

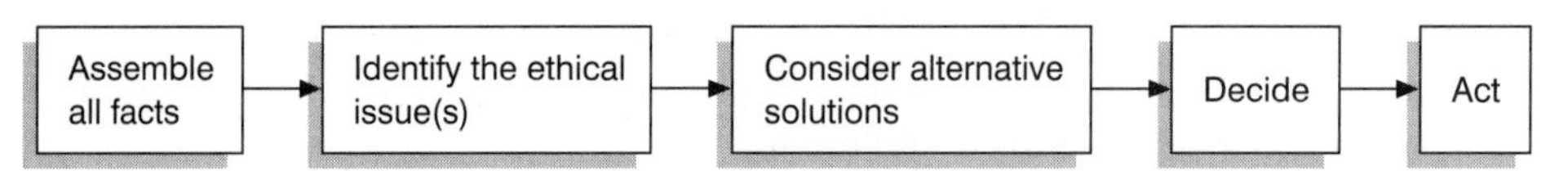

After reading of my bumbling in New Delhi, you probably are thinking, "Decision making in ethics isn't as simple as that continuum looks."

Correct. Working through that step-by-step process in search of reasoned judgment isn't simple. Beware:

Step One. As in news reporting, assembling *all* the facts requires deep probing. It's seldom that the obvious, superficial facts reveal the true dimensions of your ethical dilemma.

Step Two. Identifying the ethical issues also requires probing inquiry. *Several* ethical issues often are beneath the surface, overlapping and blurring each other. Sometimes, the way you resolve one ethical dilemma creates a new one!

Step Three. Considering alternative solutions often reveals you have an agonizing choice of many different—and tempting—ways to handle your ethical crisis. Study your full range of choices. There may be a better resolution available than the one that first pops to mind.

Steps Four and Five. Deciding and acting can be painful. Often you must choose from options that are all *un*desirable, and it's not pleasant to decide on a course of action simply because it is the least undesirable afforded you. Acting—and taking responsibility for your decision—can require courage. You may be criticized by your public, by your peers or your boss or, indeed, you may risk losing your job over a judgment call you've made.

Obviously, there are many influences on your decision making process. Let's look at them.

INFLUENCES ON DECISION MAKING

For many ethicists, Dr. Ralph Potter showed the way to structured moral reasoning in his 1965 Ph.D. dissertation at Harvard University. His "Potter Box," depicting step-by-step examination of influences on decision making, has been used (and revised and adapted) by scholars in ethics.[4]

I would adapt the Potter approach to our case study as shown in Figure 1–1.

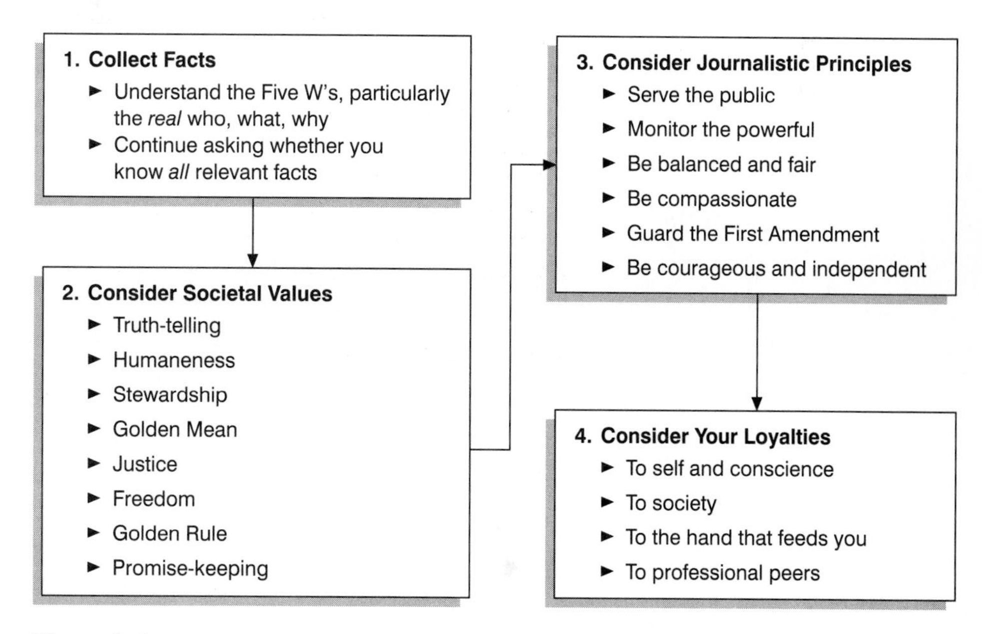

Figure 1–1
Steps toward decision

Values and principles listed in Figure 1–1 are important signposts along your route toward decision making, whether you're a media professional or media consumer.

CONSIDERING SOCIETAL VALUES

For our study, let's understand *societal values* to be standards generally accepted by a majority of citizens as important characteristics of a civilized society. To have no values—no underlying standards—is to invite moral anarchy, societal instability and philosophical chaos. A society without values is a society adrift.

Since the time of the ancient Greeks, humanity has debated what is good or bad, right or wrong, in search of values—principles or standards—against which human conduct can be judged. Here's a quick look at important contributors to that debate.

Socrates

Socrates argued that "justice" and "good" are identifiable through methodical reasoning. The Socratic Method is teaching by asking questions that inevitably lead the answerer to conclusions foreseen by the questioner. Lesson for journalists: *Reasoned dialogue* is required in ethical debate; impassioned, unreasonable insistence on one point of view renders methodical reasoning inoperable. Socrates died in 399 B.C.

Plato

Plato identified cardinal virtues—wisdom, courage, temperance—from which justice flows. Plato, who died in 347 B.C., argued "good" exists as an independent value, regardless of how society conducts itself—a precursor of the view among journalists today that an individual reporter must interpret personally what is right or good, then take a virtuous path even if that requires defying current thinking in society.

Aristotle

Aristotle's Golden Mean holds that moral virtue lies between extremes; virtue is in moderation, temperance. But journalists shouldn't seek weak, unprincipled compromise by merely taking consensus positions an equal distance between extremes; Aristotle (384–322 B.C.) warned no middle ground exists when confronting some evils, such as murder. Aristotle probably would counsel today's journalists to seek a Golden Mean by, for example, publishing or broadcasting an investigative story but also minimizing harm to innocent bystanders of the news event. Aristotle also would counsel

- to recognize your own extremist positions, then lean the other way in your reporting to ensure your stories represent all viewpoints.
- that the individual is responsible for taking virtuous action through free choice.

- that in exercise of virtue, the end does not always justify the means (perhaps it's wrong to masquerade as a police officer even if that uncovers an important story), and doing what is morally right can be measured by the price paid—sacrifices made, happiness given up (good guidance for journalists who brave jail to protect a pledge of anonymity given news sources).

Saint Augustine

Saint Augustine was an early (A.D. 354–430) contributor to the Judeo-Christian ethic, which provided a momentous turn in our ethical debate. His principles include the following:

- Love God and all humanity ("Love thy neighbor as thyself").
- It's God's will that all persons be respected, whatever their race, color, creed or what we today call their socioeconomic status (journalists must respect individuals thrust into the news).
- Each person must interpret God's will (again, the journalist has personal responsibility to determine what's right).
- There must be action-oriented love and care for others (journalists must forcefully wield the power of the press to aid the weak and suffering, to attack social injustice, to change things for the better).

Thomas Hobbes

Hobbes (1588–1679) identified fear and selfishness as prime motivators of conduct. His essentially pessimistic view of human nature held that individuals must give up certain rights under strong governments if society is to control selfishness and violence. Also, he argued a radical theme for the time: People possess true power and sovereigns, then all-powerful, don't have divine rights. It's not a big leap from that to journalists' view today that the people must be informed and, as surrogate of the people, the print and broadcast media have special roles in society.

John Milton

Milton's *Areopagitica,* published in 1644, defined an "open marketplace of ideas" where all could freely express themselves. Milton (1608–1674) said a "self-righting process" would enable truth to survive while false, unsound ideas would be vanquished. Journalists today echo this in asserting that if they publish facts, readers and viewers will ascertain truth.

David Hume

Hume (1711–1776) is associated with empiricism, a scientific approach to ethics—knowledge is gained through experience, verification through experimentation or observation alone. Hume doubted good can be found through reason; he argued humans instinctively feel charitable toward others. Important concept: Human activity is aimed at achieving happiness, and usefulness—"utility"—is the measure for any ethical principle in determining its place in society (for example, justice serves the good of humanity and thus is utilitarian).

Immanuel Kant

Kant (1724–1804) wrote of duty and the "categorical imperative" in what *ought* to be done. Codes of conduct and morality must be reasoned out and be applicable to all societal environments at all times. Kant's absolutist approach is called *deontological ethics,* from the Greek word *deon,* meaning duty. This implies universally valid rules of conduct and requires adherence to them, regardless of who or what may be harmed. For example, this would mean truth-telling is a universal virtue and journalists always must tell the truth, even if that hurts individuals. Kant argued each individual is free to act and must measure up to codes of conduct. Also, the moral worth of an act is determined by rational intention, the will to be moral, not consequences of the act.

John Stuart Mill

Mill (1806–1873) argued what counts are consequences of an act, and interpreted utilitarianism to mean moral conduct must aim at general well-being—creating greatest happiness for the greatest number of people. Nevertheless, Mill strongly defended the rights of minorities. Should a reporter invade the privacy of an unwilling individual—thus inflicting unhappiness—to obtain a story for the larger populace, the larger good? Mill probably would tell the reporter to proceed but respect the individual's rights insofar as possible.

John Rawls (Contemporary)

This contemporary thinker is associated with egalitarianism: All individuals have equal rights and should have equal opportunities; fairness is the core of justice. In a just society, there should be agreement (a "societal contract") on preventing—or minimizing—harm to weaker persons or groups. Rawls doesn't directly contradict utilitarianism but his fairness-based approach gives journalists another avenue in decision making. That's important because utilitarianism can be unfair. For example, a story attacking a prominent though unliked person might make the majority happy but be unfair to the individual. Rawls urges decision makers in ethics to place themselves behind a hypothetical "veil of ignorance," where divisive factors such as class, race and sex don't exist. For example, journalists would imagine themselves as economically or socially deprived, which would help them ensure poor and unknown people receive equal and thus "fair" coverage. The rich and famous would not get favored treatment simply because they are wealthy and well-known.

THE IMPACT OF SOCIETAL VALUES ON JOURNALISM

Our society, then, generally agrees on basic values that flow from 2,500 years of humanity's debate, from Socrates to Rawls, over ethics. The following values are crucial immediately to our study of media ethics.

TRUTH-TELLING

Honesty is fundamental to any workable societal mechanism; indeed, without truth-telling no moral framework exists.

In journalism, truth-telling is at the very core of what we do. To lie, to fabricate, to shade the truth—all are cardinal sins in journalism.

JUSTICE

Impartial, fair treatment for all is essential in a civilized society. Justice promises reward or punishment as deserved, not based arbitrarily on race, color, creed or social or economic status.

Principled journalists strive to be just in their work and to monitor whether society applies justice even-handedly to others.

HUMANENESS

It's basic to ordered, civilized conduct: Don't harm people; help them when you can and, particularly, assist the needy—the weak and vulnerable members of society.

Ethical journalists don't intentionally harm people and try to minimize harm to those thrust into the news. And, it's a tradition in American journalism: Use your power to assist those in need.

FREEDOM

It's woven into our social fabric: Freedom, independence, autonomy—liberty—for the individual are essential.

Principled journalists make every effort to remain free of any association, ideology, group or person that might restrict freedom of the press or their personal freedom to cover the news as it must be covered.

STEWARDSHIP

Stewardship requires citizens to respect and guard the rights of others. If you benefit from a system—justice or freedom, for example—you have a responsibility to protect that system and extend its benefits to others.

The following are other values central to our society:

- Christianity's Golden Rule (behave toward others as you would have them behave toward you)
- Aristotle's Golden Mean (don't be extremist; don't ignore political inequity, for example, but don't call for rioting and arson at the courthouse, either. Strive for change with a solution somewhere between those extremes.)
- Promise keeping (all must keep their word and fulfill contracts)
- Loyalty (faithfulness to your obligations and commitments, to your group, peers, employer and so forth)

CONSIDERING JOURNALISTIC PRINCIPLES

Job-related principles in journalism flow from our wider societal values and actually are adaptions of those values to the occupational tasks at hand.

For example, truth-telling as a societal value means, basically, honesty. In journalism, the job-related principle of truth-telling requires you to develop skilled techniques as a reporter and writer to ensure your news stories are accurate, complete and meaningful to readers and viewers.

Ethical debate in Britain and America, beginning in the late 1600s, yielded such concepts specifically applicable to newspapers and magazines and, now, television. We draw from those beginnings in discussions today about media ethics.

Libertarianism

This implies belief in the people's ability to make rational, intelligent decisions—to find truth—if sufficient information is available through a free press in a free society that protects free expression. Early on, the press assumed the role of enlightening the public, guarding against government infringement on personal liberties and fighting off all but the broadest outside limitations on how the press operated. The sense of press freedom extended even to freedom from any responsibility to the public: The press would provide information and, later, advertising—and in that way serve the political and economic systems while making a profit. Today, the broadest libertarian attitude of virtually unrestricted freedom is rejected by principled journalists.

Objectivity

This is an ideal developed in the late 1800s and still central to media ethics. Reporters who strive for objectivity attempt to write balanced accounts of all sides in news stories. They avoid activist involvement, don't inject partisan views into their copy and write as dispassionately as possible. True objectivity was (and is) impossible to achieve but the ideal became core philosophy of The Associated Press when it was reorganized in 1894 into the forerunner of today's mammoth international news agency. There was a business imperative: As a membership organization, AP had to serve newspapers of all political persuasions, in all sections of the nation, without hint of partisanship. Today, many media organizations try to follow AP's ideal for similar business reasons but also because they regard balanced journalism an ethical responsibility.

Social Responsibility

In the early 1900s came a rising sense of community conscience among journalists, a concept that responsibility to society was a corollary to press freedom. This strengthened in 1922 with creation of the American Society of Newspaper Editors (ASNE). At its first meeting in 1923, ASNE adopted a statement of newspaper ideals—service to the public, independence, truthfulness, sincerity, accuracy. That same year, radio stations formed the National Association of Broadcasters (NAB) and in 1929, established the first radio code. Although NAB's code dealt primarily with advertising and programming standards, a sense of social responsibility was present. (NAB's television code was established in 1952.) Though vague, early codes signaled American journalism was emerging from libertarianism and heading into a new era in which press freedom was linked in the minds of many with social responsibility. In 1947, the so-called Hutchins Commission, financed principally by Henry R. Luce of Time, Inc., warned that the press was becoming extremely powerful and engaging in practices that could lead to societal regulation.[5] A journalism professor, Theodore Peterson, subsequently wrote that the press enjoyed privileged position in our society and "freedom carries concomitant obligations." It was Peterson who injected the term *social responsibility* into our dialogue.[6] Rights became tied to duties, and American journalism never was the same again.

People's Right to Know

After World War II, Kent Cooper, then general manager of The Associated Press and a vigorous critic of barriers to free flow of information, spoke widely of the "people's right to know."[7] This concept holds that although the First Amendment gives the press the right to freely print the news, the people's *right* to know gives the press the *duty* to print it. The people's right to know is not expressly stated in the Constitution; neither is the idea that the media have the right of access to news. But Cooper and others pushed the idea of a press serving as surrogate of the people and demanding access to news, as well as freedom to print it, on behalf of the people.[8] By the 1950s, both "rights" were regarded widely in the media and public as guaranteed. The media were the Fourth Estate—a fourth branch of the system that (with the legislative, judicial and executive branches) governs the country.[9]

The Credibility Gap

The American media never have been short of critics. Even that champion of freedom, Thomas Jefferson, complained about an unrestrained "spirit of falsehood" in newspapers and suggested libel suits as weapons against writers who were "prominent offenders." Public esteem for the media fluctuated widely in subsequent generations, but by the 1980s opinion polls showed many Americans deeply doubted media accuracy and fairness. A survey for the American Society of Newspaper Editors revealed in 1991 that if American voters were asked to again ratify the Bill of Rights, freedom of the press likely would not be included. Two thirds of survey respondents failed to give unqualified support to the press in criticizing politicians or the military or reporting past mistakes of public figures.[10] A serious credibility gap was widening between public and media. Journalists today cannot ignore the reality that their reporting and writing, their motives and ethics, are regarded suspiciously by many Americans.

In sum, it's possible to follow ethical debate from the late 1600s into the 1990s and trace emergence of journalistic principles specifically applicable today to conduct of newspapers, magazines, television and radio.

For example, the following job-related principles, widely accepted in journalism, flow from societal values we discussed earlier.

Serve the Public

It echoes through the Judeo-Christian ethic: Assist the needy, comfort the afflicted, attack social injustice, *change things for the better.*

Many journalists regard themselves as surrogates of the public, particularly the needy and voiceless. Reporters often frame their search for information within the context of what they think would interest their readers or viewers. Indeed, career success in journalism flows from being able to put yourself in the position of your readers or viewers and report stories crucial to them. Understanding what your audience wants and needs is the first step any journalist must make in selecting stories to cover.

Serving the public also is a high-priority corporate goal for many media companies. In our market-driven capitalistic society, profit is a corporation's primary goal, of course, and serving the public well is how newspapers, magazines and broadcast companies make their profit. So there is obvious self-interest in serving the public. But the history of American journalism has many inspirational examples of media companies serving the public even to their financial disadvantage—by, say, rejecting advertisers who want to influence news content or force changes in editorial positions.

Monitor the Powerful

A fundamental principle of American journalism is that the media must monitor other institutions in society—particularly government, but also other institutions of great power, such as business and organized religion.

This watchdog attitude requires principled journalists to do more than merely monitor power brokers with enormous influence on our daily life. The media also must hold the powerful accountable to the public.

Thus, high premium is placed by journalists on uncovering criminality or malfeasance in official circles and then requiring officialdom to account to the public. The media feel obliged sometimes to probe into even the private affairs of powerful people or companies whose products or conduct affect, for example, the health or financial well-being of readers, viewers and listeners.

Be Balanced and Fair

Principled journalists strive mightily to ensure their reporting and writing are balanced and that all viewpoints receive the coverage they merit. This, simply, is only fair. But what's "fair"?

Philosopher John Rawls would say being fair requires equal treatment for all subjects of a news story. The famous and wealthy should not be treated more favorably than the anonymous and impoverished.[11]

The journalist's challenge comes in trying to sort out such seeming contradictions as serving the public—the majority—and simultaneously protecting the minority.

Few journalists today accept "objectivity" as a workable, all-encompassing concept they follow faithfully to ensure balance and fairness. Most recognize no one is truly objective, that we're all the product of our past and that we all have preconceived notions and attitudes when approaching a news story. Many journalists, however, say objectivity is an ideal worth striving for and that reporters should cover the conflicting ideas that arise in the news without being unduly influenced by one side or the other—or by their own attitudes.

Be Compassionate

The societal value of humaneness can be translated into the journalistic principle that reporters should be compassionate for all who figure in the news and, particularly, for those who might be harmed by how news is covered.

Should our cameras capture a widow's grief at graveside? Is intrusion into such a private moment necessary to telling the story? Should the glare of news coverage be directed at innocent bystanders—say, the wife and children of a public official caught stealing public money?

Principled journalists try to cover news as it must be covered and, simultaneously, deal compassionately and respectfully with those in the news.

Guard the First Amendment

Look to the societal value of stewardship for guidance on the journalistic principle, firmly held by many journalists, that the media have special responsibility for protecting the First Amendment—not simply for themselves but for the public as well.

Obviously, there is self-interest in this. If the First Amendment's guarantee of free speech disappears, so does the free press vanish. But even cursory examination of the media's continuing efforts to shine public light on the public's business will reveal a higher motive often is at work.

Major media organizations are prime movers in efforts to guarantee free flow of information for all citizens. At considerable expense, news organizations wage continuing legal battles to penetrate bureaucratic secrecy at local, state and federal levels—to open a school board's deliberations to the public, not just to reporters; to use the Freedom of Information Act to open federal files in Washington, not just for newspapers or broadcast stations but all citizens, as well.

Be Independent

Independent thinking—and taking personal responsibility for it—is an accepted societal value. *Autonomous moral reasoning,* ethicists term it.

As a journalistic principle, being independent means covering news without fear or favor. Most reporters avoid any action that could create public perception that they are subservient to any political, economic or social group. Some newspapers and TV stations won't endorse political candidates for fear that could compromise their neutrality.

Being independent requires reporters to avoid any action that smacks of personal conflict of interest—not investing in companies they cover, for example, or even declining free lunch from politicians who are news sources.

Journalistic societies—the American Society of Newspaper Editors and the Radio and Television News Directors Association, among them—have codes that are explicitly clear on this issue: Avoid any conduct that creates actual or, in the eyes of the public, perceived conflict of interest.

Being independent is, really, fundamental to all principles so firmly held by journalists. For example, reporters whose conduct or associations compromise their independence and integrity cannot pretend to serve the public or act as stewards of the First Amendment or, obviously, be fair and balanced.

Be Courageous

It's been implicit throughout the debate over moral values: You must have the courage to decide independently what is "good" and "right" and then to stand by your convictions.

Well, they probably weren't thinking of Socrates or Kant at the time, or maybe even journalistic principle, but 56 journalists died in 1993 while covering the news. Scores die somewhere in the world every year—all willingly putting themselves in harm's way because of a sense of duty.

A struggling small-town publisher or TV station owner shows another kind of courage in rebuffing advertiser attempts to influence news coverage—particularly if a major advertiser, whose support is the difference between a profitable or red-ink year, is on the telephone, screaming for preferential treatment by the newsroom.

Yet another form of courage is required from journalists who do what they think is right in defiance of pressure from people to whom they otherwise would give loyalty—their bosses, colleagues or friends. Let's look more closely at this.

Considering Your Loyalties

To whom—or what—does a reporter owe first loyalty?

Who—or what—has first call on an editor's allegiance?

Does a publisher or broadcast station manager owe first loyalty to shareholders interested in profit? To serving an audience or community? Or, is first allegiance due to truth or doing good?

In advertising or public relations, must your first loyalty always be to your client? Or, must you be loyal first to the public or to truth—even if in some cases telling the truth conflicts with the client's interests?

Because we all have many—and often conflicting—loyalties, answering such questions is one of the most difficult aspects of decision making in ethics.

For example, you and your friends probably can agree quickly that honesty is a societal value to be cherished. But can you agree so quickly on, say, whether you should officially report classmates who cheat on an exam? Can you agree your first loyalty is to your peers, or to the integrity of the course you're taking, or to the honor system of your university? Indeed, can you agree whether your first loyalty must be to friendship or to the value of honesty and every individual's duty to exercise stewardship in protecting it?

The following are loyalties that will tug and pull you in the decision making process.

Self and Conscience. A sense of personal integrity and professional conscience often is only awakening in campus journalists. The concept of professional integrity—professionalism—often is only embryonic in students majoring in newspapers, magazines, broadcasting or the advocacy arts, advertising and public relations. But the beginnings of personal and professional conscience generally are there.

Two thoughts:

First, even though you've not fully developed your own structured approach to ethical decision making, you may hear a whisper in the back of your head or experience a feeling when questions of right and wrong arise. Such instinctive signals often are your first suggestion on how you should proceed. Listen to those whispers; think deeply about those feelings.

Second, whatever course you decide to follow, be loyal to your sense of self, to your professional conscience, to your personal definition of integrity. A seemingly "right" decision likely will be wrong if it leads you to betray yourself. Bluntly, a judgment that makes it difficult to look in a mirror won't be satisfactory.

Of course, sorting out loyalty to yourself and your conscience can be difficult. For example, listen very carefully and you may discover that that whisper really is telling you to be loyal first to your career, to first protect your job—and to serve only secondarily the truth or your other loyalties. And, as a journalist you do have significant other loyalties besides self.

Loyalty to Society. Here, we confront loyalty on three levels:

First, journalistic duty demands loyalty to social responsibility and people's right to know. Broadly, principled journalists are loyal to the greater good of society, a utilitarian view that obviously can create conflict with your other loyalties. For example, your conscience can tell you to respect an individual's desire for privacy but your loyalty to society simultaneously can demand hauling that person into the spotlight in stories, say, on government corruption.

Second, loyalty to society also relates to readers, viewers, listeners. The American Society of Newspaper Editors' Statement of Principles says: "The primary purpose of gathering and distributing news and opinion is to serve the general welfare by informing the people and enabling them to make judgments on the issues of the time." ASNE warns that journalists "who abuse the power of their professional role for selfish motives or unworthy purposes are faithless to that public trust." It's an obvious betrayal, for example, if you buy shares in a company and then write favorably about it in the expectation that your readers or viewers will bid up the company's stock and, thus, improve the value of your shareholdings. (Such a moral betrayal also can be highly illegal and land you in jail.)

A third—and especially important—level of loyalty to society is your responsibility to individuals who will be affected or, particularly, harmed by what you write. An individual highlighted in, say, an exposé on official corruption may be entirely innocent of legal wrongdoing, yet be grievously harmed through guilt by association. A story on inner-city conditions may strengthen the stereotypical view that blacks and Hispanics sell dope—and soft pedal (or ignore) the reality that white, affluent suburbanites are among those who buy the stuff. In journalism, you can wittingly—or unwittingly—inflict enormous harm on individuals or entire groups of individuals.

Loyalty to the Hand That Feeds You. Face it: Journalists are hired not to do their own thing but, rather, to help get newspapers on the streets, newscasts on the air.

Whether written or implied, a contract exists under which you agree to work as directed in return for a paycheck.

Do you, therefore, have a moral responsibility to give your newspaper or TV station your loyalty, as well as your labor? Many journalists argue you do. In fact, reporters and editors often display great pride in their organizations and work with a loyal intensity and competitive zeal not found in other lines of work.

But, let's say your editor's interpretation of loyalty requires such competitive zeal you are pressured to write a news story before you have all the facts pinned down, simply to ensure your newspaper gets into print first and beats a cross-town competitor.

Let's say loyalty to a TV station requires injecting hyped-up urgency and drama into every newscast, whether or not the news at hand warrants it, simply to defeat other stations in the fight for audiences.

Thus does newsroom environment create many opportunities for conflicting loyalties.

More broadly, must media companies have special loyalty to those who provide financial support?

Well, here, too, contracts—and potential conflicts—exist. Subscribers agree to pay for newspapers and magazines; publishers agree to provide, in return, certain news, information, entertainment and advertising. Increasingly, newspaper and magazine reporters are assigned to select content carefully to attract principally only those readers who are attractive to advertisers. TV and radio editors select news and entertainment programming designed to attract viewers and listeners who can be sold to advertisers.

Should the media serve only audiences whose income and education make them desirable to advertisers? Or, must the media be loyal to a higher principle, traditionally very strong in America, of serving all sectors of society, including audiences less attractive in the commercial marketplace?

If society demands loyalty to the tradition of educating the untutored and uplifting the downtrodden, should media owners be forced to pay the cost? Increasingly, advertisers won't. By refusing to pay for such audiences, advertisers put very real dollars-and-cents pressure on media loyalties in this marketing problem.

Loyalty to Professional Peers. In the newsroom, loyalty to professional peers unquestionably is the strongest influence on many reporters and editors. In judging their own performance, journalists seek approval of their colleagues more than anything else.

In media countinghouses, one extremely important measurement of success is how well a company performs in comparison to other media companies. Many publish annual reports with charts showing how their profit and dividends compare to those of other media companies.

In the media as an institution, first loyalty is to the media institution itself, not government, business or other power structures in our society. Indeed, the media institution rejects suggestions that it should be held accountable by other institutions, particularly government. Although the media watchdog holds other societal institutions accountable, the media demand the right to judge their own performance by their own standards.

Let's look at how overlapping—and often conflicting—loyalties can affect you.

Acting Ethically in a "Messy" World. In a media career, you will be a moral agent in these roles:

- As a reporter, you will sort out ethical intricacies of a story assignment and decide how to proceed through the thicket of values, principles and loyalties we've discussed.
- As an editor or news director, you will act as a moral agent shaping ethics guidelines for your staff. You will juggle journalistic principles held by your reporters, by yourself, by your employer.
- As a media manager, you will decide how your newspaper, magazine or broadcast outlet will resolve major ethical quandaries.
- As an advocate in advertising or public relations, you will wrestle with professional principles, your employer's interests and standards, the public's interests and the higher societal values of truth-telling, honesty, courage and so forth.
- As a media consumer—a reader, viewer or listener but not a media professional—you will examine the ethical conduct of newspapers, magazines, tele-

vision and radio in deciding which to support with your subscription fee and time, and which to reject. And, you will judge the media in general as a powerful institution in our society.

A MORAL AGENT'S MOTIVATION

Understanding what motivates moral agents—what motivates you—is crucial to evaluating whether decision making is reasoned and independent or merely self-centered and careerism.

Plainly, what purport to be ethical judgments sometimes are neither independent nor principled. These factors often intrude into the decision making process.

FEAR

"My editors said to write it that way—or else. My job was at stake, so I did what they said."

Fear of losing a job often is a reality in newsrooms. Principled editors will listen to your ethical concerns; some will even relieve you of an assignment that you fear will confront you with a crisis of conscience. But you're paid to perform as directed, and your alternatives might be to resign—or get fired.

DESIRE FOR REWARD

It's easy to calculate what your editors want, then report and write—without threat or prompting—in conformity with their expectations. It's also easy to convince yourself that their way is the right way, even when your conscience is whispering that it isn't.

Rewards for being a team player can be salary increases or promotion. Those who buck the system can become known as difficult to work with, and their career future can become dark.

THE HERD INSTINCT

We all like to be part of a group, accepted by colleagues. In journalism, this can create the herd instinct, with reporters mindlessly following the lead of other reporters, with editors accepting the news values and judgments of other editors.

Danger lies in unthinkingly accepting as valid the values and principles of those around you. Read newspapers as you travel across the country and you'll find disturbing conformity in news selection, writing styles, layout and design. Watch the evening news on a local TV station and you may not be able to tell whether you're in Seattle or Savannah, Miami or Minneapolis.

Following the herd sometimes creates instant trends in American journalism and dampens independent thinking.

THE RULES

Many journalists avoid personal responsibility in ethics and justify decisions on grounds that "This is company policy" or, absent a policy, "Well, that's the way things are done around here."

In broadcasting, decision making often is based on rule of law, not independent moral reasoning. As federally regulated media, both radio and television matured in a belief that what's "right" is meeting Federal Communications Commission regulations. That slowed—stunted—development of independent ethical thinking by some in broadcasting.

THE MARKETING CONCEPT

Except for a few nonprofit organizations, American media must fight for profit in an intensely competitive commercial marketplace. That requires courting readers, viewers, listeners, communities—markets all.

Increasingly, news judgments are based on what the market wants, not what trained journalists think the market needs. Reader opinion surveys have supplanted editors' judgments at some newspapers.

Ask yourself whether your moral reasoning truly stems from higher principle, or is born of ethical-reactive instinct—a very human tendency to react not to what is right to do but, rather, to think first of what your boss, your readers or viewers or the market might want you to do.

TIMING AND CONTEXT OF DECISION MAKING

You may desire to be a free thinker who is independent in moral reasoning, but you cannot be truly free. None of us can be.

We all live and think within a context of our culture, of socioeconomic pressures, historical and political factors. We cannot step aside from history, spurn Aristotle, ignore Kant.

Neither can we avoid being influenced by the timing of our decision making.

For example, you probably agree in general that it's right—a good thing—for a newspaper or TV station to present in-depth, analytical coverage of increases in violent crime in a city's streets. That's what good journalism is all about, right?

But, how about coverage *during* the mayor's reelection campaign? What if coverage starts one week before voters go to the polls and continues until election eve? What if the timing of coverage implies—or voters infer from it—that increased violence somehow is the mayor's fault, and the challenger thus wins in a landslide?

Is timing important in decision making? You bet!

Important, too, is cultural context—the societal influences we've discussed and local norms of behavior, such as your employer's policies, peer pressure and the attitudes of friends.

Things can get really complicated when the cultural context of decision making is completely foreign.

For example, The Associated Press once assigned me to a team of reporters covering a big story in Indonesia. We rented a house in Jakarta, then discovered the owner, a high-ranking government official, demanded payment not in Indonesian currency but in U.S. dollars, deposited not in a local bank but in a foreign land. The official was asking us to help him evade—break—his own country's tax codes and foreign exchange laws!

In the United States, we would have refused his demands. In the cultural context of Indonesia such practices were then common. We AP correspondents, all old Asia hands, knew such squeeze was an accepted cost of doing business. We made the deal.

Philosopher Kant would argue we were wrong, that moral values are universally applicable and that we shouldn't do anything in Asia that we didn't want adopted as a principle in America.

Were we wrong? You make the call.

On another assignment, in India, I *tried* to break the law. I tried to sneak past Indian army sentries posted to prevent correspondents from approaching U.S. transport planes landing to deliver weapons. India, a self-proclaimed neutral nation, had begged for U.S. help during a border war with China, high in the Himalayas.

Indian officials were chagrined at relying on America, a nation they often maligned. For their own political purposes, they barred correspondents from witnessing an event of compelling importance to our readers back in the United States.

Back home, I wouldn't have broken U.S. law. But these were the options I saw: protect the sensibilities of Indian politicians (not high among my priorities) or try to elude those sentries and, as surrogate of my readers, reach that airfield.

Is mandatory respect for the law—all laws, everywhere—a universal moral value? Even if it's a seemingly irrational regulation in a far-off land designed to prevent American readers (and taxpayers) from learning something they should know about U.S. foreign policy?

Kant, again, would not be pleased with me. He would argue that respect for the law must be a universal value and that Americans shouldn't break a foreign country's laws unless they want law-breaking condoned in the United States.

What do you think? Consider moral values and journalistic principles. Reflect on all the pressures I felt from my professional peers, my employer (AP's foreign desk in New York wanted that story). Then, you act as a moral agent and judge my conduct. (Incidentally, an alert sentry nabbed me; I had to write the story from second-hand accounts.)

THE IMPACT OF YOUR DECISION MAKING

As a journalist, your decision making will have enormous impact on people. The power of the press is not an idle phrase.

Media professionals make judgment calls that can tumble stock markets, overturn governments, ruin careers, besmirch reputations. And, those decisions often are made quickly, under deadline pressure and without much discussion or reflection.

Indeed, many journalists regard their job as simply printing the news—ensuring its accuracy and balance, of course, but not agonizing very much over whether someone or something will be hurt by the fallout.

Understand: Few media professionals today subscribe to a print-and-be-damned philosophy. Many, however, say they cannot—and should not—agonize over possible impact of stories. After all, newspapers must be rushed to readers; TV and radio newscasts must be ready on time.

Yet, all we've studied, from Socrates forward, strongly implies that moral agents must reflect, must take time to consider whether their moral judgments, as in the Judeo-Christian ethic, are displaying love and respect for persons in the news—or whether, as in John Rawls' teaching, they are dealing fairly with people and preventing or at least minimizing harm to weaker persons or minority groups.

Often, of course, a news story's likely impact is clear and a decision indeed can be made quickly with complete journalistic validity: Will a priest be ruined if a newspaper or TV station reports charges that he's a child molester? Very likely. But if the charges are official, if the priest is under arrest, few editors will hesitate for long.

Sometimes, however, the likely impact is not so obvious and the question arises of just how much reflection, how much discussion is needed before the decision is made to go with the story.

For example, a guest on CNN's *Larry King Live* talk show made unsubstantiated assertions that his wife's brain tumor was linked to her use of a cellular telephone. Within eight days, there was a 17 percent drop in the price of shares of Motorola, Inc., largest U.S. supplier of cellular equipment. Shares lost millions of dollars in value.[12]

Should King have anticipated such impact? Could he have anticipated it?

MORAL AGENTS MUST ACT

Whatever your motivation as a moral agent, however long you agonize over likely impact, you accomplish nothing in ethics unless you act.

Justice remains an abstraction, for example, unless journalists act to ensure their writing gives fair and equal treatment to all in the news. Social utility—utilitarianism—is a meaningless concept unless journalists act to bring about the greatest social benefit, the greatest good for the largest number of people.

So, our study must move forward, in Chapter Two, to steps you can take in acting in accordance with your decision making.

First, a caveat.

JOURNALISM'S LORE: MYTH OR REALITY?

Before proceeding, note: Many Americans don't believe the media subscribe wholly and selflessly to the societal values and journalistic principles we've been discussing.

Indeed, some Americans believe this country's media subscribe generally to no motive more worthy than profit and that naked self-interest comes first for journalists and media owners alike.

Further, some see more myth than reality in journalism's lore, which holds that the history of our press is of unceasing and selfless labor on behalf of freedom, justice and other "right" causes since Colonial days.

These doubts aren't simply knee-jerk reactions from angry citizens in a street poll after the latest media hoax or outrage. Responsible social scientists, media critics and, of course, journalists themselves find weaknesses in media performance.

So, we cannot leave this chapter's discussion of values and principles without underlying three realities that somewhat deflate myths:

Reality Number One

Anyone who really understands reporters knows that generally their biggest single motivation is desire to take over front pages or the evening news with a big story.

Idealistic search for truth and belief in the people's right to know are important. But even greater influences are prized by-lines and a TV stand-up on the White House lawn.

Of course, even aggressive careerism (sometimes called *ethical egoism*) isn't all bad. It often uncovers stories that inform and enlighten the public on important matters.

Reality Number Two

If you read a couple of books on ethics you may dedicate more time and thought to moral reasoning than do many working journalists.

Judgment calls on ethical issues made more through instinct and habit than out of structured moral reasoning are only part of journalism's problem. Many news organizations have no formal ethical guidelines, and some editors and news directors even avoid structured discussion of ethics in their newsrooms. These newsroom chiefs say they are paid to make decisions by themselves, not to consult rule books or hold round-table discussions with staffers every time an ethical problem arises.

Reality Number Three

Although many media companies claim public service is their top priority, the reality is that, with very few nonprofit exceptions, the media are businesses operated first for the economic self-interest of their owners and second for the public.

News thus is collected and shaped for sale, a product created by human beings for the commercial marketplace, not a holy thing produced through divine intervention.

It cannot be otherwise, of course. The totally unacceptable alternative to profit-oriented, free-enterprise journalism is journalism subsidized—and thus controlled—by government or special interest groups. Nevertheless, some critics would be more comfortable if the media openly acknowledged their business interests and didn't claim special societal status and benefits, such as preferential postal rates for print publications, or free use of public airways by TV and radio.[13]

So, let's take a balanced, dispassionate view of media lore as we continue our study.

Summary

Decision making in ethics can be visualized as a continuum: First assemble the facts, then identify the ethical issues, consider alternative solutions, decide and act.

Assembling all relevant facts requires deep probing beneath obvious details. Often, you'll identify more than one ethical issue. Sometimes, there are several different—and tempting—ways to resolve your ethical dilemma. Or, you may have only undesirable options and be forced to choose the least offensive. Acting in ethics can be painful because you often must take a position that draws criticism.

Dr. Ralph Potter showed one way to structured moral reasoning with his Potter Box. Adapted to our purpose, this envisages the following:

1. Collect all facts, understand the five Ws, particularly the real who, what, why.
2. Consider societal values: truth-telling, humaneness, stewardship, the Golden Mean, justice, freedom, the Golden Rule, promise keeping.
3. Consider journalistic principles: serve the public, monitor the powerful, be balanced and fair, be compassionate, guard the First Amendment, be courageous and independent.
4. Consider your loyalties to self and conscience, to society, to the hand that feeds you, to professional peers.

As moral agents, reporters judge ethical intricacies of a story; editors shape ethics guidelines for their staffs; media managers decide how their newspapers, magazines or broadcast outlets resolve ethical quandaries.

Acting as a moral agent in public relations or advertising forces you to wrestle with loyalties to self, employer's interests, the public's interests and the higher societal values of truth-telling, honesty and so forth.

Even as a media consumer you act as a moral agent, judging the ethical conduct of publications you read or television you view.

Moral agents are motivated by fear (of losing your job, for example), desire for reward (promotion or raise), the herd instinct (a tendency to unthinkingly follow the lead of other journalists), the rules of employers and the marketing concept, which leads some journalists to evaluate news not for its intrinsic importance but, rather, for what audiences might want.

The timing, context and likely impact of decision making are extremely important. How the story will affect people must be considered, too.

A balanced study of ethics must consider the view of many that much of journalism's lore is myth. Some critics regard journalists as self-centered and not concerned first with serving the public.

Notes

1. Reporters' news-gathering techniques are discussed in detail in Conrad C. Fink, *Introduction to Professional Newswriting* (White Plains, N.Y.: Longman, 1992) and Conrad C. Fink and Donald E. Fink, *Introduction to Magazine Writing* (Columbus, OH: Macmillan, 1994).
2. Journalistic myth vs. reality is discussed in meaningful detail in Edmund B. Lambeth, *Committed Journalism* (Bloomington: Indiana University Press, 1986). Note particularly pp. 4–6.
3. Tebbets retired a general and died years later, still tied to the Enola Gay. Newspaper obituaries mentioned prominently that he flew the plane that destroyed Hiroshima.
4. The Potter Box and reasoning processes that flow from it are covered well in Clifford G. Christians, Kim B. Rotzoll and Mark Fackler, *Media Ethics, Cases & Moral Reasoning,* 3rd ed. (White Plains, N.Y.: Longman, 1991).
5. The Commission on Freedom of the Press, *A Free and Responsible Press* (Chicago: University of Chicago Press, 1947).
6. Theodore Peterson, Fred S. Siebert and Wilbert Schramm, *Four Theories of the Press* (Urbana: University of Illinois Press, 1956).
7. Kent Cooper, *Barriers Down* (New York: Farrar and Rinehart, 1942).
8. For fine treatment of right to know, see *The Public's Right to Know* (Washington, D.C.: Media Institute, 1980).
9. See particularly Douglas Cater, *The Fourth Branch of Government* (New York: Vintage Books, 1959).
10. Significant polling in this subject has been conducted by the Gallup Organization under commission from Times Mirror Co., Times Mirror Square, Los Angeles, Calif. 90053. Dr. Robert Wyatt of Middle Tennessee State University was principal researcher for the ASNE poll on the Bill of Rights.
11. John A. Rawls, *A Theory of Justice* (Cambridge, Mass.: Harvard University Press, 1971).
12. "Wireless Wonder," *Forbes,* April 26, 1993, p. 12.
13. I discuss marketing attitudes of all media in *Inside the Media* (White Plains, N.Y.: Longman, 1990).

PART 2

ETHICS IN THE PURSUIT OF NEWS

Let's get personal.

It's time you personally started interpreting the values and principles we studied in Chapter 1—time you began building your personal code of ethics.

I suggest this: Just as you are building personal skills in news reporting and writing, or any other subject, so must you sharpen—simultaneously—your skill at decision making in ethics. It's not enough to enter journalism simply as a skilled reporter and wordsmith; you also must be equipped to think ethics on the job.

We'll start this detailed process in Part 2, a three-chapter examination of factors you may want to include in your personal interpretation of what's right and wrong, ethical and unethical, in hands-on daily journalism.

In Chapter 2, "Your Personal Code: Troubling Concepts," we'll look at basic issues confronting working journalists—objectivity, conflicts of interest, invasion of privacy, good taste and others.

Chapter 3, "The Ethics of Technique," looks at honesty in reporting and writing, the adversarial stances some reporters take, how to deal ethically with sources, and generally how journalists should conduct themselves on a story.

In Chapter 4, "You and Your Editor," we confront a reality: You and your personal sense of ethics must mesh with your editor's approach to ethics. We'll discuss ways to handle that reality.

Let's start with troubling concepts you'll inevitably encounter.

CHAPTER 2

YOUR PERSONAL CODE: TROUBLING CONCEPTS

If you think it was difficult in Chapter 1 to sort out vague societal values and sweeping journalistic principles, wait until you see what's ahead!

We're going to grapple in detail with some of journalism's most troubling concepts, just as print and broadcast reporters must do every day. This is certain to inject new complexities into your own effort to build a personal code of ethics.

For example, most of us in journalism agree the societal value of humaneness is good and that justice is right. But there is no unanimity on some concepts we'll now look at, such as objectivity. Yet, mastering a personal approach to such controversial concepts is what thinking ethics is all about in daily journalism.

Let's start with one of the toughest.

OBJECTIVITY: THE WORTHWHILE GOAL

Whatever your personal beliefs or political persuasion, there are publications and broadcast operations somewhere in this country that reflect your views. You could happily report for one of them as a liberal or conservative—or anything in between. To express personal views on many topics, you could write editorials for newspapers or television or do a signed column.

Such *advocacy journalism* offers exciting, rewarding, meaningful careers. However, if advocacy is your choice, you should consider two factors:

1. It is unethical to blur the distinction between advocacy journalism and the fair and objective reporting that is the goal of much newspaper and televi-

sion journalism today. If you want to be an advocate, work for an advocacy medium.

2. If advocacy is your choice, openly put your advocate's label on now and display it for all to see. Don't masquerade unethically under the title of objective reporter or secretly carry your crusade into a newsroom that is trying to do an objective job of reporting.

True objectivity is impossible to achieve, of course. Each of us is shaped by background and experiences that inevitably influence how we see things and act as journalists. But objectivity is a worthwhile goal, and as a journalist you must recognize—and overcome—the very human tendency to let personal feelings influence your reporting and writing. If you are a conscientious journalist, this can be a struggle as long as you are in the newsroom.

Be particularly alert at five key points in the sequence of events leading to publication or broadcast of a news story.

STORY SELECTION

Hundreds—thousands—of story ideas are available to a newspaper or television news department. The *New York Times'* editors look each day at millions of words in news and feature copy; on an average weekday they publish only 200,000 or so. Obviously, some stories must be covered—the hard news about government, accidents, trials and so forth. But the individual journalist often has great discretion in choosing which nonspot or timeless stories will be covered.

Will you do a personality profile on a new, rising political star? A feature on abortion clinics? A background piece on crime in the streets? Examine your personal mindset, your prejudices. You have an ethical problem if you are selecting, even subconsciously, only stories that fit your own way of thinking. Are you intentionally picking stories to prove a point? Or, more properly, are you selecting stories with news merit that truly are important to your readers or viewers?

Space and time limitations often mean only stories of compelling importance to the largest number of readers or viewers can be covered. But serving the greatest news needs of most readers or viewers is not always the only yardstick against which a story's news merits should be measured. Your ethical responsibility as a journalist includes spotting, highlighting and explaining stories you know to be significant, even if most of your readers or viewers do not understand that.

SOURCE SELECTION

There is a danger of subconsciously seeking news from only sources who agree with you. If you believe abortion is immoral, news sources who agree probably will sound more logical. Whatever your views, beware you don't gravitate unthinkingly toward only those sources who think as you do.

Tapping sources on all sides of a story is just common sense, of course. What often is overlooked, however, is that you have an ethical responsibility to ensure that those representing contrasting viewpoints hold equally authoritative credentials. A Democrat dog catcher indeed represents part of the other side of a story

VIEWPOINT

Right to Publish versus Right Thing to Do

"The trouble with you journalists is that you are all mixed up between what the Constitution gives you a right to publish and the right thing to do."

Potter Stewart, late U.S. Supreme Court Justice, quoted by Fred W. Friendly, former president of CBS News[1]

involving your Republican mayor. But the dog catcher cannot authoritatively comment on how the mayor is handling citywide expenditure of millions of dollars.

FACT SELECTION AND ARRANGEMENT

Back in the newsroom, your notebook full of facts, you must write a lead and structure a story as objectively as possible. Obviously, not every argument you have heard on, say, abortion can be in your lead. In broadcast, you may have 30 seconds or so for a story.

You must select facts, gained from equally authoritative sources, that will present a balanced story. Devoting your lead and the subsequent 10 paragraphs to the proabortion viewpoint, and quoting the other side only in the 12th paragraph, is failing your ethical responsibility to present the facts in a balanced manner.

LANGUAGE SELECTION

The language you use in writing a story can be highly prejudicial.

Consider the different effect if you write that a source "admitted nervously" as contrasted with "acknowledged." What different pictures you paint if you write that a witness "walked" or "strutted" to the stand! What enormous difference there is in describing a person as "antiabortionist" or a "right-to-life advocate."

In one story, the *Wall Street Journal* prejudiced readers by stating a woman "began lamely" to explain her viewpoint. The *New York Times* said a man "brazenly admitted" an advertising agency's strategy had changed (making it sound criminal). The *Times* also said a political candidate used "spicy rhetoric" and "skewered" one opponent and "mocked" another.

When Oliver L. North began campaigning in 1994 for Virginia's Republican Senate nomination, a *New York Times* reporter, Maureen Dowd, wrote that he was a "swashbuckling Marine" with an "altar-boy gaze" who had "lied" to the U.S. Senate about his involvement in the Iran-Contra affair during Ronald Reagan's presidency. The front-page story, titled "Political Memo," said that North, in an interview, "showed the charm that made him a television hero to many—smiling that famous Mad Magazine gap-toothed grin a lot—but exhibited little of his old cowboy 'charge up the hill' side." Could you draw a negative mental image of North from this *news* story?

VIEWPOINT

Another View of Bias

"Could it be that bias sometimes is in the eye of the beholder? Do we sometimes have slanted readers?

"People are so committed, so involved, so agitated in this age of change and controversy and instant communications that many of them look for newspaper accounts of events—from Nicaragua to South Africa—to reinforce and agree with their own views, even their prejudices. If they don't get that, they often feel the press is not credible."

Warren H. Phillips, then chairman and chief executive officer, Dow Jones & Co., Inc.

Sometimes, the ethical call is extremely close on whether language crosses from *reporting* into *editorializing.* You judge this (emphasis added): " . . . Mr. [H. Ross] Perot faced a battery of questions that finally provoked him to *sharp replies,* which seem to be *typical of his style when he is challenged by reporters.*"[2]

You also can go astray when you write how people *feel* or *think,* instead of what they *say.* Example: "*Negative feelings* also emerged from Republicans who took no position." That was from the *New York Times.* In the same story, on opposition to Zoe Baird, President Clinton's Democratic nominee for U.S. Attorney General, the writer quotes Sen. Bob Dole of Kansas, Republican leader in the Senate: "Mr. Dole said, 'We're reserving judgment,' and then grinned as he stared at the ceiling." What did *that* signal to readers?[3]

Achieving complete neutrality in language is, like achieving total objectivity, arguably impossible. But even-handed, fair use of language must be a goal for any writer dedicated to presenting a balanced account.

TIMING AND CONTEXT

A spot, or "breaking," news story sets its own timing and rhythm. If the President of the United States speaks on U.S. involvement in Bosnia, that's news *right now.* The story's timing and the context in which it's published are out of a journalist's hands.

But for much of the news, a journalist selects timing and context, and that can be crucial in determining the impact a story will have.

For example, coverage of Paul Tsongas' physical health *in 1991* wouldn't have created widespread impact (indeed it's unlikely it would have been a major national story at all). However, *in 1992,* Tsongas was a leading candidate for the Democrat presidential nomination and there was detailed coverage of his bone cancer. Clearly, timing of coverage was instrumental in Tsongas' decision to withdraw from the race.

The context of coverage varied widely. Some stories depicted one man in a courageous struggle against disease. Other stories were more pointed. For exam-

VIEWPOINT

Truth and Objectivity

"Truth is the ultimate goal.

"Objectivity in reporting the news is another goal that serves as the mark of an experienced professional. It is a standard of performance toward which we strive. We honor those who achieve it."

"Code of Ethics," Society of Professional Journalists, adopted 1926, revised 1973, 1984, 1987

ple, candidates' health was discussed by William Safire of the *New York Times* in a column that started, "The last time a dying man ran for President of the U.S. was in 1944." The column actually unfolded as a dispassionate, balanced discussion of an issue—candidates' health—essential to voters. But within the context of that lead paragraph, Tsongas' health took a very special meaning.[4]

None of this means a journalist's news judgments and ethical decision making should be based only on the impact publication likely will have. It does mean an ethical journalist must understand that timing and context can have dramatic effect.

Objectivity is a highly complex concept. Two alternative views, one from inside the media and another from outside, illustrate that:

Jay T. Harris, executive editor of the *Philadelphia Daily News,* argues American journalists are "becoming reluctant to harp on that which is wrong or dangerous in our society and to continue to harp on it until it is made right." Further, he argues journalists should be "conscious, open and continuing advocates for that which is right and necessary . . ."[5] The weakness in Harris's position: Who shall determine what is "wrong or dangerous" and "right and necessary"?

A greater challenge comes from Roberto C. Goizueta, chairman of Coca-Cola Co., often the subject of media coverage. Goizueta told an editors' meeting,

> . . . the single most damaging trait in today's journalism, in my opinion, is that in the search for, and preoccupation with, objectivity and balance, the important elements of context, perspective and judgment often suffer. I will even be so blunt as to say that with some reporters and editors, it may be the result of just plain taking the easy road intellectually.
>
> Understanding and reporting the importance of events in their proper context surely is a heavy responsibility to place on anyone, but in fact, I believe the journalist has that obligation. . . . The consumers of print journalism want to see an editor's opinion on the editorial page, but we need his or her judgment as to significance, relevance and truth reflected in news stories.[6]

Goizueta thus argues the journalist's ethical responsibility is to not only judge the news merits and facts of an event, but also its truth.

YES. BUT IS IT TRUE?

Do reporters have an ethical responsibility to determine the truth of stories they report? Is it enough to state facts and quote authoritative sources? Or, must reporters determine the underlying validity of those facts and quotes?

Those questions resurrect a journalistic nightmare out of the 1950s, when a Republican senator from Wisconsin, Joe McCarthy, manipulated reporters through shrewd understanding of what in those days was their very narrow interpretation of objective reporting. It was sufficient—indeed, for many required—to limit reporting to who said what and when. A U.S. senator could be quoted at length and virtually without challenge if, for example, he scurried about the country, making unsubstantiated charges of communist infiltration in high places and assassinating with abandon previously unblemished reputations.

And that, of course, is precisely what McCarthy did—and what the media did. A U.S. Senator was saying it, and that meant it was news; it was somebody else's job to determine whether it was truth.

It was agonizing for reporters of the who-said-what-and-when school. They could see the senator jumping ahead, from charge to charge, never letting rebuttal catch up. A person attacked today tried to respond tomorrow, but by that time McCarthy was attacking someone else, again seizing headlines. McCarthy, who thoroughly understood media operations, often timed news conferences just before presses rolled. Day after day, newspapers carried his latest charge before they could obtain balancing comment.

From the McCarthy experience came a true turn in American journalism, a realization that balancing charge with response by quoting the other side a day or so later was inadequate. There evolved a new, much wider definition of objectivity that requires a reporter to provide analysis or interpretation in addition to factual reporting.

This requires balancing the relative validity of charge and countercharge, expanding a "straight news" story with a wider context that lets reader or viewer judge the truth—inserting balancing material within a single story or placing an interpretive news analysis next to the spot news story.

Interpretive coverage developed further during the Vietnam War and Nixon presidency, when straight news reporting proved inadequate in revealing official lies and coverups. The complexity of other stories—in politics, science, economics—forces reporters more deeply into analytical writing.

This is dangerous business for a reporter, of course. Where is the line between reporting facts and inserting your opinion? If you transfer interpretation from editorial page to front page, how can your reader differentiate between news and opinion?

Some print and TV reporters in the 1960s and 1970s went too far. They created "new journalism," variously considered impressionistic and humanistic, or participatory and activist. Its proponents plunged into advocacy journalism, sometimes labeling their work as interpretive and sometimes not.

VIEWPOINT

Living with the Consequences

"We see ourselves as driven professionals, informed by good intentions and purposes. Readers see us as moral vigilantes, driven only by the desire to sell newspapers. We protest our meritorious intentions. But the public does not understand. We protest that we bear no responsibility for the consequences of our journalism. It is a world, many of us feel, we never made. We only report.

"Baloney. As human beings, editors and reporters ought to be terribly burdened, haunted, by the very real consequences of our decisions to publish. We ought to live uncomfortably with the fact that our journalism does damage. It can only be redeemed by the knowledge that, on balance, it helped more than it hurt."

Arnold Rosenfeld, then editor of the *Dayton (Ohio) Daily News*

In its worst form, new journalism featured made-up quotes and composite—that is, fictional—characters. This was considered acceptable as long as the result was a story of "truth." Today, it is a technique rejected by ethical journalists.

How—or whether—a reporter should attempt to divine truth can be hotly debated. There can be no quarrel, however, with the proposition that in seeking fairness and balance, the journalist must be open and frank with reader or viewer. For example, an individual accused in a story of wrongdoing obviously should have right of reply in that same story; if that individual cannot be reached, or declines comment, the story should explain.

However, the writer who goes beyond that, with a paragraph or two on how a story was researched or which sources were contacted, can add for reader or viewer a dimension of understanding that helps establish trust in the story, and thus in the journalist and the newspaper or television station.

Within the context of the media's credibility problems, it is not enough to know in your heart that you are practicing ethical journalism. A journalist must be *perceived by the public as being ethical.*

CONFLICT OF INTEREST: REAL AND PERCEIVED

A small-town newspaper sports writer in south Georgia simultaneously worked as general manager of a local radio station and served on both the school board and county board of commissioners. Nobody in town, including his newspaper employer, seemed to think worse of him for wearing four hats. "I don't see any conflict of interest," said the journalist-radio manager-public official.[7]

At the *New York Times,* a wine critic resigned when it was revealed he had written a book for a wine importer. Said a *Times* spokesperson, "We really don't feel comfortable with a critic doing a subsidized book." Said the ex-critic, "The *Times* clearly overreacted. . . . What I did was write an objective book. . . . I have never endorsed a product. . . ."[8]

The two cases illustrate ethical questions long plaguing journalists: Where does professional life end and personal life begin? Must one dictate how the other is conducted? Must the reporter give up rights—and responsibilities—of citizenship, such as political work, to avoid conflict of interest? Must a journalist become an emotional, psychological and social bystander in pursuit of dispassionate, balanced reporting and writing?

It clearly is unethical for journalists to let personal views influence their reporting. But many newspapers and TV organizations go beyond that, insisting journalists avoid any outside activity that creates perception of conflict of interest.

ABC News, in a staff policy statement, puts it this way:

> Individuals should recognize that the same rules of conduct followed in their professional lives must also be observed in their private affairs. The distinction between professional and private is too fine to admit any essential difference. For example, a compromising offer is no less so if it involves vacation time instead of a work situation. Both must be refused.[9]

The *Charlotte (N.C.) Observer* treats the issue this way in its code of ethics:

> It goes without saying that no *Observer* staffer would ever show favoritism in the news columns in exchange for gifts or favors. So in most circumstances our concern is the appearance of conflict of interest, not actual conflict.
>
> The best general guide to conduct is that we accept nothing of value for which we do not pay. To be specific: You go to lunch with a news source who picks up the tab. That's fine, and next time you pick up the tab and put it on your expense account. Someone courts you as a pipeline into the paper and wants to give you a bottle of whiskey. Decline, with thanks, as gracefully as you can. We don't want to be sanctimonious about this, but we want our people to carry their weight.
>
> In addition, there's an obvious reason not to write stories concerning outside interests in which you are involved unless your editors know of your involvement and your story discloses that involvement.

The *Observer* code also covers outside conduct by journalists:

> You have the right to determine what you do in your private life, and so does your spouse, but that private life might affect what newsroom duties you could take on.
>
> Whenever a potential for conflict between personal and professional activities arises, prudence dictates open discussion with supervisors.
>
> In general, be wary of political commitment, although this need not mean civic isolation. Part of our obligation as citizens is to make decisions about candidates and issues and act on them.
>
> But it is also clearly part of our obligation as journalists to insure that our reputations as objective fact-finders are not blemished by a display of our political views.
>
> Generally that means the public ought not to be able to tell by our behavior how we feel about an issue or candidate. . . .[10]

VIEWPOINT

Journalist or Social Worker?

Do journalists compromise their objectivity if they publicly identify themselves as partisan supporters of a controversial issue?

Nancy Monaghan, publisher of the *Chambersburg (Pa.) Public Opinion,* says they do. After some journalists joined a pro-choice demonstration in Washington, D.C., Monaghan wrote:

"There are plenty of hard questions involved in journalism ethics, but marching in a demonstration about abortion isn't one of them . . .

"You have to decide whether you want to be a journalist or a social worker."

Gannett Co., owner of the *Public Opinion,* endorsed Monaghan's position by reproducing her statement in *Gannetteer,* a company magazine distributed to thousands of employees in its 81 (1994) newspapers, broadcast stations and other operations.[11]

Note the *Observer*'s preoccupation with public perception of newsroom staffers and their conduct because of corporate concerns for the image of the newspaper itself. Many news organizations similarly write codes primarily to protect corporate image, and only secondarily to present precise ethical instructions for individual journalists attempting to frame personal approaches to ethical issues.

That is—again—you are on your own in fashioning a personal code.

In avoiding conflict of interest, several key areas are particularly troublesome.

CONFLICTING PUBLIC PRESENCE

You will find it difficult to stay independent in your own mind if, like the south Georgia sports writer, you participate actively in a political process or event you cover. And, you cannot expect readers or viewers to accept you as a truly dispassionate reporter if, even in off-hours, you demonstrate political commitment by, say, working for the local Democrat or Republican party. Can you trust yourself—can any discerning reader or viewer trust you—on the education beat if you are a member of the city board of education? Obviously, no.

Not so obvious is that high-profile involvement in any partisan endeavor outside the newsroom likely will prejudice your position. If, for example, you become a community activist, even in such worthy endeavors as the United Way or local blood bank, you join the structure—the system—on which you report; you leave the ranks of observers and join the activists.

Reporter activism *while on the job* made news during the 1994 Super Bowl in Atlanta. About 50 football writers (black and white) demonstrated briefly against the Georgia state flag flying atop the stadium. The flag contains a Civil

War Confederate symbol. A black sports columnist for the *Detroit News,* Terry Foster, said, "I remember growing up with my great-grandfathers and great-grandmothers saying how the South was and how they hated that flag." The Atlanta demonstration quickly faded from view, although it clearly took reporters across the line of objectivity and into political activism, if even for only a few minutes.

The issue of public presence versus professional detachment extends even to spouses. A Seattle newspaper warned its managing editor he would be fired if his wife worked as the mayor's press secretary. (She quit.) CBS News warns its staffers they "must avoid any conflict between their personal interests and the interests of CBS," adding, "Each employee will be held responsible for seeing to it that neither he nor she nor any member of his or her immediate family has any interest, or engages in any activity, which is in conflict with this policy."[12]

CONFLICTING PERSONAL INTERESTS

Explosive growth of business news coverage focuses new attention on whether reporters can invest in the stock market and still be dispassionate observers of the business scene.

Obviously, it is grossly unethical for a reporter to manipulate news coverage or use inside information for personal profits. That's clearly treason to the higher calling of every journalist and fundamental betrayal of everything a principled newspaper or TV news operation stands for.

But ethical questions arising out of a conflict of interest seldom are so clear cut. For example, business reporters obviously should not trade in, say, stock of an auto manufacturing company they cover; a single favorable story could raise that stock's price, creating profit for its shareholders (including the reporters).

But, should reporters not trade in stock of *any* auto companies? Should reporters avoid holdings even in the companies, such as tire manufacturers, whose fortunes rise and fall with the auto companies?

Indeed, should journalists avoid any outside investments? Some newspapers require staffers, particularly those in business reporting, to reveal to their supervisors any private investments that might create a conflict of interest. However, none requires of its own staffers the same public revelations of personal finances required of candidates for major government office. As vice president and editor of the *St. Paul (Minn.) Pioneer Press and Dispatch,* John Finnegan argued journalists should publicly divulge their private interests, perhaps even publish periodically a statement of net worth listing stock holdings and other investments.[13] Since such forced revelations by reporters logically would compel editors and publishers to likewise tell all, there was not much support in the news industry for Finnegan's position.

Clearly, however, a journalist serious about establishing a personal position of trust should (1) discuss any possible conflict of interest with an editor/supervisor and (2) decline any assignment that conceivably could create a conflict.

CASE STUDY

The Reporter and "Inside" Information

You are a 35-year-old reporter for a highly profitable newspaper owned by a media conglomerate. You are paid $575 weekly, barely enough to live on in your high-cost city.

You frequently write a column reporting what you have heard from stockbrokers and corporate executives about publicly traded stocks. Many "fat cat" speculators on Wall Street make money by reading your column for tips, then trading before the public, always slow in such matters, can trade.

You realize you can make money (and you sure need it) by trading before your column is printed and before the fat cats can act. You also can profit on your advance knowledge of what other reporters will publish.

Your paper warns employees against trading in stocks they write about or telling outsiders about their work. Of course, such work rules are laid down by executives made wealthy in the company's employ. And, who's kidding whom about company rules? Everybody knows they are broken daily—editors telephone home and charge the company, executives take a friend to lunch and put it on their expense account as "business luncheon."

Questions Is it unethical to bend the rules yourself by trading privately on your inside information, and beating the fat cats to the draw? If you thus augment your income, are there any victims of your action? You gathered the facts for columns under your byline. Who owns the product of your labors? Do your superiors, most of whom have investments of one kind or another, really expect you to live on $575 weekly?

That scenario developed at the *Wall Street Journal* in New York City when R. Foster Winans, frequent writer of the popular column "Heard on the Street," was charged with providing advance information to trader friends, and with them enjoying about $675,000 in profits. After an investigation by the Securities and Exchange Commission, Winans was sentenced in Federal District Court in 1985 to 18 months in prison, five years' probation and was fined $5,000 on charges of securities fraud and mail and wire fraud for misappropriating privileged information from the *Journal.* His confederates also drew jail terms and fines.

Said the *Journal*:

> We are saddened and shocked by this betrayal of trust. The *Journal* has stringent policies designed to protect against ethical abuses, including use of inside information. . . . When an individual breaks faith and casts a blot on the paper's reputation, it can only inspire a deep sense of hurt and outrage among all who have labored so hard to build that reputation.

What is a reporter's moral obligation to protect an employer's reputation? Were *Journal* readers betrayed?[14]

CASE STUDY

News or a Freebie?

You are a general assignment reporter who doubles as travel editor. Winter is just ahead when you get a tempting invitation: Would you like three days in the sun, all expenses paid, to attend a birthday party of a famous resort? You may bring a guest free. The invitation is equivalent to $2,000 in travel, hotel, food and entertainment costs. No strings attached; you need not write about the trip. Your paper has no policy on such things.

Question Will you accept?

More than 5,000 news people from many countries did in 1986, when Disney World in Florida celebrated its 15th anniversary. Disney said the $7.5 million in costs were shared with 17 airlines, 26 hotels, the State of Florida and 2 county governments trying to enhance central Florida's image.

Questions Does such wider sponsorship change your attitude toward the invitation? Would paying $150 for the trip, or even all costs change your mind? Disney offered those options.

The U.S. Chief Justice was there to talk about the bicentennial of the U.S. Constitution. Also there were other notables, including a *U.S. News & World Report* correspondent recently freed in Moscow, where he had been accused of espionage.

Questions Does inclusion of newsy events in the program change your attitude toward a free trip? Isn't Disney World legitimate *news* in your hometown? Don't many of your

FREEBIES, JUNKETS AND OTHER DISGUISED BRIBES

Whether it's a $900 airline ticket to a South Seas vacation or a $9 bottle of liquor, it can be construed as a bribe if offered you free by a government official, public relations person or news source. And forget trying to establish dollar limits, such as "anything under $9 is an acceptable gift, anything over that isn't."

Whatever their value, junkets and freebies are intended to influence news coverage. And, remember, it's not you they are trying to capture; they're romancing you only to capture your newspaper or newscast.

And, if you work for a newspaper or TV news operation that expects you to accept free press tickets to the opera or free rides on the team bus, you have the option of moving on to a new job where ethical professionalism meets your standard.

But, wait. As with most ethical issues, there are gray areas. I encountered many in my reporting career. For example, free transportation sometimes must be accepted. They include riding free into battle on a U.S. Army helicopter.

neighbors dream of taking their families there? And was Disney's publicity director correct in suggesting that ethical standards for hard news, such as government coverage, should not be applied to "entertainment news"? Could you go at Disney's expense but write or broadcast without a pro-Disney slant?

Reactions of journalists varied.

An editor from a small New Hampshire paper told a *New York Times* reporter (covering the affair at his paper's expense) she brought her husband and, "I hope the paper will give me a full page for it."

A Rochester, N.Y., radio station news director told the *Orlando Sentinel*: "We are going back and we are going to talk about it. If you lived in Rochester and it was 50 degrees and rainy, would you turn down a free trip?"

The president of the American Society of Newspaper Editors: "I am disappointed that so many reporters and editors aren't troubled by the acceptance." The executive editor of the *New York Times*: "I thought we had cleaned ourselves up and we haven't. It is astonishing."

Mike Royko, *Chicago Tribune* columnist, condemned "freeloaders" with "no qualms about grabbing a freebie." (He noted freebies often are part of political life, and added: "Who ever thought Mickey Mouse would be acting like a Chicago alderman?")

Question If you worked for a small paper or station that never could afford to send you on such an assignment would you then be justified in accepting a free trip?

Postscript It was at Disney World that the Associated Press Managing Editors Association met in 1975 and adopted an ethics code calling on journalists to "accept nothing of value from news sources or others outside the profession." It specifically termed expense-paid junkets as conflicts of interest.

(That's quite different, of course, from accepting free rides in a press plane following Air Force One and its important passenger, the President of the United States; news organizations pay for seats on that plane.)

Another gray area is created when a news source presses a gift on you in apparent ignorance of the ethical problem thus created. If you fear offending—and losing—the source, estimate the gift's value and send a check to your favorite charity. Advise the gift-giver you have made a donation in his or her name as your way of expressing thanks. And, do it in a *written* thank-you note. Keep a copy for your records.

PRIVACY: A SPECIAL AGONY

If you're sensitive to human suffering (that societal value of humaneness again!), you will feel special agony many times during a news career when you drag into the public spotlight an individual who doesn't want to be there, or when you poke your intrusive reporter's notebook or cameras into an embarrassing dark corner of someone's private life.

Your rationale may be, "It's news," or, "The public has a right to know." But that won't make you feel much better when you comprehend the hurt unwanted publicity inflicts on some individuals, or when you see in the eyes of a new widow the pain caused by your probing questions at that terrible moment in her life.

Few ethical issues will cause you more difficulty than the godlike attempt to balance the individual's right to privacy, the right to be left alone, against your responsibility to inform readers and viewers about matters in which they have justifiable news interest.

The judgment call is less difficult concerning public officials, those who seek public office, and public figures, such as movie stars and athletes who choose the public spotlight.

The public has every right to be informed of official conduct, obviously. But has the public the right to know about an official's private life? Or, does the right to know extend only to private affairs that might affect official duties? If so, where is the line between private life and official duties?

Every journalist who has covered Washington knows of highly placed government officials who are secret alcoholics, secret philanderers. When such information breaks into public view through the media, the rationale usually is that private misconduct has affected official duty—the senator no longer can function in the role for which he was elected. When reporters don't cover it, the rationale is that he can drink all night but still function during the day, so why publish the information?

But who is qualified to make such judgment calls? You, the journalist? Who elected you to play God?

THE GARY HART CASE

Raging debate over these issues erupted in 1987 when the *Miami Herald* reported that Gary Hart, the leading contender for the Democratic presidential nomination in 1988, had put himself in a compromising position with a 29-year-old woman. Hart, 50, had been dogged throughout his political career by rumors that he was a "womanizer."

But, Hart's relationship with women other than his wife of 28 years had been talked about privately more than written about by Washington reporters—until the *Herald* broke its story. Acting on a tip, the *Herald* flew reporters to Washington, where, through the night, they staked out Hart's townhouse from the street and observed the former U.S. senator from Colorado accompanied by the young woman. Hart's wife was at their Colorado home at the time.

A familiar scenario went into play: A story about private behavior known to many but published by few was legitimatized for widespread publication when one newspaper published it. The floodgates opened. Hart's personal behavior became one of the biggest journalistic and political sensations in decades. The 29-year-old woman inevitably was described as a beautiful, blond, aspiring

VIEWPOINT

Journalists and Sex: Three Views

"America is an amazing country. [A politician] can completely dismiss the most menacing health epidemic in generations, deny the economy is in trouble though millions are out of work, steadfastly oppose gun control while more and more people are slaughtered each year, ignore whole families sleeping in the streets—and no reporter will ever stand up at a White House press conference and question your morality.

"But get caught screwing around outside your marriage and journalistic hearts—and presses—stop. Your sex life becomes the biggest story in the country. The Pack—as modern journalists call themselves when they converge for really important stories like Gennifer Flowers—swarms all over you, howling accusations you dare not deny and can't possibly confront truthfully."

Jon Katz, contributing editor of *Newsinc.*, commenting on media coverage of Ms. Flowers' claim that she had an affair with Bill Clinton before he ran for president

"As a general rule, I'm not at all sympathetic to those who say that we in the press are too nosy. I'm for being nosy. I don't even rule out the prospect that if a guy will cheat on his wife, he'll cheat on a lot of other things. I don't make any apology for feeling that there is a connection between character, keeping promises and telling the truth in private life and applying those principles to public life."

James Reston, long-time *New York Times* columnist, commenting on press coverage of politicians' private lives during his years in Washington

"High-caliber professional coverage of public affairs, be it in criminal justice or other areas, requires that serious, ethical journalism establish a zone of decency that effectively distinguishes rigorous, responsible reporting from sleazy, haphazard rumormongering and reckless endangerment of the quality of information reaching the public, not to mention the rights of individuals in such stories."

Everette E. Dennis, executive director, the Freedom Forum Media Studies Center[15]

actress. She was pictured on front pages and evening newscasts in a skimpy bikini. The *Washington Post* reported Hart had had a long-standing relationship with yet another woman. Reporters swarmed to the Hart home in Colorado seeking comment from the obviously distraught Mrs. Hart.

Hart fought back, accusing the *Herald* of sloppy, untruthful reporting and refusing to publish his side of the story. Then, with his standing in public opinion polls plummeting, Hart quit his campaign for the presidency with a statement that struck at the privacy issue.

He accused reporters of distorting stories about his personal life but ignoring his public policies. His private life had been overemphasized, he said, and, "I refuse to subject my family and my friends and innocent people and myself to further rumors and gossip." He added:

> We're all going to have to seriously question the system for selecting our national leaders, that reduces the press of this nation to hunters and presidential candidates to being hunted, that has reporters in bushes, false and inaccurate stories printed,

> photographers peeking in our windows, swarms of helicopters hovering over our roof, and my very strong wife close to tears because she can't even get in her own house at night without being harassed.

First, was Hart's personal conduct legitimate news? Did the media have a responsibility to place it before voters attempting to assess the character and judgment of a man who wanted to be president? Or was the coverage unprincipled, sensationalistic prying into sordid details of a man's private life?

Second, should the *Herald* and other media have resorted to secretive techniques—nighttime stakeouts and what *New York Times* columnist A.M. Rosenthal criticized as "hiding in the dark, listening for squeaking bedsprings"—to get the story?

The *Herald's* executive editor, Heath J. Meriwether, defended the paper's coverage: "With the ethics and morals of our leaders under such intense scrutiny today, people want to know about a candidate's character . . . we think the issues raised by our stories are germane to any consideration of a presidential candidate."

THE BILL CLINTON CASE

A similar scenario developed in 1992 with rumors about extramarital activities by Bill Clinton, then governor of Arkansas and, of course, leading Democratic contender for the presidency.

One huge difference: Rumors about Clinton were published first by the *Star,* a supermarket tabloid, not by a newspaper with the *Miami Herald's* reputation for journalistic excellence.

This time, the floodgates of media coverage didn't at first automatically swing wide open. Many journalists didn't want to follow the lead of the *Star.*

Then, two New York City tabloids, the *Post* and *Daily News,* carried the story. Columnist Michael Kinsley wrote in *Time* that the Clinton sex story "thus became fair game for everyone else."

Kinsley said the incident illustrated a "process whereby the daintier elements of the press can enjoy sex while claiming to have preserved their virginity: they simply wait for their less fastidious brethren to report something, then report—with distaste—that it has been reported."[16]

Then, the *Star* held a press conference featuring a woman who claimed she had a 12-year affair with Clinton, and the herd instinct took over: Clinton's private life was displayed on front pages and evening news, coast to coast.

Some coverage was sordid. "Did the governor use a condom?" one reporter yelled at the woman put on stage by the *Star.* At another press conference, Mrs. Clinton was asked for her reaction to the allegations. (An aide interrupted before she replied.)

Much coverage, however, dealt—carefully, professionally—with a larger issue: Should a presidential candidate's character be scrutinized publicly by the media? If so, is sex life indicative of character?

Another huge difference between the Hart and Clinton cases: Hart's political career was destroyed. Clinton survived, of course, as the electorate subordinated the character issue to concerns over the economy and other issues.

In the Hart and Clinton cases, the media confirmed a journalistic principle widely held in the press corps: There will be—must be—full coverage of the private lives of public figures.

NOW, *YOU* MAKE THE CALL

Judge for yourself the media's conduct in the Hart and Clinton cases. Remember the five-step decision-making process discussed in Chapter 1:

1. **Assemble all facts.** For this exercise, assume you have all the facts.

2. **Identify the ethical issue(s).** Was the issue simply invasion of an individual's privacy? Or did both men voluntarily give up privacy when they competed to be president? If the latter, what was the ethical issue? A betrayal by reporters of the societal value of humaneness? Whether reporters were truly serving the public? Or monitoring the powerful? Both are important journalistic principles. What do you see as the crucial issue?

3. **Consider alternative solutions.** Did *Herald* editors have alternatives in the Hart case? Were alternative reportorial techniques available, as Rosenthal of the *New York Times* suggested in criticizing reporters for "hiding in the dark, listening for squeaking bedsprings"? How else could the story have been dug out? *Should* it have been dug out? In the Clinton case, once the *Star* broke the story did other media have alternatives? Could they have ignored the *Star's* "exclusive"?

4. **Decide.** Are you forced, in both the Hart and Clinton cases, to decide between undesirable options? Or, is your decision clear and unequivocal in your mind? Is there a right decision?

5. **Act.** In their real-world roles, reporters and editors in both cases had to act and take responsibility—on front pages and the evening news—for their decisions. In our exercise I'm going to ask you to announce your decision(s) to your class and colleagues. Do so, note their reaction—and you'll get a feel for what it is to act on ethical dilemmas in the real world!

Incidentally, if you think it was tough making decisions on Hart and Clinton, two men who spent a lifetime seeking public exposure, just imagine the difficulty reporters have in deciding how to cover private individuals thrust unwillingly into the public spotlight by circumstances beyond their control.

If your camera catches a woman survivor running naked from a hotel fire do you air that footage because it dramatically depicts a news story in which the public has justifiable interest? Is a minister's arrest as a teenager on a morals charge *news* today, 40 years later?

CASE STUDY

Was It News or "Sleaze"?

You hear rumors that 21 years ago, an 18-year-old college freshman in a distant city, now a prominent local businessman, shot to death his mother, father and sister. Your investigation reveals he was found mentally incapable of standing trial, and hospitalized. After seven years of therapy, he was tried and acquitted on grounds he was insane at the time of the shootings. He was released from the hospital, won a college degree and married and took his wife's surname. He moved to your town and, it appears, has lived a blameless life ever since.

There is no news peg—no current development that makes this story hot news. But, the man indeed is prominent—he is publisher of 13 suburban newspapers with 200,000 circulation and 200 employees.

Question Will you publish what you learned?

Here is how that question was answered in Denver:

Patricia Calhoun, editor/publisher of *Westword,* a weekly with 90,000 free circulation that tries to present alternative approaches to news published by dailies, broke the story on her front page "because no one else had done it. . . . It always struck me as being a fascinating and absolutely newsworthy story . . ."

Editor David Hall of the *Denver Post* also knew details but said, "It's not a story. . . . There was no reason and purpose to run it. . . . There are lots of things people know that they don't put in the newspaper."

Editor Ralph Looney of the *Rocky Mountain News,* Denver's other daily, said, "This is the kind of thing that gives our whole industry a bad name. If you have someone who has led an exemplary life, it gets to the point of sleaze and sensationalism [if you publish]."

Joe McGowan, Denver AP bureau chief, said, "I'm not sure the story should have been published. How did it pertain today? He had paid his debt, done what society required. There was no impropriety. He was not in a sensitive government position."

The *Denver Post* never did run the story; the *Rocky Mountain News* did after *Westword* broke it, explaining it considered the publisher's past private until he spoke out—which he did when the story broke. AP then carried the story, and it was used by hundreds of newspapers and broadcast stations.

The publisher, H. Garrison Cochran of Sentinel Newspapers, told AP: "I have been trying to prepare myself to be strong enough to handle this when it arose." His own papers published a 17-inch story on his past.

What do you think? Was Cochran's occupation as a publisher a factor in whether to publish? *Westword's* Calhoun said, "I think how the media deals with it is a media story. I do think, in covering the media, the media does use a different set of standards." Also, did the *News,* AP and other media let *Westword* set the ethical standards on this story? Which societal values and journalistic principles (Chapter 1) were at play here?

VIEWPOINT

Good News Is No News?

" . . . one must always make allowances for the media's perverse determination to look on the gloomy side of things. To a journalist, good news is no news. Only bad news is news, and he [or she] will hunt for it with the relentless enthusiasm of a hog rooting for truffles."

Conservative syndicated columnist William Rusher[17]

Journalism of Hope

"The issue, very simply, is whether the 'old journalism' of despair, the derisive technique of leaving readers discouraged, or sad or indignant, can or should survive . . . Or whether a 'new journalism' of hope—a technique that chronicles the good, the bad and the otherwise—leaves readers fully informed and equipped to judge what deserves their attention and support can and will prevail in decades ahead."

Al Neuharth, then chairman of Gannett Co., criticizing journalists who "out-bad-news" each other

Infinite variations of such ethical dilemmas arise in privacy issues. Here, you will have no precise guidelines, and often will find little solace in what other journalists did in similar past cases. Make your best judgment call, balancing your responsibility to your reading or viewing public against the individual's right to privacy, and expect to awaken in the night, even years later, with the gnawing feeling you made the wrong call.

GOOD NEWS VERSUS BAD NEWS

Question: Is news by definition mostly bad, shocking, negative exceptions to expected behavior?

Or, is news just as frequently positive, upbeat—the good human beings perform every day in conforming to expected behavior?

How you answer is central to your personal code of ethics because the issue constitutes an important fork in the career path where you must decide which direction to take as a journalist.

Some reporters' reasoned professional judgment is that news mostly is aberrant behavior—crime, corruption—and the wars, natural disasters and other calamities that befall the world. Some reporters intentionally seek out bad news as part of a rampant careerism that feeds off front-page bylines and the top spot on the 6 P.M. news. These reporters know the journalism fraternity rewards its members more frequently for stories on sheriffs who beat prisoners than on sheriffs who patiently, gently try to reform their wards. The rewards are better assignments, promotions and more pay.

For readers and viewers, the result can be an unremitting, overwhelming drumbeat of death, disaster and doom. And, many readers and viewers don't like it. They tell researchers the media are prisoners of a bad-news syndrome. Responding, editors strive to present more "good" news. Some newspapers even set aside a good-news page for the Boy Scout promotions, church dinners and other nice things that happen.

But, is nice news news?

Despite what they tell pollsters, readers and viewers are attracted to bad news. For readers as for journalists, conflict, disaster and death still are news.

For you as a reporter, the dilemma: If your basic technique is to emphasize the positive as well as the negative, are you distorting the news in accordance with some personal yardstick on which good and bad are measured? Are you failing in your journalistic responsibility if you set forth intentionally to find good news, rather than taking the world as it comes and balancing events—good and bad—to create a discerning, meaningful daily report of what is important?

Answer these questions by again walking through the Potter Box in Chapter 1. Do the societal value of truth-telling and the journalistic principle of be balanced and fair conflict?

GOOD TASTE: BLOODY BODIES AND MORE

Journalists must begin thinking early in their careers about what their fundamental stance will be on matters of good taste and sensationalism. Both frequently give rise to major ethical crises.

First, the public suspects your motives. Many readers and TV viewers tell pollsters that reporters frequently overdramatize the news, that the bloody body is videotaped at the auto wreck simply to sensationalize an otherwise dull newscast, that lurid sex-crime details are published to lend shock value to an otherwise ho-hum front page.

Second, many responsible journalists fear the public often is correct. Every journalist knows of stories that were overplayed in extremely poor taste.

Often, newspaper and TV journalists must make difficult judgment calls quickly on stories that clearly are news but are horribly grisly. For example, in Harrisburg, Pennsylvania, on January 22, 1987, state treasurer R. Budd Dwyer, due to be sentenced the next day on a bribery conviction, called a news conference and, when reporters were assembled and the cameras rolling, put the barrel of a .357 Magnum pistol in his mouth and pulled the trigger.

The networks had the entire episode on videotape, but declined to use it. CNN said, "You can tell the story without showing the shooting." NBC said, " . . . too unsettling for our viewers." Some TV stations used it. One that did, WPXI-TV in Pittsburgh, said, "It's an historic event. We've seen JFK [President John F. Kennedy] shot to death 200 times. We've seen Bobby Kennedy shot to death. So it's a reflection of a very important man in Pennsylvania society and what he did." The station later edited the videotape, letting viewers hear the pistol shot but not see Dwyer's last moments. Stations that used the episode in full reported receiving hundreds of protest calls from viewers.

VIEWPOINT

A Photo That Offended

"In the first two days we had a total of 500 complaints. There were also hundreds of protest letters, canceled subscriptions, an attempt to boycott the paper and a bomb threat that forced us to evacuate the newspaper building."

Staff photographer John Harte after his photo of a drowned child was front-paged by the *Bakersfield Californian*

Newspapers had complete still photo coverage—an Associated Press series that gave editors the option of showing the entire sequence or omitting the most graphic parts. Gannett surveyed its 93 newspapers and found 51 used AP's photo of Dwyer holding the pistol and waving back reporters; 12 used one of Dwyer with the pistol in his mouth; the rest used other versions or, in the case of seven, no photos at all.

There was, then, no clear consensus among professionals that day on the ethics of news versus poor taste.

Societal attitudes shift rapidly on what is good taste or bad. Many journalists, even after years of wrestling with the issue, have difficulty deciding where the line lies between responsible—or, at least, necessary—journalism and bad taste or sensationalism.

For example, consider how wide open ABC News leaves the issue in this statement to its staff:

> ABC News believes that good taste must prevail in its broadcasts. Morbid, sensational or alarming details should not be included unless they are essential to the factual report. Obscene, profane or indecent material must also be avoided. The broadcast of material deemed to be obscene by the courts may also run afoul of the law as well as the canons of good taste. . . . Questions of taste cannot be answered in the abstract, but when specific problems involving objectionable material arise, they must be resolved in light of contemporary standards of taste, the state of the law and the requirements of newsworthiness. When these considerations come into conflict, consult ABC News management and request a decision.[18]

Language generally held in poor taste—vulgarity or obscenity—is used by journalists only if central to the meaning of an important story.

One presidential expletive was considered important news. During a photo opportunity at the White House, when photographers were permitted to take pictures of then President Reagan in the Cabinet room, reporters pressed questions about the Philippines, at the time in political turmoil. Reagan said to an aide, "Sons of bitches." Videotape was used on television; the language, in quotes, was used by many newspapers.

VIEWPOINT

No Swearing on Your Own

"Editorial policy at *U.S. News* forbids use of profanity, obscenity and vulgarity unless it is in a quote and the use of the quote is considered essential to the story."

The Editors, *U.S. News & World Report*[19]

In this case, journalists decided the expletive was indicative of presidential mood on an important story, the U.S. position on the Philippines, as well as a commentary on the press corps.

If such language is used, how will it be displayed and where? Many newspapers bury such language deep in a story or run the story itself only on inside pages.

Some television newscasters introduce video clips of obscenities or vulgarity by warning, "the following contains language objectionable to some . . ." Federal regulation limits use of indecent language by TV and radio.

Good taste quickly becomes a major ethical consideration in covering stories involving grief. Families of U.S. Marines killed abroad are in the news. The family of a villager killed in Bosnia is in the news; pain inflicted by war on the innocent is important to the story.

But, how to handle that grief, that pain? How to avoid what columnist George Wills calls the "pornography of grief," the brutal exploitation of the grief and pain of others?

The camera—television's or a newspaper's—is the worst offender; it intrudes, it catches and exploits the tears on the cheek, the tremble across the lips. But word journalists who crowd around the grave, who push into the church as the dead are eulogized are part of the problem, too. Happily, there are many examples of journalists discharging their truth-telling responsibility to cover a significant story but doing so with compassion and good taste.

When covering grief, you must judge whether it belongs in public view or is one of those stories that should not be published. If you must publish, move in with sensitivity, get your story and get back out as quickly and gently as possible.

Care is essential in covering sex crimes or trials. Heinous crime is important news, and not covering it in the name of good taste is abdication of ethical responsibility.

The dilemma is *how* to cover it.

Question: Should you be guided by whether readers or viewers need to know? For example, if a rapist is assaulting women in your town, do your readers need to know how and when he operates? If children in a day care center have been sexually abused, do parents among your readers and viewers need to know what warning signs to look for, what protective steps to take?

VIEWPOINT

Good Taste and Bad News

"We live in the era of news-media overkill.

"It isn't enough to acknowledge the ubiquity of barbarism; we are forced to see it in color. Local television news assaults our sensibilities with graphic details of incineration, rape, infanticide, gruesome murders, and every horror that the well-developed imagination of a masochist can conceive.

"It isn't that these events don't occur. Everyone living in New York City and every other city is aware of them. The issue is not whether these stories are news—technically whatever occurs is news—but whether they are newsworthy.

"I am not arguing here for censorship, albeit any concern for human decency ultimately involves some limits on what television allows us to observe. What I am demanding is tastefulness."

Herbert London, dean of New York University's Gallatin Division[20]

Societal revulsion over sex crimes is so great that special ethical problems are created in covering anyone connected with them—accused or accuser.

Many journalists, for example, routinely withhold names of rape victims but often identify alleged rapists. Journalists protect sexually abused children. But should men arrested for, but not convicted of, sex crimes on the testimony of children be photographed being led handcuffed into a courtroom?

As you develop your personal code for handling such stories, recall our Chapter 1 discussion of the societal values of truth-telling and humaneness. Do they conflict? How about the journalistic principles of be balanced and fair and be compassionate? Can you be both if you identify the accused but not the accuser?

Those are tough calls. Suggestion: Treat each incident as unique. Seldom will ethical decision making involved in one neatly cover another. Coolly assess the need to cover the story, then if you must publish, proceed carefully in determining language to use, details to present, pictures to publish and timing and context of publication.

A complication in covering some crimes and suicides is that some criminals and unbalanced people are subject to copycat impulses. Given graphic details of a crime or suicide, they sometimes are triggered to copy.

Two days after treasurer Dwyer killed himself before the cameras in Harrisburg, Pennsylvania, a teenager in nearby York, Pennsylvania, shot himself to death in precisely the same manner.

In New Jersey, four youths killed themselves in a suicide pact by running a car engine in a closed garage until overcome by carbon monoxide. A week later, two acquaintances tried to commit suicide in the same garage—and similar teenage suicides erupted across the nation.

The *New England Journal of Medicine* reports teenage suicides increase following a suicide heavily covered by the media. The U.S. Food and Drug Adminis-

CASE STUDY

Is It Different on TV?

You report for a television station in a major city where a sensational kidnap trial is under way. Evidence shown the jury in open court includes videotapes of the bound, helpless kidnap victim just prior to being raped. Reporters are given complete transcripts of dialogue on the tapes.

Questions Should you show the videotape on your evening newscast? Does public interest—the journalistic principle of serve the public—override the victim's desire for privacy? Do you see greater societal good flowing from screening the tapes of this horrible event? Is publishing transcripts in newspapers different from showing videotapes of the actual event? Should all judicial records be available to the media and public?

In Minneapolis, where the trial was held, two television stations asked a federal court for the right to copy and use the tapes. The judge refused—and drew editorial support from the *Minneapolis Tribune.*

Don Dwight, then publisher of the *Tribune,* noted:

"The *Minneapolis Tribune* said the judge 'exercised his discretion rationally and justifiably.' By supporting an individual's right of privacy in this case, did the *Tribune* yield its position in the front lines defending the right of the press and the public to judicial records?

"We think not. The tapes had been shown in the courtroom 'for all to see,' as the judge's decision pointed out. Complete transcripts of the dialogue were furnished to the press at that time.

"The *Tribune* did express real concern about precedent setting, but it also noted: 'Even when not compelled to do so, Minneapolis news media have usually respected individual privacy when that consideration was compatible with their duty to inform the public. Such responsible behavior is not entirely altruistic. The press usually recognizes that when it abuses its power, it jeopardizes its credibility—and its ability to gather information for which the public has a legitimate need.'

"We think that's another very good way of saying a press that is responsible will help ensure a press that is free and strong."

Who was right—publisher Dwight or the TV news directors who wanted to use the tapes? How far must an editor go in such cases to present the news but also protect the sensibilities of viewers or readers? Where did the *Tribune*'s loyalties lie in this case?

tration finds heavy coverage of food tampering causes a wave of tampering complaints nationwide.

Sometimes, you can risk contributing to copycat behavior indirectly. For example, a new book specified names and doses of drugs a woman used to help her terminally ill mother commit suicide. Book reviews by the Associated Press and the *Washington Post* reprinted the specifics—a prescription for suicide.

Now a warning:

If you judge newsworthiness in part by your sense of good taste, there is danger of overlooking your first ethical responsibility, the news needs of your readers or viewers. A striking example occurred when AIDS burst widely into view in the United States.

Coast to coast, journalists agonized over handling graphic details of how the disease, acquired immune deficiency syndrome, is transmitted. The story was handled so delicately that the public was denied essential details.

In sum, high risk of AIDS infection comes from exchange of semen through anal intercourse, thus the high rate of incidence among homosexual men. That preceding sentence contains words—*anal intercourse*—that many journalists would do almost anything to avoid using in a news story. And that's what many did in trying to explain, with euphemistic indirection, what AIDS was all about. One result was a huge health scare that left millions wondering whether they could contract AIDS from drinking fountains, the air they breathed or from little children who got it quite innocently from blood transfusions.

The lesson: Good taste, humaneness, compassion—all are essential but cannot develop into prudishness that denies your readers or viewers essential information on important stories. Even the most explicit story on a subject normally deemed offensive can be used in a newspaper or newscast if written in considered, responsible language and displayed appropriately.

But how to handle gory details in stories that are not of earth-shaking importance but are, well, bizarre and titillating? From 1993 to 1994, newspapers covered the arrest and trial of a Virginia woman charged with cutting off her husband's penis with a kitchen knife after he allegedly raped her. For many newspapers, it was an occasion to use a word seldom headlined: *penis.* For others, however, the woman "mutilated" her husband or severed his "offending organ." (He was found innocent of rape; she was found innocent by reason of temporary insanity.)

Summary

Each aspiring journalist must build a personal code of ethics as part of giving readers or viewers fair, balanced coverage of the news. These following areas are fundamental:

1. *Objectivity* arguably is impossible to achieve, but the effort must guide journalists in deciding which stories to cover, selecting sources, arranging facts, writing and, then, timing publication or airing of the story. Some argue journalists also must decide what is right or truth in the news, but who is qualified to make those judgment calls?
2. *Conflicts of interest,* real or perceived by the public, can destroy the relationship of trust each journalist must create with readers or viewers. Avoid particularly any outside involvement, as in politics, that would compromise your independence. Also beware unethical personal investments and accepting gifts that might influence your news judgment.

3. *Privacy* forces you to balance the individual's right to be left alone against the public's right to know about matters of important news interest. It's not difficult to make judgments concerning public officials, those who seek the public spotlight. Much of their lives should be open. But it gets tougher when you understand that unwanted publicity inflicts great hurt on many private individuals who want only to be left alone.
4. *Good taste* must enter your value judgment on stories involving, for example, vulgarity or obscenity, grief, sex crimes and other crimes or suicides that might trigger copycat behavior. At times, however, explicit stories normally deemed objectionable must be told—in considered, responsible language—if you are to fulfill your greater responsibility of meeting the public's need to know details of important stories.

Notes

1. Fred W. Friendly, "Gays, Privacy and a Free Press," *The Washington Post,* April 8, 1990, p. B-7.
2. Steven A. Holmes and Doron P. Levin, "A Man Who Says He Wants to Be Savior, If He's Asked," *New York Times,* April 13, 1992, p. 1. For the Oliver North story see Maureen Dowd, "Oliver North Looking to Join the Senate He Once Defied," *New York Times,* national edition, Jan. 28, 1994.
3. Adam Clymer, "Opposition to Baird Grows as Senators Hear the People," *New York Times,* national edition, Jan. 22, 1993, p. A-10.
4. William Safire, "Candidates' Health," *New York Times,* national edition, April 23, 1992, p. A-15.
5. Jay T. Harris, executive editor, *Philadelphia Daily News,* speech to Society of Professional Journalists, Phoenix, Ariz., Nov. 15, 1985.
6. Roberto C. Goizueta, chairman and chief executive officer, Coca-Cola Co., speech to Associated Press Managing Editors, San Francisco, Oct. 29, 1985.
7. Sam Hopkins, "Conflict of Interest for Journalist Holding Public Office," a detailed report on conflicts of interest on various South Carolina and Georgia newspapers, *Atlanta Constitution,* Jan. 18, 1981, p. 9B.
8. For detailed treatment, see "Wine Critic Corked," *Washington Journalism Review,* May 1983, p. 9.
9. Roone Arledge, president, ABC News, memorandum to ABC staff, March 10, 1982, American Broadcasting Companies, Inc., 7 W. 66th St., New York, N.Y., 10023.
10. "Ethics Policy" adopted in 1980 by the *Charlotte Observer,* P.O. Box 32188, Charlotte, N.C., 28232.
11. Celeste James, "Publisher: Journalists Don't Do Marches," *Gannetteer,* May 1990, p. 10.
12. CBS News Standards, CBS Inc., 51 W. 52nd St., New York, N.Y., 10020.
13. John Finnegan, speech to Morris Communications Corp., seminar on "Newspapers: Conduct and Values," Savannah, Ga., March 9, 1986.

14. For details, see Alex S. Jones, "Insider Trading Reports Focus on Journal Writer," *New York Times,* national edition, March 30, 1984, p. 29; Jonathan Friendly, "The Sticky Business of Financial Reporting," *New York Times,* April 8, 1984, national edition, p. 22-E; and Harvey D. Shapiro, "Unfair Shares," *Washington Journalism Review,* July/August 1984, p. 35—three of the more definitive accounts of the "R. Foster Winans affair."
15. Jon Katz, "Mind Your Own Business," *Newsinc.,* June 1992, p. 35; "A Perspective on Power, A Conversation with Alvin P. Sanoff," *U.S. News & World Report,* Oct. 28, 1991, p. 81; Everette E. Dennis, "Proposing a Zone of Decency in Coverage," *Communique,* February 1993, p. 2.
16. Michael Kinsley, "Private Lives: How Relevant?," *Time,* Jan. 27, 1992, p. 68.
17. William Rusher, column for Sunday papers of Jan. 12, 1992; see *Athens (Ga.) Daily News and Banner-Herald* for that date, p.6-D.
18. Roone Arledge, staff memorandum, op. cit.
19. "Crosstalk: Watching Our language," editors' note, *U.S. News & World Report,* Dec. 7, 1992, p. 6.
20. Herbert London, *New York Times,* Dec. 29, 1981, p. 21.

CHAPTER 3

The Ethics of Technique

Aristotle could not have envisaged it, of course. Neither could Mill nor Rawls nor the other philosophers we've studied. But the societal values they debated in such sweeping philosophical terms have precise and pragmatic everyday application to your role as a reporter and writer.

We now turn to that in Chapter 3—a detailed examination of how you can translate your (and their) definition of right and wrong, good and bad, into day-to-day conduct on the job in journalism.

First, we discuss the ethics of accurate reporting and honest writing. By definition, inaccurate reporting and, of course, dishonest writing are immoral. Developing accurate and honest techniques as a journalist isn't simple. We look at ways you can start developing your ethical technique.

Then, we discuss broader professional realities that you'll face in your efforts to be an honest, ethical journalist. The adversarial relationship—tension between newsmaker and news-gatherer—is one.

We also examine the line between reporting the news and making it. It's a line easy to cross.

Few relationships in journalism are as complicated—or as important—as those you'll develop with news sources. Ethical traps abound, and we highlight them.

All this doesn't look that complicated to you? Well, a question: You wouldn't steal somebody's silverware, would you—or receive and use silverware you knew was stolen? Of course not. But would you receive and use a stolen government document? Many reporters have.

Still think this stuff isn't complicated?

THE ETHICS OF ACCURATE REPORTING

Accuracy is so fundamental to responsible journalism that you can argue it shouldn't even be discussed along with ethical issues on which there legitimately can be differing opinions, or nuances of good and bad. Accuracy is good, inaccuracy is bad—and that's that.

But, accuracy must be discussed, because by definition an inaccurate journalist is unethical, too. And, certainly, the subject is central to understanding public perceptions of media ethics, because what readers and viewers consider unethical often is nothing more than sloppy, inaccurate reporting.

Becoming an accurate reporter is the first step toward a responsible, ethical relationship with your readers or viewers. It requires accepting a journalist's responsibility to above all provide accurate, reliable information. Then, you must fashion reportorial attitudes that will produce it. Among the most important are the following.

RESPECT FOR THE BASICS

In our world of stunning complexity, a reporter must dig out the meaning behind the facts, take readers and viewers gently by the hand and lead them, with interpretation and analysis, toward understanding. But the basics of ethical reporting remain balanced, factual representations of the five Ws and how, tightly attributed to authoritative sources: Who is involved? What is happening? When? Where? Why? Plus, How is it all coming together? And, importantly, Who says so?

For many journalists, the temptation is overwhelming to explain true meaning at the expense of reporting the facts. That can break down the line between reporting and opinion.

For readers or viewers, the result often is a feeling they are being manipulated. Repeatedly, they tell pollsters: Report the facts, and we'll decide on meaning and make up our own minds.[1]

RESPECT FOR DETAIL

There is greater danger, by far, of being inaccurate on "little" details than on "big" ones. It's more likely you will catch accurately the central thrust of the evening speaker's argument than the precise spelling of the speaker's name, age, title, address, corporate affiliation and the name of the club that sponsored the visit.

Reporters tend to let down, to get sloppy on the little details (libel lawyers defending the media in lawsuits arising out of "little" inaccuracies say the same thing). Yet, no details are unimportant, and if you fail with any of them, you fail as an accurate, reliable and, thus, ethical reporter.

RECOGNITION OF YOUR OWN WEAKNESSES

No reporter can possess strong background in all sectors of news, or even more than a couple. Forget what you've heard about fabled general assignment

VIEWPOINT

Beware Manipulation

"As a reporter, you have to recognize that there is a tremendous potential to be manipulated. You can't get lazy."

Jonathan Alter, senior editor of *Newsweek,* in interview with *Folio* on danger of using unnamed sources

reporters of days bygone who boasted ability to cover fires, floods or bank failures with equal skill. They covered them all right, but not always well.

It is your ethical duty to recognize where your academic preparation or on-the-job training left you unprepared to cover a story properly. Seek out authoritative sources, frankly acknowledge if you don't know the difference between a Federal Reserve Bank and the Federal Reserve System, or why movement in the prime interest rate affects local home construction costs. Large numbers of your readers or viewers, increasingly sophisticated in financial, technical and scientific matters, do know the difference, and your credibility will plunge dramatically if your reporting shows weakness.

So, ask someone who knows. *There are no dumb questions—just dumb reporters who fail to ask.*

HEALTHY SKEPTICISM

It's not that all your sources want to mislead you, although some do, of course. Some will lay the baited trap, attempting for their own purposes to mislead you with misinformation or disinformation.

But even those who honestly want to give you accurate information sometimes fail. A busy police officer, a court clerk or the U.S. Secretary of State easily can err as they talk with you while trying to direct traffic at an accident site, hurry into the judge's chambers or depart Andrews Air Force Base for Manila. So, check and double-check. Pose the same question another way to another source to see if you get the same answer—and whenever possible go to documentation, the public records, a piece of paper, for facts,

Facts—precise numbers, lots of names, dates, addresses, exact quotations—are mainstays of accurate reporting.

A warning about healthy skepticism: If you're not careful, it can evolve into cynicism, a disbelief in everything and everybody. If that becomes apparent in your reporting, you won't bridge the gap with news sources or your readers or viewers.

The more you prepare to cover a story, the more accurate your reporting will be. Move into a story unprepared and at half-speed and you risk being overwhelmed by it. And out of that come errors—factual and ethical.

VIEWPOINT

Closets and Corpses

"It can be very hard for a journalist who has been knocking around for a couple of decades, or even a couple of weeks on some assignments, to take anything at face value anymore. So the error often comes in raining down sardonic doubt on some assertion that it just does not seem possible is true. We are morally certain that if we just yank open one more closet door the corpse will fall out. And maybe we don't give enough attention to things that are going well."

Meg Greenfield, *Newsweek* columnist

THE "NO COP-OUT" ATTITUDE

There never is enough time in daily journalism to collect all the facts, never enough newshole or air time. Those are realities of your craft. But it is a cop-out to cite them as excuses for less than accurate, fair reporting.

To your readers or viewers, there are no excuses for anything less than sound, complete, ethical reporting.

THE ETHICS OF HONEST WRITING

Honest writing is a crucial tool in building trust with readers or viewers.

In print, honest writing is the ceremony of transmittal, the reporter's hopeful leap from page toward reader comprehension. In television, it must be substance behind smile, meaning behind glitter.

In either medium, trust is established through sound, honest writing that effectively communicates. Without it, trust vanishes.

Writing rates high among ethical priorities because writing that is dishonest obviously defeats best attempts to be objective, balanced and fair in reporting. Accurate, unbiased reporting withers in dishonest writing.

There obviously is no justification for intentionally and covertly slanting a story through choice of language, selective inclusion or omission of facts, improper emphasis, misquotation or, worse, "creative" use of quotations with prejudice to prove a point. Writers who do that are propagandists, not journalists.

It is dishonesty by oversight, by error, that must concern us. For it is here, ambushed by carelessness and amateurism, that most of all we fail as honest writers,

Broadly, honest writing does two things:

First, it ensures the internal dynamics of each story communicate fairly, dispassionately and with balance.

Second, it ensures an open, honest relationship with readers or viewers, leveling with them not only within each story, but also in a wider sense over a period of time. This requires learning to say, in effect, "The facts aren't available on this one," rather than trying to pirouette around factual weaknesses with fancy writing. It also requires saying on occasion, "Sorry, but I was wrong."

THE SIN OF OMISSION

An intentionally dishonest writer easily can skew a story away from accuracy through sin of commission—by including erroneous, unfair biased material in a story.

However, a writer with the most honest intentions just as easily can commit the sin of omission, skewing a story by omitting material that should be included. This is a dangerous trap in newspaper and broadcast news writing because time/space constraints are so severe; not everything can be shoveled into a story that will get only six column inches or 45 seconds airtime.

But if the mayor is charged with official corruption and a noted business leader rushes to his defense, take space, take time to mention they have been friends for 30 years and play golf together on weekends. Excluding those essential details is to commit the sin of omission.

Deciding what to include and what to omit can be pure agony for a young writer trying to do an honest job. Be comforted: Seasoned writers wrestle with the same agony of choice on many stories.

THE SIN OF DISGUISED OPINION

Our earlier discussion of objectivity covered dangers of letting opinion penetrate the reporting process. They will confront you in the writing process, too. (I make the distinction between writing *news* copy, where your opinions don't belong, and *advocacy* copy, openly and honestly labeled, where your opinions do belong.)

In striving for honest news writing, beware of adjectives. Opinions sneak into your writing on their backs. For example, don't tell your readers there was a "bitter picket line battle." Describe how rocks were thrown, cars overturned. Let readers discover the meaning for themselves.

Be particularly alert on stories dealing with issues on which you have strong personal feelings and those that send you back to the newsroom breathless over the passion, danger, bitterness and bloodshed you have witnessed. Sit back for a moment, settle down, then do an honest writing job.

THE TRAP OF SELECTIVE QUOTATION

You can write a story almost exclusively of direct quotations and still unethically distort what was said—in effect, use the speaker's own words to slant a story.

If the mayor tells Rotary Club there are promises and dangers in your town's economic future, and you quote only comments on bright spots ahead, you are dishonest both with the mayor and your readers or viewers.

You even can reverse the meaning of what was said through selection of quotations. Beware particularly if you break up a long quotation, paraphrasing and using only a portion in direct quotes.

Consider: The mayor tells Rotary, "We're headed into a short-term recession in our economy, but in the distant future are rosy times." You're dishonest in writing, "Mayor Fred Smith said today 'rosy times' are ahead for Our Town."

THE ERROR OF ASSUMING TOO MUCH

To communicate honestly and effectively, each news story must be self-contained, give background and explain the news as well as report it.

A common error among writers is to assume readers or viewers know more than they do, even about stories frequently in the news. Not everyone knows what the foreign trade deficit is; not everyone remembers (or ever knew) the background of U.S. involvement in the Middle East. Brief explanation can bridge the gap between writer and reader or viewer—and meet your journalistic responsibility for truth-telling.

RUMORS TO REPORTS, SOURCE TO SOURCES

A mark of an ethical writer is being open and honest with readers and viewers. You must level with them. It is patently unethical to write in a manner that conceals—or distorts—facts or nuances important to true understanding.

You are dishonest if a rumor you hear from a secretary in the City Hall's cafeteria escalates, in your story, to a "report from City Hall." And if, in the writing, a single Pentagon briefing officer rises to a tidal wave of "high-ranking sources in the military," more dishonesty is afoot.

Obvious, perhaps; yet, writers every day busily escalate rumors to reports, and multiply a source to sources. It's dishonest, unethical—and can be extremely damaging. A rumor of a corporate takeover, perhaps let loose by a single investor who stands to gain, can move mountains of money on Wall Street if elevated to a "report," and if precise identification of the source and his or her motives are lost in the writing.

WATCH THOSE PRESS REPORTS

Quoting other news writers is a dangerous habit. Plagiarism aside, with each retelling by successive writers, the rumor from the cafeteria line gains stronger credibility until you, unless careful, will serve up to reader or viewer a glob of baseless gossip disguised as news.

If compelled to quote your colleagues, do so with precision, as AP does in this Washington story: "The *Washington Post,* quoting unidentified government sources and citing intelligence documents . . ." That AP writer was honest with readers that day.[2]

EXPLAIN THE HOLES

If there are holes in your story, if you don't have all the facts pinned down, say so, openly and honestly.

Note how AP explains why it must quote "diplomatic sources" and "conflicting reports" in a story on Afghanistan: "Accounts were pieced together from reports by Western diplomats in Kabul, Afghans who claimed to witness the disaster, and rebel sources in Pakistan. Independent accounts were impossible to obtain because Afghan authorities sharply restrict foreign reporters."[3]

In writing on politics in Honduras, *New York Times* writer Barbara Crossette explains why she quotes an anonymous rancher even though he willingly spoke openly: " . . . after hearing his tales of corruption and brutality, it seemed prudent to give him anonymity."[4]

Not only do these AP and *New York Times* writers explain holes, they strengthen their stories by helping readers understand the news-gathering process.

And, always explain apparent lapses in fairness. If the mayor charges the police chief with corruption and you cannot reach the chief, say so: "The chief did not return four telephone calls to his office." If you get through to him and he still declines comment, write that, too: "The chief, reached at his office, declined to comment."

Now, let's look at broader professional realities that affect your efforts to be an honest, ethical journalist.

ADVERSARIAL RELATIONSHIP: A REALITY

It's often cautious, frequently tense: the relationship between reporters and the structure they cover—whether that structure be government, business or even those cheerful volunteers who run United Way fund drives in your town. Sometimes, it bursts into bitterness. Should it be this way?

Two views are expressed by Michael O'Neill, former editor of the *New York Daily News,* and Benjamin C. Bradlee, former executive editor of the *Washington Post*:

> O'Neill—The press has become so adversarial in its relationship with government that it threatens the democratic process.[5]
>
> Bradlee—Mike talks about the press's harshly adversarial posture towards government. I'd like to talk about the selling of the presidency, the manipulation of the public, where the press is a captive, if not willing, victim. . . . Does anyone really want to make peace with government? Do you really want us to formalize a "more positive, more tolerant" attitude with government? More tolerant of what? More tolerant of lying? More tolerant of misrepresentation? More tolerant of manipulation, photo opportunities? That can't be serious. That's a pact with the devil.[6]

Widespread adversarial attitudes—those of your media peers and your news sources—will be major realities shaping your reportorial technique. Like it or not, the relationship between reporters and those who generate news in this country largely is one of tug and pull, push and shove.

Many journalists consider adversarialism fundamental to success: News must be found and the story dragged out, over the objections—often active resis-

VIEWPOINT

Tradition of Defiance?

"I believe that the journalistic tradition of skepticism and even defiance toward political power is valid today. After all, the pamphleteers were ahead of the politicians in the fight for independence of the country, and this tradition still dominates the press, radio and television today."

James Reston, after decades of covering Washington for the *New York Times*[7]

tance—of those who for their own and sometimes nefarious reasons want to keep it hidden.

Hardened by years of battling for the news, many journalists regard adversarialism inevitable, natural even, in the relationship between newsmaker and news reporter in a free society. The media—and, thus, the people—have been led astray by officialdom, even lied to, on many stories of compelling national interest, creating visceral suspicion among journalists that the facts simply will not emerge from anything less than head-on confrontation.[8]

As to the form the adversarial relationship should take, opinions differ among journalists. Bluntly, some start assignments thinking they must blast their way into the story, confront and even threaten sources and gut officials. For these reporters, every story is a brawl—and no prisoners are taken.

After the media hit hard at several factual errors President Reagan made at news conferences, the mood became so tense that David R. Gergen, White House director of communications, said each news conference was "like going into the arena of the lions again."

In 1993, the Clinton Administration experimented with televised daily news briefings—then quickly dropped the idea. The live briefings seemed "unnecessarily combative," said Dee Dee Myers, President Clinton's press secretary. (Clinton then hired Gergen as his communications director.)

The opposite—and equally unacceptable—extreme of mad-dog adversarialism are the reporters who passively accept, with grateful thanks, the prepared statement—and who swallow hook, line and handout the official version of the story.

Be comforted. Somewhere between those extremes of reporting techniques is a more decorous but equally effective relationship (a Golden Mean?) you can build with news sources. It starts with your own strongest possible commitment to an ethical, professional technique, coupled to a bulldog—but responsible—determination to get the news and fulfill your journalistic responsibilities to your readers or viewers. Get close to the newsmakers but never on their team; work with them, travel with them, but always remember you are there as a surrogate of readers or viewers—and thus maintain your independence, the professional principle (and societal value) so essential to ethical journalism.

VIEWPOINT

And Who Will Keep Score?

"The government always wants the reporters on the team. But if the journalists are on the team, who will report the game?

" . . . There can't be any freedom of inquiry without irreverence. All presidents seek to capture the press and the two defenses against that are professionalism and independence."

James Deakin commenting on 25 years as White House correspondent for the *St. Louis Post-Dispatch*[9]

A skilled, multibillion-dollar industry is devoted to breaking down the adversarial relationship by enlisting you on the team. Thousands of information specialists and public relations consultants in government and private sectors devote careers to handling the media and steering coverage in certain directions (and not always toward the news). Don't think this happens only in big league journalism, on the White House lawn; it happens also in the mayor's office, on the school board, in the sheriff's department, on all those news beats where you likely will draw your first reporting assignment. Given experience—and unceasing vigilance—you will spot efforts to manage you and the news.

More difficult to spot is a subtle breakdown in the adversarial relationship that can create grave ethical crises for you. For example, you inevitably will develop friendships among news sources or grow sympathetic with the efforts of those you are covering—whether they are trying to win ball games or protect U.S. interests in foreign policy.

Get too friendly, too sympathetic, and you'll find the adversarial relationship crumbling; you'll find it difficult to write objectively, dispassionately.

Another danger: You will become dependent on sources for news tips and background explanation of highly complex matters. Sooner or later, you will find yourself weighing the news value of a story against whether publishing or airing it will embarrass a source and close down an information pipeline important to you.

Adversarialism is far from the perfect technique. It may force you into uncomfortable confrontations, make you feel like an unethical inquisitor. Certainly, it can be embarrassing to you and damaging to the media's image when television captures grown men and women shouting at the President of the United States for the sake of the people's right to know, or ambushing unsuspecting innocents and thrusting them with gross insensitivity into the glare of publicity because they, through no fault of their own, have become "news."

But adversarialism may be the only way, given the importance of your job of getting the news and the unfortunate tendency of those in power to hide it. Tempered but forceful, courteous but insistent, adversarialism should continue to distinguish American journalists from the captive reporters or the willing, active media propagandists in authoritarian societies.

CASE STUDY

How Do You Top a Pulitzer?

A Pulitzer Prize–winning photographer and a reporter are assigned to a team of 90 *Detroit Free Press* staffers reporting the effect crack cocaine has on their city in one 24-hour period.

The photographer and reporter spend the entire day with three addicts. They are in the photographer's car—and the addicts want money for more drugs.

The photographer agrees to buy a Walkman from one addict for $20. They spend the $20 on crack and he photographs them smoking it. The resulting photo is spread dramatically across the front page, kicking off the in-depth examination of city-wide dope dealing.

The reporter notes in the accompanying story that the addicts got money from selling a Walkman—but the reporter and photographer agree not to tell their readers or editors who provided the $20.

Questioned later by editors, the reporter and photographer reveal their role in the drug buying. The photographer tells *Washington Journalism Review*:

"There was tremendous pressure to get the story. Here I am, I win the Pulitzer eight months ago. The bases are loaded, and I'm expected to hit a home run.

"There's me, trying to top the Pulitzer. It's a problem we face as journalists. Are we worried about what our readers think or what our peers think?"

One editor acknowledges "we weren't giving ourselves time to reflect, polish and edit."

Executive Editor Heath J. Meriwether goes public in his weekly column:

- "Did we cross the line between cultivating sources and steering them?" Yes, he says.
- Should the photographer and reporter have told their editors about the $20? Yes, Meriwether says, and the two had broken " a bond of trust . . . that is crucial to the way we do our job."

Meriwether notes the photographer had said the affair started when he decided to drive the addicts to a crack house.

"It's a close (ethical) call about driving the addicts around," the editor says. "We talked about it and decided they were going to get to those crack houses anyway."

NEWS: MAKING IT OR REPORTING IT?

Whip out your reporter's notebook or point a camera at the world around you and you start making news. You become a participant, a catalyst even, in the newsmaking process. Things happen when a reporter arrives on the scene.

Therefore, to report a balanced, fair view of what was happening before you arrived and what likely will happen after you depart, you must develop methods

But, the editor says later, giving the addicts money "was a mistake and going too far. . . . When a person knows that the money changing hands is going immediately into buying crack, that person is facilitating. He is getting involved [in making news.]"

The *Free Press,* in addition to telling all in public, suspended the photographer and reporter for several days without pay.

Now, *You* Make the Call

Judge the conduct of the *Free Press* reporter and photographer in this case study. Turn again to the adaptation of the Potter Box in Chapter 1:

1. Collect the facts. For purposes of this exercise you have the facts.
2. Consider societal values. Recall the first we discussed was truth-telling. Was that basic value betrayed? Or, did the reporter and photographer actually deliver what a practitioner of new journalism might call the essential truth? After all, those were addicts in the back seat. They did smoke crack. Were the reporter and photographer untruthful in, shall we say, assisting the addicts so the resulting coverage would give *Free Press* readers a portrait of the drug world? Do you see conflict here with other societal values—humaneness, the Golden Mean, promise-keeping and so forth?
3. Consider journalistic principles. Did—or did not—the reporter and photographer betray the first we discussed in Chapter 1, serve the public? Was providing $20 to the addicts, then concealing that from readers, a betrayal of a journalist's duty to serve the public? Or, was the overall impact of the coverage—the inside look at the terror of addiction—a service to the public? Did other journalistic principles come into play here? Be balanced and fair, for example? Be compassionate?
4. Consider your loyalties. Our Chapter 1 discussion covered four: to self and conscience, to society, to the hand that feeds you, to professional peers. Which dominated the thinking of the *Free Press* reporter and photographer? Was the photographer's obsession with the Pulitzer prize an egocentric concern with first loyalty to himself and his career? Or was it, simply, overwhelming peer pressure? What about loyalty to the *Free Press* and society? In going public with a detailed explanation of what happened, was editor Meriwether serving any journalistic principle or loyalty? Was he being loyal to society—his readers—at the expense of the hand that feeds him, the *Free Press*?

of getting the story as unobtrusively as possible. It will be a great challenge as you try to construct an ethically sound reportorial technique.

Meg Greenfield, distinguished editorial page editor of the *Washington Post* and *Newsweek* columnist puts it this way:

> To the extent that it is working at all, the press is always a participant. Our decisions on where (and where not) to be and what (and what not) to report have enormous impact on the political and governmental life we cover. We are obliged to be

VIEWPOINT

TV Gave Him a Stage?

"I don't know whether Andrews would have done this had they not given him a stage."

Police Chief Paul Locke after 37-year-old Cecil Andrews set fire to himself as an Anniston, Alabama, TV crew filmed his "protest against unemployment"

selective. We cannot publish the Daily Everything. And so long as this is true—so long as we are making choices that 1) affect what people see concerning their leaders and 2) inevitably therefore cause those leaders to behave in particular ways—we cannot pretend we are not participants.

But of course we do, or at least some of us do. The "Shucks, I'm just a simple country stenographer, writing it all down as it happens" affectation is still with us, even though most people would agree that reporters (not just editorial writers and political columnists) must make subjective judgments every step of the way and are not merely walking tape recorders. The question, of course, is how honest, fair and professional those judgments are—and that is what the argument over journalistic participation in our national political life has been all about.[10]

Not only in covering politics is being honest, fair and professional required. Your story can move financial markets, shake large institutions, cause angry debate; your camera can inspire otherwise normal football fans to leap from their seats, wave their arms and make insane faces. Your mere presence can make news. Elements to watch:

PRESENCE AND NUMBERS

In the chemistry of reporter influence on the newsmaking process, one plus one does not equal two. It equals five.

That is, two reporters arriving to cover a story more than doubles the impact of one; if one of the two reporters is from the *New York Times, Washington Post* or *Wall Street Journal,* the impact widens exponentially, for those papers legitimize a story; they set the national news agenda. A reporter from one of those papers will draw competing special correspondents, TV cameras and news agency reporters.

It's called herd journalism, and no matter how you try to make independent news judgments or follow your own instincts, you will find it difficult to go against the flow. Your editor or news director will wonder why you are proceeding in one direction while the *New York Times, Washington Post,* AP and the networks are moving in another. Then *you* will begin to wonder why.

THE EGO FACTOR

Nothing in journalism causes more news to be made than the ego gratification of getting your byline on a front-page scoop or doing a standup for the 6 p.m. news in front of city hall. Great reporters are driven to find and tell, dig and reveal—and win appropriate applause, a prize or two, from peers and public.

It is creative but dangerous, this ego factor. More than money, more than anything else, it drives great reporters to uncover important stories. It also can become rampant careerism, which leads unethical reporters to manufacture news where none exists, to "hype" stories with importance they don't deserve, to press for front-page display of stories that are page-20 caliber.

Recognizing that you feel such stirrings (and that other reporters do, too) is half the battle of controlling the ego factor.

You'll also feel considerable external pressure to make news (although it will be called developing an enterprise piece). Faced with a slow news day, your editor will have you on the telephone or out on the beat, initiating interviews, working up a feature or two. And then you must guard against manufacturing news—particularly if you are proud to be a reporter who on a slow day can be counted on to find a bell-ringer for the front page.

George V. Higgins of the *Wall Street Journal* describes such distortion of the newsmaking process:

> The journalistic tendency to react to a paucity of events amounting to news, by instigating some news, is most pronounced among television reporters and gurus because dead air is exponentially more excruciating for them to endure than dull columns are for us ink-stained wretches. TV journalists are likelier to go around making trouble than are members of the pencil press, not because they are more mischievous but because their need is greater and more urgent. They commence therefore, very gingerly, to reverse the polarity of media and politics, by their analysis prodding the drowsy politicians from their dozes onto their feet to do a little barking. The print media do not find this cruel sport. We troop happily right along behind the television folks, duly perpetuating in the papers the next day the news which is thus made.[11]

MOVING CENTER STAGE

A former president of the Associated Press said being a reporter is to have a front row seat watching history being made.[12] Sometimes, however, reporters move into center stage—or are thrust there—to help make history, and that can raise complex ethical questions.

For example, few would doubt a reporter or photographer must intrude into the story to prevent a deranged person from a suicidal plunge off a bridge. But can suicide be a political statement into which reporters should not intrude? That was the judgment of AP reporters who watched—and photographed—a Buddhist monk immolate himself at a busy intersection in downtown Saigon to protest his government's policies during the Vietnam War. The burning monk photos had immense impact on world opinion and created antiwar sentiment in the United States.

Reporters sometimes become involved in police work: Prisoners seize guards and insist on making public statements through reporters (it happened at Ossining, New York, prison, and the governor's top aide says television "became a part of the process"); a deranged man seizes hostages in the Washington Monument and demands that a reporter serve as intermediary with police (an AP man does, with considerable courage, but also with concern over being part of the story, not an observer, and with being asked to do police work by getting a description of the man and a detonator-like device he is holding).[13]

The difficulty in judging whether reporters should play such roles is summed up in AP's statement after the Washington Monument incident:

> The involvement of our reporter, Steve Komarow, in the siege at the monument brings home again the lesson that terrorist-hostage situations defy the normal journalistic ground rules.
>
> Steve performed bravely, calmly and responsibly. One could not have asked for more from the young AP newsman.
>
> Yet, the whole scene is troublesome. Reporters don't belong in the middle of these situations, as Steve himself observed later in describing his own reaction.
>
> Perhaps all that can be said now of crises like the one at the monument is that as journalists we must judge the circumstances that confront us each time and respond in a way compatible with our professional role.[14]

STUNTING

Reporters sometimes court arrest or break laws in search of sensational copy—breaking through guard lines to test airport security, stealing to research a story on shoplifting or even dealing in narcotics on the streets for an inside view of the underworld.

In all but the most exceptional cases, such stunting is unethical, probably illegal—and can get you shot.

SOURCES AND YOUR ETHICAL TECHNIQUE

Reporters without news sources are like soldiers without rifles or cowboys without horses; they lack the essential tool of the trade. So important are sources that complex ethical considerations govern their care and feeding. These considerations divide roughly into two parts:

First, the ethics of your relationship with sources themselves.

Second, the ethics of what you reveal to your readers and viewers about your sources.

In developing sources, you must get close to power centers, find out where the button is pushed and by whom. Be alert. Sources will help you for various motives—not all ethical. For example:

- The fun of the game. People sometimes genuinely want to help get a story on the front page or on the 6 p.m. news, simply for the fun of it. Treated cautiously, such people can become helpful, ethically sound sources.

CASE STUDY

Reporters or Policemen?

The U.S. Attorney asks to meet secretly with you, managing editor of the city's only daily newspaper, and the general manager of its only television station. The official explains police want to trap a man trying to hire a "hit man" to kill a local cattle farmer. Payment has been promised when the killing is reported in the news.

The U.S. Attorney wants you to publish a false story—he calls it a "deception"—reporting the farmer's bloodstained truck has been found and police are searching for him. Your television competitor agrees. Police fear that if TV carries the report and your paper does not, the "deception" will fail. The U.S. Attorney is more forceful: He tells your publisher he might be responsible for deaths.

Question Do you cooperate with authorities by actively engaging in the hoax?

Confronted with that question, Frank Sutherland, managing editor of the *Hattiesburg (Miss.) American,* told police they had presented him with three options, "all of them bad": Publish the hoax and damage his newspaper's credibility, expose the officials' secret maneuvering, or write nothing, "which will look funny when people, including the guy you're trying to catch, see something on TV and nothing in the newspaper."

Sutherland and Publisher Duane McCallister finally decided to publish a single sentence that was true but wouldn't deceive readers: "Police are seeking information concerning suspected foul play directed toward Oscar Black III [the farmer]."

WDAM-TV broadcast the "victim's" name and described how his truck was found with apparent bloodstains in it. WDAM carried the false story for several days, but an informant told police the case had been "blown."

Police went public to praise WDAM and condemn the *American.* WDAM General Manager Cliff Brown said he had chosen ethics of life over ethics of journalism. In a single two-hour call-in show, 2,000 viewers telephoned about the incident, and WDAM said 80 percent agreed with its action.

Managing Editor Sutherland said, "Not many people understand our ethics. . . . The problem gets confusing if someone thinks we are not being a good citizen. But if we lie to them, they will always be able to wonder—say perhaps the next time we run a police story—are they telling us the truth?"

Publisher McCallister said, "Once you break that bond of trust with the reader, you can never put it back together."

Postscript Months later, using more traditional methods, police arrested a Hattiesburg man and charged him with trying once more to have the farmer killed. He was sentenced to 17 years in prison and fined $10,000.

What is a journalist's obligation as a citizen in such a case? Did Sutherland and McCallister put their newspaper and its reputation above a man's life?

VIEWPOINT

The Thorniest Issue?

"There is no thornier issue in journalism than the ethics of when and how to use anonymous sources."

Alex S. Jones of the *New York Times* on publication by the *Seattle Times* of charges by eight unidentified women that U.S. Sen. Brock Adams sexually harassed them

"This was the only way we could tell the story. Obviously, it would have been better to have published the names of the women but this was the only chance we had. We've been chasing this story for three-and-a-half years in an effort to be responsive to the people."

Executive Editor Michael Fancher of the *Seattle Times* to *Editor & Publisher* on coverage that caused Adams to halt his re-election effort

- The public interest. These are whistle blowers who believe they serve a higher cause by leaking news of graft, corruption and malfeasance. Washington is full of them, and they break a great deal of important news. Your guard should be up. Mixed in with true dedication to public interest there often is a heavy component of self-interest.
- Self-interest. Individuals, bureaucratic cliques, political parties feverishly leak news to advance their own careers or causes. In Washington, around budget time, when the armed forces scramble for more tax dollars, a Navy source will reveal shipbuilding in China threatens to world peace; an Air Force source will reveal the real threat comes from bombers and missiles. And, both will provide irrefutable evidence! The same dynamics motivate sources on Main Street; only the scale is different. There is nothing ethically unsound in accepting news tips from partisan sources; just remember precisely where you got the news and why it was given to you—then write a balanced, fair account.
- Jealously, hatred, revenge and other motives not so nice. Huge ethical problems arise when sources use news tips to strike at enemies and subject them to the special agony of twisting slowly in the glare of unfavorable media coverage or, even, by getting them fired or sent to jail. For reporters, the dilemma is acute if the source clearly is acting out of personal hatred but is leaking a story that just as clearly belongs in the public view.

On my first reporting job, I was tipped by a county treasurer that the sheriff was misusing county cars, a big story in small-town journalism in Illinois. The treasurer hated the sheriff, waited patiently for years until he made a misstep and then contacted me. The treasurer's motive may have been unethical, but the story—carefully double-checked—indeed was news important to the public. It was published.

VIEWPOINT

Informed Sources and Other Games

"It allows that well-known unknown, the 'informed source' or 'high administration official,' to get his knife into an opponent or float a trial balloon without political danger. It permits a reporter to write a story which proves he is in the know, but protects him from the consequences of error, since he is simply relaying what the person behind the mask has said. And it provides useful reading for all the other participants in the Washington game, since they usually know enough to be able to make out, at least hazily, the identity of the source and the meaning of the message.

"The problem is that the average reader or viewer can't do the same thing . . ."

Hodding Carter III, former State Department spokesman[15]

When a source bares fangs in revealing a story, proceed extremely carefully, but always keep in mind the greater news needs of your readers or viewers—to whom first loyalty is due.

SOURCES AND GROUND RULES

Often, sources impose ground rules for use of information given to you. Frankly, much important news enters public view only because reporters agree to the restrictions. So, sometimes you must go with "informed sources," unnamed "officials" or another of the anonymous labels sources often duck behind to avoid public responsibility for your story.

This can raise many ethical issues. For example, sources spurred by hatred or other personal motives will insist on avoiding, almost without exception, any connection with the story. But also—and more importantly—playing the informed sources game opens you to manipulation by sources and distances you from your basic mission of providing readers and viewers with important, reliable news tightly attributed to authoritative sources by name, rank and serial number. Readers and viewers deserve to know the source of the information you place before them so they can judge for themselves its reliability.

In dealing with sources, your best stance is that of a reporter who talks openly, aboveboard with sources and names them in print or on the air. Don't offer to go off the record.

If sources insist on anonymity, you should consult a supervising editor before agreeing. You also must decide whether the story's news value warrants departure from your stance as a reporter who tightly attributes news.

Is there another way to dig it out? If not, insist on attribution that will reveal to readers or viewers as fully as possible the authoritative credentials of your source and, importantly, make clear the source is in a position to know the accuracy of the information. That is, deep background, a ground rule against any

VIEWPOINT

Jail or Conscience

"I would be betraying my sources. It's a matter of conscience."

Loretta Tofani, 31-year-old reporter for the *Washington Post,* when warned she faced six months in prison for refusing to identify her sources in a story on sexual assaults in the Prince Georges, Maryland, county jail

". . . I'm quite proud of Tim for his courage and his commitment to this very important principle. This principle is not only important to journalists, but to citizens in general."

Executive Editor Paul Trash of the *St. Petersburg (Fla.) Times* as he escorted reporter Tim Roche to jail to serve 30 days in 1993 for refusing a judge's order to identify a confidential source. Trash added that he had asked Roche to write columns from jail "on what life inside jail is for someone who wouldn't expect to find himself there"!

identification, is least satisfactory. The source is insisting you use the information as your own. So, informed source is somewhat better than no source; a "high-ranking administration official" is an improvement; a "top aide in the President's inner circle of advisers, who declined to be identified," is even stronger.

Warning: Be certain you agree explicitly with the source in advance on attribution. Deep background means one thing to some officials, quite something else to others. It is unethical to agree to protect sources, then publish descriptions that identify them even if names are not used. A few such betrayals and your sources will vanish.

Never promise to protect a source's anonymity unless you are prepared to go all the way—to jail, even—to keep your promise. Whatever the source's motives, you must be known as a reliable, ethical reporter who stands by a promise. Many of your journalistic predecessors went to jail on contempt of court charges because they refused to identify confidential sources. No reporter can work effectively without complete trust from sources. Such trust is a foundation principle of a free press in a free society.

THE ETHICS OF NEWS-SLEUTH TECHNIQUES

The age-old debate over what means are justifiable to reach worthwhile ends is becoming heated for journalists. The equation is complex: Polls report readers and viewers want reporters on guard, digging out wrongdoing. But they disapprove of undercover techniques such as secret tape recorders or cameras. Editors generally don't want reporters acting like undercover sleuths either . . . unless a major story of high public importance is at stake and there is no other way to get it.[16]

As you sort out your ethical position, you must wrestle with your conscience and your supervising editor on a case-by-case basis. The following are areas of concern.

VIEWPOINT

The Reverse Spin

"We pose as whores, we pose as pimps, as burglars, thieves, murderers and drug dealers. This is perhaps a new low in our career, but there's nothing illegal about it."

Police Chief Bob Stover explaining to the *Albuquerque Tribune* that one of his officers posed as a reporter to catch a criminal

CONCEALING IDENTITY AND MASQUERADING

Let's say you're a reporter doing a story on the mood of a city. Is it ethical to walk around, talking to people, without identifying yourself as a reporter? No problem, right?

Now, let's say you're doing a story on, for example, cost of auto repairs. Is it ethical to take your car to 10 garages, without revealing your identity, and write a story comparing cost estimates for an engine overhaul? Still no problem?

How about checking into the local hospital's emergency ward and complaining about a fierce pain in your side—to research a story on medical practices in your town. See any ethical problems yet?

Let's take another step: Would you not only conceal your identity, but walk over to witnesses after a bank holdup and identify yourself as a detective to obtain an exclusive interview? No? Well, would you talk to those witnesses and passively deceive them by letting them assume you are a detective?

Ethical issues arising from such questions are equalled in number perhaps only by the differing answers journalists have.

On one extreme is the reporter who impersonated a police officer to interview a prison inmate (an illegal act for which the reporter spent 10 days in jail).[17]

In the middle are some editors who support undercover techniques if the story is profoundly crucial to the public and not available through other, more open means.

Some newspapers follow a third option and firmly oppose masquerading. The *New York Times* is among them—but the *Times* permits restaurant critics to sample food without alerting the chef in advance.

Can you articulate a Golden Mean solution?

Concern among journalists over news-sleuth techniques was summed up by J. Russell Wiggins, former editor of the *Washington Post*: "Deceit of this kind may now and then produce a story not otherwise obtained. The more often used the less effective the tactic will be and the greater the public distrust of the press."[18]

SECRET RECORDERS, HIDDEN CAMERAS

Conflicting ethical (and legal) arguments arise over whether reporters should use secret recorders.

CASE STUDY

Reporting or Eavesdropping

Is a reporter ethically responsible for warning public officials that what they say may be damaging or that a private off-the-cuff remark has been overheard?

In 1992, Bill Clinton, then campaigning for the U.S. presidency, was told by a reporter that the Rev. Jesse Jackson, whose political support he had sought, was campaigning for another presidential hopeful.

Clinton said to an aide, "It's an outrage, it's a dirty, double-crossing, back-stabbing thing to do."

Without his knowledge, Clinton's comment was picked up by a TV crew waiting to interview him and broadcast in Phoenix.

Clinton subsequently learned Jackson had not endorsed his opponent and telephoned Jackson an apology.

Should reporters have warned Clinton he had been overheard? Not important, you say? Politics as usual?

Well, what if such electronic eavesdropping records the president of the United States making a flippant—but potentially damaging—comment during the Cold War?

It happened in 1984 when network technicians were arranging a broadcast by President Reagan. During a routine microphone test they asked him to say a few words so they could adjust sound levels.

"My fellow Americans," he said, "I am pleased to tell you I just signed legislation which outlaws Russia forever. The bombing begins in five minutes."

Ask anyone who was there: During the Cold War, bombing other countries was no joke. But in this case, laughter erupted in the studio. The joviality helped reduce pre-broadcast tension.

Reagan's remark and the laughter were transmitted—not to the public, but to recording equipment outside the studio.

For example, all reporters take notes during telephone conversations with news sources. Isn't it logical to use a tape recorder to catch those quotes verbatim? Isn't it an excellent defense to have an electronically precise record of the conversation in case of a libel suit? But is it ethical—honest—to secretly record a conversation?

There generally is unanimity among journalists, readers and viewers: By large majorities, they disapprove of secret taping.[19] But dissenters ask why replacing pencil with recorder, even secretly, creates an ethical problem. State laws differ (and check yours before proceeding). In some, participatory taping—one party using a recorder in a two-party conversation—is legal; wiretapping—a third party listening secretly to two others—is illegal.

Question Should the President's obviously jocular but nevertheless startling remark have been treated as news to be reported publicly?

CBS, which recorded the remark on a Saturday, didn't use the tape until AP broke the story and printed the quotes. CBS then quoted the President on its late Sunday news. On Monday, after lengthy internal deliberations, CBS ran the actual recording on Dan Rather's *Evening News.*

CBS President Edward Joyce emphasized two points:

First, broadcasting the taped comment offered an explanatory dimension not created by merely quoting from the transcript: "There's a very clear indication of the jocularity around the mike when the laughter comes up. One of the questions we asked was, 'Does this in some way advance, clarify, further develop things?' Because of the jocular tone, and the laughter that developed, we felt it did."

Second, Joyce made a technical distinction: CBS and other networks would feel free to use the President's comments *if they left the studio*—which they did, on CBS transmission facilities.

Larry Speakes, White House spokesman, furiously charged that off-the-record ground rules had been broken. The networks claimed they had rejected any ground rules two years earlier when Reagan made a similar off-the-cuff remark before broadcast. That time, he referred to Poland's military government as a "bunch of no-good lousy bums." Later, in his actual broadcast, Reagan used the term, "a military dictatorship." But the "bums" remark was widely used.

Questions Should a reporter consider the international implications—the Cold War context—of such off-the-cuff remarks before using them? Is a reporter obligated to protect public officials from repercussions from their own casual remarks? Did AP stampede CBS? In answering, consult the societal values and journalistic principles discussed in Chapter 1.

There is little doubt: Secret tapping is unethical. Indeed, even when merely taking pencil notes, it is proper to point out the conversation is on the record.

Using hidden cameras creates different questions. As any foreign correspondent knows, openly photographing on the streets during, say, a riot can lead to cameras—and heads—being smashed. Secretly photographing from a second-story window in such cases clearly is not only ethical but wise.

But, let us say you are investigating drug dealing in your town. If you witness drug sales in a playground or park, photographing secretly from a nearby house or parked car would be acceptable. The action is taking place in public and thus is obvious to all who care to look. Many journalists agree, further, it is ethical to use a secret camera if, say, a drug dealer comes to your apartment to offer nar-

VIEWPOINT

When the Press Presses In

"The Salt Lake City hospital's public relations staff had been overwhelmed by the requests for information by news organizations and, in some cases, by the behavior of journalists. At the Utah hospital, a photographer had leaped out of a laundry hamper where he had been hiding and snapped pictures of the medical team that later appeared in a Japanese newspaper."

Alex S. Jones describing coverage of a human heart transplant, the *New York Times*

cotics. However, secretly photographing unsuspecting persons in their private home, where they have the right to privacy, is unacceptable to many.

CBS News outlines for its photographers just those distinctions: Use hidden cameras in public or your own home or office. But don't secretly intrude into the private domain of others.[20] Yet, ABC broke an important story in 1993 only by smuggling a camera into the meat department of a grocery chain store and revealing extensive adulteration of food.

Clearly, news the public should have sometimes comes into view only through tactics that will make you feel ethically uneasy.

The *Chicago Sun-Times* made the public versus private distinction when it established a tavern—a licensed public place—for use in investigative reporting. The tavern became a watering hole for corrupt city employees shaking down local businesses. *Sun-Times* reporters worked as bartenders and overhead conversation; *Sun-Times* photographers caught the whole thing from a hidden room. (The paper also invited in CBS's "60 Minutes.") The *Sun-Times* was expected to win a Pulitzer prize, but two members of the Pulitzer advisory board blocked it—Ben Bradlee, then editor of the *Washington Post,* and Eugene Patterson, then managing editor of the *St. Petersburg Times.* They explained honoring the *Sun-Times* would signal journalists across the country that misrepresentation was acceptable technique.

THE CASE OF THE PURLOINED DOCUMENTS

Stealing somebody's dining room silver is a crime. So is receiving stolen silver. Not many people will defend either.

Yet, many reporters obtain official or private documents without permission if the resulting story is deemed to serve the public interest. That is, many reporters will receive and use what technically are stolen goods.

As in most ethical issues, there are nuances.

It is to be hoped, for example, that few journalists will break into an official's office to obtain a document (although that has been done, and although some reporters might make a questionable distinction between a nighttime burglary

VIEWPOINT

More to It Than That

"The old notion that you 'get the story, and to hell with everything else' has no responsible defenders in American journalism today."

John Hohenberg, media scholar[22]

and entering uninvited during office hours). Some will read a document on an official's desk if invited in but left alone for a while (White House press aides once left documents out that way, and planted on a few reporters a minor scoop that turned out to be a major hoax).

Many reporters will consider a document a prize catch if they find it, say, after a meeting in an open conference room where the official absentmindedly left it (at one seminar on ethics where this scenario was presented as a case study, the major reservation among attending journalists was only whether to give the official advance word his document would be published).[21] And, many journalists gleefully accept a document—or a detailed report on its contents—if it is obtained by a "news source" (and no questions asked about how the source obtained it).

If you've already decided never to use purloined documents (particularly those stamped "secret"), consider the most celebrated instance in which they were used. That, of course, was publication in 1971 of the so-called Pentagon Papers, a massive official analysis of U.S. involvement in the Vietnam War. A former Defense Department analysis leaked them to the *New York Times, Washington Post, St. Louis Post-Dispatch* and *Boston Globe,* which published them despite vigorous legal efforts by the government to keep them secret.

Today, it is clear the Pentagon Papers were improperly classified secret, that publication of excerpts did not jeopardize national security, that the public had a right to know what was in them and that the newspapers served well the principle of a free press. But none of that disguises the fact that the documents were stolen goods.

Never forget your responsibility to explain to readers or viewers how you obtained confidential documents—and, particularly, the motives of those who leaked them to you.

On April 11, 1993, the *New York Times* broke a major story: Experts sent to Bosnia by President Clinton urged Washington to seriously consider military intervention.

In their first three paragraphs, the writers listed no attribution, leaving discerning readers to wonder how the *Times* got the story. The writers answered in their fourth graf:

CASE STUDY

Taking Readers Backstage

A metropolitan daily assigns you to write a Sunday wrap-up on an explosive local political development—the discharge of a well-known woman who had chaired your city's Housing Authority.

Throughout the week, daily stories reported charges that she misused Authority funds. What was not reported is that the woman was betrayed by subordinates offended by her harsh treatment. They tipped reporters on where to look for irregularities.

Should you take readers backstage, showing how this story developed? How can you report details of confidential arrangements between sources and reporters that often break big news?

Calvin Sims of the *New York Times,* writing that Sunday wrap-up in 1992, took his readers straight in with this lead:

> It was not the pink leather sofa ($3,070), the trip with seven aides to Puerto Rico ($16,000), or the chartered helicopter to Atlantic City ($1,500) that precipitated (the woman's) fall from the chairmanship of New York City's Housing Authority last week. It was her abrupt, often harsh treatment of subordinates who opened the door for reporters who had been tipped to what they would find.
>
> Behind the news reports of [the woman's] lavish public spending was a deliberate and skillful plot to unseat her by disgruntled staff members at the Housing Authority, which she headed, and the Metropolitan Transportation Authority, whose board she served on.

Note author Sims skillfully weaves a story of fact and reporter technique, thus serving the journalistic principle of honesty with readers. Then, Sims expands his explanation of how the story was broken *and* tells readers that, to be fair, the woman was asked for comment:

> Reporters who filed Freedom of Information Act requests for public documents detailing her expenses had lists of which reports and dates to ask for. Still-angry members of [the woman's]

> An executive summary of a draft report, prepared in March, was obtained by the *New York Times* from an official who believes the material should be part of the public debate on policy towards the crisis . . .[23]

NEW TECHNOLOGY AND THE ETHICS OF YOUR TECHNIQUE

So, *Spy* magazine takes this photo of a model dressed in leather and a very revealing bra—and holding a whip—and they stick Hillary Rodham Clinton's head on it!

> staff said last week that they helped reporters in order to retaliate for times they had been publicly humiliated. "We vowed to get her back, and we did," said one staff member who, like the others, spoke on condition of anonymity.
>
> [The woman], 53 years old, declined to be interviewed for this article. She resigned from her posts last weekend and is now being investigated by the Inspector General of the Federal Department of Housing and Urban Development and other agencies.

Sims goes further to ensure fairness and balance in his writing:

> [The woman], a gruff, hard-driving bureaucrat whose political allies say she had made it clear she wanted to be mayor some day, had won praise for winning Federal dollars for housing and ridding some projects of drug dealers.
>
> Her friends say she is a dedicated civil servant who is often misunderstood because she is aggressive. "Most people think that [she] is arrogant, because she believes in herself," said [a friend], an insurance executive who has known her for 25 years. "But she's just taking care of business. If she were a man, there would be no problem. But a woman cannot have an opinion. And that's what she has, an opinion."

Charges *against* the woman are from unidentified sources. Is that fair? Sims obviously doesn't think so. He adds *independent verification* of the charge that the woman is unduly harsh with subordinates:

> Many reporters have seen [the woman] upbraid people. At one overcrowded meeting, she arrived 45 minutes late, took a seat and immediately interrupted the chairman to demand that the meeting be adjourned, saying the room was too hot and she feared that photographers behind her would drop a camera on her head. When the chairman went on with his briefing about a fatal subway fire, she got into a shouting match with a television reporter who asked her to be quiet and then reprimanded the reporter for not knowing who she was.

Lessons:

The *techniques* of reporting can be fascinating news that's valuable to your readers and their understanding of your story.

Never forget, in the heat of covering a big story, to seek balancing comment, particularly from an accused person.[24]

You see, *Spy* uses a computer to manipulate photo elements and create a hilarious cover photo. You can't even tell it's not Hillary's body.

It's okay for *Spy* to do that, isn't it?

No, it's not okay. Furthermore, it's a frightening demonstration of how new technology introduces whole new dimensions of ethical problems in journalism today.[25]

For word journalists, computers and new high-speed communications technology change the techniques—and impact—of collecting and disseminating information. For example, information that once took months, then weeks, days or hours to travel around the world now can be transmitted globally in seconds.

A.

B.

Can you spot the difference between Photos A and B? In Photo A, an outfielder jumps for a ball, and misses by a wide margin. In Photo B, he misses it just narrowly—thanks to computer manipulation that moved the ball closer to his glove.

Experimental manipulation by
Harold G. Buell of The Associated Press

Imagine the impact important business news has when transmitted simultaneously in seconds to brokers and traders throughout the world. There is instantaneous impact on stock market prices and—literally—fortunes can change hands in minutes on the news. Imagine the impact of delivering—immediately—to one nation's leader what another leader says. Reporters (and their new high-speed transmission facilities) *are part of the diplomatic process*!

But, it's in new photo technology that particularly serious dangers of ethical transgressions arise.

Photo editors always could change what the cameras captured. Editors cropped photos and used other darkroom techniques to highlight one element in a photo or subdue others. But that was cumbersome, time-consuming and seldom yielded fully satisfactory results. For certain, it was difficult to put someone's head on another's body and make the darkroom surgery look authentic.

Today, in just seconds at a computer terminal, an editor can manipulate any element in a photo, changing substantially its content, meaning and truth. Believe it: Today, the camera—or, at least, its manipulated product—can lie.

A.

B.

In the original shot, Photo A, the player kneels dejectedly after being thrown out in a double play. Note he didn't get even close to second base. In Photo B, however, it was a close call—thanks to computer manipulation that moved the base closer!

Experimental manipulation by
Harold G. Buell of The Associated Press

One of the nation's top photo editors, Harold G. Buell, assistant to the president of the Associated Press, provided for this book two examples of how easily photos *can* be manipulated (see photos on pp. 84 and 85).[26]

It took Buell less than *five* minutes to manipulate the photos in our examples. And you'll note the results are perfect; you cannot tell which photos are doctored. Buell used a standard Leaf computerized photo editing system that most newspapers now have—and keyboard skills that anyone could learn in five minutes.

Unlike those who put Hillary Rodham Clinton's head on another woman's body, editors can have innocent motives for manipulation such as those in our illustrations.

For example, say you're an editor holding a sports page for a late baseball game. You've kept open room for a two-column photo. But when the photo arrives, just minutes before deadline, it's a three-column shot—wider than you expected because the ball is far from the player's glove, wider because the base is far right of the kneeling player.

What to do? Rip up the entire page and remake? That's a lengthy, laborious process that will delay presstime. Nah, why not just manipulate the photo elements a bit? Who will know—or care? What's the harm?

Indeed, what is the harm? You make the call:

- You have a great feature photo of a small boy, but his fly is unzipped. You can zip it up for him—and save him embarrassment—with a few touches on your computer keyboard. You don't have any problem with that, do you?
- You are a photo editor with a clean, neat photo of a Pulitzer prize-winning photographer. But smack in the middle, on a desk, is a soft drink can. Is it all right to tell a computer operator to eliminate the obtrusive can and clean up an otherwise great shot?

Okay so far? Let's escalate the stakes a bit:

- You're at *TV Guide* doing a cover story on Oprah Winfrey, and an editor suggests attaching somebody else's body (Ann Margret's) to Oprah's head. Sure looks better that way.
- You're at *National Geographic,* doing a story on the pyramids of Giza. An editor promises a much better cover photo can be arranged by moving one of the pyramids a bit to get tighter composition. That's okay, isn't it?

Those scenarios are true: The boy's fly was zipped up; the soft drink can was removed; Oprah got a delicious new body, and a pyramid was uprooted and moved across the sand.

Note the gentle escalation of ethical challenge in those four scenarios. You are escalated from a seemingly innocent attempt to prevent embarrassment to a little boy to major tinkering with truth.

Once even innocent manipulation begins with the truth—with reality—there is no telling where it will end. Therein lies, many photo journalists say, a major ethical dilemma: Is any manipulation of photo elements ethical?

By a wide margin, surveys show editors disapprove of any manipulation of photos other than traditional darkroom techniques of "burning" and "dodging." The Associated Press is unequivocal in a policy statement to its photo staffers: "The content of a photograph will *never* be changed or manipulated in any way."[27] Equally adamant is the executive committee of the National Press Photographers Association: "As journalists we believe the guiding principle of our profession is accuracy. Therefore, we believe it is wrong to alter the contents of a photograph in any way that deceives the public."[28]

Bottom line: Photo journalists who manipulate photos are violating fundamental truth-telling responsibilities that all journalist have—including those who work with cameras, rather than notebooks and pencils.

(Incidentally, want to check your reactions to the four scenarios above against reactions of editors who were shown the photographs? They voted overwhelmingly against manipulation in each case—although there did seem to be some sympathy for the little boy whose pants were zipped up!)[29]

Briefly, other ethical issues confronting photo journalists:

- *The one-shot problem.* Word journalists have hundreds, perhaps thousands of words to tell a story; a photojournalist may get one shot published. Does that single shot adequately tell the story? Can it represent all dimensions of complex issues? If not, the photojournalist has a major ethical problem.
- *Which angle to choose?* From one angle, a photo of, say, a political rally can show a candidate and 1,000 cheering supporters. From another angle, the photo can show the candidate and 5 or 10 supporters. For a photojournalist, choosing the correct angle is like a word journalist choosing the correct language. Bad calls in either case can result in irresponsible—and, thus, unethical—journalism.

- *The problem of context.* A widow can be photographed *smiling* at her husband's funeral—but perhaps she's smiling bravely at her children, off camera and not shown. Unexplained, in the caption or otherwise, the smile is out of context. See the problem?
- *What's too strong?* Photographers see—and catch—unimaginable blood and gore. Well, that's reality, right? But when is reality too strong for readers and viewers? And, if editors intervene—edit out the blood and kill the gory pictures—are they censoring reality and thus, in an ethical sense, failing their truth-telling responsibilities? During the Gulf War, AP refused to distribute a color photo—close-up and graphic—of an Iraqi soldier burned to death while fleeing Kuwait. Said AP: " . . . too gruesome for average newspaper readership." Said photographer Ken Jarecke: "If we're big enough to fight a war, we should be big enough to look at it." You make the call: principled editing in good taste, or self-censorship?[30] In San Francisco, KQED-TV applied for permission to televise the execution of a death row inmate. Strong, courageous journalism? Or, unethical, unprincipled pandering to base instincts? (Permission was refused.) A poll in 1993 by *Broadcasting & Cable* magazine indicated that wasn't an entirely popular decision. Of TV news directors polled, 49 percent said their station would consider airing televised coverage of a state-sanctioned criminal execution.
- *The posed shot.* Is any posed shot—even, "Look at the camera, please"—making news, rather than reporting it? Many leading photojournalists won't pose anything; they shoot what's happening spontaneously or they don't shoot at all.
- *Free press, fair trial.* Word journalists are admitted to courtrooms; so should photojournalists be admitted, or so goes the argument. Some state court judges agree, but not federal judges. Former U.S. Supreme Court Justice Warren Burger set the tone for federal judges: " . . . show business and judicial business just don't mix." Photojournalists say new cameras and film permit still photography without disruptive flash equipment. Television editors say their cameras are small and can be controlled from fixed positions without operators being in the courtroom.

Finally, you'll note there is no extended discussion in this book of the admission by NBC News in 1993 that it rigged a pick-up truck explosion being videotaped to illustrate an "exposé" on truck safety. That and similar hoaxes on the viewing public are for books on journalistic fraud, not journalistic ethics.

Summary

In building a personal code of ethics you must consider not only your ethical intent but also the ethics of technique.

Ethical reporting technique requires respect for the basic facts of a story because, by definition, an inaccurate reporter also is unethical.

Reporters must deal carefully with little as well as big details of a story, and recognize their own weaknesses—in background information about the story, for example—and correct them. Develop healthy skepticism as you search out facts for your readers; beware sources who try to trap you with misinformation.

The ethics of honest writing require you to include all relevant facts in a story and keep your own opinion out of your copy.

Beware of how you select quotes for your story. You can skew a story if you don't select quotes that represent the speaker's true intent.

One important influence on reportorial technique is the adversarial relationship, the always cautious, sometimes tense relationship between reporters and the structure they cover. Some reporters seek head-on confrontation with news sources; others passively accept news handouts. It's possible, however, to build a decorous but effective relationship—a Golden Mean—by getting close to sources but never joining their team.

One ethical dilemma for reporters is that their mere presence at a news event can make news, involving them in much more than an observer's role. Each reporter must carefully avoid getting involved in a story.

News sources are critically important, and complex ethical considerations have grown up around reporter-source relationships. It's important to understand the source's motives in giving you news. Some do so to advance their personal interests, others to damage a foe. To be fair to your readers you must identify your sources, whenever possible. If it's not, you should describe the source's authoritative credentials as fully as possible so the reader or viewer can decide on the reliability of your information.

The ethics of undercover reporting are hotly debated. Readers, viewers and editors like the result of investigative reporting, but disapprove of such techniques as using secret tape recorders or cameras. Editors also increasingly frown on journalists concealing their identity as reporters or masquerading under an assumed identity.

Notes

1. This sentiment began appearing strongly in reader/viewer polls of the early 1980s. Note particularly "Relating to Readers in the '80s," a 1984 survey by Ruth Clark, president, Clark, Martire & Bartolomeo, Inc.
2. "Leak About CIA Operation against Khadafy Angers Congress," AP story for morning papers, Nov. 5, 1985, published in *Atlanta Constitution* that day, p. 9-A.
3. "2,700 Killed in Afghan Tunnel," AP story for morning papers, Nov. 10, 1982, published that day in *Athens (Ga.) Daily News,* p. 1.
4. Barbara Crossette, "On Honduran Coast, A World Apart," *New York Times,* July 2, 1983, p. 2.
5. Michael J. O'Neill, speech to American Society of Newspaper Editors, Washington, D.C., May 5, 1982.
6. For a full discussion of this exchange, see "The Adversary Press," a report on an Ethics Center Seminar, p. viii, 1983, Modern Media Institute, 801 Third St. South, St. Petersburg, Fla., 33701.

7. James Reston, "Reagan and the Press," *New York Times,* March 21, 1982, p. 23.

8. One particularly fine wrap-up on government deception is Anthony Marro, "When The Government Tells Lies," *Columbia Journalism Review,* March/April 1985, p. 29.

9. James Deakin, *The Right Stuff: The Reporters, the White House and the Truth* (New York: William Morrow & Company, Inc., 1984).

10. Meg Greenfield, "When the Press Becomes a Participant," Annual Report 1984, The Washington Post Co., 1150 15th St. N.W., Washington, D.C., 20071, p. 21.

11. George V. Higgins, "TV: The Democratic Oratory Contest," *Wall Street Journal,* July 23, 1984, p. 13.

12. The full quote is, "I would not want to be a newsman at any other time. . . . Man's aspiration was never higher in reaching for the stars, his material wealth never greater, and his chance for survival in a nuclear age never thinner. And we, in the AP, sit in front row seats to report all this." The quote is from Wes Gallagher and can be found as the introduction to Charles A. Grumich, *Reporting/Writing from Front Row Seats* (New York: Simon & Schuster, Inc., 1971).

13. The burning monk was photographed by Malcome W. Browne, then AP Saigon bureau chief, on June 11, 1963. The photos created a tremendous stir over whether their use was in good taste. For details on the Ossining story, see Jonathan Friendly, "Officials and Newsmen Discuss TV's Ossining Role," *New York Times,* Jan. 15, 1983, p. 16. Steve Komarow describes his role in the Washington Monument incident in "Eyewitness to History," *AP Log,* the Associated Press, 50 Rockefeller Plaza, New York, N.Y., 10020, Dec. 13, 1982, p. 1.

14. Lou Boccardi, "A Note of Caution," *AP Log,* op. cit.

15. Hodding Carter III, "The 'Informed Source' and Other Masked Men," *The Wall Street Journal,* Jan. 20, 1983, p. 25.

16. Reader disapproval of undercover techniques is reported in a number of surveys, in none so clearly as "Newspaper Credibility: Building Reader Trust," research report, 1985, American Society of Newspaper Editors, P.O. Box 17004, Washington, D.C., 20041. Several studies of editor attitudes reveal this ambivalence. Note Guido H. Stempel III, "New Studies Explain Credibility, Secret Taping of Calls," *presstime,* Nov. 1985, p. 55; Ralph S. Izard, "Technique: Certain News Procedures Found to Bother Journalists," a special report on ethics, Associated Press Managing Editors, 50 Rockefeller Plaza, New York, N.Y. 10020; and, "Editors Say Journalists Should Not Use Hidden Recording Devices," research bulletin, Southern Newspaper Publishers Association, P.O. Box 28874, Atlanta, Ga., 30328, June 16, 1983, p. 1.

17. "Reporting Subterfuge," *The APME Red Book* 1983, Associated Press Managing Editors, 50 Rockefeller Plaza, New York, N.Y., 10020.

18. Ibid. Also see Tom Goldstein, "The News at Any Cost," *Washington Journalism Review,* Sept. 1985, p. 48.

19. "Editors Say Journalists Should Not Use Hidden Recording Devices," Southern Newspaper Publishers Association Bulletin, op. cit., and "Newspaper Credibility: Building Reader Trust," ASNE research report, op. cit.

20. *CBS News Standards, a policy manual,* CBS Inc., 51 W. 52nd St., New York, N.Y., 10020, April 14, 1976.

21. Seminar in media ethics sponsored by Morris Communications Corp., Savannah, Ga., March 9–11, 1986.

22. John Hohenberg, *The Professional Journalist* (New York: Holt, Rinehart & Winston, Inc., 1978), p. 320.
23. Michael R. Gordon with Stephen Engelberg, "President is Urged to Consider Force to Help Bosnians," *New York Times,* national edition, April 11, 1993, p. 1.
24. Calvin Sims, "A Commissioner Done in by a Staff She Offended," *New York Times,* national edition, March 1, 1992, p. 6-E.
25. For a full discussion, see "How *Spy* Magazine Makes Its Hilarious Covers," *Imaging Magazine,* Aug. 1993, p. 38.
26. Buell, for years an editor overseas and at home, then head of AP's entire photo service, is a leading commentator on photo ethics.
27. Vin Alabiso, executive photo editor, "The Ethics of Electronic Imaging and Photo Content," *AP Log,* Nov. 26, 1990, p. 1.
28. This statement was released at an NPPA Electronic Photojournalism Workshop on Nov. 12, 1990, and reprinted in "NPPA Releases Ethics Statement," *SixShooters,* the Region 6 publication of NPPA, Nov./Dec. 1990, p. 9.
29. Significant research in this subject was published by Sheila Reaves, assistant professor of journalism and mass communication at the University of Wisconsin-Madison. See "What's Wrong with This Picture?," *Newspaper Research Journal,* Fall 1992/Winter 1993, p. 131. AP's Buell also cites these four scenarios as examples of unethical electronic manipulation.
30. Jon Fine, "Spiked," News*Inc,* March 1992, p. 33.

CHAPTER 4

You and Your Editor

It's reality time: Not only must you develop a personal approach to the ethics of technique that we discussed in Chapter 3, you also must ensure your code meshes with your editor's.

Either you and the hand that feeds you agree on ethics in reporting and writing, or you (not your editor) will be a very unhappy employee—or unemployed.

Ideally, you can avoid a clash on the job about ethics by carefully selecting the type of newspaper or broadcast station you work for. Study the reporting and writing of prospective employers and try to select one whose attitude toward ethics is similar to yours.

If, for example, you don't want a career of writing about moon men landing in the pumpkin patch, avoid those supermarket tabloids. If ambush journalism—jumping from behind a hedge and thrusting a camera into someone's face—isn't your idea of responsible TV journalism, avoid those stations that will do anything, including unethical stunting, to win in the ratings on the 11 p.m. news.

Unfortunately, even with the perfect employer, tension can arise as you try to relate your personal sense of right and wrong to your editor's. We turn now to some particularly delicate areas where that can happen.

WHO'S IN CHARGE HERE?

Editors today generally set standards of conduct for everyone in their newsrooms and decide ethical issues once thought properly left to individual reporters. This stems from a widespread feeling among newspaper editors and TV news directors that they must take firm control of what is happening in their own newsrooms.

In the 1970s and 1980s, many editors feared that insufficient supervision was permitting some reporters to practice advocacy journalism, where objective reporting once was the goal, or, even worse, get into print and on the air with phony stories.

Fears became reality when a reporter, Janet Cooke, managed to slip through the *Washington Post*'s editing safeguards with a nationally acclaimed—and phony—story about a child heroin addict. What shook journalists most is that on this hoax, the *Washington Post*'s renowned editors simply lost control of a reporter's performance in their own newsroom, and the story got into print.

Michael J. O'Neill, then editor of the *New York Daily News,* called for stronger, more vigilant editing:

Editors, he said,

> need to be ruthless in ferreting out the subtle biases—cultural, visceral and ideological—that still slip into copy, into political stories, mostly, but also into the coverage of emotional issues like nuclear power and abortion. Lingering traces of advocacy are less obvious than Janet Cooke's fiction but, for that reason, are more worrisome. Editors—myself included—have simply not exercised enough control over subeditors and reporters reared in the age of the new journalism.[1]

Lee Hills, a leading architect of the principled journalism for which Knight-Ridder, Inc., is noted, called on editors to prevent such "journalistic felonies" as the Janet Cooke story:

> Be more rigorous on editorial standards and less self-righteous when something goes wrong. . . . Use blind sources sparingly. . . . The editor trusts the reporter but the reporter must also trust his or her top editor and tell them everything. . . . Insist on corroboration. The reporter wants to protect his source. But the editor must protect the very reputation of the newspaper itself. He cannot delegate it. If the *Post* had taken this precaution, or any one of several others, the scandal of the [child addict] story would not have happened. Never forget that our most precious and fragile asset is credibility. In a society running short on trust, we are one of the trustees.
>
> If an editor has given up control of his newsroom to reporters, get it back. If the editor is too weak to insist on carrying that responsibility, get a new editor.[2]

Hills' comments illustrate the pressure on many editors to exert firmer administrative control over their newsrooms. For reporters, this can raise several ethical issues.

THOSE ANONYMOUS SOURCES AGAIN

Many editors take solely to themselves all decisions whether news sources will be granted anonymity. Reporters who once granted anonymity with relative impunity or made deals with sources now must seek permission.

As editor of the *Chicago Tribune,* James D. Squires claimed editors and reporters too long were "duped and manipulated" by news sources who attacked enemies through the press, and who "simply want to cower behind the walls of a reporter's privilege and throw rocks in anonymity." He said his reporters could not unilaterally agree to protect a source's identity:

VIEWPOINT

Editors Warned to Edit

"*Post* editors simply failed to do their job. They trusted a gifted liar; a kid from Ohio who had even faked her background to get her job only nine months before. Everyone in our profession was injured some because it gave ammunition to critics who want the press somehow controlled."

Lee Hills, former chairman of Knight-Ridder, Inc., warning company editors to control their newsrooms because of the Janet Cooke hoax on the *Washington Post*

> [T]he time has long since passed when that pledge by an individual reporter can bind and incapacitate a news organization to the point where it supersedes all other ethical considerations. Readers deserve honesty as much as sources deserve loyalty. And there is no greater editor's responsibility than the life and credibility of the newspaper.[3]

The *Youngstown (Ohio) Vindicator* suspended a reporter because he signed an agreement with a news source promising confidentiality in return for exclusive information. The agreement permitted the source to read any news story written from the information *before* it was published and committed the paper to other restraints. An arbitrator rejected the Newspaper Guild's contention that the suspension was without "just cause."[4]

When a reporter unilaterally committed the *Athens (Ga.) Banner-Herald* to an embargo—not using a story until a time set by the source—the paper's associate editor, Rick Parham, wrote a lengthy signed column explaining to readers what happened. His lead: "There is a story that you didn't read in today's paper." He wrote that his reporter had to make a quick judgment on whether to accept the embargo, that he didn't agree with her decision, "But we'll keep our promise on the embargo."[5]

For example, reporters sometimes are subpoenaed to testify in court cases or turn over notes, under threat of contempt of court. That, in turn, can lead to employers being threatened with contempt unless reporters comply.

In New Jersey, reporter Myron Farber refused to turn over his notes in a murder case. That, he said, would have identified sources to whom he pledged anonymity. Farber went to jail for 47 days—and his employer, the *New York Times,* was fined $286,000. (Farber and the *Times,* which backed him all the way, were pardoned four years later, and the newspaper got back $185,000.)

Is a reporter's right to protect sources more important than ensuring all evidence is available in a murder trial? Was there conflict between societal values and journalistic principles in the Farber case?

A classic example of how editors get involved in a reporter's protection of sources exploded on front pages and the evening news in 1991. Sources in Wash-

CASE STUDY

Would You Print or Hold?

In this case, move to the other side of the copy desk—into an editor's slot, to gain understanding of how supervisors must handle ethical crises of reporters.

You are a sports editor in a town gone crazy over professional football. It appears the local team can win the league championship.

Then, one of your reporters drops a bombshell on you: He heard rumors of drug problems on the team, but couldn't verify details so he asked the coach. The coach said his players "tested clean," and he hadn't seen drugs affect performance. He agreed to give your reporter background if the story were held until after the season. Your reporter agreed, only later informing you and saying he didn't think he could have gotten the story any other way.

Questions Are you bound by the reporter's deal? Must you consider what revealing a drug scandal would do to the team's championship drive? What would your readers, many of them sports fanatics, think if you broke this story with a championship in reach? Also, your competitors might sniff out the story. Should you break it while it still is exclusive?

It happened at the *Boston Globe* in 1986 when reporter Don Borges made the deal with Coach Raymond Berry of the New England Patriots.

Vincent Doria, *Globe* assistant managing editor for sports, decided breaking the commitment "would have damaged us—our integrity as reporters." He said he worried the story was "potentially libelous. . . . There was no boosterism involved." Doria said he had thought the Patriots would lose their battle for the league championship, and then he could use the story quite quickly. In fact, they extended the season by going to the Super Bowl, and Doria had to sit on the story much longer than expected, which made him "uncomfortable." After losing the Super Bowl, Patriot players voted to be the first NFL team with a voluntary drug-testing program.

Boston TV stations learned that and broke the story, scooping the *Globe.* Criticism of the *Globe* was widespread:

Producer Mark Williams of WRKO Radio in Boston: "Callers wondered if the paper would have held on to the information in other situations, like something involving a politician. And there was a feeling that the reporter knew and the bookies knew and that's why the point spread was so wide."

Publisher Patrick Purcell of the competing *Boston Herald*: "Regardless of whether the story is about politics, business or sports, the paramount concern should be the public's

ington leaked word to Timothy M. Phelps of *Newsday* and Nina Totenberg of National Public Radio that a University of Oklahoma law professor, Anita F. Hill, had made sexual harassment charges against Clarence Thomas, then seeking confirmation as a U.S. Supreme Court justice.

The U.S. Senate launched an investigation of the leaks, but both reporters refused to identify their sources. Then, the Senate's special counsel questioned

right to know. I believe it was wrong for the *Globe*'s reporter to make a deal to delay the story until after the Super Bowl in return for verification. If the reporter could not get verification of the story through diligence and hard work, so be it. He shouldn't have struck the deal."

Now, *You* Make the Call

Who was right? The *Herald*'s Purcell or *Globe*'s Doria?

Before you answer, a question: Should we really spend time on this case study? After all, aren't we talking here about only a sports story? It's not the Fate of the Western World at stake. Should we make the same moral judgments about sports coverage that we do about reporting on, say, White House policy or another really serious issue in the news?

Assuming you think (as I do) that all news coverage—front page, sports page and on TV—should come under equally intense ethical scrutiny, proceed now to judge the *Boston Globe* case with our five-step process:

1. You have the pertinent facts.
2. Can you identify a central ethical issue? Is it the reporter's loyalty to the team vs. loyalty to readers? Boosterism vs. dispassionate news coverage?
3. Could the reporter and editor consider alternative solutions? Is a Golden Mean available? What solution would you consider?
4. How have you decided? Print and be damned? Or, does the *Globe* really have to stand by the reporter's pledge to hold the story until season's end? Indeed, does the *Globe* have a responsibility to the team's championship hopes? Would mid-season coverage of the drug scandal have ended those hopes?
5. Has editor Doria of the *Globe* acted correctly? Is it correct to sit on the story?

Refer to the Chapter 1 adaptation of the Potter Box: Which societal values are involved in this case? Truth-telling? Promise keeping? Look closely at journalistic principles in the box—serve the public, be balanced and fair, be compassionate.
And which loyalties come into play? To self and conscience? To society?

For many editors, the basic issue is simple: Who is in charge of newsroom operations, editors or reporters? Increasingly, editors—backed by top management—are taking firm charge.

More than managerial principle is at stake: Editors fear their newspapers or TV operations can land in big, expensive trouble if individual reporters are permitted to enter into binding agreements to protect a source's identity.

Anthony Marro, *Newsday*'s editor, for more than five hours. Though facing possible contempt citation, Marro also refused to cooperate, arguing that journalists are protected from such inquiries by the First Amendment's guarantee of press freedom. (The inquiry eventually died.)

Lesson: Expect your editor to demand that you consult in advance of any pledge to your sources.

VIEWPOINT

You, Your Editor, Your Source

"Refusal to tell your editors where you got a story is grounds for dismissal."
Wayne Sargent, then editor, the *San Bernardino Sun*

"(O)n request, a senior editor must be able to learn the identity. The request is made only intermittently, when a story is sensitive or shocking."
Allan M. Siegal, news editor, the *New York Times*

"To assure maximum protection for sources who have been guaranteed anonymity, the editor who gives the copy its first reading *may not* reveal the identity of the source—even to other editors—without the permission of the author. Consequently, reporters will routinely reveal their sources only to one editor. Sources should be assured their identities will be protected."
Champaign-Urbana (Ill.) News-Gazette policy statement

The *Roanoke (Va.) Times & World-News* grants anonymity only if (1) a supervising editor determines there is no other way of getting information the public needs, (2) the reader is told as much as possible about the source, without revealing identity, (3) extensive efforts have been made to corroborate the source's information, and (4) the editor knows the source's identity.

If your editors ask the identity of your source you should seek assurances that they—and your newspaper or TV station—will protect the source. Your credibility with sources, the main tool of the reporting trade, is at stake.

But what if your editors overrule a pledge of anonymity you've already given and order the source identified in print? It happened at the Minneapolis *Star Tribune* and *St. Paul Pioneer Press,* where editors required reporters to print stories identifying a man who, under a secrecy pledge, leaked damaging information about his political rival.

The "burned" source fought all the way to the U.S. Supreme Court, contending he should be able to sue the newspapers for breach of contract. The Court ruled the First Amendment does not protect newspapers from such a lawsuit, and sent the case back to the Minnesota Supreme Court. The Minnesota court ruled in 1992 for the burned source, who won $200,000 in damages.

Lyle Denniston, who covers the U.S. Supreme Court for the *Baltimore Sun,* notes that for journalists it's "normal ethical duty to keep promises of source secrecy" and that the press "might improve its chances with the law if it were truer to its own code of ethics."[6]

WHO OWNS YOUR BYLINE?

Editors are paid to assign you to stories, edit your copy and oversee your training. In return, you draw a salary for helping get the paper out or the evening news on air.

VIEWPOINT

When You and Your Boss Disagree

"If your reasons conflict with your firm's objectives, you've got a problem that's a lot deeper than this decision; either your values must change or your job should. Beware if you're frequently rearranging your values to align them with those objectives; you may be learning how to do business in an unfamiliar environment, but you may also be prostituting yourself. You can't be happy if you've surrendered your dignity. That's when it's time to get out."

Peter A. Reinhardt, management expert[7]

Fair enough, except that on occasion an assignment may offend your personal code of ethics—interviewing that grieving widow at graveside may not be your idea of journalistic integrity, for example. Or, your ego will be bruised if your elegant prose is heavily edited—butchered, you will think—and your personal code of ethics compromised if editing changes the story's meaning.

If that happens, consider several factors:

First, maybe—just maybe—your editors know what they are doing. Maybe there is important news in that assignment, and that by virtue of greater experience, your supervisors see it; maybe you did mess up the writing. So, don't automatically blow your ethical top.

Second, assignments must be covered, stories must be written, the newscast must get on the air, the paper must get out—and you are paid to help. You are not a free-lancer, after all; you're a member of a news team.

Third, however, you still may see fundamental ethical problems. If so, negotiate. A reasonable editor will be sensitive to your crisis of conscience. Perhaps the story can be assigned to someone else; perhaps you can convince your supervisor you do have a point on the editing. Perhaps your byline can be removed from a story you feel was botched in editing. However, some editors claim the newspaper owns your byline while you are on the payroll and that its usage is at their discretion; under the Copyright Act, the newspaper or TV station paid for and owns the story itself.

Fourth, your editor may have an inflated sense of self-importance or lack of sensitivity to your ethical dilemma, and you may have no choice but to refuse an assignment on a point of personal integrity. That, of course, can lead quickly to unemployment, a high price to pay for courageous journalism, particularly if you have car payments and college debts to pay off. But it is a price paid by others before you.

The Newspaper Guild, a union for journalists and others, attempts to force publishers to contractually recognize reporters' rights in matters of ethics and integrity. Many publishers refuse, but the Guild issues model contract language its members should strive for in negotiations:

> An employee shall not be required to perform, over the employee's protest, any practice which in the employee's judgment compromises the employee's integrity. An employee shall not be required to use the employee's position as an employee for any purpose other than performing the duties of the employee's position. An employee's byline or credit line shall not be used over the employee's protest. Substantive changes in material submitted shall be brought to the employee's attention before publication. An employee shall not be required to write, process or prepare anything for publication in such a way as to distort any facts or to create an impression which the employee knows to be false. If a question arises as to the accuracy of printed material, no correction or retraction of that material shall be printed without prior consultation with the employee concerned. An employee whose work or person is mentioned in a letter to the editor shall be informed of such letter immediately and shall have the right to respond to such letter simultaneously and adequately on the page on which it is published.[8]

In the Minnesota burned-source case, one reporter, enraged that her confidentiality pledge was being broken, pulled her byline off the story.[9]

At Knight-Ridder's *Journal of Commerce,* many reporters withheld their bylines from stories for three days, protesting what they said was an unnecessary front-page apology to an advertiser for unflattering coverage. Editors used "Journal of Commerce staff" as bylines, instead.[10]

YOUR EDITOR'S OTHER CONCERNS

Editors and news directors have other concerns that influence whether you mesh with them on ethical issues. To understand their views, understand the following concerns.

MONEY

Solvency must be the first goal of any newspaper or magazine or television or radio operation, and your editor or news director is on a strict budget. There may not always be enough money to do the job journalistically as you think it should be done.

You may feel it irresponsible—unethical, even—if you cannot travel to Hong Kong to round out your reporting on a story. Your supervisor may agree, but simply be unable to afford to get you there.

You may feel you need at least 15 column inches or three minutes of air time to do an honest writing job—and be told to do it in nine inches or one minute. A newspaper editor often has no more than 35 to 40 percent of a newspaper's total space for news; in television, your news director may have only 30 minutes, minus time for commercials, to cover the entire world.

THE LAW

No editor or news director today can make any important decision—in ethics or anything else—without considering legal implications.

It's called the *chilling effect:* Defending against a libel suit, let alone losing one, can be stunningly expensive. As a result, some stories quite frankly are not covered or, perhaps, are covered in a certain way.

If this happens on a story of yours, you may argue that it is irresponsible, unethical to pull punches because of a threatened lawsuit. But your supervisors' decision must be whether your story is worth hundreds of thousands in defense lawyer's fees or, perhaps, millions in judgments if a jury decides against you.

That is a harsh reality in every newsroom today, and here's why: The Libel Defense Resource Center reports that in 1990–1991, the *average* award for compensatory and punitive damages in libel suits that went to juries was about $9 million! Juries awarded two huge judgments against the media in that period—for $58 million and $34 million—which pushed up the average. But even without those two, awards would have averaged almost $5.2 million.[11]

Even in relationship with you, your editor or news director is severely constrained in what can be done or said. Hours you work, conditions under which you work—all are mandated by law and, perhaps, union agreements, as well.

In other words, what you see as purely an ethical issue, may be to your supervisor an ethical issue in a complex legal wrapping.

THE CORPORATE IMPERATIVE

Your editor or news director must perform—as a manager as well as journalist—in keeping with corporate guidelines.

News strategists set goals in such things as tone and image to be achieved with a newspaper or news program. Often, these goals are designed to capture certain market segments—chosen readers, viewers or advertisers—so the newspaper or television news operation will achieve marketplace success.

That is why the *New York Times* and other similarly elitist newspapers take one approach to news coverage while, for example, the *New York Post* or *New York Daily News,* both mass appeal newspapers, take quite another.

Call it what you will—tone, policy, guidelines—you and your supervisor are expected to conform, and that could directly influence discussions between you on ethical issues.

For example, your editor must serve as intermediary between you and the public. A complaint about one of your stories must be answered by your editor. Forgive editors if they adopt a, shall we say, placating tone when dealing with public complaints. Readers and advertisers are customers and customers pay the bills—including your salary.

James K. Batten, chairman and chief executive officer of Knight-Ridder, Inc., one of the nation's leading newspaper groups, told his editors, "We have tended too much to take our customers for granted. . . . We prided ourselves on our ability to tell our critics to go to hell. After all, we were the press—beholden to no one and proud of it."[12]

Batten, a former reporter and editor, made clear his editors must serve the public, making newspapers more attractive and customers more satisfied.

CASE STUDY

Tough Calls Editors Must Make

You are an editor whose Washington reporter learns the White House is directing secret talks with certain elements in Iran, a nation the United States officially terms a terrorist state.

One goal is release of American hostages, including an AP correspondent, being held in Lebanon. A small Mideast publication breaks the story, but the White House nevertheless warns that if you publish details, you could jeopardize hostages.

One already-freed hostage, the President at his side, tells reporters: "In the name of God, will you please just be responsible and back off. Unreasonable speculation on your part can endanger their lives. . . ."

Question Will you order your reporter to probe for details? Will you publish a story? How does the societal value of humaneness play here against the value of truth-telling as defined by Kant?

It happened in 1986, and newspapers indeed probed and published, eventually forcing President Reagan's administration to reveal the real story was much larger than hostages.

Despite pledges he never would negotiate with terrorists, Reagan acknowledged he had approved arms sales to Iran, then at war with Iraq. He said goals were to improve relations with Iran, establish ties with moderates who eventually might govern the country and end Iran's support for international terrorism, as well as free hostages. Money from Iran was diverted to supply Contra guerrillas in Nicaragua. There was an uproar in Congress, which had not been informed of the arms sales, and among American allies, who had been pressured by the United States not to deal with Iran.

An editor's responsibility for the public image of a newspaper can have direct impact on newsroom ethics and individual staffers.

At the *Houston Post,* in 1991, editors denied a columnist permission to reveal in his column that he is homosexual. When he gave interviews to other publications on his conflict with his editors, they fired him.[13]

There was a different twist in 1992 at the *Atlanta Journal and Constitution*: Editors published a news brief reporting that the papers' traffic columnist was charged with driving under the influence of alcohol—just as they publish stories about public figures arrested for DUI. The next day, the writer began his column this way:

> This is a column I told my boss I need to write.
> It is not humorous and it is not going to help you deal with traffic . . .

More questions In such tense times, must reporters and editors consider whether they jeopardize a President's conduct of foreign policy by reporting his secret moves? Would knowing of the Iran deal but not publishing make reporters and editors participants in official covert policies? Did the small Mideast publication, in revealing some details, relieve American reporters and editors of moral responsibility for considering the impact of their stories?

The response among American print and broadcast journalists was to publish as many details as possible.

Ralph Langer, executive editor of the *Dallas Morning News,* said the media could not get enlisted in covert policies; official charges that reporters might endanger lives were "very sobering," but "I'm not sure how reporting something the other side already knows could endanger [hostages]. The only ones who did not know were the American people."

Ben Bradlee, executive editor of the *Washington Post,* said Washington publicly tried to draw European nations into promising not to negotiate with terrorists, but then did so itself. "You can't do it then tell me I can't report it," Bradlee said.

Warren Hoge, *New York Times* foreign editor, said, "I think our responsibility is to give an accounting to our readers about what the government is doing, especially when it's doing the opposite of what it says it's doing."

President Reagan told *Time* magazine, "What is driving me up the walls is that this [foreign policy initiative] wasn't a failure until the press got a tip from that rag in Beirut and began to play it up. I told them that publicity could destroy this, that it could get people killed. They then went right on. . . . This whole thing boils down to a great irresponsibility on the part of the press . . ."

Were editors, who could not know all the facts in such situations, justified in printing the story? Such reporting can have enormous impact on governments and nations. Does that carry journalists across the line from reporting into policy-making?

> I wish from my feet to my forehead that I was not writing this about me. But I am, in the hope that my story might help others.
>
> I was arrested for DUI early Friday morning . . .

The four-column headline on that story was, "No Excuses, Road Warriors: I Was Arrested for DUI."[14]

Thus did *Atlanta Journal and Constitution* editors serve notice that no individual staffer is above the same news judgments and treatment accorded any member of the public.

YOU, THE UNKNOWN

Look at yourself as your editor or news director must: inexperienced, a hard charger and, journalistically, an unknown factor.

Yet, on any given story the reputation of the newspaper or television news operation—plus your supervisor's own reputation—could depend on how well you perform. One misstep by you could damage corporate image or purse.

So, be understanding if your editors suggest you conform to ethical guidelines they have laid down.

TIMES WHEN YOU'LL NEED BACKUP

Loyalty must run both ways in newsrooms because just as your editor needs your agreement on ethical principles, so do you need firm support from your editor.

Let's look at situations where you'll need loyal backing.

WHEN COURAGE IS NEEDED

It took courage for Myron Farber of the *New York Times* to refuse that New Jersey judge's order to turn over his notes. He knew he faced jail. And he was right. Farber spent 40 days in jail.

William Farr of the *Los Angeles Herald Examiner* spent 47 days in jail for refusing to identify sources in a murder trial he covered.

Courage and self-discipline are essential to ethical journalism, along with honest reporting and honest writing. But no reporter can succeed without strong, loyal backing from editors.

For Farber and Farr, crisis of conscience arose over a principle fundamental to journalism in a free society—that reporters must be permitted special relationships with news sources, including the right to grant them anonymity, if the press is to function properly. Their defense of that principle at enormous personal cost brought much of the media to their support. Their cases drew national interest.

For you, courageously defending ethical principle may be a lonely affair. Perhaps you will have to make your stand over an issue that, although of compelling importance to you, holds no significance for your media colleagues or interest for the public. Perhaps you will face ethical issues lacking the clarity of those faced by Farber and Farr. And, wrestling with nuances of right and wrong and shades of meaning can leave you doubting the wisdom of your course.

If you see an ethical problem looming, make sure your editor is informed before a crisis arrives.

DEFIANCE OF AUTHORITY

Few things require more courage for journalists just starting their careers than defying authority—pushing your way into an improperly closed meeting of the school board, pressuring police to open public records, insisting that officialdom conduct the people's business in the open sunshine.

Push you must, of course—politely, professionally, but very firmly as surrogate of the people.

Again, you'll need your editor's backing because that puts the institutional strength of your newspaper or TV news operation behind you. This is particu-

CASE STUDY

An Editor's Dilemma: When Bad News Hits Good Guys

You are editor of a metropolitan daily and your reporters pick up rumors that a high-ranking officer in a local Salvation Army post, an ordained minister, has been misappropriating donated goods—a car, boat, motorcycle and other things—for his own use.

Your reporters confirm the rumors, and you tell Salvation Army officials what you discovered. They are candid: It in fact happened. They plead with you not to publish, citing damage that would be done to the Army, itself innocent, although one of its own has gone astray. They offer to open to you their own internal investigation so you will be satisfied that the wrong has been righted.

The Salvation Army has an outstanding record of public service in your city, is regarded highly by the public and has a board directors that is a who's who of local philanthropic, civic and business leaders—including the president of the company that owns your paper.

Questions What societal values and journalistic principles are at play here? Do you publish the story? If not, why not? If so, why—and will you give it special handling?

Editor Burl Osborne of the *Dallas Morning News* faced those questions in 1985. He describes in a letter for this book what the *News* did:

> We . . . explained that we had to publish; that not to publish would cause greater damage to the institution since rumors already were about, and that, further, not to publish could be construed as vigilante journalism, with us in effect going around threatening people with exposure if they don't do what we say. . . . That decision was reached quickly. What was more difficult, at least for me, was deciding *how* to publish the story, doing what needed to be done, without unfairly painting an entire organization as tainted. There also were the standard forces working against the concern: Reporters had invested a lot of time. That circumstance generally produces an overlong story and expectations of second-coming play, whether or not it is merited.
>
> Here is what we did:
>
> We ran the story on page one, with a very carefully written headline, not at the top of the page. We made certain that the Army's response was high. We followed up with a story in the same place on the page when corrective action was announced. We wrote an editorial focused on the Salvation Army's value to the city, and trying to insure the problem was viewed in context. And we undoubtedly will find a good Salvation Army Christmas story to tell. This isn't a big-deal event to a newspaper. There is a common view that our responsibility is to get it right. I am not sure responsibility ends there.
>
> This case *was* a big deal to the Salvation Army.

When the good guys—and everybody knows the Salvation Army is among them—slip up, should editors look the other way? Was Editor Osborne justified in what he did?

Do you think Osborne arrived at a Golden Mean with his handling of the story? Did any journalistic principle suffer as a result?

larly important if, as with Farber and Farr, you risk defying a judge or see threat of a libel suit.

A common form of confrontation places you in defense of a story against attack by officialdom. American correspondents, some of whom were young, who reported that the Vietnam War was not going well repeatedly found themselves defying unending optimism from the combined authority of the armed forces, Pentagon, State Department and White House. It took courage for those correspondents to stand by the accuracy of their reporting when such formidable authority was arrayed against them. It also took courage from editors and publishers.

MAINTAINING INDEPENDENT NEWS JUDGMENT

Sticking by your own evaluation of a story's news merits and covering it in accordance with your own judgment often takes courage—and firm backing from your editor.

In early days of the Watergate story, young reporters for the *Washington Post* revealed misdeeds in the Nixon administration while others failed to find such skullduggery. Indeed, some media even reported all was well.

Being exclusive for too long on such a story can put great strain on the courage of an entire news organization, particularly if it is depending, as was the *Post,* on relatively inexperienced reporters. That magnifies the strain on the reporters themselves.

Enormous pressure built on the *Post,* both from the Nixon administration and other media which began to doubt the *Post*'s accuracy. *Post* reporters stuck to their story and, of course, eventually were proved correct.

Inexperienced reporters, often feel great pressure from many sources to move in a certain direction with a story. In covering school affairs, for example, you will feel it from the board of education, parents, teachers—all of whom want the bond issue passed so a new high school can be built. Their news judgment will be that the merits of the issue already have been proved; yours should be that the story still must be covered objectively and dispassionately.

At every level—from White House to local school board—you cannot resist that kind of pressure unless you mesh with editors who agree with your sense of ethics.

WHAT? DEFY YOUR EDITOR?

Yes, there will be times when you'll feel you must resist extraordinary pressure from within the newsroom—from your editor.

Let's hope that doesn't happen too often or, particularly, that you and your editor don't clash over ethical fundamentals that can lead to something rash happening—like you getting fired.

But tension with your editor will occur. Here are two areas where it might happen first—and most often.

LEARNING WHEN TO HOLD 'EM

Picture it: Your editor is calling for the story; your training, your every instinct, is to go with it, get into print, get on the air.

Yet, you have a nagging concern that you don't quite have it pinned down; there are a couple of loose ends, a few facts unsubstantiated, a source or two you haven't had time to check—and you feel strongly that inaccurate journalism is unethical journalism.

Whoa! If you doubt the story's accuracy or honesty, hold it—don't go with it. Many times, you'll be forced to go with an incomplete story, one that could be improved with more time. But never go with one that is inaccurate.

Learning when to hold a story takes self-discipline of the first order. It also requires you to keep a cool head, to explain patiently to your editor why the story isn't ready.

RESISTING THE SCOOP MENTALITY

In competitive situations—two newspapers going head-on for circulation or TV stations fighting for ratings—great pressure builds on reporters and editors to bring in scoops.

Frequently, this drives coverage toward the sensational and trivial, and away from substance. It also can lead to grossly unethical behavior—invasion of privacy, playing loosely with facts, overwriting or hyping a story beyond its news merits, all to score a competitive beat.

Standing firm against such pressure can require enormous self-discipline for a reporter-editor team.

As always in ethics, however, you alone must take personal responsibility for your behavior. So, yes, do try to understand your editor's position; do consider the corporate context the editor operates in; do understand the need for profit and keeping the customers happy. But always remember it is you that you must look at in the mirror every morning.

Summary

It's reality time: You must ensure your personal approach to ethics meshes with your editor's. Otherwise, you will be an unhappy employee—or unemployed.

Editors, backed by top management, increasingly are taking firm charge of newsrooms, setting standards of conduct and deciding ethical issues once left to individual reporters.

Many editors take solely to themselves decisions whether a news source will be granted anonymity. At stake sometimes is the reputation of the editor and entire newspaper or TV operation; but, also, employers can be cited for contempt of court if reporters refuse a court order to identify sources.

If supervisors ask you to identify a source to them, you should ask whether they—and your newspaper or TV employer—will uphold your pledges of confidentiality.

There are examples of editors overruling reporters' pledge of anonymity. The U.S. Supreme Court ruled the First Amendment doesn't protect newspapers from being sued for breaking such a pledge, which is regarded as a contract. In Minnesota, a source who was pledged anonymity but was later "burned" on an editor's order, was awarded $200,000 in damages.

Your employer owns the product of your labor—a story, for example. Less clear is who owns your byline. Some reporters withhold bylines from stories they think have been improperly edited, or as a protest against their newspaper's actions.

Editors have many concerns that influence their relationship with you on ethical issues.

Solvency must be the first goal of a newspaper or TV station, so your editor works on a tight financial budget. That can influence journalistic quality and integrity.

The chilling effect of the law is such that no important decision can be made in a newsroom without considering it. For example, $9 million was the average award in libel cases that went before juries in 1990–1991, and when your editors look at your story they must consider whether it is worth hundreds of thousands of dollars in libel defense fees or millions in judgments.

The corporate imperative influences your editors, too. They are required to perform as newsroom managers, as well as journalists.

Often, you'll need loyal backup from your editors, just as they need it from you. For example, an ethical reporter must push through closed doors to reveal the public's business to the public. You'll need the editor's institutional strength to accomplish that.

Sometimes, you'll be in ethical conflict with your editor. For example, you can be pressured to go with a story before you have ensured its accuracy. When that happens, hold firm. Nothing justifies publishing an inaccurate story.

Notes

1. Michael J. O'Neill, speech to American Society of Newspaper Editors, Chicago, May 5, 1982.
2. Lee Hills, speech to annual meeting of shareholders, Knight-Ridder Newspapers, Inc., One Herald Plaza, Miami, Fla., 33101, April 21, 1981.
3. James D. Squires, "When Confidentiality Itself Is Source of Contention," 1985–86 Journalism Ethics Report, National Ethics Committee, Society of Professional Journalism, Sigma Delta Chi, 53 W. Jackson Blvd., Suite 731, Chicago, Ill., 60604, p. 7.
4. "Arbiter Upholds 3-Day Suspension of Reporter for Signing Agreement with News Source," *presstime,* Nov. 1985, p. 60.
5. Rick Parham, "The Story That Isn't—Yet," *Athens (Ga.) Banner-Herald,* March 5, 1986, p. 4.
6. Lyle Denniston, "The High Cost of Burning a Source," *Washington* (now *American*) *Journalism Review,* May 1992, p. 51.

7. Peter A. Reinhardt, "Manager's Journal," the *Wall Street Journal,* Sept. 9, 1985, p. 24.
8. Article XXII, "Employee Integrity," U.S. Model Contract, The Newspaper Guild (AFL-CIO), 1125 Fifteenth St., N.W., Room 550, Washington, D.C., 20005, July 15, 1984, p. 23.
9. Bill Salisbury, "Burning the Source," *Washington Journalism Review,* September 1991, p. 18.
10. George Garneau, "Reporters at *Journal of Commerce* Staged Byline Strike," *Editor & Publisher,* Nov. 11, 1989, p. 35.
11. "Average Jury Libel Award Rises to $9 Million," *New York Times,* Sept. 20, 1992, p. 14.
12. M. L. Stein, "Newspapers Urged to Please the Reader," *Editor & Publisher,* April 15, 1989, p. 11.
13. Roberto Suro, "Writer Ousted after Saying He's Homosexual," *New York Times,* Aug. 31, 1991, p. 9.
14. Tom Opdyke, "Traffic Report," *The Atlanta Journal/The Atlanta Constitution,* March 1, 1992, p. D-2.

PART 3

ETHICS IN PURSUIT OF PROFIT

Reporters and editors, our subject in Part 2, work within a corporate context that strongly influences ethical imperatives in the newsroom. We must explore that context more fully because corporate concerns about profits and other countinghouse factors can overwhelm even the most conscientious effort to do the right thing in handling the news.

In Part 3, we focus on the corporate entity—the newspaper or broadcast company—and its ethical stance as an institution of major economic, political and social influence.

Chapter 5, "Social Responsibility and Codes of Ethics," examines whether newspapers or TV stations in fact have social responsibilities beyond making a profit. We also look at codes of ethics many have for newsroom employees.

Chapter 6, "Corporate Profits and Newsroom Ethics," focuses on the profit motive driving all free enterprise media and its impact on ethics.

In Chapter 7, "Ethics in the Countinghouse," we turn to advertising—lifeblood of the media—and ethics in other sectors of newspaper and broadcast operations.

In Chapter 8, "The Changing Face of the Media," we look at huge media conglomerates that now control mass communications in America.

Caution: In none of this can we stray far from this book's underlying theme: Ethics is an intensely personal subject, and the individual journalist, even in a corporate cocoon, retains ultimate responsibility for (and, really, the only meaningful influence over) newspaper and television journalism ethics.

Can you operate within the corporate context and still do the right thing? Let's see.

CHAPTER 5

Social Responsibility and Codes of Ethics

In times bygone, corporations gained good-citizen status by selling customers suitable products at acceptable prices, providing employees with decent wages and working conditions, and ensuring fair profits for shareholders.

Today, that won't guarantee good-citizen status for even obscure manufacturers of nuts and bolts, let alone the highly visible and enormously influential print and broadcast media.

In Chapter 5, we examine the widespread societal conviction that corporations have ethical and moral responsibilities far beyond making customers happy and improving profits.

Even Henry Ford II, whose family pursued personal profit with remarkable dedication for several generations, saw it coming: He went to the Harvard Business School, where profit is king, to say, "The terms of the contract between industry and society are changing. . . . Now we are being asked to serve a wider range of human values and to accept an obligation to members of the public with whom we have no commercial transaction."[1]

That means media corporations have social responsibility parallel to an individual journalist's obligations and duties.

Let's look more closely at how the responsibilities of media corporations are tied to the rights and freedoms of our craft—and how you can learn to operate ethically as a journalist within the parameters of corporate activity.

THE ARGUMENT OVER SOCIAL RESPONSIBILITY

Management theorists don't agree whether corporations in fact have social responsibilities beyond caring for their own customers, employees and profits.

VIEWPOINT

Profits and Responsibility

"There is one and only one social responsibility to business—to use its resources and engage in activities designed to increase its profits so long as it stays within the rules of the game . . ."

Milton Friedman, Nobel laureate in economics

Well into the 1930s, a traditional or classicist view was dominant: A firm is socially responsible if it creates jobs, thus strengthening a community's social structure, and through profits, wages and bank deposits broadens its economic base. This view still has support, despite rising opinion that corporations must serve wider societal values beyond their own, more narrow goals.

Milton Friedman, a Nobel Prize winner in economics, is a leading proponent of the traditional view that the societal responsibility of any business is to increase profits.[2] This view holds that a profitable corporation by definition is socially responsible. Society evaluates its product or service in the marketplace, consumers judge its value and purchase it, ergo the corporation performs a socially responsible task.

The classicists view a profitable corporation as socially responsible because its profits are invested, by the corporation itself or shareholders, in other endeavors aimed at increasing profits. This creates new jobs, new products, new demand—and society benefits.

For a manager, this traditional measure of success simplifies scorekeeping: Profits and new products and jobs are all easily measured.

Such easy scorekeeping is denied newspaper and television managers who must measure progress in wider, far less tangible social sectors. How, for example, does a media manager measure progress toward such socially responsible—but intangible—goals as informing the public on important issues or defending the people's right to know?

Critics attack the concept of corporate social responsibility in two broad areas.

BUSINESS PRAGMATISM

"Business is the business of business." Profit, not social reform, is the goal, so media companies should get on with making money.

Critics also maintain social responsibility is costly and penalizes shareholders. Consider, for example, professional managers for Knight-Ridder, Inc., or CBS, who donate company money to a good cause or spend for news coverage they view as socially responsible. Those executives are spending dollars that belong to thou-

VIEWPOINT

Profit versus Public Service

"Can a newspaper simultaneously be both a business serving its own interests and affect to be a quasi-public institution serving everybody's best interests as defined by the newspaper itself?"

Leonard Silk, economic correspondent, the *New York Times*

"[A]vailable evidence does not suggest that the most socially responsible firms are the most profitable."

Jack W. Duncan, *Management,* Random House, Inc., New York, on cost of social responsibility

sands of shareholders who own Knight-Ridder and CBS—and it's unlikely anyone determined their views on whether to cut into profits for social responsibility.

Anyway, critics say, charging business with social responsibility is futile. Managers know they are judged (and rewarded) for business, not societal, success. And, that means most managers give only lip service to social responsibility.

JOURNALISTIC PHILOSOPHY

Some critics argue that if social responsibility is the measurement of success in journalism, freedom of the media will disappear, along with independent news values and judgments.

These critics see societal responsibility leading newspapers and television toward bland, consensus journalism that follows—and doesn't lead—public opinion. Such critics long for the days of libertarian journalism (again see Chapter 1) when newspapers determined themselves what course to follow in news and business, rather than reacting to public mood. Some critics see voluntary abrogation by the media of true freedom with acceptance of social responsibility. The critics fear conformist media merely responding to current public whim or political ideology, rather than being independent and adversarial.

However, life has changed dramatically since such traditionalist views were formulated.

ARE TRADITIONALISTS OUTDATED?

The classicist view that corporations have no social responsibility is outdated by fundamental changes within individual companies and the society in which they operate. Change is particularly striking in three sectors:

First, public attitudes change as corporations grow larger, more visible and, particularly, when they are perceived as having enormous impact on daily life.

VIEWPOINT

Press and Public Opinion

"You no longer shape public opinion, you have supplanted it."

Kurt Luedtke, former executive editor *Detroit Free Press* and later a prize-winning screenwriter, on role of newspapers

This happens with industrial firms—society, for example, no longer asks only whether a chemical company makes a profit; it also asks whether the firm pollutes rivers and skies.

Certainly, public attitudes toward the media change with bigness. A hometown newspaper or TV station that joins a multibillion dollar media conglomerate becomes a major influence on how government is run, life is lived. And, any corporate giant that affects the lives of millions will receive more public scrutiny than did the hometown paper or station.

A second major change eroding the classicist view is change within American corporations. Social consciousness rises as ownership shifts from private to public status, and as managers are drawn from society, not owning families.

Nonfamily managers tend to take a wider view of what a corporation must achieve. It's good business to do so. Professional managers expanded tremendously the social responsibility horizons of formerly family-owned media companies such as Knight-Ridder, Gannett and others.

Workforce attitudes also change. Employees win improved job security and higher living standards, which permit them to switch from preoccupation solely with economic survival to also demonstrating concern over wider social issues.

In the media, both factors are operative: The largest, most influential newspapers are in multibillion-dollar, publicly owned companies run by professional, not family, managers; television networks and the largest stations are publicly owned. And, for both newspaper and television journalists, wages and job security are improving, permitting social consciousness to become a daily concern.[3]

A third significant change: Government attitudes and the law—themselves expressions of society's thinking—require a corporation to take wider, more meaningful view of social responsibility.

As a regulated industry, broadcasting must be alert to letter of the law in such matters. Newspapers and magazines, though free of direct regulatory supervision, nevertheless also must respond to government agencies, such as the Occupational Health and Safety Administration, and to societal pressure that is reflected, for example, in libel judgments against them or moves by special interest groups to influence how the news is covered. Newspapers and television companies must build the financial strength that, in turn, permits journalistic independence.

SOCIAL RESPONSIBILITY: OTHER VIEWS

Those who argue the concept of social responsibility covers the business of journalism say there is strong reason to institutionalize it, formalize it, as a driving motivation in newspaper and broadcast operations.

GOVERNMENT INTERVENTION

First, U.S. business history clearly shows that any industry unresponsive to societal demands risks government intervention. This is an argument that society grants rights to an industry and, in turn, expects certain conduct—and government, representing society, will intervene if the industry doesn't perform as expected.

Thus, the Equal Employment Opportunity Commission, established to help implement the 1964 Civil Rights Act, is society's response to industries that fail to voluntarily prohibit discrimination on basis of race, age, sex, religious beliefs or national origin. Many newspapers and television stations are forced into affirmative hiring under the act because they did not move voluntarily on their own.

The Occupational Safety and Health Act (OSHA) of 1970 reflects society's demands for healthy, safe workplaces; OSHA inspectors fine newspapers that do not clean up their own production departments.

IMPROVE BUSINESS

Second, supporters of social responsibility see in the concept a way of improving business conditions. Business is in the business of meeting societal demands, so if society demands social responsibility in the media, that's what newspapers and television stations should provide—or so goes the argument.

THE "RIGHT THING"

Third, of course, supporters see social responsibility as the right—ethical—course for a newspaper or television station.

So, arguments for social responsibility in the media have strong support. But it clearly does not come first with media corporations.

Whenever publishers or broadcasters meet, due deference is paid the need for socially responsible media behavior, for protecting the public's right to know.

Be it the *New York Times*' slogan, "All the News That's Fit to Print," or CBS's claim that Dan Rather's evening newscast "Keeps America on Top of the World," there runs through the media's self-esteem a theme of public responsibility and service. Unquestionably, many individual journalists feel strongly theirs is a craft with a higher calling. Editors are wont to express their desire to sell newspapers in terms of serving the public.

YET, SOCIAL RESPONSIBILITY ISN'T NO. 1

The concept of social responsibility and, beyond that, ethical behavior, do not get top billing in statements of corporate goals. For example:

Tribune Company, a multibillion-dollar communications conglomerate built around the *Chicago Tribune,* other newspapers and television stations, says in its annual report to shareholders:

> [W]e measure success by our ability to attract audiences by informing and entertaining, to produce results for advertisers, and to attain a return on stockholders' investment competitive with that being achieved by other media companies. Tribune Company is in excellent position to fulfill these objectives in the years ahead.[4]

Knight-Ridder, owner of some of the nation's most outstanding newspapers, is more balanced in stating its company goals:

> The basic operating goals of the company are systematic and orderly profit growth, diversification via acquisition and entrepreneurial startups in the media communications field, and maintenance of the highest standards of professionalism and editorial quality. The company is dedicated to serving the communities where it operates, providing its employees with an opportunity to make their lives more productive and rewarding, and enhancing the investment of the company's shareholders.[5]

Dow Jones, publisher of the *Wall Street Journal,* dailies in 22 communities and internationally renown high-quality financial news services, says

> Dow Jones is a unique blend of the old and the new. Old in the sense that the company is committed to those values on which its success has been built—values that stress high standards of quality, service, ethics and individual achievement. New in that the company, in a constant quest for improvement, embraces the most up-to-date concepts and technology to produce and deliver the *Wall Street Journal* and other publications and services.[6]

In stating their objectives, broadcast corporations must give major billing to conformity with government regulation because they are in a federally regulated industry. For example, an ABC policy handbook for employees states:

> Broadcasting is . . . a regulated industry. We operate in a thicket of legal decisions that may not allow the freest rein on news operations. So, while we want to be flexible and imaginative and allow for individual initiative, before you set out on a bold new path, check with someone in the management. Do not set policy on your own. Sometimes there are problems you didn't think of.[7]

Now, all four companies—Tribune, Knight-Ridder, Dow Jones and ABC—enjoy among journalists strong reputations as socially responsible practitioners of high-quality journalism. But, clearly, service to society is not the number one corporate goal for any of them; service to shareholder is.

This is not to suggest the media should put social responsibility first, becoming public utilities that put service even at a financial loss ahead of service at a profit. Long-term journalistic success can rise only from financial success, journalistic independence only from financial independence. Financially weak newspapers or television stations become easy prey for special interest pressures that distort the news process.

Nevertheless, some response to societal pressure is required by any newspaper or television station.

SETTING RESPONSE LEVELS

In self-interest, any corporation must audit influences on its business. This involves identifying external and internal pressure, measuring its intensity and judging the response necessary to deal with it.

Important external pressure comes from national, state and local governments and their official agencies and regulatory bodies; special interest groups, and the general public. Company attorneys and regulatory specialists judge government pressure; public opinion surveys are one way of judging public attitudes.

Internally, adjustment must be made to pressure from employees (and unions), customers, suppliers, competitors and, of course, the profit expectations of owners, whether private or public.

The social audit must evaluate company operations that might draw fire and determine how the company can preempt hostile moves by government or other forces. In most companies, a board of directors establishes policy guidelines for the chief executive officer, who is responsible for efficient, profitable operation of the company.

For many media companies, then, social responsibility attitudes don't just happen; more often, they are established carefully after detailed analysis of what the corporate stance should be.

Response levels vary widely.

THE MINIMUM RESPONSE

This is a defensive move to build corporate image, not truly meet any social responsibility. It really is designed to improve business conditions, to sell newspapers and advertising or, in television, sell air time and meet requirements from regulatory bodies. Handing out company t-shirts or sponsoring the local soap box derby are minimum response ploys.

THE GOOD CITIZEN MOVE

Here, the newspaper or television company escalates its response. Company executives and employees, for example, are given time off to participate in community affairs. This response level is characterized by company commitment of significant resources—time, money, employee effort.

FULL SOCIAL RESPONSIBILITY

This requires high-level commitment to aggressively meet social challenges with the same dedication that business problems are met. This can involve substantive change in corporate structure and direction—special minority training programs, for example, or socially oriented trusts or scholarship funds. Of course, self-interest is at work here, too: tax advantages or recruiting benefits flow from social responsibility.

Sometimes, difficult dollars-and-cents questions flow from social responsibility. For example, should a newspaper spend heavily to achieve circulation in low-income neighborhoods, whose residents are of only marginal interest to advertisers? The business of newspapers, after all, is selling news to attract readers who are sold, in turn, to advertisers—and the more affluent the readers, the happier the advertisers.

Does the newspaper have a social responsibility to penetrate those poorer neighborhoods with its uplifting, educational news, even at financial loss? Try finding the elitist *New York Times* for sale on slum street corners in its own city.

Should a television news show maintain its own correspondents in foreign capitals at the cost of hundreds of thousands of dollars each annually? Will covering those cities firsthand attract more viewers? More advertisers? Note the number of news shows that use talking head anchors who read AP dispatches from those capitals.

Social responsibility is expensive. Luckily, many newspapers and television news operations still accept—at considerable cost—such social responsibilities.

Externally, it's good for business. A newspaper or television station out of sorts with readers, viewers or advertisers is headed for financial difficulty. Socially irresponsible conduct in the marketplace adds enormously to the credibility gap we discussed in Chapter 1, and that's bad for business. Irresponsible conduct also can attract direct government intervention in corporate affairs, which newspapers—despite their First Amendment protection—cannot risk lightly these days, any more than can television companies.

Internally, enlightened policies can benefit a media employer over the long run. Providing employees with better work environments, creative jobs and involving them in how things are run can produce more efficient work performance.

Finally, adopting a socially responsible corporate policy is the right thing, the ethical thing, to do.

Although the concept of social responsibility has been around a long time, the idea that corporations can—or should—operate under codes of ethics has won acceptance only relatively recently. Let's look at current thought in the newspaper and television news industry.

CORPORATE ETHICS

It was traditional: Sometime after first walking into the newsroom a new reporter would be introduced to "the way we do things around here." There might be a company handbook on vacation policy and health insurance, or a short session with someone from the personnel department.

But the company ethos—its collective characteristics and beliefs—seldom was formalized. It passed haphazardly in bits and pieces to new reporters by word of mouth, learn-as-you-go. That was industrywide custom.

VIEWPOINT

"They Don't Work"

"Everyone, so it seems, has been adopting codes over the past decade or so, ranging from the simplicity of the Ten Commandments to the complexity of a corporate prospectus. All have one thing in common: They don't work.

"A bad person does not become a good person because his newspaper has an ethics code . . .

"(I)f readers don't like what we're doing they'll quit buying our papers. The marketplace is the best regulator the press can have."

Michael Gartner, ex-president of the *Des Moines Register,* former editor of Gannett's *Louisville Courier-Journal* and former president of NBC News

Today, media executives increasingly are formalizing corporate policy and writing precise directives on specific ethical principles that require adherence, especially by reporters, editors and news directors, as a condition of employment.

This trend arises in part from external, societal pressure, but also from growing awareness within journalistic circles that a haphazard approach no longer is sufficient. In 1974, the Associated Press Managing Editors Association surveyed members and found only 9 percent of respondents had written ethical codes; in 1992, a survey for the Society of Professional Journalists found 44 percent of editors and 49 percent of news directors at 304 newspapers and television stations had written codes of ethics.[8]

The trend is not without controversy.

THE CONTROVERSY OVER CODES

There is general agreement on corporate codes in two areas:

First, a newspaper or broadcast operation must not only ensure its conduct is legal, but also that it conforms to accepted ethical principles of right and wrong.

Second, it is top management's responsibility to shape and enunciate those principles and ensure they are followed in all corporate activity.

That is, ethical considerations are regarded essential to both journalistic and business endeavors and to employee training. But there general agreement ends, and controversy begins over which principles to adopt, how to enunciate them and, indeed, whether formalizing corporate ethical attitudes—in say, a written code—is dangerous self-censorship.

Proponents of written codes argue ethics is too important to leave to individual whims and interpretation, and that only writing them down will ensure every employee understands and conforms to them.

VIEWPOINT

Codes, Who Has Codes?

A Society of Professional Journalists survey of 304 newspaper editors and TV news directors showed:

- 44% of newspapers had written codes
- 49% of TV stations did also
- 60% of newspapers with codes wrote them in-house
- 45% of TV stations produced their own
- 22% of newspapers used codes from parent companies
- 27% of TV stations used parent's or network's
- 40% of newspapers had amended their codes between 1990 and 1992 when the survey was made
- 12% were revising codes when the survey was made
- 33% of TV stations had just revised their codes since 1990
- 25% had revisions under way during the survey

Opponents, who include some of the nation's leading editors, argue there is danger that any definitive and widely accepted code, particularly if endorsed by major newspapers or television operations, could become—in the eye of judges, legislatures or the public—a general standard of behavior to be enforced on all media. These opponents view written codes as a self-inhibiting first step toward licensing the media under a universal standard of conduct.

Opponents say written codes could be used against the media in court. In a libel case, for example, wouldn't a lawyer be well on the way to victory if it were proved a reporter deviated from written company policy while covering a story? If a code called for, say, double-checking every fact produced by an anonymous source, and a reporter under deadline didn't, wouldn't that be damaging evidence the newspaper broke its own rules?

This seems more a fear than reality. Various studies show that media codes of ethics rarely come up during litigation.

More often, opponents argue that codes simply are insipid window dressing, nothing more than grudging concessions to public anger at the media—and are so regarded by management, staff and public.

And further, opponents argue that if a code purports to represent the totality of a newsroom's ethical stance, it necessarily will be general to the point of being

VIEWPOINT

Journalistic Wimps?

"Journalists should actively censure and try to prevent violations of these standards, and they should encourage their observance by all newspeople . . ."

Code of Ethics, Society of Professional Journalists

"The Society of Professional Journalists has turned wimpish toward its own code of ethical standards . . ."

Casey Bukro of the *Chicago Tribune* and the society's former ethics chairman, commenting on the society's reluctance to strictly enforce its own code of ethics

vague and, therefore, of little use in the daily struggle over countless fine points of journalistic ethics. (Note sweeping generalities in the codes, addenda at the end of this book, for the Associated Press Managing Editors Association, the Radio-Television News Directors Association and other organizations.)

Also, the argument continues, newsroom values shift, ethical thought evolves, and calling the shots under deadline pressure requires judgment in an editor or news director, not a code hanging on the wall. (Ethical absolutists would counter, of course, that absolute moral laws exist, regardless of time or place, and that they can be defined and followed. Recall our discussion of Kant in Chapter 1.)

The tendency of editors to rely on their judgment—their professional instinct—and not a written code was underlined in an Associated Press Managing Editors survey in 1993: Of 573 managing editors responding, only 17.8 percent said they have a copy of the APME Ethics Code and know where it is. Just 7.2 percent said they read the code for guidance when a question of ethics arises in their newsrooms.

Opponents of written codes argue that codes generally lack any enforcement provisions and, thus, have no punch. That indeed is true for industrywide codes. Unlike those drawn up by physicians, attorneys and other professional groups, codes adopted by journalism associations lack provisions for expulsion or other discipline (leading some social commentators to deny journalism the label *profession)*.

But ethical policies of many individual newspapers and television stations are being enforced. An American Society of Newspaper Editors survey revealed that of 226 newspapers responding, 48 dismissed employees for ethical violations and 30 suspended employees for varying periods.[9]

Most importantly, code opponents say, it is management example, not a written document, that changes corporate attitudes toward ethics. Only open, unmistakable corporate commitment to ethical conduct will bring along a newspaper or broadcast staff.

TOP-LEVEL ENDORSEMENT VITAL

The tone of any company's response to its challenges—journalistic, business or ethical—is set at the top and transmitted to each employee through a managerial chain of command leading from board chairperson down to the lowest first-level supervisor.

Over the long run, no newspaper or broadcast station will outperform expectations of top management in news or business. And, no newsroom will develop ethics policies and adhere to them unless management insists.

Corporate statements of ethics policy vary widely.

Knight-Ridder, explicit in public acceptance of social responsibilities and enormously successful journalistically, is unmistakably clear in stating of its ethics policy. Knight-Ridder's flagship, the *Miami Herald,* gives each employee an ethics code ("The *Herald* and You") that opens:

> We strive to attain the highest standards of journalism and to publish a newspaper that is fair, accurate and objective. We try to avoid all conflicts of interest. That, simply, is our goal. It is not a goal easily achieved. It requires from each of us decisions of conscience on matters both professional and personal. Often there are no clear answers or precise precedents.
>
> We ask that you use your own best judgment. We ask that you act in good faith and that you recognize the best interest of *The Herald.* Whenever in doubt, inquire. Talk to your department head.[10]

Eugene Patterson, as chairman and chief executive officer of the *St. Petersburg Times,* an editor widely known for producing high-quality newspapers, took a different approach:

> We have no written code of ethics because I can't imagine any manageable code that would be comprehensive enough to cover the ethical judgments that have to be made at a newspaper in the course of a given half-day.
>
> Specific areas of ethical decision are too unpredictable to be covered by any imaginable list of right answers. To try to compose one, therefore, would in my judgment produce much gas but little lift.
>
> Instead we talk about fairness and balance, accuracy and sensitivity, honesty and candor. And we try to teach by example; the reporter who sees the kind of story his editor puts into print, and the kind of story he kicks back as unacceptable, learns our code of ethics over time.[11]

However the *Times is* managed under a forceful "Standards of Operation" drawn by Nelson Poynter, chairman of the paper from 1969 until he died in 1978. The standards state:

> Our Mission: To set and maintain the highest standards of excellence in the field of journalism, through independence, enterprise and commitment to the public interest.

> Our Strategy: While maintaining a national perspective and reputation, to operate our newspapers in accordance with a philosophy of community involvement and public service. To preserve their independence from conglomerate ownership so as to maintain a direct responsiveness to the needs of the community of which we are a part . . . to sustain freedom from any pressure that could alter our commitment to service to the nation's citizens through impartial political research and unbiased coverage of the government . . .

The statement demands integrity in news coverage and sensitive discharge of community obligations, and concludes: "Our publications' policy is very simple—merely to tell the truth."[12]

The *Chicago Tribune*'s policy makes no sweeping statement of ethical philosophy, opening instead with this proposition: "All professional staff members of the *Tribune* are expected to avoid any compromises of their journalistic integrity. This must include even the appearance of compromise, which can be equally damaging to the credibility of the newspaper." The policy deals with specific ethical problems such as free gifts, outside employment and involvement in public affairs.[13]

The *Los Angeles Times* is similarly broad in its code of ethics: "[T]o try to avoid embarrassment or conflicts with your responsibilities to *The Times,* and to answer questions which arise from time to time, here are some general guidelines to confirm and clarify our existing practices . . ."[14]

A completely different approach from Bob Haring, executive editor of the *Tulsa World*: "I don't have a written code of ethics here. Frankly, it's not been a problem. . . . In general, I tell people to do what they think is right, what they feel comfortable with. *In most cases, they're more restrictive than I would be*" [emphasis added].[15]

COMPONENTS OF A POLICY

Regardless of how it is structured, whether written or not, an ethics policy must address key issues if management's corporate philosophy is to be translated effectively into day-to-day operations.

WHO IS COVERED?

The *Los Angeles Times* directs its ethics policy at "editorial staff"; the *Chicago Tribune* addresses "all professional staff members"; the *Miami Herald* has a code for "newsroom staff members," and the parent corporation, Knight-Ridder, has another for "key executives." The 26,000-circulation *Longview (Wash.) Daily News* has written policy guidelines for each department in the newspaper.

WHAT IS COVERED?

For newspapers, the essentials are news and advertising policy. Most newspaper managers lay down explicit rules for both. In television, goaded by federal regulation, policy direction is much broader. The networks, for example, issue highly detailed rulebooks covering personnel (and such matters as objectivity, gifts, etc.), production (interview technique, confidential sources, investigative reporting), the law and regulatory practices (libel, copyright).

WHY ETHICS?

Each policy needs explicit explanation of why it is necessary. Policies generally bow toward social responsibility, meeting community obligations, serving reader and advertiser. But, above all, in both newspapers and broadcast, they make clear that corporate integrity is at stake and that the commercial position of the newspaper or station must be protected in the marketplace. Though laced with undeniably sincere desire to do what is ethically correct, most corporate ethics policies clearly are defensive gestures designed to counter external pressures.

WHO IS ACCOUNTABLE?

With striking unanimity, newspaper and broadcast ethics policies place squarely on the individual employee full responsibility for conforming to corporate policy—even if policy is not explicitly laid out in writing. Look again at the *Chicago Tribune's* language: "All professional staff members of the *Tribune* are expected to avoid any compromises of their journalistic integrity." The *Tribune*'s policy, understandably, doesn't try to discuss the hundreds, if not thousands, of challenges to integrity every newsperson meets during a career; rather, the *Tribune*'s policy states general philosophy in just a page and a half.

Repeatedly, ethics policies instruct employees to "talk it over with a supervisor" in questionable circumstances. ABC News cautions employees, "The burden of acting sensibly in most situations rests on each of us."[16] What is questionable, what is sensible, is left to individual interpretation. Clearly, each employee in communications today must possess a highly developed personal sense of ethics; corporate policy cannot cover all bases.

HOW IS POLICY ENFORCED?

Here, ethics policies are noticeably silent. For legal reasons, employers find it unwise to spell out precisely how an employee will be disciplined for an ethical breach. Newspapers and broadcast stations do fire or suspend employees for policy transgressions, but prefer to handle each case separately and, mostly, quietly. Sometimes, explicit policy is unnecessary. I recall an era in the Associated Press when a foreign correspondent could disappear on a binge for a few days and be welcomed back when it was all over, the steam all let off. But by word of mouth, tradition, osmosis—however you want to describe the process—every employee understood instant dismissal was the penalty for compromising the integrity, honesty, objectivity of the news report.

Nothing stays simple, however, and today many ethical questions arise in truly gray areas where tradition (or osmosis) are inadequate in alerting employees to what is right or wrong, acceptable or unacceptable.[17]

IMPLEMENTING ETHICS POLICY

Some editors involve employees in creating and implementing policy as a means of elevating the dialogue over ethics from unfocused conversation to a focused effort with meaningful impact on how things are run.

John Murphy, executive director of the *Portland (Maine) Press Herald, Evening Express and Sunday Express,* recommends editors approach newsroom ethics from several angles:

1. Develop a newsroom policy manual.
2. Discuss ethical problems as they arise with individual employees, then at staff meetings and finally codify them in a book of ethical standards.
3. Ensure ethics are discussed in orientation programs for new employees.
4. Establish an ethics committee that included all newsroom departments, the city desk, reporters, the editor and the publisher.[18]

The Newspaper Guild, a union of editorial and other employees, opposes codes written solely by management on grounds that makes them enforceable work rules designed to protect company interests. The Guild argues codes threaten employee job security and should not be imposed unilaterally by management but, rather, should be negotiated with employees and jointly written—as ethical guidelines or ideals, not enforceable codes.

Some management theorists recommend widest possible staff participation in drafting codes.[19] The theory is that a staff that helps create a code is more likely to follow it. For many publishers and editors that smacks of abrogating managerial responsibility. Editors meeting in a Southern Newspaper Publishers Association seminar on standards and the credibility gap put it this way:

> Solving the credibility problem, everyone reluctantly agreed, is a managerial problem. The people at the top set the tone; to act on this problem we must rediscover ourselves as managers. Perhaps we are too reluctant to be autocratic when necessary as we run our participatory management newsrooms.[20]

CBS makes it clear who originated its TV standards and who is to follow them: "Meetings of senior management to consider the policy and operating questions these new circumstances raised were held, and standards and guidelines to cover them were decided upon and circulated to the appropriate personnel."[21]

THE LIMITATIONS OF CODES

Newsroom codes today aren't much more profound than the few that existed a generation ago. Many are limited to pragmatic, situational ethics—what to do if this narrow situation arises, what not to do if that one does.

Almost without exception, the central thrust of codes is guidelines for individual conduct. But the goal is protection of corporate image and marketplace position.

VIEWPOINT

Freebies Are Out

"No one who works here will accept work for pay from an auto maker, its advertising agency, or any other of its agents . . .

"We would prefer that you not grace us with any gift that goes beyond the souvenir/memento level. This translates to no jackets, no luggage, no press kits inside luggage, no CD players, no binoculars, no cassette recorders, none of the many things a generous auto industry has sent our way in the years past."

William Jeanes, editor, *Car and Driver,* the nation's largest auto magazine, in letter to car companies

"[I]t is not intended that the guidelines inhibit employees to the point of foolishness such as, for example, refusal of a cup of coffee or anything equally insignificant. But the basic concept the guidelines seek to implement is clear: Employees may accept no favor, overt or otherwise, which can compromise their roles as newspersons or give the appearance of doing so."

CBS News Personnel Standards

Rarely do editors or news directors sketch for their staffs the wider philosophical question of profit versus journalistic excellence or establish an ethical tone that reflects top management's commitment to excellence. Most written codes are much more limited.

Here are examples of how some codes handle particularly sensitive subjects.

GIFTS

Codes leave the impression that newsrooms are under siege by regiments of special interest pleaders trying to subvert reporters with gifts of everything from free calendars to cases of imported wines—and, further, that reporters are easy prey.

The *Los Angeles Times*: "Shun gifts from news sources or subjects of coverage, except those gifts of insignificant value. Books or records received for review should not be sold by staffers."[22]

Chicago Tribune: "Gifts of significant value should be returned with a courteous explanation that acceptance constitutes a violation of this policy. Gifts of insignificant value such as pencils, key chains and unavoidable surprises such as birthday cakes or anniversary flowers are acceptable. However, even these should be avoided and discouraged whenever possible."[23]

JUNKETS, FREE MEALS AND TICKETS

Existing codes show editors regard this area of freebies as troublesome, particularly for news organizations that assign writers to frequent travel in covering politics, say, or sports.

VIEWPOINT

A Guideline, Not a Rule

"A policy is a guideline, not a rule. A guideline is not an undeviating course that must be followed invariably. This is not to say that deviation from all policies is permissible, but rather to allow the flexibility that is necessary oftentimes to deal sensibly with unusual or unexpected situations."

Longview (Wash.) Daily News, "General Policies"

The Miami Herald provides its staff with detailed guidance:

> As a general rule, we pay our own way. We also act with common sense and good manners. . . . Common sense should prevail in situations where it may be socially awkward or even impossible to pay at the time. In most instances, department heads should make payment arrangements before an event. . . . Free tickets to movies, plays, sports events and other entertainment attractions for which admission is normally charged shall not be solicited or accepted. There are some exceptions: private screenings or special press showing for which tickets are not sold to the public; registration fees at seminars or conventions attended with specific story coverage in mind; passes to special press box facilities, photo galleries and other areas available exclusively to the press, provided these are used only by those assigned to cover the event. Generally, the *Herald* will pay all transportation expenses incurred on assignment. In certain circumstances, such as use of military transit, a staffer may accept free transportation if it is the only way to effectively complete the assignment. The executive director should be advised as quickly as possible.[24]

OUTSIDE CONDUCT

The *Miami Herald* puts it bluntly: "Staff members should avoid outside activities that conflict—or appear to conflict—with their jobs." The *Herald* warns employees against endorsing political candidates or contributing to their campaigns and, indeed, instructs staffers not to run for office themselves.

The *Los Angeles Times* goes into considerably more detail, noting *Times* staffers "are being offered increased opportunities these days to use their expertise for outside publications or the electronic media. . . . These offers can bring career enhancement and personal satisfaction, and we do not seek to discourage either." The *Times,* however, forbids writing for competing publications or for groups *Times* reporters cover. It also bans paid sports scoring by reporters (once a favorite means for sports writers to profitably spend time in the pressbox), and "with rare exceptions," paid record or book jacket reviews not published in the *Times.* As for appearing on broadcasts or in other outside events:

> All such appearances for pay should be carefully examined from the aspect of possible conflicts and embarrassment to yourself or the newspaper. In general, regu-

larly scheduled appearances or those under any other circumstances which might confuse the staffer's primary identification as a *Times* person should be avoided.

Note this is a *Times* statement that it has vested interest in the professional identity (not just the byline) that it helps each staffer build.

OTHER INCOME

Explosive expansion of business news coverage raises the question of whether reporters should be restricted in their outside investments. Most newsroom codes cover moonlighting (clear it with your supervisor, do it on your own time, and it's okay), but few wrestle with this central issue: News moves market prices for everything bought or sold in this world, and the temptations for misusing that news are extraordinary.

An unethical reporter who invests on inside information—news learned on the job but not yet available to the public—can make a fortune (if not arrested under federal laws prohibiting such conduct).

The *Los Angeles Times* code comments: "Staff members with investments or stockholdings in corporations should avoid making news decisions that involve these corporations. If it is impossible to avoid them, these potential conflicts should be disclosed to a supervisor." (The *Times* also forbids staffers from entering any "business relationship with their news sources.")

The *Chicago Tribune*'s ethics policy doesn't deal directly with stock market investments. The language: "Outside employment *or compensation* [emphasis added] is permitted when it is compatible with the newspaper's right to the full time and efficient service of its employees and does not constitute a conflict of interest." The code adds: "Each year all *Tribune* staffers will be asked to fill out and sign a disclosure statement detailing all civic and political involvement *and identifying the sources of outside income*" [emphasis added].

As is to be expected, the *Wall Street Journal* pays great attention to staffers' outside investments. It is newspaper lore: If readers could obtain—today—a copy of tomorrow's *Journal,* they could be millionaires. On occasion, that occurs to staffers, including R. Foster Winans, the *Journal* columnist imprisoned for illegally attempting to enrich himself and investor friends who traded on inside information obtained working at the *Journal* (see, again, the Chapter 2 case study). Reproduced at the end of this book are sections of the policy laid down by the *Journal*'s parent company, Dow Jones. The code will not guarantee all staffers live honest, ethical, responsible personal and professional lives. No code will. But its precision language is a model for editors anxious to explain clearly how conflict of interest must be avoided. Note: All Dow Jones staffers are asked to sign statements that they understand the policy and agree to abide by it. Not abiding by it is cause for dismissal.[25]

PLAGIARISM

The American Society of Newspaper Editors surveyed 225 newspapers and found plagiarism is a major problem. One of every six editors said they discovered instances of plagiarism by staffers in the previous three years.

VIEWPOINT

If You're Wrong, Correct It

"Our reputation for accuracy in reporting rests on diligent efforts to get it right, and if we are wrong, to broadcast a correction. Significant errors of fact must be corrected in a clear and timely manner.

"There is another cause for corrective action. Sometimes the error is not of fact but of balance, when we leave out something important or give too much prominence to the wrong thing. That, too, calls for a report to redress the balance."

CBS policy handbook

Appropriating as one's own work the language, ideas and thoughts of another author and out-and-out fabrication of a story were among the serious ethical problems that led ASNE to report, "The extent of unethical behavior is disturbing."[26]

If any rule is part of the journalistic fabric, it is that a reporter should not steal or rewrite another reporter's story. Many codes don't spell that out. Perhaps they must in the future, particularly because news work can create conditions where reporters unthinkingly commit plagiarism. The unwary, for example, can dip into a news morgue for background on an event and incorporate into their story another reporter's work. On fast-breaking stories particularly, reporters tend to build on developments revealed by other reporters. The solution is tight attribution—giving credit—to what other reporters have done.

SO, ARE LIMITED CODES ENOUGH?

The question remains: Are limited codes in effect in newsrooms across the country enough? Aren't they, as written, so painfully obvious, so basic—don't take bribes, don't cheat—as to be useless?

And, even with best intentions, can the *Chicago Tribune* more than touch major issues in an ethics policy of one and a half pages? Can the *Los Angeles Times* in its two and a third pages?

Editors obviously must set personal examples and use other devices—staff seminars, one-on-one meetings, speeches, periodic memos—to create an environment of ethical, socially responsible journalism. They need to construct—and implement—a checklist for excellence.

Michael J. Davies, former publisher of the *Hartford (Conn.) Courant* and *Baltimore Sun,* told an editor's seminar on ethics they should create a newsroom environment that ensures the following:

- compassionate understanding of readers
- fair and accurate reporting and writing
- fast, full correction of errors

CASE STUDY

Bradlee and the *Post*

As executive editor of the *Washington Post,* Benjamin C. Bradlee was one of the nation's most influential journalists. Below is Bradlee's definition of the *Post*'s responsibilities and the staff's obligations under them.

As you read, identify basic themes in Bradlee's writing. Refer to the Potter Box adaptation in Chapter 1.

Do you see references to societal values—stewardship and so forth?

Which journalistic principles can you spot? Serve the public? Be compassionate? Monitor the powerful?

How about loyalties? Does Bradlee incorporate loyalty to self and conscience? To society? To the hand that feeds you (the *Post*)?

Note particularly five factors:

- Pledging acceptance of the *Post*'s ethics code (second paragraph) is a condition of employment.
- Staffers must avoid even appearance of conflict of interest and discuss with supervisors any conduct by family members that might "compromise our integrity."
- There will be no masquerading, no making of news; identify yourself as a *Post* reporter, Bradlee says, and cover the news.
- Granting anonymity to sources is an editor's prerogative, and when a secrecy pledge is made, the *Post* will defend it.
- Balanced, complete reporting—fairness—is central to the *Post*'s policy.

Standards and Ethics of the *Washington Post*

The *Washington Post* is pledged to an aggressive, responsible and fair pursuit of the truth without fear of any special interest, and with favor to none.

Washington Post reporters and editors are pledged to approach every assignment with the fairness of open minds and without prior judgment. The search for opposing views must be routine. Comment from persons accused or challenged in stories must be included. The motives of those who press their views upon us must routinely be examined, and it must be recognized that those motives can be noble or ignore, obvious or ulterior.

We fully recognize that the power we have inherited as the dominant morning newspaper in the capital of the free world carries with it special responsibilities:

- to listen to the voiceless.
- to avoid any and all acts of arrogance.
- to face the public politely and candidly.

Conflict of Interest

This newspaper is pledged to avoid conflict of interest or the appearance of conflict of interest, wherever and whenever possible. We have adopted stringent policies on these issues, conscious that they may be more restrictive than is customary in the world of private business. In particular:

- We pay our own way.
- We accept no gifts from news sources. We accept no free trips. We neither seek nor accept preferential treatment that might be rendered because of the position we hold. Exceptions to the no-gift rule are few and obvious—invitations to meals, for example, may be accepted when they are occasional and innocent, but not when they're repeated and their purpose is deliberately calculating. Free admission to any event that is not free to the public is prohibited. The only exception is for seats not sold to the public, as in a press box. Whenever possible, arrangements will be made to pay for such seats.
- We work for no one except the *Washington Post* without permission from supervisors. Many outside activities and jobs are incompatible with the proper performance of work on an independent newspaper. Connections with government are among the most objectionable. To avoid real or apparent conflicts of interest in the coverage of business and financial markets, all members of the Business and Financial staff are required to disclose their financial holdings and investments to the assistant managing editor in charge of the section. The potential for conflict, however, is not limited to members of the Business and Financial staff. All reporters and editors, wherever they may work, are required to disclose to their department head any financial interests that might be in conflict or give the appearance of a conflict in their reporting and editing duties. Department heads will make their own financial disclosures to the managing editor. We free-lance for no one and accept no speaking engagements without permission from department heads. Permission to free-lance will be granted only if the *Post* has no interest in the story and only if it is to appear in a medium that does not compete with the *Post.* It is important that no free-lance assignments and no honoraria be accepted that might in any way be interpreted as disguised gratuities.
- We make every reasonable effort to be free of obligation to news sources and to special interests. We must be wary of entanglements with those whose positions render them likely to be subjects of journalistic interest and examination. Our private behavior as well as our professional behavior must not bring discredit to our profession or to the *Post.*
- We avoid active involvement in any partisan causes—politics, community affairs, social action, demonstration—that could compromise or seem to compromise our ability to report and edit fairly. Relatives cannot fairly be made subject to *Post* rules, but it should be recognized that their employment or their involvement in causes can at least appear to compromise our integrity. The business and professional ties of traditional family members or other members of your household must be disclosed to department heads.

✣ CASE STUDY, *continued*

The Reporter's Role

Although it has become increasingly difficult for this newspaper and for the press generally to do since Watergate, reporters should make every effort to remain in the audience, to be the stagehand rather than the star, to report the news, not to make the news.

In gathering news, reporters will not misrepresent their identity. They will not identify themselves as police officers, physicians or anything other than journalists.

Errors

This newspaper is pledged to minimize the number of errors we make and to correct those that occur. Accuracy is our goal; candor is our defense. Persons who call errors to our attention must be accorded a respectful hearing.

Attribution of Sources

The *Washington Post* is pledged to disclosure the source of all information when at all possible. When we agree to protect a source's identity, that identity will not be made known to anyone outside the *Post.*

Before any information is accepted without full attribution, reporters must make every reasonable effort to get it on the record. If that is not possible, reporters should consider seeking information elsewhere. If that in turn is not possible, reporters should request an on-the-record reason for concealing the source's identity and should include the reason in the story.

In any case, some kind of identification is almost always possible—by department or by position, for example—and should be reported.

No pseudonyms are to be used.

However, the *Washington Post* will not knowingly disclose the identities of U.S. intelligence agents, except under highly unusual circumstances, which must be weighed by the senior editors.

- two-way dialogue with the public and accountability for what is reported (he recommended an ombudsperson, or reader representative, be appointed on the staff)
- good and bad news are presented with balance
- the context of events and wider meanings are explained
- the newspaper covers itself and other media just as it covers any other major story
- the newspaper cares about its community
- activists whose personal view color their copy are weeded out[27]

Plagiarism and Credit

Attribution of material from other newspapers and other media must be total. Plagiarism is one of journalism's unforgivable sins. It is the policy of this newspaper to give credit to other publications that develop exclusive stories worthy of coverage by the *Post.*

Fairness

Reporters and editors of the *Post* are committed to fairness. While arguments about objectivity are endless, the concept of fairness is something that editors and reporters can easily understand and pursue. Fairness results from a few simple practices:

- No story is fair if it omits facts of major importance or significance. Fairness includes completeness.
- No story is fair if it includes essentially irrelevant information at the expense of significant facts. Fairness includes relevance.
- No story is fair if it consciously or unconsciously misleads or even deceives the reader. Fairness includes honesty—leveling with the reader.
- No story is fair if reporters hide their biases or emotions behind such subtly pejorative words as "refused," "despite," "quietly," "admit" and "massive." Fairness requires straightforwardness ahead of flashiness.

Opinion

- On this newspaper, the separation of news columns from editorials and opposite-editorial pages is solemn and complete. This separation is intended to serve the reader, who is entitled to the facts in the news column and to opinions on the editorial and "op-ed" pages. But nothing in this separation of functions is intended to eliminate from the news column honest, in-depth reporting, or analysis or commentary when plainly labeled.

Summary

Management theorists don't agree American corporations have social responsibilities beyond profitably serving customers and employees.

Traditionalists say business is the business of business, and that social responsibility is too expensive, a disservice to shareholders and, anyway, not the function of any corporation. Traditionalists fear social responsibility leads to bland, consensus journalism and the media's voluntary abrogation of independence.

However, society now demands more of huge corporations, which strongly influence everyday life. Professional managers of publicly owned corporations

CASE STUDY, *continued*

The National and Community Interest

The *Washington Post* is vitally concerned with the national interest and with the community interest. We believe these interests are best served by the widest possible dissemination of information. The claim of national interest by a federal official does not automatically equate with the national interest. The claim of community interest by a local official does not automatically equate with the community interest.

Taste

The *Washington Post* as a newspaper respects taste and decency, understanding that society's concepts of taste and decency are constantly changing. A word offensive to the last generation can be part of the next generation's common vocabulary. But we shall avoid prurience. We shall avoid profanities and obscenities unless their use is so essential to a story of significance that its meaning is lost without them. In no case shall obscenities be used without the approval of the executive editor or the managing editor or his deputy.

frequently regard social responsibility as important; so do employees when job security and higher living standards permit. Government enters the equation, reflecting societal pressure for certain standards of performance.

Supporters of social responsibility argue corporations face government intervention unless they perform as expected and, anyway, business is in the business of meeting societal demands. Also, social responsibility is considered the right course for newspapers and broadcast stations to follow. But that concept still comes second to service to shareholders.

The concept of social responsibility is old; widespread acceptance of the idea corporations must follow precise ethical policies isn't.

Opponents of written codes argue they could lead to general standards of behavior—licensing, perhaps—for all media. Also, some consider written codes dangerous because they could be used against the media in court if, say, reporters were proved to have broken their own company's policies. Opponents argue codes necessarily are vague window dressing and that what is needed is an editor or news director with judgment, not a code hanging on a wall.

Whether or not they're written, ethical policies need endorsement by top level management and should state explicitly who is covered, which activities are acceptable, and how they will be enforced. Although industrywide codes have no enforcement provisions, individual newspapers and broadcast stations increasingly fire or otherwise discipline employees who compromise the integrity of the corporation.

The *Post*'s Principles

After Eugene Meyer bought the *Washington Post* in 1933 and began the family ownership that continues today, he published "These Principles":

> The First mission of a newspaper is to tell the truth as nearly as the truth may be ascertained.
>
> The newspaper shall tell the truth so far as it can learn it, concerning the important affairs of America and the world.
>
> As a disseminator of the news, the paper shall observe the decencies that are obligatory upon a private gentleman.
>
> What it prints shall be fit reading for the young as well as the old.
>
> The newspaper's duty is to its readers and to the public at large, and not to the private interest of the owner.
>
> In the pursuit of the truth, the newspaper shall be prepared to make sacrifices of its material fortunes, if such course be necessary for the public good. The newspaper shall not be the ally of any special interests, but shall be fair and free and wholesome in its outlook on public affairs and public men.

"These principles" are re-endorsed herewith.[28]

Benjamin C. Bradlee

Notes

1. Thomas Donaldson, *Corporation and Morality* (Englewood Cliffs, N. J., 1982, p. 6).
2. See Milton Friedman, "The Social Responsibility of Business Is to Increase Its Profits," *New York Times Magazine,* Sept. 13, 1970, p. 32.
3. Among commentators on the social responsibility of business, I found particularly helpful: Michael A. Hitt, R. Dennis Middlemist, Robert C. Mathis, *Effective Management* (St. Paul: West, 1979); W. Jack Duncan, *Management* (New York: Random House, 1983); George A. Steiner and John B. Miner, *Management Policy and Strategy* (New York: Macmillan, 1977); Davis L. Kurtz and Louis E. Boone, *Marketing* (New York: Dryden Press, 1981). Also see Milton Friedman, *Issues in Business and Society,* G.A. Steiner, ed. (New York: Random House, 1972) and J.W. McGuire, *Business and Society* (New York: McGraw-Hill, 1963).
4. Annual report to shareholders, Feb. 14, 1986, p. 3, Tribune Company, Tribune Tower, 435 North Michigan Ave., Chicago, Ill., 60611.
5. Annual report to shareholders, Feb. 3, 1986, p. 2, Knight-Ridder, Inc., One Herald Plaza, Miami, Fla., 33101.
6. Annual report to shareholders, March 1, 1986, p. 1., Dow Jones & Company, Inc., World Financial Center, 200 Liberty Street, New York, N.Y., 10281.
7. ABC News Policy, an employee handbook, March 10, 1982, preface, American Broadcasting Companies, Inc., ABC News, 7 West 66th Street, New York, N.Y., 10023.

8. The APME 1974 report can be obtained from the Associated Press, 50 Rockefeller Plaza, New York, N.Y., 10020; Dr. Ralph Izard, professor of journalism, E. W. Scripps School of Journalism, Ohio University, Sigma Delta Chi survey. For trends in the early 1980s, see C. David Rambo, "Codes of Ethics," *presstime,* February 1984, p. 20. For 1993 results, see "Conduct on Codes," *presstime,* February 1993, p. 13.
9. John R. Finnegan, senior vice president and editor, the *St. Pioneer Press and Dispatch,* and an ASNE official, in speech at Morris Communications Corp. seminar on ethical issues, Savannah, Ga., March 10, 1986.
10. Richard G. Capen, Jr., chairman and publisher, *Miami Herald,* One Herald Plaza, Miami, Fla., 33101; letter to author, Oct. 2, 1985.
11. Eugene Patterson, chairman and chief executive officer, *St. Petersburg Times and Evening Independent,* P.O. Box 1121, St. Petersburg, Fla., 33731; letter to author, June 11, 1985.
12. Eugene Patterson, "Standards of Operation," June 15, 1979.
13. Jim Squires, editor, *Chicago Tribune,* 435 N. Michigan Ave., Chicago, Ill., 60611, "Ethics Policy," June 24, 1982; and letter to author, Oct. 7, 1985.
14. William F. Thomas, editor, *Los Angeles Times,* Times Mirror Square, Los Angeles, Calif., 90053, "Code of Ethics," Nov. 16, 1982, and letter to author, Feb. 4, 1986.
15. Bob Haring, executive editor, *Tulsa World,* P.O. Box 1770, Tulsa, Okla., 74102; letter to author, Nov. 6, 1985.
16. Roone Arledge, memo to staff on "News Policy," ABC News, 7 West 66th St., New York, N.Y., 10023, March 10, 1982.
17. Ethical issues in business are discussed with skill by Fred Luthans, Richard M. Hodgetts and Kenneth R. Thompson, *Social Issues in Business* (New York: Macmillan, 1984) and Thomas Donaldson, *Corporations and Morality* (Englewood Cliffs, N.J.: Prentice Hall, 1982).
18. See report of Professional Standards Committee, APME Red Book 1984, The Associated Press Managing Editors Association, 50 Rockefeller Plaza, New York, N.Y. 10020, p. 169.
19. W. Jack Duncan, *Management,* op. cit., comments on this.
20. A report on this seminar, "Closing the Credibility Gap," was written by John Dillion, special assignment editor, *The Richmond Times-Dispatch,* and is available from SNPA, P.O. Box 18875, Atlanta, Ga., 30328.
21. CBS News Standards, memo to personnel, April 14, 1976, CBS Inc., 51 W. 52nd St., New York, N.Y., 10020, p. 2.
22. "Code of Ethics," *Los Angeles Times,* dated Nov. 16, 1982; and letter to author from editor William F. Thomas, Feb. 4, 1986.
23. "Ethics Policy," *Chicago Tribune;* and letter to author from editor James D. Squires, Oct. 7, 1985.
24. "The *Herald* and You" an ethics code, *Miami Herald,* One Herald Plaza, Miami, Fla., 33101; and letter to author from Richard G. Capen, Jr., chairman and publisher, Oct. 2, 1985.

25. "Conflicts of Interest Policy," Dow Jones & Company, Inc.; and letters to author from Lawrence A. Armour, Oct. 17, 1985.

26. "Newsroom Ethics: How Tough Is Enforcement?" a survey by American Society of Newspaper Editors, P.O. Box 17004, Washington, D.C., 10041, released April, 1985.

27. Michael J. Davies, speech at ethics seminar held in Savannah, Ga., March 9–11, 1986, by Morris Communication Corp., P.O. Box 936, Augusta, Ga., 30913.

28. Reprinted with permission from Benjamin C. Bradlee.

CHAPTER 6

Corporate Profits and Newsroom Ethics

Profit is the number one goal for all free-enterprise media that must scramble for survival in our highly competitive commercial marketplace.

And, in that truism lie enormously important implications for any journalist dedicated to ethical reporting and writing of high-quality—and thus expensive—news and information.

Why is profit so important? Aside from the reality that media owners like to make money, why must newspapers, magazines and broadcast stations be profit-driven?

Because without profit, talented employees cannot be hired. Newsrooms starve for funds to pay for credible journalism.

Because without profit, the media (a capital-intensive industry) cannot pay for new presses, new technology—or attract the investor capital necessary to prepare for the future.

Bottom line: News organizations scrambling to stay afloat financially cannot shine journalistic light in dark corners.

So, it's futile to discuss, as we have, efforts by individuals to practice ethical journalism without examining the corporate profit motive and its impact on those efforts. To that we now turn in Chapter 6.

ETHICS AND THE MARKETING CONCEPT

Three developments changed forever the economics of news media in America and, thus, the character and practice of journalism.

First, starting in the late 1960s, costs began to soar for newspapers, magazines, radio and TV stations. Payrolls climbed steadily, as did cost of newsprint and the even more expensive paper most magazines use.

Second, competition intensified for reader and viewer time and, especially, advertiser dollar. The fight grew hotter between traditional print and broadcast media but increased even more with the surge of newcomers, such as cable television and direct mail.

Third, despite all these problems, delighted media owners found that newspapers and TV stations could be hugely profitable—more so than almost any other type of business in America.

Clearly, the media business became Big Business. Local mom-and-pop owners of newspapers began selling out for astronomical prices to publicly owned media conglomerates managed from remote headquarters in the name of thousands of distant, anonymous shareholders. Television and radio stations and magazines also were snapped up by publicly owned groups. And the money began pouring in.

Yet, many media companies still were being run haphazardly by poorly trained executives—by, for example, former newspaper editors who, though great journalists, had little experience in financial or managerial techniques of big business.

The solution for many companies: Import nonjournalist managers—accountants, lawyers and financial analysts—and convert from news and service-oriented corporate strategies to profit-driven business strategies.

Thus arrived in the media world the "marketing concept," a business approach long before adopted by many American industries but generally not fully developed by media firms, particularly news-oriented newspapers and magazines.[1]

The impact on newsroom ethics and media social responsibility was profound.

FOCUS ON PROFITS

Applied to the media, the marketing concept requires setting profit goals, then integrating all operating departments—including news—in a total effort to achieve those goals.

This requires, in a newspaper, for example, a planned, disciplined drive for financial success, involving teamwork by advertising, circulation, production, promotion and news.

Newspaper, magazine and broadcast editors, who traditionally isolated themselves from "business-office" matters, now are expected to construct news strategies within a unified marketing effort that will exploit the economic potential of the marketplace. Editors must create news and information packages that will lure sufficient numbers of readers or viewers with income and spending habits attractive to the advertisers who foot the bills.

But, can editors or news directors be harnessed to the marketing concept by profit-oriented news strategies and still remain true to higher ethical standards and social responsibilities of journalism?

VIEWPOINT

Don't Let Profit Surprise You

"It often comes as a surprise—particularly to foreign journalists—that the media in the United States are essentially commercial ventures. I do not view this as a liability.

"On the contrary, I view our 'capitalist' foundation as one of our greatest strengths. Financial success provides the dollars needed to create quality. And financial success provides the independence the press needs to pursue the news without fear or favor at home.

"It can be quite costly. Take Watergate. When the *Washington Post* was reporting the Watergate story, the Nixon Administration attempted to intimidate us by, among other things, bringing about challenges to our television station licenses. That caused our stock to plummet and cost over a million dollars to defend.

"An organization with fewer financial resources could not have paid this price. It also would probably have been harder without family control, but still possible, I believe. An organization that depended on governmental subsidies in one form or another certainly would have abandoned the story.

"So our existence depends on meeting the needs of enough people who are willing to pay for our survival with their hard-earned dollars.

"We don't have the luxury of being ideologues who parade as journalists in order to advance their own ideas and agendas. We have to satisfy the specific demands of a specific audience for information, perspective or entertainment."

Katherine Graham, then chairman, Washington Post Co.

Can editors hotly pursue affluent readers, often to the neglect of the less affluent, because that's what advertisers want, and still cover the world as their news instincts and training—and accepted journalistic principles—dictate it should be covered?

Can TV news directors hold true to their journalistic responsibilities and still pursue the larger numbers of viewers promised by happy-talk news shows and the other silliness that so often afflicts TV news organizations driving for better ratings?

Is ethical conflict fundamentally inherent in all of this?

THE RISING TIDE OF SHAREHOLDER EXPECTATION

If shareholders push unceasingly for ever more profit, either because they need it or simply because they like it, can ethical, socially responsible journalism flourish?

This rising tide of shareholder expectation, the constant pressure for better financial results, is the most compelling ethical issue facing policy-makers in American newsrooms today.

WHY THE TIDE RISES

Newspapers properly managed in economically strong markets yield great profit, particularly if they face no competing newspapers of like size and characteristics.

Under the right conditions, some—particularly small and medium-sized newspapers—convert 30 percent or more of total revenue to operating profit. That is, of every dollar received from advertisers and subscribers, 30 cents or more goes to pretax profit.

Other U.S. industries boast annual profits only a fraction of that. General Motors averaged 4.3 to 4.4 percent in the late 1980s and early 1990s, Exxon 5.8 to 9.4 percent, and so on.

Even in 1990, during the worst economic recession to hit newspapers in 40 years, 13 publicly owned newspaper companies tracked by analyst John Morton averaged 16.5 percent operating profit.

"All that is really happening," Morton said, "is that instead of being two or three times more profitable than most businesses, newspapers this year are reduced to being only one or two times more profitable."[2]

Television's profit potential can be even greater. A network affiliate in a major market such as Richmond, Virginia, could convert *50 percent* of gross revenue from advertisers to operating profit during the 1970s and 1980s (although profits slipped lower in the 1990s).[3]

In Wall Street parlance, communications companies for years were cash cows. Not surprisingly, all this attracted investor attention.

Medium-sized newspapers without competition in growing markets sold for three to five times gross revenue. That is, a newspaper taking in, say, $10 million annually from advertisers and subscribers could sell for $30 million to $50 million. That price multiple is extraordinary high compared to other industries.

Major market TV stations sold for hundreds of millions of dollars. In 1993, Times Mirror Co. sold four network affiliates for $335 million; H & C Communications agreed to sell two for $165 million (to a newspaper company, Pulitzer Publishing).

Communications companies, particularly those diversified in both print and broadcast, today are attractive investments on stock exchanges.[4]

GROUP CONTROL GROWS

Newspapers and broadcast stations are passing quickly from private ownership into large, publicly held communications conglomerates. More than 75 percent of all dailies are owned by groups. Groups control over 80 percent of all daily circulation and nearly 90 percent on Sundays.

Inheritance taxes prevent many owning families from passing newspapers or stations to succeeding generations. High profit potential lures groups into offering attractive prices. Tax breaks provided companies that expand through acquisition give groups additional incentive to acquire more and more.

For many reasons, then, newspaper and broadcast families of generations of journalistic commitment to a community are being succeeded by professional, profit-oriented managers who, in some cases, have no particular allegiance to community or, indeed, journalism itself.

NEW BREED MANAGERS

This does *not* mean automatic degradation of journalistic quality or social responsibility. Publicly owned groups such as Knight-Ridder, Dow Jones, The New York Times Co., Times Mirror Corp. are producing the finest journalism ever seen in this country. Those companies are as eager as any for higher profits but, fortunately, they commit to journalistic excellence as means of achieving it.

Nevertheless, the switch from family to group ownership has brought to top-level management of communications companies a new breed of managers who by training are accountants, lawyers, business school graduates, not the editor-turned-publisher of old who received early training in the newsroom.

And some new breed managers are less concerned with covering news on Main Street than with responding to Wall Street, to their distant group headquarters and its profit demands on the local "property." For this type manager, it is axiomatic that gaining a dollar in new circulation or advertising revenue through improved news content carries with it certain costs, so only a portion of that dollar will descend to bottom-line profit.

However, a dollar stripped out of existing operating costs is added almost intact to the bottom line—and thus are born careers devoted not to imaginative, expansive, community-minded journalism of high quality but, rather, to squeezing a few bucks out of costs here, there and everywhere—including the newsroom.

All this means moral issues of what is good or bad, right or wrong in the newsroom could be decided mostly outside the newsroom.

GOOD JOURNALISM ISN'T CHEAP

The first move toward ethical, responsible journalism must come not from the newsroom but, rather, the executive suite. There must be owner commitment to excellence, and that means commitment of money. Good journalism isn't cheap.

Witness three world-class newspapers (all members, incidentally, of profit-oriented, publicly owned communications groups) and their *newsroom* budgets: The *New York Times* reportedly spent $80 million covering the news in 1986; the *Los Angeles Times,* $68.6 million; the *Washington Post,* almost $50 million.[5] Those newspapers, among the prestigious handful that set the news agenda in the United States, demonstrate management commitment to excellence.

By one estimate, ABC, NBC and CBS at the time were spending $750 million or more annually on news programming.[6]

The biggest individual newsroom spender in newspapering is the *New York Times.* A. M. Rosenthal, until 1987 executive editor, is clear on what he regards as the first essential ingredient of ethical, responsible journalism. Commenting on the *Times'* very considerable journalistic achievements under his direction, Rosenthal says:

VIEWPOINT

Good Journalism is Good Business

"[W]e believe good journalism is good business. As an information company, our success depends on the excellence, reputation and usefulness of that information which is our product. We want our readers and viewers to have the highest possible confidence in what we produce. This is essential to maintaining our credibility and consequently the loyalty and following of our readers and viewers."

Alvah H. Chapman, Jr., then chairman of Knight-Ridder, Inc., in letter to author

> This could not have been done without cooperation between the business and the news side, and it most certainly could not have been done well without the participation and encouragement and adventuresomeness of the publisher, [Arthur Ochs] Punch Sulzberger.
>
> As a matter of fact, looking back it seems to me that perhaps the most important single thing in the success of a newspaper is the willingness of a publisher to invest his mind and money to improve the quality of the newspaper. Not just promotion, not just circulation, not just advertising, but quality. When in trouble you can either put more water in the soup or more tomatoes—the *Times'* publishing tradition has been to add tomatoes.[7]

When A. H. Belo Corp. decided in the early 1980s its *Dallas Morning News* would attack Times Mirror's *Dallas Times Herald* in all-out war for dominance of the city, Belo's owners recruited talented—and expensive—newsroom managers, writers and reporters from top-flight newspapers throughout the country. Then, they *doubled* the newsroom's budget in one year. Within three years, the *Morning News* achieved superiority over the *Times Herald,* and won nationwide acclaim for journalistic quality.[8] In 1991, the *Times Herald* folded. Other factors, including a natural advantage to the *News* as a morning paper, contributed to the outcome. But massive amounts of money wisely spent by Belo were key.

Knight-Ridder management repeatedly urges its newspapers toward journalistic quality and responsibility, then puts money where its slogans are. As of 1993, Knight-Ridder won 61 Pulitzer Prizes.

Few of the nation's 1,556 daily newspapers (1993 count) spend on news as do the *New York Times* or *Dallas Morning News.* To be fair, not many have the strong economic base offered by New York City or Dallas markets.[9] And, *no newspaper can perform for long above the economic strength of its marketplace.* If advertising and circulation revenue isn't there, principled, ethical, high-quality journalism won't be, either.

Market strength aside, however, American journalism is characterized by enormous variances in management commitment to ethical, responsible news coverage.

MEASURING COMMITMENT TO EXCELLENCE

American newspapers range from world-class journalistic quality to shoddy dogs. For every Knight-Ridder or New York Times Co., there is a company that publishes low-quality (but often highly profitable) newspapers.

Television's performance swings equally wide. For every news special combining space-age communications technology with superb reporting, there is a silly, happy-talk local anchor team that wouldn't know news if it dropped on its blown-dry coiffures.

In either medium, which it will be—excellence or shoddy journalism—is up to top management. There are ways to measure which way management is moving.

STAFFING

One measure of management commitment is the number of employees made available to the newsroom. In newspapers, it generally varies from 0.7 to 1.04 or more newsroom staffers per 1,000 circulation. In its drive for excellence, the *Dallas Morning News* had 1.05 per 1,000 circulation.[10] Personnel accounts for generally 46 to 49 percent of a newspaper's total costs and most of a newsroom's costs, so a management that commits people to news is committing substantial money.

In television, the choices are handling news relatively cheaply with a talking head in a studio, augmented by a few stringers and lifting news from local newspapers, or commitment of expensive mobile units and large outside reporting staffs.

NEWSHOLE

One crucial indicator of newspaper management commitment to excellence is newshole—total space given news and information. Newshole is not determined by flow of news or newsroom judgments of how news should be covered; rather, newshole is established by amount of advertising sold.

Thus, on heavy advertising days—Wednesdays and Sundays in most cities—papers are fat. If big news breaks for fat days, there is a better chance it will be covered in full. Chances aren't so good for lean days, such as Mondays, Tuesdays, and Saturdays.

With newsprint at $685 per ton (in 1993) and climbing, only managers truly committed to social responsibility and journalistic quality will provide news pages for a big story even without supporting advertising.[11] That eats into profits, unappealing to many shareholders and their surrogate managers in publicly owned companies. *New York Times* managers, and those of a few other great newspapers, routinely make space available for important stories, regardless of advertiser support—to their great credit among serious journalists.

The news-to-advertising ratio within a newspaper is thus an indicator of quality—and commitment to ethical, socially responsible journalism. It varies widely from paper to paper. In some metropolitan dailies on heavy advertising days, news gets as little as 25 percent of total space; in small town dailies on slow advertising days, 70 percent or more can go to news (or, frequently, meaningless but inexpensive filler mailed from a syndicate).

A ratio traditionally regarded about right, 60 percent advertising and 40 percent news, is breaking down under pressure to sell more advertising. In 1992, for example 66.3 per cent of Sunday newspaper content nationwide was advertising. If news content over a prolonged period runs substantially under 40 percent, readers simply are being cheated. (Of course, if news runs heavily over 40 percent for lengthy periods, the newspaper may be starved for advertising and facing a financial crisis.)

A critical problem is the increasing swing by many advertisers from pages of the newspaper itself into preprints, those colorful minicatalogs inserted in many newspapers, particularly on Wednesdays (food day) and Sundays. This reduces dramatically the number of pages available to news. Unfortunately, most publishers don't use profits from preprints to support a larger number of news pages in the paid-circulation paper.

THE COST OF AIRTIME

In television, there is equivalent tension in the news versus advertising equation. TV's version of newsprint—time—is expensive, too, and there is struggle over who gets it.

The plain fact is that although news programming can attract advertising and be profitable, entertainment programming generally is more profitable, and really is what television is all about.

For news directors concerned with ethical, responsible journalism, the conflict takes many forms. Most visible is whether news, particularly an unexpected fast-breaking story, can preempt scheduled entertainment programming. At network level, preempting entertainment can cost hundreds of thousands of dollars, millions even; in local TV, it's almost unheard of.

Another source of conflict is whether network evening news should be extended from the current half-hour to a full hour. The issue is not whether Peter Jennings and Tom Brokaw each evening need more than 22 minutes for news (30 minutes minus commercials). They do; the world simply cannot be covered in any meaningful depth in the time given network news teams. The real issue is that local network affiliated stations profitably sell that extra 30 minutes to local advertisers and are unwilling to turn it over to Jennings, Brokaw or anyone else, whatever the news needs.

AP VERSUS LOCAL

In both newspapers and broadcast, an important signal of management's commitment to excellence is whether the newsroom is forced to rely heavily on external news resources such as news agencies and syndicates.

Bluntly, the cheapest way to put out a newspaper is to fill it with Associated Press copy, tucking in around the edges yards of syndicated columns and features. AP, a membership cooperative, is relatively inexpensive because its prices are controlled by the newspaper publishers who pay them. In the 1980s, AP costs were only 4 percent of the *Baltimore Sun*'s newsroom (*not* total) budget; yet, AP provided 24 percent of news the *Sun* published. The *Phoenix Gazette* and *Arizona Republic* drew 37 percent of their news content from AP and paid AP 4 percent of their newsroom budget. At the *Kansas City Star and Times,* it was 7 percent of newsroom budget for 39 percent of content. Smaller papers and broadcast stations pay AP much less. For both newspapers and broadcast, supplemental news agencies and syndicates are even cheaper.[12]

Now, AP is one of the world's premier news organizations. Supplemental agencies such as The New York Times News Service and Los Angeles Times-Washington Post News Service are excellent. And, any editor who makes discerning use of AP and leading supplements to augment local coverage can do the reader a great service.

Problems arise, however, when profit-oriented managers of smaller papers realize AP or a supplemental agency costs less than an experienced local reporter or two. That can lead to newspapers, even of 20,000 to 25,000 circulation, maintaining local reporting staffs of only four or five persons and stuffing their pages with inexpensive, albeit often high-quality, copy from distant cities on esoteric subjects of little local consequence.

Management's commitment to socially responsible journalism really is signaled in major part by total dollars allocated to newsrooms. The range is enormous—anywhere from 7 percent of total expense to 20 percent for papers of 20,000 circulation to over 100,000.[13] It is impossible to predict what level of spending on news will yield excellence. Competition, market, owner profit expectation—all vary, as indeed does the definition of excellence itself.

QUALITY AND PROFIT: BASIC DILEMMA

Search as they will (and must), editors and news directors concerned with ethical, responsible journalism cannot find proof that spending heavily to produce high-quality reporting and writing will assure profitability. No such provable link exists.

However, with management increasingly staffed by accountants, lawyers and other nonjournalists, the need to cost-justify excellence is no idle exercise. Convincing that type manager to pay for quality becomes crucial to everything else—including ethics—that follows in a newsroom.

Those who believe ethical, responsible, high-quality news coverage is essential to long-term financial as well as journalistic success (and I am among them) can point to much evidence. In newspapering, names jump easily to mind: the *New York Times, Philadelphia Inquirer, Washington Post, Chicago Tribune, Los Angeles Times, Dallas Morning News, Wall Street Journal.* All spend heavily on news, producing ethical, responsible, outstanding newspapers—and, to boot, enjoying substantial profits.

In television, the networks spend heavily on evening news shows, and profitably so. CBS's "60 Minutes," expensive to produce, always is among most-watched and most profitable shows.[14]

VIEWPOINT

Quality Journalism and Economic Success

"Editorial awards don't automatically translate into economic success. But they are the symbols of quality journalism that help our newspapers grow in circulation and reader acceptance without which economic success is improbable."

Erwin Potts, president and chief executive officer, McClatchy Newspapers, Inc., in company's 1993 annual report to stockholders

However, American newspaper history is filled with examples of journalistically outstanding newspapers that withered even in economically good times, then keeled over dead during bad times. The *New York Herald Tribune,* "a newspaperman's newspaper," was filled with fine writing and reporting, even when it had a death rattle in its cash register. The *Philadelphia Bulletin, Washington Star, Cleveland Press, Minneapolis Star* and many others died not because their news products were poor. Rather, they died for complex reasons of economics, competition, changing lifestyles—and mismanagement—that not even outstanding journalism could overcome.

Conversely, there are many examples of low-quality newspapers producing high profits. The Thomson, Park and Donrey newspaper groups, among the nation's largest in number of newspapers owned, specialize in small newspapers with no direct print competition and that, therefore, can extract maximum economic reward from their markets for minimum investment in journalistic quality.

There is some question whether such tactics succeed over the long haul. Disaffected readers of poor-quality newspapers seek other sources of news and advertising; competitors slip into the market. But particularly in small towns without alternate sources of local news and advertising, cut-rate journalism can produce enormous profit ratios.

THE GRESHAM LAW OF TV

In television, sheer perversity is at work—a sort of Gresham's Law of Journalism: poor-quality, low-cost entertainment shows drive out high-quality, high-cost news programming. First-rate network news shows lose viewers when opposed in the same slot by entertainment such as "Wheel of Fortune." Superb news specials in the Edward R. Murrow tradition of thoughtful, responsible broadcast journalism vanish before stampedes of sitcoms and cops-and-robbers shows.

Clearly, the newsroom ethicist dedicated to socially responsible journalism must take the fight outside the newsroom itself, well beyond the ethical issues met in the daily struggle to get the newspaper on the street and evening news on the air. The fight must be carried to higher management in terms nonjournalist managers understand—how better, more responsible (and, thus, more expensive) journalism can help the newspaper or broadcast station reach its overall strategic goals of increased share of reader or viewer time and advertiser dollar and profit.

As he tracked profit slippage in the recession of the early 1990s, analyst John Morton warned that unrealistically high profit expectations could lead to long-term harm.

> The real danger in this problem is that some newspapers might therefore try to do too much to shore up profitability by trimming staff, newshole and journalistic effort. Some moves in these directions may be advisable, but going even a few steps too far damages product quality—a consequence liable to far outlast the difficulties of the current recession.[15]

LEARN TO TALK THEIR LANGUAGE

Editors or news directors seeking top management's commitment of resources necessary for quality journalism can think ethics and social responsibility, but on entering the executive suite it's more productive to talk dollars and cents. They must express their journalistic needs in countinghouse language.

The business imperative for newspapers today is simple: On behalf of advertisers, attract (at acceptable cost) readers in sufficient numbers and affluence who live in the right places (near advertisers' stores), then help influence them to purchase advertisers' goods and services.

Many enlightened corporate business strategists also think ethics and social responsibility; we've mentioned great newspapers they publish. But their challenge is to get, hold and persuade the right kinds of readers who, in turn, are sold to advertisers.

Most advertisers want their message delivered into homes where more than one reader awaits, especially women aged 18 to 49, the big spenders. So, in addition to attractive demographics—income, education and spending habits—advertisers seek household penetration.

Note the game is no longer simply adding more circulation; in fact, circulation among the "wrong" types of readers (the demographically unattractive) in the "wrong" places (distant from advertisers' stores) will not gain advertiser support. Thus, for the newspaper that type circulation is not a revenue producer, but, rather, a cost factor that drains profits.

Understanding these basic facts of modern newspaper (and magazine) marketing, editors can express their journalistic needs and ethical imperatives in terms of what will yield not only responsible journalism but also—music to publishers' ears—deeper household penetration and improved demographics. Editors can produce newspapers that salve their professional consciences, meet their ethical and social responsibilities and fit productively into the corporation's overall marketing concept.

"ATTRACTIVE" READERS WANT NEWS

Attractive readers by definition want superior news coverage. They are, compared with TV viewers, for example, well educated and sophisticated in news interests;

they are affluent and adventuresome in lifestyle and way of thinking. Constructing a newspaper to reach that type reader with improved political coverage, strong business news and thoughtful editorials and commentary can be delightful for editors, profitable for publishers—and socially responsible for both.

This is more difficult to achieve in television news and, consequently, high-quality network journalism faces perilous times. Numbers of viewers—huge, raw, undifferentiated numbers—are the goal of network television. Millions of men who want a close shave, tens of millions who drink more than one beer, and women of all ages and types who use detergents are what the television advertiser wants. Whether they earn $12,000 annually, or $120,000, went to college or not, is immaterial—just so they shave, drink beer or wash dishes.

To the despair of responsible television journalists, playful game shows, cheap to stage and easy to watch, sometimes produce larger numbers than thought-provoking (and expensive) news specials on important issues of the day; mindless sitcoms rival in popularity the hard-hitting, award-winning, million-dollar-a-year evening news anchor.

TV NEWS CUTS BACK

All this bodes ill for network television journalism. After all, it is—with the exception of CNN—strictly an adjunct in an entertainment-oriented medium managed at the top almost exclusively by nonjournalist executives raised in an industry scarcely 45 years old and, compared with newspapers, lacking a long tradition of journalism.

ABC, NBC and CBS have made major cutbacks in their superb news staffs; more likely are ahead. Combined with expansion of local television news, this may mean current star anchors are among the last who will become household fixtures coast-to-coast.

Growth of CNN, Fox and other independent networks is fractionalizing television—each network's slice of the viewer and advertising pies is getting smaller. And that means less money is available for high-quality news produced by major networks.

The reality, then, is that profit as the leading motivation in modern communications corporations has fundamental importance to the practice of ethical, responsible newspaper and television journalism. Yet, many editors and news directors resist the thought that they are involved in a business manufacturing a product that must compete and win in the marketplace just like any other product.

EDITORS AND BUSINESS: CONFLICTING ETHICS?

For 32 years, Charles W. Bailey worked for the *Minneapolis Star and Tribune.* He was editor when bad times arrived in the 1980s. The morning and afternoon papers, in serious financial difficulty, were merged and the staff cut 15 percent.

Bailey, whose reputation as a principled journalist extended far beyond his upper midwest base, resigned in protest with a public statement that spoke the concerns of many editors:

> I think there are some new threats to the independence and public utility of newspaper editors. One is the growing tendency to encourage, in fact, to require, editors to become businessmen—to be part of a "management team," to concentrate on things that involve business rather than journalism.
>
> An editor has to know where the money comes from, and it is currently fashionable to talk about "the total newspaper," but speaking from personal experience, I don't think most editors are especially qualified in matters of business and finance. And even if they were, I do not think they should spend most of their time and energy on such matters.
>
> They have more important things to do. There will always be people around to tell a publisher how he can do things more cheaply, more profitably, less controversially. He needs someone to explain, from time to time, why things have to be done more expensively, less profitably, and in ways that create rather than avoid controversy.

PROFIT DRIVE CAUSES TENSION

For some editors, conflicting demands of newsroom and countinghouse create major job tension. An Associated Press Managing Editors Association survey of 902 editors found most stimulated by the journalistic challenges of their jobs, but suffering emotional stress when their publishers imposed profit-oriented policies that compromised newsroom ethical integrity or denied resources necessary for responsible, high-quality journalism.

Robert H. Giles, then editor of Gannett's Rochester, N.Y., newspapers, and now publisher of the *Detroit News,* directed the survey. He explained:

> Fifteen years ago, editors were editors. Today, they are editor-managers. They direct the editing of the newspaper with one hand and, with the other, they are deeply involved in business management.
>
> The editor is expected to carry on in the best traditions of journalistic excellence, but also is expected to share the responsibility for the newspaper as a "profit center." Many editors discovered that this dual obligation created unfamiliar stresses, stresses born of a conflict between the need to be good and the need to be lean.

Whether editors and news directors should be inducted into the integrated management team can long be argued; in fact, many are—and, along with other department heads, must assume responsibility for the marketplace success of their newspapers or television news shows. Their performance is measured in businesslike terms: whether they expand circulation properly and achieve deeper household penetration or, in TV, pull in more viewers—and meet budget.

Corporate cross-pollination—making editors responsible, in part, for marketing the product as well as creating it—is reflected in the increasing number who also carry corporate titles. "Vice president and editor" is a favorite combination, and it very clearly signals dual responsibilities. Alex S. Jones, then the *New York Times'* perceptive media reporter, noted in 1986 the top four officers of the American Society of Newspaper Editors, ***which officially won't even admit publishers to membership*** (some in fact are members), carried corporate, as well as newsroom, titles, or once served as publishers. Jones wrote from Washington:

VIEWPOINT

The Integrated Editor

"[N]ewsroom strategy must be integrated with the strategy of the entire newspaper. The editor and the publisher and the marketing director and the operations manager must be a team. . . . The day is gone when the editor can be going in one direction while the marketing director is going in another and the operations director in a third."

Michael Gartner, then president and editorial chairman, *Des Moines Register and Tribune,* letter to author

> Many of the nation's editors, gathered in record numbers here this week for an annual convention, grumbled in hotel corridors with the sophistication of publishers about flat advertising revenues that threaten to squeeze news budgets.
>
> In the modern newspaper, top editors who once shunned business concerns have had to become knowledgeable about corporate finance as well as news coverage, and the American Society of Newspaper Editors reflects that change . . .[16]

Just a year earlier, at the Society's convention, Jones reported:

> [T]he job of being a newspaper editor has changed so dramatically in the last decade that the society is no longer sure precisely what a newspaper editor is or should be. . . . One of the traditional pleasures of being a newspaper editor has been the role of defending the sanctity of the paper's news operation from encroachment by the business side of the paper, represented by the publisher. At conventions in past years, editors would often grumble about their publishers and bask in the sense of muscular brotherhood that made the society almost an executive-level union.
>
> But that adversarial atmosphere has almost completely disappeared from the society's annual meeting.
>
> As newspapers have been consolidated into chains and the chains have grown into communications conglomerates, editors have increasingly become key executives in a corporate structure whose product is news, and there are fewer single-minded, hard-bitten editors of newspapers. For instance, editors now frequently use the jargon of publishers to describe their newspapers; what was "a good newspaper" a few years ago is now described by editors as a "quality product."
>
> [E]ditors expressed concern that they now spend too much time pondering budgets and the company's bottom line and are distracted from their duties as editors.
>
> The editor's role now often includes participating in such corporate functions as strategic planning and marketing. Many editors have assumed corporate titles that suggest relatively little of their time is spent editing.[17]

Rather than sullenly resisting inevitable induction into corporate affairs, newspaper editors and TV news directors should use such cross-pollination to battle meaningfully and where it counts—in the business office—for ethical, socially responsible journalism. If editors and directors don a vice-president hat at the planning table, they can fight for the resources—people, money, time, newshole and air time—they need to produce that kind of journalism.

EDITORS AGREE . . . YET

Many editors and news directors accept close interaction between their news and corporate business responsibilities. They see need for producing newspapers or news shows that succeed financially, as well as journalistically. They accept organizational responsibilities outside the newsroom.

Yet, curiously, few write newsroom codes reflecting this fact. Few deal effectively, for their staffs, with the wider question of profit versus ethical, responsible journalism. Few present newsroom and corporate imperatives as synergistic—not conflicting—forces. However it is done effectively in the small lumbering town of Longview, Washington.

From 1923, when founded, until 1985, when sold to a group, the *Longview Daily News* was published by John M. McClelland or his son, John, Jr. They were of a rapidly vanishing breed of owners who lived where they published the *Daily News* and felt personally responsible for the newspaper's business and journalistic direction.

In a policy statement, the McClellands addressed the troublesome question of how to balance the twin objectives of ethical, responsible journalism and profit:

> Our newspapers' only license to publish is the freedom of the press clause in the Constitution. As such, their first obligation is to publish the news, to broadcast the truth, to keep the people informed. Their primary obligation is to serve the readers.
>
> Secondly, they are business and manufacturing enterprises depending on the sale of their products for the financial success which enables them to continue publishing the news. That success is necessary to provide compensation for employees, to furnish reserves for improvements in productive capacity, to provide for the payment of taxes necessary to maintain the government, and to allow the shareholders whose capital has made the business possible a reasonable return on their investment.
>
> To assure this success, it is essential to produce newspapers that are as good as we are capable of producing, to increase continually our family of readers and to provide, through well planned advertising, a means of serving effectively the sales objectives of our customers.
>
> Talented, truthful, energetic journalism; well-prepared advertising and the finest printing our employees and machines are capable of producing—these shall be our objectives.[18]

CORPORATE PROFITS AND JOURNALISTIC ELITISM

Implicit in American journalistic tradition—and, certainly, in the concept of social responsibility—is a mission to inform and educate, to uplift.

Newspapers claim special societal (as well as Constitutional) status on grounds they inform and enlighten, which, in turn, strengthens our society. Because of this sense of mission, many types of preferential societal treatment, such as favorable postal rates for newspapers, are justified by publishers and editors alike.

Yet, newspapers are positioning themselves journalistically to best yield profit, and that requires attracting well-educated, highly affluent readers.

But, how about the less-well-educated, not-so-affluent citizenry? Who exists to inform and uplift them?

THE ELITIST NEWSPAPER

Marketing directors at many leading newspapers would panic if large numbers of low-income, poorly educated readers began subscribing to their newspapers. Such newcomers would "dilute" the "purity" of reader demographics on which high advertising rates are based.

How pure?

A 1993 survey for the Newspaper Association of America shows 81 percent of college graduates read a Sunday paper; for noncollege graduates, the figure is 76 percent. In households with $60,000 or more annual income, Sunday readership hits 81 percent; in households with less than $40,000, readership slumps to 63 percent.[19]

It's axiomatic: educated, high-income "upscale" people read newspapers (and magazines); TV is the medium of choice of "downscale" people.

Newspapers are quick to take advantage of such information, of course.

ATTRACTING THE CHAMPAGNE CROWD

Dow Jones boasts of the elitist audience attracted to its *Wall Street Journal*:

> The quality of the *Journal* audience . . . remains unsurpassed among major publications," says a Dow Jones promotional ad directed at advertisers. "Household income of the *average* (author's emphasis) *Journal* subscriber is $107,800 and average net worth exceeds $750,000. The typical *Journal* subscriber is in the ranks of top or middle management, with diverse job responsibilities in key areas. He or she also is an active investor, with an average personal portfolio of more than $600,000.[20]

Well, one might say, the *Wall Street Journal* is a special publication aiming at the carriage trade audience. So, obviously, is the *New York Times*:

Walter E. Mattson, then president and chief operating officer of New York Times Co., told securities analysts his paper's national edition " . . . is aimed really at maintaining the position of the *New York Times* in the marketplace as a newspaper of national and worldwide influence and as a newspaper that delivers to its advertisers an influential and affluent market."[21] The *Times* aims at upper-income, well-educated professionals and executives—seeking perhaps the top one percent, in demographic terms, of the nation's population.

The *Los Angeles Times* boasts households taking its daily paper are "84 percent more likely" than non-*Times* households to "serve wine/champagne once a week or more"; on Sundays, the figure is 98 percent.[22]

VIEWPOINT

Covering Upscale Murders

"I remember being trained as a green police reporter to understand, through repetition, that a murder on Park Avenue was big news and a murder on Dean Street in Brooklyn wasn't worth interrupting the card game for."

Sydney H. Schanberg, then a *New York Times* columnist

In Dallas, the *Morning News* claims it is read by "the right people. . . . People advertisers are most interested in reaching . . . more families with household incomes of $50,000+ and $35,000+, more professionals and more people with a college degree."[23] The *Washington Post* claims its Sunday magazine reaches 265,000 households with incomes of more than $50,000.[24]

What's all this talk about serving the champagne crowd, the rich, the "right people"? In city after city, the pattern is the same: On behalf of the all-important advertiser, newspaper strategists seek the affluent, and editors develop special approaches to the news that will help.

It's nice to be a journalistic servant of the people; it's nicer to serve the rich.

AFFLUENCE VERSUS RESPONSIBILITY

Some leading big-city newspapers, those on everybody's list of the "best," are moving upscale so rapidly in search of more affluent readers that they are leaving behind great sectors of their publics. Serious questions of social responsibility are raised.

For most metropolitan papers, the business necessity today is to leapfrog out of the socioeconomic deterioration of their core cities and develop new circulation and advertising in affluent and growing suburbs.

Left behind in center city are many low-income families, blacks and Hispanics—in whom advertisers have less interest, and for whom upscale newspapers have little relevance.

Evidence of this upscale shift is in the shallow household penetration major newspapers achieve in their own home counties. The weekday *New York Times* penetrates as many homes in Connecticut's affluent Fairfield County and New Jersey's rich Bergen County as it does in its home boroughs. The *Los Angeles Times* penetrates (in 1993) just 25.4 percent of households in its home county; the *Chicago Tribune,* 23.1 percent; the *Dallas Morning News,* 32.5 percent. The *Miami Herald,* one of the nation's finest papers, penetrates just 38.7 percent in its home county, Dade, which has many Spanish-speaking residents.

An exception is the *Washington Post,* with 65.7 percent penetration in the District of Columbia. However, detailed analysis of circulation within the district

VIEWPOINT

Profitability versus "The People"

"The newspaper industry claims the right to put vending machines on public streets and in airports, the right to sit in courtrooms, the right to see public records, the right to question the president, the right to have a front row seat at the war—all on the basis that it is an institution exercising the people's right to know.

"Never does it claim the right to such access on the basis that it is in the business of delivering advertising information for profit. But nowhere does the Constitution define 'the people' as the predominately white, 35 percent of the population from 25 to 50 years age making $50,000 or more a year . . .

"By reducing circulation efforts among low income, minority readers, newspapers actually improve the overall demographic profile of their audiences, which they then use to justify raising advertising rates. Thus, with few exceptions, the profitability of newspapers in monopoly markets has come to depend on an economic formula that is ethically bankrupt and embarrassing for a business that has always claimed to rest on a public trust: The highest profitability comes from delivering advertising sold at the highest rates in a paper containing the least number of pages and sold for the highest possible retail price to the fewest number of high income customers necessary to justify the rate charged to advertisers.

"Of course, such a strategy can't possibly produce anything but declining market penetration, for which television and illiteracy are getting the blame."

James D. Squires, former executive editor of the *Chicago Tribune* and a critic of the marketing concept's influence on newsroom strategies[25]

shows the *Post* achieves only shallow penetration in large pockets of low-income areas.[26]

To meet advertiser demands—and reduce their own costs—newspapers eliminate "inefficient" circulation in distant areas of no interest to home-base advertisers. Thus, the *Atlanta Journal and Constitution, Minneapolis Star Tribune, Miami Herald* and other newspapers that once circulated statewide pull back closer to home. The *Boston Globe,* once circulated throughout New England, now identifies an area within 50 miles of downtown as its primary circulation target.[27]

Editors employ marketing strategies to attract the "right" readers. *New York Times'* editors create a journalistic tone appealing to readers who buy fur, not cloth, coats; those who vacation in the Caribbean, not Coney Island. That means covering serious books, music and drama and in other ways positioning the entire paper for the $60,000+ audience.

When advertisers demand—as many do—that 90 percent or more of all households in a market be reached, most newspapers provide total-market-coverage vehicles (usually, direct mail services or free-circulation shoppers) to do the job. They avoid "diluting" content of the newspaper itself or positioning it downscale.

WHO ISN'T BEING REACHED?

American newspapers today sell roughly 70 or so copies per 100 households. In 1950, it was 124 copies for each 100 households. Who isn't being reached? Mostly, it is the low-income and minority sectors.

Most big-city newspapers do not try to deliver both the affluent suburban audience and low-income, city-core residents. For most, the strategy is not to reach down, in a journalistic sense, but rather to wait until the less affluent achieve middle-class education and income—and become attractive to advertisers. At that point, the elitist newspaper, in content and tone, becomes relevant.

Fashioning mass appeal, downscale newspapers made fortunes for Hearst and other press barons 50 years ago. Editors who try that today are headed for financial disaster. For example, incapable of competing against the *New York Times* for the elitist audience, both the *New York Daily News* and *New York Post* position themselves downscale in content and marketing strategies. Both are barely profitable.

Unquestionably, their inability to attract affluent readers contributed strongly to the deaths of the *Cleveland Press, Chicago American, Baltimore News-American* and other blue-collar papers.

NOW, *YOU* MAKE THE CALL

If an elitist paper dominates its upscale market and enjoys financial strength, does it have a moral responsibility to reach downscale, to present news content appealing to all sectors of the public?

If intent on doing an ethical, socially responsible job, must an editor or TV news director represent, in good as well as bad news, all constituencies of the market?

Not to suggest silliness such as yardstick editing—allocating, say 12 percent of newshole or air time for news about blacks because blacks are 12 percent of the population. But is an editor morally obliged to ensure that over a prolonged period all sectors of the community are covered and served?

Are managers of publicly owned media corporations morally responsible for putting social responsibility on a par with profit-making? Are the shareholders to whom they report equally responsible, in a moral sense, to put aside their money concerns and insist media companies spend more heavily for ethical, socially responsible coverage?

Should editors and news directors withdraw from the countinghouse, spurn the marketing concept and concern themselves solely with newsroom matters?

Return once more to societal values and journalistic principles discussed in Chapter 1:

- Do upscale newspapers serve the values of stewardship and justice? Do they serve the first journalistic principle we discussed, serve the public?
- If a newspaper or TV station courts advertisers in a profit-oriented marketing strategy is it courageous and independent, an important journalistic principle?

- Consider loyalties discussed in Chapter 1. Is a marketing-oriented media company loyal to self or society?

Now, walk through the five step decision-making process:

- Which ethical issues did you identify in reading, here in Chapter 6, about profit-oriented newspapers, magazines and TV operations?
- If newspapers fail financially without profit-oriented strategies, what alternatives do you see to courting advertisers in a marketing approach that includes the newsroom?

These are tough calls, aren't they? Well, be comforted. Even editors with years of experience find them tough, too.

Many editors instinctively seek balance and fairness—reporting all sides of a controversy—in a news story. Ensuring geographic balance by covering all areas of a market, country as well as city, is second nature. Producing subject diversity—covering science as well as politics, economics as well as sports—for many is second nature.

However, even casual study of American newspapers and TV news reveals many editors don't do as well covering the poor along with the rich, minorities as well as the majority, elderly as well as the young.

Summary

Operating profitably is essential for any newspaper or broadcast station. Without profit, no news organization can sustain itself.

But can ethical, socially responsible journalism flourish in any organization whose owners—whether a private individual or thousands of shareholders of publicly owned corporations—push unceasingly for ever more profit? This is the compelling ethical issue facing policy makers in American newsrooms today.

Growth of large, publicly owned communications conglomerates does not mean automatic degradation of journalistic quality. Some of the nation's finest journalism is produced by groups. But group ownership has brought many nonjournalists into key management positions, and journalists interested in ethical, responsible reporting must learn their language.

For good journalism is not cheap, and editors and news directors must convince top management to make the first step toward excellence by committing sufficient resources—money, newshole or air time and personnel.

A basic problem is that high-quality, responsible journalism does not guarantee financial success. Indeed, some newspaper managers achieve higher profits, at least short term, by intentionally holding down costs, and, thus, journalistic quality and responsibility.

Many editors are assuming corporate titles in an integrated marketing scheme that makes them responsible in part for not only creating the news product but also, in a sense, selling it. Though seemingly inevitable, this expansion of editors' roles is highly controversial. Some editors feel corporate titles and duties detract from their function as editors.

Newspapers claim special societal—and constitutional—status because they inform, educate and uplift. But to meet advertiser demands for more affluent readers, many newspapers are moving upscale in journalistic tone and market positioning. These newspapers boast of well-educated, high-income readers.

But who serves the poor along with the rich, the elderly along with the young, the minorities as well as the majority? Serious questions of ethics and social responsibility are created because less-attractive readers are left behind by elitist newspapers.

Notes

1. I discuss the marketing concept more fully in Conrad Fink, *Strategic Newspaper Management* (New York: Random House, 1988).
2. "Recession in Some Quarters Dampens Newspapers Profits," *presstime,* December 1990, p. 6.
3. The Richmond example and background on newspaper-operating profits are drawn from my experience in media management.
4. Ibid.
5. Figures for 1986 are from David Shaw, "Foreign Correspondents: It's On-the-job Training," *Los Angeles Times,* July 2, 1986, p. 7. For comparison, Executive Editor Ben Bradlee of the *Washington Post* stated in a July 11, 1983, letter to the author that his newsroom budget that year was $38 million. The *Los Angeles Times* 1982 newsroom budget was put at $45 million in "Coast Paper Feeling Pinch of Recession," the *New York Times,* Aug. 15, 1982, p. 13. In 1980, the *New York Times* spent $53 million covering the news.
6. Desmond Smith, "Is the Sun Setting on Network Nightly News?," *Washington Journalism Review,* January 1986, p. 30.
7. A. M. Rosenthal, letter to author, March 28, 1983.
8. Dallas insights were developed by author from a variety of sources, notably extended correspondence and conversations with Burl Osborne, president and editor of the *Dallas Morning News,* 1984–1986.
9. The count on daily (and weekly) newspapers in the United States fluctuates constantly; I use *Facts about Newspapers '94,* Newspaper Association of America, The Newspaper Center, Box 17407, Dulles Airport, Washington, D.C., 20041.
10. A very helpful look at various staff-to-circulation ratios is in "Newsroom Management Committee Report, 1979, Continuing Studies," Associated Press Managing Editors Association, 50 Rockefeller Plaza, New York, N.Y., 10020.
11. Newsprint prices escalated from $179 per metric ton in 1970 to $535 in early 1986, then to $685. See *Facts About Newspapers '94,* op. cit., for year-by-year price changes.
12. Figures on AP costs were developed in 1985–1986 by the Associated Press, 50 Rockefeller Plaza, New York, N.Y., 10020, to show the cost-benefit ratio for AP membership.

13. For excellent background see "Editors Need Larger Role in Budgeting Practices, INCFO Told," *Southern Newspaper Publishers Association Bulletin,* July 7, 1983, p. 3, and C. David Rambo, "Excellence," *presstime* November 1984, p. 15.
14. Desmond Smith, "Is the Sun Setting on Network Nightly News?" op. cit., quotes Don Hewitt, "the $1.5 million-a-year executive producer of '60 Minutes,'" as saying the show's profit for CBS in 1985 was $70 million.
15. "Recession in Some Quarters Dampens Newspaper Profits," op. cit.
16. Alex S. Jones, "Stagnant Revenue Worrying Editors," *New York Times,* April 14, 1986, p. 13.
17. Alex S. Jones, "Newspaper Editors on Business Role," *New York Times,* April 14, 1985, p. 11.
18. *General Policies,* a handbook, Longview Publishing Co., P.O. Box 189, Longview, Wash., 98632.
19. *Facts about Newspapers, '94,* op. cit.
20. Annual Report 1984, Dow Jones and Company, Inc., World Financial Center, 200 Liberty Street, New York, N.Y., 10281.
21. Walter E. Mattson, Morton Newspaper Forum, Montreal, May 3, 1984.
22. "Our Readers Have Big Appetites For Spending," *Los Angeles Times,* advertisement, *Advertising Age,* May 9, 1983, p. M-15.
23. "Fact Is, The People with Money and Influence in Dallas Read *The Morning News,*" advertisement, *Advertising Age,* Aug. 15, 1983, p. 30.
24. "'Post' Time For Revamped Sunday Book," *Advertising Age,* April 21, 1986, p. 35.
25. Excerpts from James Squires, *Read All about It* (New York: Times Books division of Random House, Inc., 1993).
26. Penetration figures from *Circulation, '93,* published by Standard Rate & Data Service, 3004 Glenview Rd., Wilmette, Ill., 60091.
27. Tom Winship, then *Globe* editor, letter to author, March 11, 1983.

CHAPTER 7

ETHICS IN THE COUNTINGHOUSE

The integrated marketing concept fashionable in media management tightly links the newsroom with countinghouse departments in a team effort to assure financial success of a newspaper, magazine or broadcast operation. That means journalists work within a profit-driven context that inevitably bears directly on the day-to-day quality—the principles and ethics—of their reporting and writing.

In Chapter 7, we examine strategic business imperatives that have major influence on the newsroom and all who labor in it.

Advertising supports all free-enterprise media, so we'll pay particular attention to the media's role in carrying buyer and seller messages into the commercial marketplace. Understand the dynamics of advertising or you cannot understand the corporate ethos of the media or how you and your ethical principles can fit in as a journalist.

We'll also look at other business-side activity—particularly in the executive suite—and how that affects journalists trying to do the ethically "right thing."

ADVERTISING: THE MOTHER LODE

Get used to it: Your newsroom colleagues probably will grumble about advertising department "business types" who vigorously chase up and down Main Street after ad dollars. But that chase is the core of the management strategy directing newspaper, magazine and broadcast operations—and those dollars will pay your salary.

Advertisers contribute about 75 to 80 percent of most daily newspapers' total revenue. With their purchases, readers contribute about 20 to 25 percent—not

Table 7–1
Competition for advertising dollars

	Total Ad Dollars (millions)	Percentage of Total
Newspapers	$31,906	23.1
Television	30,600	22.2
Radio	9,390	6.8
Magazines	7,420	5.4
Farm publications	245	0.2[1]

enough to cover the newsprint on which news is printed, let alone other operating costs.

In magazines, 49 to 50 percent of revenue generally comes from advertisers. Although they've increased subscription rates, most magazines cannot live without advertising, either. Only a few—*Ms.* and *Consumer Reports* among them—carry no ads.

Commercial television and radio are free to viewers and listeners, of course, so advertisers contribute 100 percent of broadcast's revenue. That increases advertisers' importance to—and thus influence over—how networks and stations are operated.

Some cable-TV systems are supported primarily through subscriber fees but will be more advertiser-oriented in the future—as will new electronic media just over the technological horizon.

An increasingly competitive fight is under way for advertising dollars—a mother lode that exceeded $137 billion in 1993. See Table 7–1 to show how the lode was divided.

In addition to fighting each other, the traditional media battle two other advertising competitors:

- *Direct mail,* with $27.4 billion or 19.9 percent of the total, is America's most rapidly expanding advertising medium. Its strength is ability to precisely target consumers for advertisers: reaching the homes of wine drinkers (but not beer drinkers) for wine advertisers, focusing on Cadillac lovers (not pickup truck buffs) and so forth. Traditional media select content that will attract such niche audiences. Newspapers produce zoned editions for special audiences, for example; magazines construct an editorial tone sure to attract certain readers (*Forbes* positions itself as a "capitalist tool" for millionaires); TV and radio preselect audiences through programming—golden oldies for older radio listeners, for example, rock for youthful audiences.
- *Yellow Pages,* with $9.5 billion or 6.9 percent of the total, challenge classified advertising, which provides 50 percent of total advertising revenue for some newspapers. Your generation of journalists will work for, or compete against, news and information media using telephone company technology. All traditional media today are preparing for a new electronic highway of two-way interactive circuits that will link American homes to computerized reservoirs of news, information—and advertising.

MONEY, EDITORS AND ETHICS

Highly complex ethical questions arise in a media environment structured around the vast sums of money in advertising and the competitive fight for it.

For editors, principal concern is that under the integrated marketing concept, advertising's importance to the financial success of any newspaper or television operation creates tight linkage between newsroom and advertising department, between editor and sales director. Editors must fashion news, information and entertainment packages that attract readers or viewers who, for their affluence or other attributes, are designated by advertising strategists as important.

Often this is only implicitly agreed between editors and advertising executives. It is considered very bad form at most newspapers and television networks for the advertising department to explicitly suggest how journalists should treat a story or create the news product.

But, as editors join integrated management teams, willing cooperation develops between departments in joint design of marketing strategy for news content, journalistic tone and audience segments sought.

Nevertheless, there are occasions—and every experienced journalist knows of some—when advertising considerations overtly intrude into, distort even, the news process.

ETHICS IN ADVERTISING

The basic ethical question: Are consumer and society served by advertising or, as critics argue, is advertising wasteful, unnecessary and simply devoid of any redeeming social value?

Advertising's defenders—media executives among them, naturally—argue it helps consumers make intelligent choices by communicating to them valuable information on products and services.

Defenders see advertising creating consumer desire that stimulates consumption that, in turn, permits the free enterprise system and mass production with all its efficiencies and lower prices.[2]

Without advertising, its defenders say, business, commerce and industry would slow and the consumption-oriented American economy—richest in the world—would falter.

Importantly, advertising revenue gives American newspapers and television the financial independence from government or political groups that's essential to journalistic independence. Being able to avoid government or political subsidies gives American media extraordinary freedom compared to state-supported (or state-dominated) media of many other countries.

Of course, relying heavily on advertisers can create dependence on them and expose newspapers and television operations, particularly those marginally profitable, to economic pressure. That pressure sometimes is intense.

In most cities, for example, just a few advertisers provide most newspaper revenue. The *New York Daily News,* only narrowly profitable despite circulation then of 1.3 million, lost $11 million in annual revenue when just two companies, Gimbels and Ohrbachs, closed department stores in New York City. The *News'* publisher said, "Survival is at stake and there is no time to lose." Scores of employees were laid off; the newsroom budget was slashed—and the paper slid into financial disarray that, by 1993, left it in jeopardy.

Many newspapers that failed did so for lack of ad dollars, not reader support. The *Philadelphia Bulletin, Washington Star, Cleveland Press* and other famous but now-defunct newspapers had circulation in the hundreds of thousands when they folded.

Television networks also rely heavily on multimillion dollar contracts with relatively few national advertisers. This can expose TV to heavy outside influence on programming. For example, in 1987, Chrysler Corp. objected to content of an ABC miniseries, *Amerika,* which depicted a Soviet takeover of the United States. Chrysler pulled $7 million worth of commercials from the program, which cost $40 million to produce.

WHAT THE CRITICS SAY

Advertising critics argue the following:

- Advertising adds enormously to selling costs eventually paid by consumers, without adding actual value to goods or services produced.
- Advertising, particularly on television, doesn't fill an information need because its often sketchy slogans and 30-second jingles (such as Coca-Cola's "It's the real thing") don't truly inform consumers about a product; advertising, in fact, is designed only to sell, not inform.
- Advertising doesn't create consumer desire; rather, it simply shifts desire from one product to another. And this, critics say, negates claim that advertising engenders mass consumption and its resultant benefits to society.
- Advertising creates unnecessary materialistic consumer desires that are psychological in origin and, thus, advertising is manipulative and wasteful. Economist John Kenneth Galbraith claims, for example, an individual's physical needs, such as food and shelter, are finite and quickly met, so much advertising is aimed at creating expandable desire for such things as social acceptability, sexual attractiveness or personal beauty.[3]

Advertising permits large, financially strong firms to dominate an industry because only they can afford high-cost advertising. With small firms thus effectively barred from an influential role, the few companies dominant in the market can raise prices at will.

Neither supporters of advertising nor its critics can prove its true social effect. Some critics argue, for example, advertising helps small firms enter the market against larger competitors.

And, far from clear is whether advertising creates societal values or merely reflects them. Nor is it possible to measure accurately advertising's impact on consumer desires. After all, some products and services flourish without formal advertising (illicit drugs and prostitution are two).

PUBLIC WORRIES ABOUT ETHICS

It is possible to get a firm grasp on consumer perceptions of advertising: the widespread belief it raises costs, which consumers must pay; that it creates unnecessary demand; and sometimes is untruthful, misleading and often insultingly strident, intrusive, unpleasant and simplistic.

Further, the perception persists that advertisers influence news coverage in unethical ways.

Newspaper researcher Ruth Clark finds, "A majority [57 percent] of men and women believe news coverage often is influenced by advertisers or other business interests. Only 30 percent disagree, and 13 percent are not sure."[4]

Television gets even lower marks, consistently ranking behind newspapers in such things as believability of advertising (68 percent of respondents in one poll found newspaper advertising "believable and very believable"; only 34 percent so voted for television).[5]

Other evidence of societal concern over advertising erupted when civil rights groups pressured newspapers to insist advertisers show minorities in ads. The Lawyers' Committee for Civil Rights under Law said one study showed minorities were depicted in fewer than 2 percent of the *Washington Post*'s real estate ads. The *Post* subsequently wrote advertisers they had to show blacks in at least 25 percent of display ads and prominently feature the equal housing logo. The *New York Times* and other newspapers have similar policies.

For media executives—and journalists—all this raises important questions: how to improve public perception of the media, protect corporate self-interest, guard advertising's huge revenues—and still operate in an ethical, socially responsible manner.

ETHICS AND CORPORATE SELF-INTEREST

In advertising departments, more than in newsrooms, it is difficult to isolate for examination how newspaper and television executives truly regard many ethical issues. Corporate self-interest is so intertwined with advertising ethics that it is nearly impossible to tell where ethics begin and self-interest ends.

The primary reason for this linkage, of course, is the enormous financial importance of advertising. But other factors enter the linkage, too.

First, many media executives say advertising is a significant portion of the total information service provided to readers or viewers. They say public perception of their newspaper or television operation depends on the accuracy, reliability, tone and, yes, ethical quality of advertising content, as well as news content. Newspaper executives know, for example, that substantial circulation is with readers who buy the paper as much for advertising as news; classified advertising ranks as popular reading material. So, many statements of ethical principle in newspaper and television advertising really are image-building efforts.

Second, executives in community newspapering and broadcasting argue advertising contributes heavily to local economic activity, introducing buyer to seller and energizing, if not creating, business and commerce. *And that more than subtly changes their view of social responsibility.* Although a news executive may see the mission of a newspaper or TV station as observing from the sidelines and commenting with disinterested detachment, advertising executives often see it as one of participating. This tends to pull advertising executives into close cooperation with business and industry, into community boosterism ("What's good for this town is good for my newspaper").

Third, this is an unprecedentedly litigious era for the American media, and extremely important legal considerations surround advertising. So, statements of ethical principle tend to reflect the need for avoiding lawsuits as much as resolving any underlying ethical issues. Also, crucial questions of First Amendment rights arise frequently in advertising and, as in the growing controversy over whether tobacco advertising should be made illegal, many statements of ethical principle actually are designed to protect in the advertising department the right to publish that is so important in the news department.

ETHICS AND SELF-INTEREST BLEND

Note the blend of ethical principle and self-interest in these statements:

- CBS Television, in its highly detailed "Advertising Guidelines," states, "CBS believes that advertising is an important element of the information presented to broadcast audiences. In this connection, CBS recognizes its responsibility to review—for truth, taste and legal requirements—all advertising submitted for broadcast."[6]
- The *St. Petersburg (Fla.) Times* introduces its "Advertising Standards of Acceptability," by stating, "The intent of these standards is to encourage and preserve believability in advertising, to multiply its impact and effectiveness, and to promote accountability in sales and marketing throughout the Suncoast market area. The Times Publishing Company advertising columns are open to competition of all legitimate advertisers."[7]

Robert P. Smith, head of the *New York Times* advertising Acceptability Department, is more specific:

> The character of a newspaper is determined not only by its news and editorial content, but also by the advertising it publishes. Those that accept inaccurate, misleading, deceptive, or offensive advertising, or that tolerate slipshod performance by advertisers run the risk of demeaning their most valuable asset—their credibility. That's just plain bad business.
>
> Don't get me wrong. It's gratifying to be on "the side of the angels" for its own sake. But nowhere is it written that concern for the welfare of the reader and sound business practice are mutually exclusive. On the contrary, self-regulation and discipline with regard to the acceptance of advertising is about as good an example as you will find to illustrate the profitability of principle.[8]

VIEWPOINT

Advertising and the First Amendment

"[A]dvertisers and agencies . . . have come to prize the freedom of speech that you and your editors have protected for us for so long. So, believe with me. Act with me. Defend me, when I say that the freedom of expression belongs to the advocates as well as the observers. Know that any limitation on the freedom to advertise is a direct obstacle to your freedom to cover a trial, write an editorial or publish a political column."

Louis T. Hagopian, then chairman of N W Ayer, Inc., the oldest U.S. advertising agency[9]

ETHICAL SCREENING OF ADVERTISING

Many newspapers and television operations protect the sanctity of their advertising as zealously as they guard the ethical character of their news content. They do so with codes of acceptability that police advertising in three broad aspects of communication:

First, codes address the originator or authors of advertising, attempting to prevent deception by the manufacturer of a product, its advertising agency and anyone involved in creating an ad.

NBC says "ultimate responsibility for advertising rests with the advertiser," and advertising agencies "should consult the Broadcast Standards Department in advance of production." It adds, "NBC accepts advertising only after securing satisfactory evidence of the integrity of the advertiser. . . ."

ABC reserves the "right to investigate the advertiser and the accuracy of all statements and claims made in commercial copy."

Codes insist advertisers not only avoid outright falsehood, but also deception through misleading ads.[10]

Second, however, codes by their very nature—and sometimes, explicitly—commit the newspaper or network, as the medium of advertising, to accept responsibility. The *St. Petersburg (Fla.) Times* says in its acceptability code that it

> does not, and will not, knowingly accept any advertisement that may be misleading, deceptive, fraudulent, unlawful, is immorally suggestive or in bad taste. Any advertising which tends to destroy the confidence of our readers is unacceptable. In order to fully serve the advertiser, the Times Publishing Company must have the full confidence of its readers. Truth and good taste must prevail.[11]

Paul Ruffin, classified ad manager of the *Eugene (Ore.) Register-Guard,* says he applies to advertising the same standards of truth applied to news: "What it comes right down to is a person delivering wood and shorting some 85-year-old widow woman. She calls me. . . . I find out what happened. . . . If [the advertis-

VIEWPOINT

Good Taste, Time and Audience

"All advertising messages should be prepared with proper consideration of the type of product being advertised, the time of broadcast, and the audience to whom the advertising is directed. Good taste must always govern the content, placement, and presentation of announcements."

ABC *Advertising Standards and Guidelines*

ers] do not make it up or give her money back, I will not accept their advertising anymore."[12]

Third, codes address the audience for advertising. Most codes consider advertising's acceptability within the context of the audience at which it is aimed.

Television network codes state, for example, that advertising acceptable for adults might not be acceptable for an audience of children unable to filter out hyperbole or misleading nuances easily recognized by adults. CBS's code states, "CBS recognizes the special obligations it has as a responsible broadcaster to insure that commercial announcements directed to children are not misleading in any way."[13]

WHAT'S ACCEPTABLE AND WHAT ISN'T

Newspapers broadly agree on which types of advertising will be accepted and which won't. Television has even stronger consensus and, particularly at the network level, has extremely detailed codes.

In its "Advertising Policy Manual" for employees, the *Miami Herald* states, "A newspaper is an invited guest in the home. Therefore, in order to maintain an atmosphere of good taste and believability for both readers and advertisers, The Miami Herald Publishing Company holds to the following restrictions." It lists 13 categories of unacceptable advertising and 22 acceptable "subject to restrictions."[14]

The *St. Petersburg (Fla.) Times*—like many newspapers—sets a moral tone for its "Advertising Standards of Acceptability": "No advertising is acceptable which, in the publisher's judgment, will irritate the sensibilities of, or result in harm or insult to, any segment of the Times Publishing Company's wide readership. Any advertising that casts unfavorable reflection, directly, or indirectly, upon any individual, group, race, creed, religion, organization, institution, competitive merchandise, business or profession is likewise unacceptable."[15]

GUARDIANS AGAINST IMMORALITY?

Inevitably, setting themselves up as guardians against immorally suggestive advertising can make censors of the media.

VIEWPOINT

Principles versus Pocketbook

"I could hardly believe my eyes when I noticed ads for German handguns and assault rifles in a recent issue of the *Constitution.* Aren't you the people who froth at the mouth editorially in condemnation of gun ownership by the citizenry? Like all of your liberal ilk, it is obvious that your loudly stated 'principles' stop at your pocketbook."

A reader's letter to the editor, *Atlanta Constitution,* May 28, 1993, p. A10

Newspapers and television stations around the country refused to accept advertising on a film titled, *Sexual Perversity in Chicago.* The film was renamed, *About Last Night.*

For years, the media rejected condom advertising on grounds that condoms were birth control devices considered immoral by some or, simply, because the product dealt with a subject offensive to many.

However, in view of increasingly explicit news coverage of sex and sexually transmitted diseases, an advertising policy change was easy for many newspapers and TV stations when health officials called for condom advertising to combat spread of AIDS. For many, condom ads stressing disease control were acceptable—if they didn't mention birth control. Condom companies quickly seized on the difference and began producing ad copy featuring, for example, a young woman saying, "I'll do a lot for love. But I'm not ready to die for it."

GROUNDS FOR REJECTION

Broadly, newspaper codes reject advertising that does the following:

- Violates any law (including libel) or encourages violation. Many, for example, refuse ads for devices motorists use to detect police radar.
- Is untruthful, misleading, indecent, offensive or in poor taste. In every case, the publisher retains the right to interpret the impact or meaning of advertising or, indeed, whether to run it at all.
- Begs, offers matrimony, escort services, or "companionship." (*Newsday,* Times Mirror Corporation's 770,000-circulation daily on Long Island, publishes many personals but rejects any deemed flaky or kinky.) Adult bookstores ads are rejected. The *St. Petersburg Times* accepts no amusement ads "that state or imply conduct that is considered morally or socially unacceptable." X-rated movie ads "can be no longer than 1 column by 1 inch in size and cannot contain illustrations." The newspaper reserves the right to change X-rated film titles considered suggestive.
- Offers get-rich-quick schemes or something of value for nothing.

CASE STUDY

Tobacco Ads: A Moral Contradiction?

On front pages, American newspapers report the latest study linking use of tobacco to cancer.

On editorial pages, American newspapers sound the alarm, calling for massive research into cancer and its causes.

Throughout their pages, American newspapers publish advertisements for tobacco products, including cigarettes, which, according to no less than the Surgeon General of the United States, are a deadly product.

A moral contradiction?

Are newspapers and magazines failing in their moral and social responsibilities by helping promote a product that, much of medical science says, *kills when used as intended*?

Or, is tobacco advertising legitimate commercial free speech? Should advertising be illegal for a product legally manufactured and sold?

If print media refuse tobacco advertising on moral grounds, would that establish a precedent of censorship that logically extended to other dangerous products—alcohol, guns, high-speed cars?

Should tobacco ads in print be outlawed, as they have been on TV and radio?

The influential American Medical Association and American Cancer Society are among those demanding a ban on tobacco advertising, particularly ads directed at young people.

- Employs bait and switch tactics under which the plan is not to sell the advertised product at the price listed—or at all—but, rather, to entice customers and then offer another product or service.
- Offers mail-order weapons, bust developers, baldness remedies, diet pills, contraceptives or, in the words of the *Miami Herald,* ads "injurious to the health or morals of a reader." (The *New York Times* also does its bit in protecting endangered species of animals; it won't accept ads for fur or leather products made from their hides.)
- Is intended as a joke or a hoax.

Some advertising is accepted only under certain conditions:

- Employment advertising must actually offer employment and state conditions. Most papers reject any that even implies religious, nationality, sex, race or age preferences.

Resisting a ban are the Newspaper Association of America (NAA) and others who say a ban would threaten commercial free speech and, thus, the First Amendment.

NAA, which packs a public relations wallop because it represents most daily newspapers, with 90 percent of total circulation, links all forms of advertising to wider constitutional right: "Commercial speech also is protected under the First Amendment . . . legal products and services should be legal to advertise . . . governmental restrictions on advertising content often infringe unnecessarily upon commercial speech. . . ."[16]

Antismoking forces argue the Constitution's framers never intended it should protect such things as tobacco advertising.

Joe B. Tye, president of an antismoking group, wrote for the *Wall Street Journal*:

> Cigarette makers like to frame the issue as one of freedom of speech. Any attempt to restrict their efforts to promote smoking is portrayed as a violation of First Amendment rights and the first step toward mass censorship of commercial speech. In fact, no other industry has abused freedom of speech so egregiously. For 60 years, cigarette firms have used unfounded health claims to encourage people to smoke despite the risk of harm.

Opinions from newspaper and magazine executives:

> For the young boy who thinks, perhaps, that smoking will make him a man, Camel offers ads and billboards with anthropomorphic Old Joe, a stud camel in flashy bow tie surrounded at the beach, near the pool table, and at the gambling casino by curvaceous young women. In other ads, the Marlboro Man oozes machismo.
>
> For girls, an ad for Newport Stripes shows a beach scene with a gaggle of giggling, healthy, swimsuit-clad young women who look no older than my 16-year-old daughter. An ad for Virginia Slims still associates smoking with female independence: A modishly dressed young woman, cigarette in hand, complements the headline—'You've come a long way, baby.'

- Political advertising usually carries many restrictions, including prohibitions against political charges made so close to an election they cannot be answered. (Without exception, newspapers require that politicians pay in advance.)
- Religious advertising must not attack other religions or imply faith healing.
- Business opportunity advertising undergoes detailed scrutiny. Many newspapers require advertisers to submit detailed verification of claims made in ad copy and proof they conform to relevant laws. The aim is to weed out fraudulent pie-in-the-sky offers.
- Service advertising is severely restricted. The *Tampa (Fla.) Tribune,* for example, requires building contractors to include in ads the number of their competency license issued by the city. This policy also was established at the *St. Petersburg (Fla.) Times* after its own reporters found 25 percent of its home improvement advertisers lacked necessary licensing.

CASE STUDY, *continued*

> . . . newspapers need not oppose the freedom of cigarette companies to advertise in order to exercise their own freedom to reject cigarette ads . . .
>
> If newspapers and magazines kicked the cigarette ad habit, perhaps Americans would find it easier to refrain from becoming addicted to cigarettes. That's reason enough for editors to ask their publications to stop running cigarette ads.

Loren Ghiglione, editor of the *Southbridge (Mass.) News* and, at the time, president of the American Society of Newspaper Editors[17]

Should editors critique advertising policy, as Ghiglione suggests? One view:

> I believe it is wrong to invite editors and reporters to censor and prune the advertising sales department's customer list.
>
> I'm troubled by the notion that Mr. Ghiglione's idea would place newspaper editors in the position of denying access to newspapers to a segment of our nation's business community.
>
> As for publishers, if they agree to drop cigarette ads to please their editor, why stop with cigarettes? How do they react when the same activist editors later demand that they ban ads from oil companies that have polluted a shoreline, or the air? What about ads for alcoholic beverages? Habit-forming drugs? Caffeine products? Airlines that lost their luggage? At *what point would editors get out* of the censorship business?
>
> Isn't it better for editors to assume newspapers and magazine publishers are grown-ups, that they've heard all the arguments for and against cigarette smoking and cigarette advertising and don't really need input from their editors on this matter?

Fred Danzig, editor, *Advertising Age* magazine[18]

Yet another view:

> . . . I agree that everything possible should be done to discourage persons from smoking. But trampling on freedom is not the way to do that, and banning ads—be it self-censorship by

It's not known how many newspapers have written codes of acceptability or subscribe to the Advertising Code of American Business (see the code, which can be found in Appendix F). However, hundreds refuse at least one type of advertising, including liquor ads.[21]

TELEVISION'S ETHICAL CONSENSUS

Television's approach to ethics and social responsibility in advertising is one of strong consensus established primarily by the three major networks.

Detailed advertising guidelines published by ABC, NBC and CBS are strikingly similar in content and clearly reflect societal pressures on television since its development as a commercial medium—really beginning, we should remem-

publishers or government-imposed censorship (as we have in broadcasting)—is suppressing freedom.

Where will we draw the line? Will we drop ads for fast food because of the fat that kills people? Will we no longer accept ads urging people to visit Florida, because of the peril of skin cancer? Will we stop ads for liquor? After all, drunk drivers are a true peril. What about ads for radar detectors? Surely, they have but one purpose—to break the law.

We fight speech with more speech, not with suppression. It's just the wrong thing to do.

Michael Gartner, then president of NBC News and co-owner of the *Ames (Iowa) Daily Tribune*[19]

Tobacco advertising is important to newspapers but yields less revenue than many other national ad categories, such as transportation/travel and automotive. Magazines took in $223 million in tobacco advertising in 1992, down from $290 million in 1991 and $373 million in 1991.[20]

Some publications voluntarily drop tobacco advertising. The *Saturday Evening Post* did in 1983, at cost of about $400,000 in annual lost revenue. It cost the *Seattle Times* over $100,000 annually to follow suit in 1993.

Now, *You* Make the Call

Questions Which ethical issue(s) do you identify in the controversy over tobacco ads? Should print media refuse tobacco ads? Should they be made illegal?

Which societal values come into play? Do newspapers and magazines run afoul of truth-telling, humaneness and stewardship in carrying tobacco ads?

Consider journalistic principles we have discussed. Are print media truly guarding the First Amendment when they decline to censor tobacco ads? Are they serving the public?

Which of the loyalties discussed in Chapter 1 influence defenders of tobacco ads? Are media that carry ads true to self or society?

ber, only in the 1950s. Newspapers, by contrast, have had many decades to develop ethical consensus.

Four sources of pressure are instrumental in shaping television's stance.

THE LAW

The Federal Communications Commission can lift broadcast licenses (though it rarely does) for rules infractions, and along with other federal agencies, particularly the Federal Trade Commission, strongly influences advertising practices.

To some extent, federal scrutiny prevents the television industry from effectively regulating its own activities. For example, the National Association of Broadcasters dropped its code suggesting limits on number and length of commercials after a federal court found guidelines violated the Sherman Antitrust Act.

No broadcast executives can ever forget the federal presence. For many in television conforming to regulatory requirements is an end in itself that has stunted individual or corporate development of ethical thinking in advertising (as well as news). For example, television faces no ethical dilemma over cigarette advertising; the federal government kicked it off the airways.

Certainly, network guidelines in advertising are heavily weighted to ensure legal and regulatory—as distinct from ethical—requirements are met.

SPECIAL INTEREST GROUPS

Law reflects societal attitudes, of course, so regulatory surveillance of television is societal pressure. But there is more to it than that.

Because of its amazing ubiquity—over 98 percent of all American homes have sets—society in general and special interest groups in particular police television with intensity. This causes every advertising executive to place pleasing them second only to conforming to the law.

Consumer advocates focus strongly on television advertising content, truthfulness, accuracy and impact on audiences, particularly children. Such pressure can further stunt purely ethical development in television advertising either by individuals or corporations. Placating the Federal Trade Commission and consumer advocates can be a full-time job for anyone.

Strong societal pressure leads television in what might appear to be self-restraining ethical volunteerism but really is designed to fend off special interests or legal pressure. For example, the networks tightly restrict beer and wine commercials (ever see one of those happy guys actually drink a beer in a TV commercial?). With beer and wine commercials worth millions annually, the networks want to preempt growing societal pressure for a total ban on any advertising of alcoholic beverages. Because most stations are owned by or affiliated with a network, the Big Three set the consensus for the entire industry.

MONEY

For any advertising medium, money is pressure—and TV advertising represents money, lots of it.

A single commercial on a top-rated network show brings in hundreds of thousands of dollars; ad revenues for one show total millions. For an evening, networks take in tens of millions of dollars.

That's why network executives hate to preempt entertainment programming—and its lucrative commercials—for news coverage. That's why a local station often won't break into afternoon soaps (and their lucrative commercials) with a hot news story and, instead, will insert a quick one-liner between commercials: "Fire strikes downtown business district. Details at 6."

COMPETITION

There is a fierce fight for TV advertising at both the national and local levels.

Nationally, the three major networks, joined recently by Fox and Cable News Network, battle not only other competitors but, particularly, each other. Conversely, until new technology in the 1980s permitted the *Wall Street Journal*, the *New York Times* and *USA Today* to launch truly national editions, there was no newspaper competition at that level.

And, whereas most cities long ago were reduced to one newspaper, direct head-on competition in local television is fierce. Most cities have three network affiliates, an independent or two, public broadcasting and a plethora of cable channels—all fighting for the same ad dollar.

Thus, the struggle for audience is all-consuming. Whoever—or whatever—pulls in most viewers wins because the higher the ratings, the higher the ad rates.

Now, if a sitcom attracts well over 50 million viewers to NBC of a Thursday evening, as "The Cosby Show" did, will CBS or ABC that night feature newsy public service programming? Of course not; that would surrender the entire evening to NBC.

At the local level, if one station's news achieves higher ratings with a jazzy set, handsome young anchors, the happiest chatter in town—and a decided soft pedal on serious, deep-dig journalism—will its competitors counter with craggy, decidedly unhandsome but truly experienced reporters who go for serious news? Of course not, again.

Thus is consensus established in local TV news programming and attitudes: The drive for ratings frequently leads to formula journalism acceptable to the widest possible audience. And if that means an "Action News" format of blown-dry anchors, helicopters in the sky and ambush interviews down here, so be it.

LEVELING WITH READER AND VIEWER

An important ethical issue in advertising is whether newspapers or television truly inform readers and viewers about what is being placed before them. Neither medium is above letting advertisers slip one over on the audience, now and then.

Networks, for example, ban commercials that attempt to lend products respectability by using pseudo reporters, fake physicians or phony scientists to do the pitch. Gone is the distinguished gentleman wearing a doctor's white coat in a laboratory who pitches aspirin.

Yet, television permits commercials implying the way to happiness with friends is to drink beer, that buying a new car will get a fellow a beautiful woman, that eating this cereal, not that one, promises health and good times.

It's in the very nature of sight-and-sound advertising that gullible viewers are thus bamboozled—and television lets it happen.

NEWSPAPER CON JOBS

Many newspapers con readers with advertorials, advertisements made to look like news copy, or an advertising insert that looks for all the world like a special news supplement. Ad executives love advertising that looks like news because, as one puts it, people are five times more likely to read editorial as ads.[22]

The ethical way to handle such copy is to clearly label it as advertising and set it in type distinctly different from type used in news columns. Special inserts should carry editor's notes informing readers the copy is advertising and stating whether the copy was prepared by qualified newspersons, advertising employees or outside stringers—or ad agency writers.

The *New York Times* did that with a notice in an insert on condominiums: "Advertising Supplement to the *New York Times.*" Each page was labeled "advertisement." Then: "This advertising supplement is sponsored by participating advertisers. The promotional material was prepared under the direction of Ernest Dickinson and did not involve the *Times* reporting or editing staff."[23]

Leveling with readers and viewers in financial advertising got a big boost—but more from federal truth-in-lending laws than the collective conscience of the advertising world. It's now possible to read some advertising and figure out, for example, the true annual percentage rate of interest you'll pay on a loan or time purchase. But it's also possible to see a salesman banging on a car hood shouting at the camera, "Only $100 a month"—and neglecting to say whether that is monthly for nearly a lifetime.

CONSCIENCE AND THE LAW CLASH

For broadcasting, conscience and the law clashed for decades over advocacy or controversial issue advertising.

For 38 years, the FCC's fairness doctrine required broadcasting to give opposing sides "reasonable opportunity" to be heard on controversial issues, a principle held to apply also to advertising. Thus, the networks and most television stations rejected issue advertising. This, of course, put television in the position of denying access by proponents of controversial ideas and denied viewers the opportunity to see or hear them.

The FCC abolished the fairness doctrine in 1987.

Newspapers vigorously defend their right to reject any advertisement, but most open their pages to issue advertising. Says the *New York Times'* Smith:

> We've published opinion advertisements representing a wide range of public discourse—from the John Birch Society to the Communist Party. In our view, the First Amendment does not only guarantee a newspaper's right to disseminate news or publish editorials and commercial messages but it also guarantees the public's right to enter into open discussion in the realm of ideas.[24]

The *Times* used its news pages to level with readers when it, along with other newspapers, was hoaxed by a bogus advertisement. A lengthy article explained why the *Times* didn't properly check the origin of the ad that "seemed to attribute anti-Israel sentiments to six relief organizations [which] later disavowed any connection with it." The ad was signed by a group that gave an address later found to be false. What it boiled down to, the *Times* informed its readers, was that checking such things prior to publication "was impeded by the fact that many advertising executives, advertisers and executives of newspapers held differing views as to whose job it was."[25]

That may not have made readers any happier, but it did level with them on what went wrong.

A similarly responsible explanation was published by the *Athens (Ga.) Banner-Herald and Daily News* when a reader wrote complaining about content. Executive Editor Hank Johnson told his readers in a Sunday column:

> She canceled her subscription, in part she said, "because of our disgust at the lack of objectivity of your 'Dining Out' column. Every week, the column gushes over a different restaurant. It appears that the restaurants must pay to have this column run, since we have yet to see a complaint about food/service—quite unrealistic. This is typical small-town 'good-boy' reporting and we do not wish to support it through subscription."

The letter writer had stumbled on a flagrant violation of advertising ethics. "Dining Out" was an advertorial, cleverly written and laid out to appear as news copy. Johnson's explanation to readers continued:

> Well, as a matter of fact, the "Dining Out" column . . . is a paid advertisement. The restaurants whose ads appear on the page sign a contract to advertise on that page. In addition to the ad which runs every week each restaurant is periodically allowed to tell its own story.
>
> Given those circumstances, it is easy to understand why the letter writer had never seen a complaint in the "Dining Out" column. Our mistake was in assuming that it would be obvious to readers that the description of the restaurant, its food and service, was not objective and clearly was not a straight story or legitimate review.
>
> Steps have been taken to correct that.
>
> While we're clearing up misunderstandings, I should point out that the "Business Review" page that runs in both Monday papers is done the same way as "Dining Out."[26]

That's leveling with readers, and it is the way newspapers should deal with the deplorably unethical advertorial.

THE PRICE TAG ON ETHICS

Ethics in advertising won't happen, of course, unless management is willing to make financial sacrifice for ethical principle.

Substantial revenue can be lost if ads are rejected on ethical grounds or the newsroom proceeds with coverage offensive to a major advertiser.

Newspaper and television lore is burdened with examples of managers who caved in before that harsh reality. But many stand firm on principle, even at considerable cost.

The *Wall Street Journal* reported on Mobil Corp., its executives and their families despite clear signs this would cause trouble. Citing "five years of problems," Mobil announced in 1984 it would not give the *Journal* any information on its corporate affairs, wouldn't grant interviews to *Journal* reporters and would cancel its advertising. That cost the *Journal* advertising worth $500,000 annually, a significant but hardly fatal loss for the hugely successful *Journal*.[27]

Lawrence Armour, *Journal* corporate relations director said, "The point is, we're not in the business of acting as cheerleaders for corporate America and

VIEWPOINT

Improper Advertiser Influence

Advertisers often try to influence news coverage—and sometimes succeed.

A 1992 survey by Lawrence Soley and Robert Craig of Marquette University found that of 150 newspaper editors responding:

- 89.8 percent said they knew of advertisers attempting to influence new content.
- 71.4 percent of editors said advertisers tried to have specific stories killed.
- 89.1 percent said advertisers withdrew ads because of coverage.
- 36.7 percent said advertisers had *succeeded* in influencing story content.[28]

A separate study by the nonprofit Center for the Study of Commercialism found widespread advertiser favoritism among newspapers. The principal author of the study, Prof. Ron Collins of Catholic University, said that with newspapers facing tough financial times, during the recession of the early 1990s, there was increased tendency to cater to advertisers.

"It's one of the best-kept secrets about censorship in America today," Collins told the *Wall Street Journal.*[29]

Cathleen Black, president of the Newspaper Association of America, commented, "Advertisers feel they have a little bit more clout when times are tough."

John Crowley, member of the National Advertising Review Board:

"There's certainly a point where an advertiser has every right *as a citizen* to influence editorial content.

"But as soon as an advertiser begins to use the threat of his money spent with the publication, it's an improper influence on editorial content."[30]

Sometimes, advertiser pressure tactics stir a backlash. For example, in 1993, a year when all media were scrambling for ad revenue, the German automaker, Mercedes-Benz of North America, wrote about 30 magazines: pull our ads from any issue carrying negative stories about our company *or* Germany, or we'll refuse to pay for the ads. Mercedes-Benz at the time was spending a significant $14.5 million annually in magazine advertising.

There is *unwritten* agreement by many newspapers and magazines to pull airline ads from any issue reporting plane crashes. Many publications also avoid placing cigarette ads next to stories about cancer. But the blatant threats by Mercedes-Benz stirred such a negative reaction that the company quickly rescinded its policy.

sometimes this offends certain people. But they seem to understand and they seem to quickly get over their immediate annoyances. . . ."

The *Journal* tangled in 1954 with powerful General Motors Corp., always one of the biggest spenders on advertising. A *Journal* reporter obtained details of new cars GM planned for the following year, a tightly guarded secret. Furious GM executives canceled all advertising in the *Journal.* The boycott lasted just one month.

Years later, it became apparent there had been an unexpected bonus in the affair for the *Journal.* Vice Chairman Donald MacDonald of the *Journal* commented, "It put us on the map. GM's actions were on radio and in newspapers all over the country. It gave us credibility. It said you couldn't buy the *Wall Street Journal*'s news columns." Said Executive Editor Frederick Taylor: "Millions of people who hadn't heard of us and the millions who had knew we weren't patsies for business. It turned out to be the best thing that could have happened."[31]

HOW ABOUT THE LITTLE GUY?

Mobil and GM advertising was just a fraction of the *Journal*'s total revenue. How about smaller newspapers that might jeopardize their financial viability in a dispute with advertisers?

Katharine Graham, then chairman of the *Washington Post,* acknowledged small-town publishers have "a particularly tough job because they cannot afford to run the risk of lost advertising . . ." Publisher Virgil Fassio of the *Seattle Post-Intelligencer* said metro dailies can "let the chips fall where they may but small-town publishers have to look businessmen in the eye every day. They don't have our anonymity." Robert Phelps, vice president of Affiliated Publications, then owner of the *Boston Globe,* said, "The most ethical newspapers are the richest and the most powerful. They can withstand economic buffeting."[32]

Nevertheless, some small-town newspapers can take ethical stands against advertiser pressure because they gain strength when acquired by larger groups.

The 36,000-circulation *Jackson (Tenn.) Sun* was boycotted by auto dealers, among the largest local retail advertisers for community newspapers, because it published articles on how car buyers can negotiate lower prices. Behind the *Sun* were the huge resources of its group owner, Gannett Co., which then had nearly 100 dailies with more than 6 million total circulation. Publisher Michael Craft said Gannett was "supportive" of his stand that the auto dealers had made "an unwise business decision."[33]

Independently owned newspapers must stand alone but sometimes find the cost of ethical conduct not as high as expected. The *St. Joseph (Mo.) Gazette and News-Press,* 45,000 morning circulation and 15,000 afternoon, instituted advertising screening and calculated its loss from rejected ads was less than one percent of annual revenue.

Larger newspapers, television stations and networks don't reveal how much revenue they turn away in rejected ads. But it should be noted that one percent of advertising at Dow Jones would have been $6.5 million in 1992. That figure undoubtedly is far below what the company actually spurned; its *Journal* will accept only ads "not offensive to good taste or public decency." Unacceptable categories include some of the most heavily advertised services and products—investment advisory services, lingerie, plus any drugs, cosmetics or other substances applied to the skin, and firearms.

At Times Mirror, publisher of the *Los Angeles Times* and other papers, one percent of 1992 ad revenue would have been $14.6 million!

To illustrate the impact on smaller papers, a 75,000-circulation daily could have $15 million to $17 million ad revenue annually, and, of course, one percent of that would be $150,000 to $170,000.

Ethics in advertising can carry a stiff price tag, obviously. For some media executives, the price is worth paying.[34] At the *New York Times,* Robert Smith said of his acceptability program, "Top management must make a commitment to be selective and realize that this will lead to a loss of some ad revenue. You can't have it both ways: All the lineage that's offered *and* a selective policy on ad acceptance."[35]

ETHICS IN OTHER COUNTINGHOUSE CORNERS

In addition to advertising, other business activities strongly influence decisions in newspaper or broadcast newsrooms on matters of principle.

For example, newspapers and, certainly, television are not in the news and advertising business alone. Both deal in entertainment. Newspapers also are in the manufacturing and transportation business (printing and distributing more than 60 million copies daily, 62 million on Sundays).

We need a wider view to understand why newsroom ethics and standards come under pressure from other departments and why publishers and network executives often act more like business than news executives.

COMMON CHARACTERISTICS

Note these characteristics that influence ethics in both the newspaper and television industries:

- Both industries are high cost. Entertainment programming can cost millions per hour to create. Newspapers' basic raw material, newsprint, is more than $685 per ton (and they used, in 1993, 11,643,000 metric tons).
- Both are personnel-intensive industries. Newspapers employed 451,700 persons in 1993. Television employs many thousands, too. And, neither industry can automate a reporter on the beat or an editor on the desk.
- Both the newspaper and television industries are high profile, exposed daily to public critique, subject to market and societal pressures, and thus are image-conscious.

Let's look at implications in all that for ethics in the newsroom.

ETHICS IN THE EXECUTIVE SUITE

Media managers must perform profitably in their business responsibilities or soon be unemployed. The rising tide of shareholder expectation forces many managers to put profit first; everything else is second—sometimes including ethical, socially responsible journalism.

Exceptions are those lucky managers whose organizations are enlightened (and profitable) enough to follow good, sound journalism as a route to financial success. But even they must keep their business priorities straight: It is important

VIEWPOINT

'Twas Always Thus?

"One of the basic troubles with radio and television news is that both instruments have grown up as an incompatible combination of show business, advertising and news. . . . The top management of the networks, with few notable exceptions, has been trained in advertising, research, or show business. . . . They also make the financial and crucial decisions having to do with news and public affairs. Frequently, they have neither the time nor the competence to do this. There is no suggestion here that networks or individual stations should operate as philanthropies. But I can find nothing in the Bill of Rights which says they must increase their net profits each year, lest the Republic collapse."

Edward R. Murrow, CBS's famed correspondent, in a 1958 speech to the Radio-Television News Directors Association

to be able to inform shareholders that company newspapers won Pulitzer prizes or, in television, Peabody Awards. It is imperative that the manager announce profits are up.

Because of the huge profits involved and sheer business complexity in the media today, a process of executive selection, under way since communications companies began going public in the mid-1960s, has pushed nonnews executives into the top ranks of many major communications firms.

The perceived need is for executives skilled in finance, accounting, long-range planning, assets deployment, advertising strategy—and, it would be nice if they knew something about news or at least are interested in it. If there is a network or major television station headed by a career newsperson, I don't know of it.

And, note the career origins of those managing important companies built primarily around newspapers: Times Mirror Co., which owns the *Los Angeles Times, Newsday* and *Baltimore Sun,* is run by a man trained in law. Tribune Co., owner of the *Chicago Tribune, Orlando Sentinel* and other newspapers, has a former accountant as chairman. Business-trained executives lead Belo, whose flagship is the *Dallas Morning News,* and Media General, owner of papers in Richmond, Tampa and elsewhere.

Three major companies have chairmen with substantial careers in news—Gannett (owner, in 1994, of 83 dailies), Dow Jones (*Wall Street Journal* and 22 other dailies) and Knight-Ridder (*Miami Herald, Philadelphia Inquirer* and 26 others.)

Regardless of whether they understand—or like—involvement in news, top media managers often are forced into profit-minded, high-profile roles. That can require them to assume community responsibilities that make it difficult to simultaneously serve as objective dispassionate news executives. It's called boosterism.

Many media executives see nothing wrong in boosterism if it involves the wider economic interests of a community (as contrasted with, say, favoritism for

VIEWPOINT

Boosterism: Four Views

"One of the biggest chasms between editors and readers today is differing concepts of what is boosterism. Boosting the opening of a new store or a shopping center can be news. To many readers, having a new place to shop is more important—and more interesting—than what is going on at city hall or with the school board or the local politicos."

Rey Hertel, managing editor, *Joliet (Ill.) Herald-News*

"Because a newspaper is usually a vital part of a community, the publisher is often asked to take an active civic role. It seems perfectly appropriate that he or she do so providing no pressure is exerted on the editorial department."

Kenneth J. Botty, vice president and editor, *Worcester (Mass.) Telegram and Evening Gazette*

"We don't join and we don't boost."

John K. Murphy, executive editor, *Portland (Me.) Press Herald*

"[T]he newspaper's first priority is public service. It is by nature the forum in which important issues can be most conveniently placed before the entire community. It is the newspaper's responsibility, more than other institutions, to articulate the community's values and to comment responsibility upon their application. To the extent this obligation is fulfilled over time, the community and its newspaper are inextricably bound together."

Burl Osborne, president and editor, *Dallas Morning News*

an individual advertiser). For example, looking back on its first 100 years, Times Mirror Co. unashamedly reported the "relentless boosterism" of its *Los Angeles Times,* which "undoubtedly lured multitudes of Easterners and Midwesterners to the City of Angels."[36]

Publishers and station managers serve the Boy Scouts, United Way and many other civic organizations, and problems can arise. One survey showed 49 percent of responding publishers acknowledge their involvement in local community groups poses conflicts of interest (42 percent said items published in their newspapers caused them "professional embarrassment" with the groups they joined).

But that doesn't hold them back: 90 percent said they were involved with local business or professional organizations, 76 percent with charitable groups. Half believed their sales managers should be required to join local business organizations; fewer made that demand on editors.[37]

The moral dilemma:

Even if assured free rein, do reporters feel completely free to investigate a charity organization headed by their boss?

Do editorial writers criticize with impunity a city planning board chaired by their publisher?

Importantly, does the public perceive reporters and editorial writers capable of fair, dispassionate coverage of activities involving the publisher?

Some newspaper publishers try to carry the concurrent title of editor; television managers often read stations editorials. Michael Craft, when both publisher and editor of Gannett's *Jackson (Tenn.) Sun,* warned against this:

> Involvement with the business community and government cause some of the most difficult ethical and soul-wrenching problems. Instincts as a newspaperman tell you that there are stories involved with your activities as publisher. An editor would jump at some of the stories or tips, sending reporters immediately on the trial of a good story.
>
> But the editor-publisher is torn by 1) his involvement in the first place in something that might be secret or confidential and 2) his inner cravings and title as a newspaper editor to get cracking on a possibly good story.

Editors-publishers must ask whether their ethics will permit having both jobs and then how they will perform when conflicts do arise.

For him, Craft said, "editor" is a "title without substance."[38]

Richard Buzbee, both editor and publisher of the *Hutchinson (Kan.) News,* said, "To be sure, there is danger of conflicts of interests. There's a certain challenge in writing an editorial reaming the mayor, and then [as publisher] sitting across the dinner table from him at Rotary that day."[39]

The real ethical challenge, of course, is to write the editorial as the facts dictate without even subconsciously pulling punches—and convince the public that you are—regardless of who the dinner companions will be.

Active involvement by managers in politics creates ethical conflict.

Warren Lerude, longtime Gannett executive and journalism professor, said the main questions are the following:

First,

> How newspaper publishers, who elect to work openly for one candidate or another, will keep the gate open for opposition points of view, fullness of reporting, editorial page comment, letters to the editor and columnists' analysis, so as to protect the strong tradition of the American press in getting to the readers all the information the electorate need.

And, second, "How publishers so involved will proceed to ensure their readers and critics of a full and balanced story . . ."[40]

Many newspapers technically prohibit any staff member from personal involvement in politics. But publishers often act—with relish—as power brokers behind the scenes.

Because their newspapers or stations are among any community's most important institutions, media managers frequently are under public scrutiny as fully penetrating as that afforded elected officials. That makes some publishers uneasy, but not Gene Roberts. As president and editor of the *Philadelphia Inquirer,* he commented, "Newspaper editors and publishers are fair game, and we should expect our lives to be open to public scrutiny as the public officials we scrutinize. We're not elected officials but we write about issues in the public domain and we, therefore, are in the public domain."

ETHICS IN THE PERSONNEL DEPARTMENT

Recruitment of the right people and their proper training are central to whether a newspaper or TV newsroom operates ethically and responsibly.

That makes the personnel—or human relations—department extremely important to our study of countinghouse influence on newsroom ethics. Two questions arise:

First, Are the newspaper and TV industries recruiting the best possible talent? Quick answer: Probably not, but things are improving.

One problem is that although bright men and women are attracted to journalism schools, low starting salaries persuade many to seek other careers. Average 1993 starting salaries for graduates with bachelor degrees in 28 majors was $26,000 annually. Highest was $40,173 for chemical engineers; the lowest, $19,114, was for journalists.[41]

Of course, salaries for established professionals are substantial: Minimum salary in 1993 in the *New York Times* newsroom was $60,264; at *Time,* $59,644; Reuters, $55,019.[42]

And, salaries at the top are even better. Total compensation in 1992 for Charles Brumback, chief executive officer of Tribune Co., was $2.4 million. Gannett's John Curley drew $2.1 million, Knight-Ridder's James K. Batten, $1.2 million.[43]

A second question central to how human relations affects ethics and social responsibility: Have the media built ethnically diverse newsroom staffs truly representative of the multicultural communities they cover (or should cover)?

Definitely not, but here, too, things are improving.

By 1993, a strong affirmative action hiring program began to show results for U.S. media. More minorities landed television jobs, and a survey of 987 daily newspapers, 64 percent of the total 1,535, showed these gains:

- In newsrooms, minorities were 10.25 percent of staff, up from 9.39 percent in 1992.
- 55 percent of newsrooms employed minorities, up from 40 percent.
- Among supervisors, 7.1 percent were minorities, up from 6.3 percent.
- Minorities were 24 percent of all journalists hired for their first full-time newsroom jobs; newsroom interns were 30 percent minority.

Importantly, major newspapers in cities with large minority populations reported success in minority hiring. In 1993, the *Miami Herald,* published in a city with a huge Hispanic population, reported 34.7 percent of its newsroom staff was minority. In Detroit, where many blacks live, the *Free Press* reported 21 percent, the *News,* 18.7 percent.

VIEWPOINT

Hiring Minorities is Smart

"Promoting and practicing equal opportunity is not only the right thing to do, it's the smart thing to do. . . . No newspaper can cover all of the community unless it employs all the community."

Al Neuharth, then chairman of Gannett Co., and industry leader in minority hiring

Among national papers, *USA Today* led in 1993 with 20.8 percent minority representation in its newsroom. The *Wall Street Journal*'s figure was 16.8 percent, the *New York Times'*, 14.1 percent.[44]

In the past, with advertisers demanding demographically attractive readers, newspapers and magazines felt little economic pressure to reach low-income black or Hispanic neighborhoods and thus had no need to actively recruit minorities to cover those neighborhoods. However, rising societal pressure, reflected in the 1964 Civil Rights Act, forced the media to expand their recruitment horizons—and that put them in direct competition with other, high-paying industries, all responding belatedly to changing times, and all trying to preempt trouble from the Equal Employment Opportunity Commission, charged under Title VII of the act with enforcing job opportunity.

A 1992 survey of 1,156 American journalists revealed how far the media have to go: The "typical" journalist is married, male, 36 years old (median), white, Protestant, holds a bachelor's degree and earns $31,297 annually (median.)[45]

ETHICS AND THE TYRANNY OF PRODUCTION

Few forces shape reporting and writing—and thus news ethics—more than production deadlines. Journalists spend their working lives trying to quickly write stories that are complete, balanced, accurate, fair. Complete or not, balanced or not, news copy must meet deadlines.

In newspapering, newsroom deadlines are set not by editors but, rather, by production and circulation departments. Newspapers must be gotten off the press and into delivery trucks in time to meet trains, buses, motor delivery drivers and 15-year-olds on bicycles—none of whom wait for late deliveries.

In television, the camera's red light blinks on immediately following the commercial and complete or not, balanced or not, the evening news is on the air—now, not two or three minutes from now.

More than the general public realizes, such purely mechanical considerations dictate how journalists perform.

Any outsiders trying to influence how news is reported are a giant step toward success if they understand newspaper and television production.

Demagogue Joe McCarthy, a Wisconsin Republican senator, understood it in the 1950s. For newspapers, he broke "news" (often undocumented charges of communist infiltration into government) just before deadlines. Repeatedly, newspapers rushed into print without time to double-check. For television, McCarthy would wave a sheaf of paper and declare he had in his hand a list of communists in high places—thus providing the dramatic video and sound bite around which so many TV news stories revolve.

Today, government officials, politicians and public relations executives also understand all this. For example, they schedule committee hearings, press conferences and "media events" for midafternoon—just in time for evening TV news but too late for afternoon papers. It's a tactic highly favored by those with ideas they would rather deliver directly to the public, through the tube, than through the analytical writing of a print journalist.

The enormous cost of newspaper and television production add to the "tyranny of production."

For a 50,000-circulation daily, production and newsprint alone soak up about 33 percent of total costs; circulation, 13 percent or so. Those two departments, representing at least 46 percent of total costs, have great clout at the planning table. (At this size paper, news represents about 13 percent of total cost; advertising, 8 percent; general/administrative, 33 percent.)

Television news production is costly, too, particularly in the field. For example, whereas a newspaper can maintain a foreign correspondent for $300,000 or so annually, the cost of a network bureau is over $1 million.

What's an editor to do?

First, newspaper editors should fight to gain for newsroom purposes every minute saved by new technology. Electronic editing speeds the production process. Electronic pagination, the computerized layout of full pages, speeds it even more. Time saved should go to extend deadlines so the newsroom has more time for thoughtful, sound, responsible journalism.

Second, new technology transfers to the newsroom many tasks formerly performed in production. Editors must demand more staff. The countinghouse tendency will be to add tasks but not bodies, thus subtracting substantially from the time and personnel editors have to do the news job.

Third, and I say it again: Editors must learn countinghouse language and ways. They must learn to justify, in terms business strategists understand, adding that $300,000 foreign correspondent or $1 million TV news bureau. Neither will be approved on a nice-to-have basis; both will be if editors translate the newsroom's needs into improved circulation or ratings and prestige with advertisers—results the countinghouse understands.

ETHICS IN CIRCULATION

Many reporters and editors seldom, if ever, visit the circulation department. They should, for out of circulation can come serious ethical questions affecting the newsroom.

Circulation considerations swing increasing weight in any upper management strategy session. Simply put, advertising executives want the paper in the hands of certain people attractive to advertisers. Circulation executives must get it there—but can do so only if editors create a product essential to those certain people.

And there, at that point in the integrated marketing concept, is where the newsroom is pressured to pull in tandem with advertising and circulation departments.

In television, of course, pressure comes from the advertising sales department to produce programming—including news—that wins higher ratings which, in turn, makes it easier to sell commercial time at higher rates.

In bygone, perhaps simpler times, newspaper editors pretty much covered the news as they saw it. The circulation department sold the resultant product to as many readers as possible; who they were and where they lived were not as important as total numbers. Using those total numbers as bait, the advertising department then sold space in the paper to advertisers.

Some papers pushed their circulation out to distant horizons, covering many states and in some cases becoming regional powerhouses. The *Atlanta Journal,* for example, promised that it "Covers Dixie Like the Dew."

Today, advertisers won't pay ad rates based on circulation hundreds of miles distant from their retail outlets. Atlanta retailers no longer are interested in circulation in south Georgia where they have no shoppers.

So, the Atlanta paper has retreated toward its home market—all in response to circulation, not news, considerations. Any societal responsibilities Atlanta editors feel to get their papers into every small town in Georgia fades before the circulation department's argument that they cannot afford to do that. Editors proud of achieving widespread circulation now hear advertising salespeople say they cannot sell that distant circulation to downtown department stores and that it therefore is a cost factor, not a generator of profit.

In sum, editors who once produced newspapers for general, widely scattered audiences now have new marching orders: create a product tailored to specific geographic and demographic targets selected to meet advertiser needs.

This zoning or target marketing has revolutionized newspaper strategy, yielding new, undreamed profits. And, make no mistake, *it requires editors to edit in response to business considerations.*

In its bluntest form, circulation pressure on the newsroom can be a memo from on high stating that subscription sales crews will be working in suburb X next month, and would the newsroom please get out there right away and cover the territory to give them something to sell? In that context, whether there is anything truly newsworthy in suburb X is immaterial. Thus do editors, in a world of war, famine and disaster, show sudden interest in handshaking Rotarians in suburb X and large pumpkins grown by householders there. (Of course, given resources, editors can produce meaningful coverage in such areas even when reacting to circulation department pressure; many metropolitan newspapers have high-quality suburban coverage.)

In its worst form, circulation pressure on the newsroom can create sensationalistic, profoundly unethical and irresponsible journalism. Newspapers and television alike have their sinners.

The *New York Post,* with its daily diet of rape, murder and arson, serves as an example of circulation-driven newspaper editors pandering to the most ignoble instincts of their street audience simply to push a few more copies at .50 cents each.

In television, inexorable pressure is toward news fare palatable to the widest possible audience, if not particularly enlightening or uplifting.

Because big money rides on winning readers or viewers, then selling them to advertisers, counting the numbers also has ethical implications for both newspapers and television.

Newspaper circulation figures historically were so chaotic—not to say intentionally inflated—that the industry and advertisers created in 1914 a nonprofit cooperative, the Audit Bureau of Circulations, to do the counting. Today, paid circulation figures for daily newspapers and weeklies, along with hundreds of magazines, are checked by full-time ABC auditors. Newspaper promotion aimed at advertisers is built around those ABC numbers.

Non-ABC papers promote numbers they have sworn are accurate in statements submitted to U.S. Postal Service officials. Generally, these numbers are far less reliable than ABC numbers.

Television measures its numbers primarily through one company, Nielsen, which uses meters wired to television sets and diaries filled out by viewers to report what they watched. Clearly, the meters measure many sets on but not watched; diaries often are filled out from memory and are inaccurate.

By some estimates, television audiences are overstated by as much as 10 to 15 percent—which could mean the three major networks, with annual billings of billions of dollars, are overbilling national advertisers by millions.

With so much money riding on the numbers, outright falsification of circulation or audience is not unknown in the media. But fudging takes other forms—newspapers giving away prizes to entice subscribers just before an ABC audit, or television pumping up its offerings just before audience surveys.

NOW, *YOU* MAKE THE CALL

Review our Chapter 1 discussion of the five-step decision-making process in ethics and the societal values, journalistic principles and loyalties involved in it. Then, to flesh out your attitudes toward advertising, answer these questions:

Do you identify a fundamental ethical issue(s) in the dependence of free-enterprise media on advertising?

For example, do you think it forces newspaper and TV editors to conform to the business dictates of integrated marketing management and thus precludes loyalty to the journalistic principle of serve the public? If you regard loyalty to both as a moral contradiction, what alternative solution do you propose? Government financial support of the media? Support by special interest groups (labor unions, business associations and so forth)?

Editors who say they serve their employer's business needs *and* their readers really are saying they have achieved an Aristotelian Golden Mean, aren't they? Do you think such a solution is possible? Can editors be loyal simultaneously to self and conscience, to society, to the hand that feeds them?

Examine this chapter's excerpts from newspaper and network codes of acceptability in advertising. Do you detect in them loyalty to self—loyalty to the cash register—or loyalty to society? Or, have advertising executives also tried to reach a Golden Mean?

Katharine Graham and other big-city publishers express sympathy for small-town publishers who come under pressure from advertisers. Should there be a two-tier ethical structure in the media—one for financially strong companies well equipped to resist pressure and a second, less demanding tier for smaller companies that are less strong financially? Immanuel Kant would argue that codes of conduct and morality must be applicable to all societal environments at all times (Chapter 1, Box 1–1). Do you agree with Kant?

Now, really step back: In light of this chapter's discussion of advertising, do you believe media companies truly have social responsibilities? Indeed, is it possible for companies to be marketing-oriented and simultaneously responsible to society or a greater good? Or, should the media give up trying to achieve a morally superior position in society and acknowledge they are just in the business of making a profit, like most companies in other industries? Should there be frank, open return to libertarianism (Chapter 1, Figure 1–1)?

Summary

Any study of newsroom ethics must pay special attention also to ethics in the countinghouse—other departments of a newspaper or television operation that influence why and how news is covered.

Because of its enormous financial importance, advertising is particularly influential. There is debate over whether advertising has true societal value or is a wasteful, costly endeavor that creates unnecessary materialistic consumer desire.

For American media, advertising creates financial independence from government or political groups and thus permits extraordinary journalistic independence. There is danger, however, of economic dependence on a relatively few large advertisers who exert undue influence on news coverage.

Newspapers and television networks go to elaborate lengths to screen advertising for acceptability and most protect the sanctity of their advertising columns or airtime just as editors try to protect the ethical character of the news. Screening codes prohibit the originators or authors of advertising from placing deceptive ads, and commit a newspaper or network, as the medium of advertising, to ensuring trust, good taste and legality. Because this can involve turning away unacceptable advertising, there is a price tag attached to advertising ethics.

Media managers must protect the business interests of their newspaper or television operation, must perform efficiently and profitably—and simultaneously administer news operations that report on many of the individuals and industries on which those business interests depend. Many managers report conflicts of interest in that equation.

In personnel, the challenge is to build a talented staff committed to ethical, socially responsible journalism and to build an ethnically diverse staff truly representative of the community it covers (or should cover). Results are mixed.

Many production factors influence the character of news reporting and writing. Newspaper and television journalists spend their working lives trying to meet production deadlines and still get into print or on the air with stories that are complete, balanced, accurate and fair. More than the general public realizes, the purely mechanical factors in production—and the cost—influence news coverage.

In circulation, ethical questions arise because of the influence circulation executives have on the geographic and demographic targets editors are given to cover. Many editors today edit in response to business, not news, considerations. There also is ongoing debate over how circulation (or ratings) figures are achieved, measured and promoted.

Notes

1. *Facts about Newspapers '94,* Newspaper Association of America, The Newspaper Center, 11600 Sunrise Valley Drive, Reston, Va., 22091, p. 10.
2. For a good discussion of advertising ethics within a wider context see Manuel G. Velasquez, *Business Ethics* (Englewood Cliffs, N.J.: Prentice Hall, 1982).
3. John Kenneth Galbraith, *The Affluent Society* (Boston: Houghton Mifflin, 1958).
4. Note particularly Ruth Clark, "Relating to Readers in the '80s," a 1984 opinion study done for ASNE, P.O. Box 17004, Washington, D.C., 20041. Also, a 1986 study done by Times Mirror Corp., Times Mirror Square, Los Angeles, Calif., 90053, found 53 percent of all Americans regard the press as " . . . too often influenced by powerful interests and institutions."
5. Helpful is a national survey in 1981 by Opinion Research Corp., for the Newspaper Advertising Bureau.
6. "CBS Television Network Advertising Guidelines," CBS Inc., 51 W. 52nd St., New York, N.Y., 10020.
7. "Advertising Standards of Acceptability," The Times Publishing Company, 409 First Ave. South, St. Petersburg, Fla., 33701.
8. Robert P. Smith, "Advertising Acceptability Policies Protect Newspaper's Credibility," *INAME News,* June 1984, p. 11.
9. Louis T. Hagopian, speech to American Newspaper Publishers Association, San Francisco, April 22, 1986.
10. "Advertising Standards and Guidelines," American Broadcasting Co., 1330 Avenue of the Americas, New York, N.Y., 10019; and, "CBS Television Network Advertising Guidelines," op. cit.
11. "Advertising Standards of Acceptability," op. cit.
12. Marcia Ruth, "Taboo Ads," *presstime,* October 1985, p. 34.

13. "CBS Television Network Advertising Guidelines," op. cit.
14. "Advertising Policy Manual," *Miami Herald,* One Herald Plaza, Miami, Fla., 33101.
15. "Advertising Standards of Acceptability," op. cit.
16. "An Overview of Current Issues," policy statement by American Newspaper Publishers Association, The Newspaper Center, Box 17407, Dulles Airport, Washington, D.C., 20041.
17. Loren Ghiglione, "It Is Time for Us to Voluntarily Give Up Cigarette Ads," *ASNE Bulletin,* September 1989, p. 2.
18. Fred Danzig, "Editors Shouldn't Be Censors of Ads," *Advertising Age,* Jan. 8, 1990, p. 22.
19. Michael Gartner, "The Bulletin Board," *ASNE Bulletin,* November 1989, p. 27.
20. Marc Boisclair, "RJR Rolling Their Own," *Magazine Week,* May 31, 1993, p. 11 and Lambeth Hochwald, "Tobacco Ads Still Smoking," *FOLIO*: January 1993, p. 17.
21. Marcia Ruth, "Taboo Ads," op. cit.
22. Stuart J. Elliot, "Advertorials: Straddling a Fine Line in Print," *Advertising Age,* April 30, 1984, p. 3.
23. *New York Times,* Oct. 10, 1982.
24. Robert P. Smith, "Advertising Acceptability Policies Protect Newspaper's Credibility," op. cit.
25. Eric Pace, "Whose Fault Is Bogus Ad?" *New York Times,* July 30, 1982, p. 16.
26. Hank Johnson, "What's Going On at One/Press Place," *Athens (Ga.) Banner-Herald and Daily News,* May 12, 1985, p. D2.
27. Details of this incident are available in Alex S. Jones, "Effects of Mobil's Journal Ban," *New York Times,* Dec. 5, 1984, p. 36; William F. Gloede, "Mobil's Still Mad," *Advertising Age,* April 8, 1985, p. 6; "Boycott Big Business," *Editor & Publisher,* Dec. 15, 1984, p. 10.
28. Peg Masterson, "Many Editors Report Advertiser Pressure," *Advertising Age,* Jan. 11, 1993, p. 22.
29. G. Pascal Zachary, "Many Journalists See a Growing Reluctance to Criticize Advertisers," the *Wall Street Journal,* Feb. 6, 1992, p. 1.
30. Black and Crowley are quoted in "Many Editors Report Advertiser Pressure," op. cit.
31. A detailed review of this incident is in "A Helluva Bureau," an historical look at Dow Jones' Detroit bureau, in *What's News,* Dow Jones employee publication, Spring 1985, p. 1.
32. Comments made at the Dec. 5, 1984, meeting in Tacoma, Wash., of Allied Daily Newspapers, a group of papers in Washington, Oregon, Idaho, Montana and Alaska.
33. This boycott is reported in, "Car Dealers Boycott Tennessee Daily," *Editor & Publisher,* Oct. 12, 1985, p. 22.
34. "Newspapers Ponder Advertising Codes," *presstime,* August 1984, p. 43.
35. Robert P. Smith, "Advertising Acceptability Policies Protect Newspaper's Credibility," op. cit.
36. "Annual Report, 1984," Times Mirror Co., Times Mirror Square, Los Angeles, Calif., 90053, p. 10.

37. Survey by John Reddy, vice president/editorial, Suburban Communications Corp., Livonia, Mich., of 207 suburban publishers; reported in *Research Bulletin,* Southern Newspaper Publishers Association, P.O. Box 28875, Atlanta, Ga., 30328.
38. ASNE survey, "Editors and Publisher: Wearing Two Hats Comfortably," *ASNE Bulletin,* October 1985, p. 4.
39. Ibid.
40. M. K. Guzda, "Ethically Speaking," *Editor & Publisher,* Sept. 29, 1984, p. 11.
41. "Outlook," *U.S. News & World Report,* May 31, 1993, p. 10.
42. William Glaberson, "House Union at Journal Revived by Salary Study," *New York Times,* May 24, 1993, p. C-8.
43. "Corporate America's Most Powerful People," *Forbes,* May 24, 1993, p. 142.
44. "Minorities Make Newsroom Gains," *presstime,* April 1993, p. 33.
45. David H. Weaver and G. Cleveland Wilhoit, "Journalists—Who Are They, Really?," *Media Studies Journal,* Fall 1992, p. 63.

CHAPTER 8

THE CHANGING FACE OF THE MEDIA

The ethical foundations and journalistic tone of most newsrooms in America—and the news you and I get every day—are influenced strongly by distant corporate forces and faraway, often anonymous people.

This influence comes from headquarters of huge media groups that are sweeping up most of the nation's significant newspapers, magazines and broadcast operations—and from shareholders who, in turn, own the groups.

Gone are yesteryear's Hearstian presslords who hurled "must-run" telegrams at their editors nationwide, directing what must be on each front page that day and in editorial columns.

Neither society nor, importantly, the increasingly complex business of media operations permits today that kind of arrogant (and often unprofitable) high-handedness.

However, a new, business-oriented breed of presslords directs today's media conglomerates—and to understand newsroom ethics you must understand who they are and what motivates them.

This new breed and the changes they're bringing about in American media are our subjects in Chapter 8.

THE GROUPS AND THEIR POWER

Ownership and management of American newspapers, magazines and broadcast companies concentrates enormous influence and economic power in a relative handful of major groups. The groups, in turn, are run by small cadres of professional managers trained together to work together and to think together.

With startling speed, independently owned media are being swallowed by huge, mostly publicly owned conglomerates. The trend gained momentum in the 1970s and 1980s and continues in the 1990s, though at a slower pace.

By 1993, groups owned 1,205 daily newspapers—about 76 percent of the total. Because they owned most of the larger papers, groups controlled 48.2 million daily circulation, 79 percent of the total, and 50.7 million or 81 percent of Sunday circulation.[1]

Television stations became extraordinarily profitable and largely disappeared into group ownership within a couple decades of TV's launch in the 1950s as a commercially viable medium.

Many magazines are highly profitable and also attractive to conglomerates. *One* company, Time Warner, brings in over $2 *billion* in annual advertising revenue alone from its magazines; Hearst, over $1 billion.

Most conglomerates are diversified in newspapers, magazines, TV, radio and cable TV, and even into industries outside news and information.

In years ahead, you'll see another face-change: Large groups will swallow others, merge or otherwise combine forces to build even greater financial, technical and executive strength. That will be necessary to exploit the hugely expensive technological innovations sure to open new forms of communication in the next century. Massively strong nonmedia firms, such as the multibillion dollar regional Bell telephone companies and AT&T, will be partners—or competitors—in using new technology to serve readers, viewers, listeners and advertisers in new ways.

BIG ISN'T ALWAYS BAD

Big is not automatically bad in media ownership and profit is not a dirty word in journalism. To the contrary. Even the media's most severe critics must acknowledge the best American journalism—and some of it is superb—is produced by large, profit-oriented corporations.

Nostalgia for the days of privately owned mom-and-pop news organizations is, in this sense, largely misplaced. Mom and pop generally had neither the vision nor financial strength to produce journalism of the quality routinely produced daily by Knight-Ridder, the New York Times Co., Times Mirror or similarly enlightened conglomerates.

However, concentration of media power makes clear that our study of journalistic ethics and social responsibility must push beyond whether a sports writer should accept a freebie bottle of whiskey, whether a small-town publisher should get into community boosterism or whether a local TV station manager should employ happy-talk anchors to boost ratings and court advertisers.

We must study the character and structure of America's leading media companies. We must move upstream along the power flow and into the boardrooms of those conglomerates to see who really creates operating policy—and ethical standards—for that sports writer, the small-town publisher, the station manager.

VIEWPOINT

"Chain" Owner and Local Loyalty

"A 'chain' owner cannot do justice to local publications or radio stations. His devotion and loyalty to any one area is bound to be diluted or divided if he has other ownerships and interests."

Nelson Poynter, late owner of *St. Petersburg Times* who severely criticized in 1947 the growth of media groups and whose successor managers at the *Times* by the 1980s had built a multistate group of periodicals

WHY THEY EXPAND AND DIVERSIFY

If you suspect modern-day Citizen Kanes are putting together these media conglomerates so they can grab power and influence the minds of America, join the crowd. Some media vigilantes and social commentators fear Hearstian manipulation of news by media magnates pulling strings that lead to newsrooms across the nation.

But, it is not ideology or proselytism that motivates the empire building. Rather, it's a highly complex combination of profit-oriented business factors and the compelling need of certain aggressive, ego-driven managers to build, to succeed, to be bigger than anyone else.

There, of course, is ideological conservatism in media management, as in management of most businesses. But most groups studiously avoid even the suggestion of a company line news editors must follow. And rare indeed is the corporate hierarchy that permits itself to become publicly identified with a politician or narrowly partisan cause—not in this era of nationwide corporate strategies designed to operate media properties profitably in areas diverse geographically, economically, socially and politically.

Following most presidential elections surveys show that Republican candidates gain more support on editorial pages than Democrats and that conservative ideas win wider endorsement than liberal ideas. But ever since the media turned so profitable and got organized as businesses, critics have been hard pressed to show any significant evil manipulation of news and editorial pages by group corporate boardrooms.

In fact, the trend increasingly is to avoid editorial endorsement of any party or candidate. *USA Today,* the epitome of the market-oriented group newspaper, a paper methodically constructed to appeal to a wide audience, avoids endorsing any political candidates. Its owner, Gannett, promotes its $3.3 billion, nationwide media network and 81 newspapers as a "world of different voices."

If any charge strikes home against the groups it is not that they wrongly intervene in the newsrooms of their distant satellites to set ethical standards and news policy but, rather, that they don't pay them enough attention and don't care what their news pages or newscasts look like, as long as the profits roll in.

The danger is not of nonjournalist managers descending into the unfamiliar terrain of the newsroom and trying to run things but, rather, that untrained in news and insensitive to its complexities or importance, they ignore the newsrooms. Many are the publishers who don't carefully read their own news columns and station mangers who don't watch their own newscasts.

This is managerial failure through noninvolvement, and it can be remedied only with appointment of experienced, motivated editors who do care and are capable of fighting in the countinghouse for the resources needed to produce ethical and responsible journalism.

The groups have come a long way since yesteryear's must-run telegrams. Any businessperson—and that's what today's media baron is—would be crazy to do such a thing. It would queer the whole glorious, moneymaking arrangement.

No, group expansion and diversification are fueled by factors much more easily explained.

A manager's first responsibility to shareholders is to create profit, to increase their return on investment (ROI). It is a fundamental principle embodied in business tradition as fiduciary responsibility and carved on MBA diplomas. ROI is how you score the game, how you win the highest salary on the block plus the limo, the private jet and other perks.

Group expansion and diversification broaden, sometimes exponentially, the revenue base on which improved profit margins and increased ROI can be built. Here is how:

DIVERSIFICATION IS DESIRED

Diversifying geographically protects a company against economic dislocation in a single region. When New York Times Co. went on an acquisition binge, most newspapers it swept up were scattered throughout the Sun Belt, faring much better economically than the northeast or midwest.

Diversifying into cities with different industrial bases also provides corporate insurance. Big city groups diversify into small towns; groups based primarily on, say, smokestack industrial towns seek other types of markets as protection against severe economic dislocation in the steel or auto industries.

Diversifying into different media reduces the danger of relying on a single source of revenue. Companies traditionally based in newspapers seek attractive television and radio stations, outdoor advertising firms, mobile radio-telephone companies—and nonmedia enterprises—for protection against dislocation among advertising-supported businesses.

Diversification permits secondary use of existing staff and resources in profitable synergism. For example, paid-circulation newspapers develop new revenue by producing free-circulation shoppers in the same plant with the same staff. Tribune Company bought the Chicago Cubs not only for profits the team produces but, most importantly, for television programming for Tribune's WGN-TV.

VIEWPOINT

Taking From Peter to Pay Paul

"The most harmful effect of chain formation may be that profits made in a community paper are not reinvested in that paper. The community daily has become a source of capital to be invested elsewhere."

Ben H. Bagdikian, author, educator and, at times, severe media critic

TAX LAW ENCOURAGES EXPANSION

Tax laws can make it financially irresponsible not to expand.

In the go-go days of the 1970s and early 1980s, when today's media empires largely gained momentum, as much as .25 cents to .50 cents in tax advantage came with every $1 invested in acquisitions, thus the irresistible temptation to buy yet more newspapers or TV stations and build far-flung media empires.

But, finally, expanding a company is heady, ego-gratifying stuff. It's fun to zoom into town in a private jet, make a multimillion dollar deal, watch the local minions snap to attention, and be known on the industry circuit as someone who builds megabuck profits. Anyone who doubts the role of ego in media empire-building should attend a convention of publishers or broadcasters and watch the wheeler-dealers at work and play. They measure each other's profit levels like gunfighters studying quick-draw techniques.

WHY DO SELLERS SELL?

Of course, buyer motivation can't change the face of the American media if sellers are not willing. Why are they willing?

High prices paid by groups are one reason. The groups, enormously profitable, have surplus they must invest or give to Uncle Sam as tax on retained earnings. And, smart group executives can improve the profitability of most privately owned (and, often, inefficiently run) newspapers and television stations. So, paying even extraordinarily high prices is justified as a means of achieving greater profit later.

Groups paid three to four times gross revenue or 30 to 40 times annual earnings (profits) for newspapers—and often more for TV stations—during the boom days of expansion. A multiple of 10 to 12 times earnings was a handsome price in many other industries.

The economic recession of the early 1990s put a damper on media acquisitions and prices, although attractive media properties still command top dollar. In 1993, New York Times Co. agreed to acquire the *Boston Globe* for $1.1 billion, highest price ever for a newspaper.

CASE STUDY

The Arithmetic of Group Growth

The impact of federal estate tax was dramatic on individually owned, locally managed daily newspapers in America: They virtually disappeared.

About 76 percent of all dailies today are group-owned. They were swept up in an acquisition frenzy in the 1970s and 1980s when heirs could not afford to pay estate taxes and ensure orderly transfer to a surviving generation.

Here's a hypothetical example of the inescapable arithmetic that worked in that era to the advantage of groups:

A privately owned daily has $10 million in annual advertising and circulation revenue. It converts 20 percent or $2 million to pretax or operating profit.

Income taxes, federal and state, take about half the operating profit, leaving earnings (or net profit) of $1 million.

With so many companies bidding for newspapers (and very few new dailies are being launched), the law of supply and demand takes over: Our daily has a fair market value—what a willing buyer will pay a willing seller—of three times annual revenue, or $30 million (that's conservative, incidentally; some buyers paid five times revenue in those days).

The Internal Revenue Service levies estate (or inheritance) tax on fair market value. The maximum rate in the era under study is 63 percent (it's now 50 percent).

At the maximum rate, heirs to our newspaper face *$18.9 million in taxes* if they want to, in effect, buy their family newspaper back from the U.S. government.

The reality, of course, is that very few newspaper families have $18.9 million stashed in a bank somewhere and available for the IRS. So, our family has two options:

First, it can borrow $18.9 million. But interest at this time is running as high as 14 to 21 percent. Borrowing $18.9 million at 14 percent will cost $2,646,000 in first-year interest alone. There is no way to finance $2.6 million interest payments out of a newspaper with $2 million pretax profit annually—and even if a loan can be financed, the total estate tax will, at current levels, consume the newspaper's profits for nearly 20 years.

The second option for our family is to sell. And that, of course, is what happens to our typical medium-size hometown newspaper—and hundreds others across the nation.

But the greatest single reason for the increasingly rapid disappearance of the family-owned newspaper or broadcast station is federal estate tax. When the principal owner dies, many families are forced to buy their newspaper or station a second time—this time from the Internal Revenue Service—if they want the property passed to heirs. If the heirs don't have sufficient cash for taxes, they must call in a buyer.

These same circumstances confront families that own gas stations, farms or other businesses, of course, except for one crucial factor: Estate taxes are based on fair market value of the property—what a willing buyer will pay a willing

In 1986, after the Gannetts, Knight-Ridders and other groups had swallowed many dailies, the maximum estate was lowered to 50 percent. Even then, the owning family would face $15 million in taxes in our hypothetical example.

The same estate taxes are levied against other types of businesses. But newspapers are particularly hard-hit because their fair market value is so high.

Now, *You* Make the Call

- Is there societal value in having a large number of U.S. communities being served by locally owned newspapers? Can a local owning family bring something to community journalism that a conglomerate, with headquarters in a distant city, cannot?
- Should society grant estate tax exemptions to families of locally owned newspapers? If so, should they also be granted other family businesses—shoe stores, gas stations, farms?
- Should groups be limited in the number of media properties they can acquire? Would you favor, for example, laws stating that no single group could reach, through print or broadcast, more than, say 25 to 30 percent of the U.S. news and information audience?
- If you favor tax breaks to family-owned local newspapers and restrictions on group expansion, how does your belief square with the First Amendment's guarantee of a free press? And, aren't you proposing interference with a free and open commercial marketplace, the very core of our free enterprise capitalistic system?[2]

As you consider these questions, refer again to the decision-making process discussed in Chapter 1.

Are societal values and journalistic principles applicable to individual journalists also applicable to media groups, executives and their conduct? If you think (as I do) that they are, ask yourself:

- Are profit-oriented, expanding media groups fulfilling stewardship, the societal value of protecting the system (a free press) from which they benefit so fully?
- Or, are they exploiting the system for gain?
- Are such groups violating the journalistic principle of serve the public?
- And, to whom or what do group executives show loyalty? To self? To society?

seller—and for reasons already outlined, newspapers and television stations have extremely high market values. Taxes based on those values frequently are more than owners can finance out of their operation.

It's ironic. We hear so much about the evils of group ownership, how family-owned newspapers or broadcast stations are scooped up by group executives run wild in their empire building, or betrayed and sold by greedy owners who simply want to pick up a huge bundle of cash. But the real villains are in tax law.

Well, then, what types of media companies come from all this? Who are the big players? Let's look.

VIEWPOINT

Taxed Into Selling

"Times change . . . costs of materials and equipment mount inexorably. The future requirements of journalism, both print and electronic, are difficult to predict. Meanwhile, tax policies make it increasingly hard for family-held corporations to maintain control from one generation to another."

Barry Bingham, Sr., announcing the family-owned *Louisville Courier-Journal* and *Times* were being sold to Gannett Co., for $305 million

THE LARGEST GROUPS

Most media companies today are highly complex, with not one corporate face, but several. The measurements of distinction are many.

To judge Times Mirror, for example, requires assessing its performance in newspapers, television, radio, magazines, cable, outdoor advertising, book publishing, real estate, forest and paper products and other areas—many beyond the scope of our study.

So, let's objectively rank the largest firms according to total media revenue, making a few subjective observations along the way but not pretending to treat all their corporate affairs comprehensively.[3] Such an appreciation is central to our study of ethics and social responsibility in the media and, certainly, to the media's role in society (see Figure 8–1).

MEDIA CONTROL EQUALS WEALTH

For one thing, people who control the companies we've been discussing are very rich. Billionaires are made through media investments.

The Newhouse brothers, who run Advance Publications, share a fortune said to be well over $7 billion made through newspapers, magazines, television and cable TV. Three members of the Cox family (Cox Enterprises, *Atlanta Journal/Constitution* and others) share a media fortune estimated at $4.2 billion. The Hearst family's fortune is put at about $4 billion. One of America's shrewdest investors, Warren Buffet of Omaha, made much of his billion dollar fortune in media stocks, principally Washington Post Co., and Capital Cities/ABC.[4]

Many of America's great family fortunes were built on media interests: Bancroft (Dow Jones), Block (*Toledo Blade, Pittsburgh Post-Gazette* (TV and cable), Chandler (Times Mirror), Gardner Cowles family (*Des Moines Register and Tribune, Minneapolis Star* and others), William Cowles family (*Chicago Tribune,*

VIEWPOINT

Media Size and Success

"The public . . . is occasionally alienated by the sheer size and financial success of the communications media today. To many, we appear to be a rather rich, monolithic, forbidding institution. Our motives become suspect. Are we in business to serve the public or increase our profits? Are they, in fact, contradictory?"

Katharine Graham, chairman, Washington Post Co.

Spokane Spokesman-Review and Chronicle), de Young (*San Francisco Chronicle*), Hoiles (Freedom Newspapers), McClatchy (Fresno, Sacramento, Modesto, Calif., *Bee* Newspapers), McGraw (McGraw-Hill, mostly magazines, books), Pulitzer (*St. Louis Post-Dispatch* and other properties), E. W. Scripps (newspapers, television), J. E. Scripps (*Detroit News,* now owned by Gannett, and other papers, television), Sulzberger (*New York Times*), Wolfe (*Columbus Dispatch* and others).

You might suspect that ocean of media money buys political power and societal influence that, if mixed with manipulation of the news, could bode ill for the future of the republic. Such potential may exist to some degree—but not much.

Most media fortunes are dispersed among many heirs not actively involved in the media properties that yielded their wealth. *Forbes,* for example, found about 30 descendants sharing the de Young fortune of $450 million. None is named de Young; one descendant, Nan Tucker McEvoy, runs the *San Francisco Chronicle.*[5]

However, some media-owning family members are deeply involved in management—Katharine Graham and her son Donald at Washington Post Co., and Sulzberger and his son at New York Times Co., are examples.

Most significant family companies—including Washington Post and New York Times—long ago went public. And although family members may hold controlling stock, the companies are managed day-to-day largely by professionals chosen not for their blood line but, rather, for ability to improve profits—for everyone, including third-generation heirs basking in the Bahamas and Mr. and Mrs. Average Investor who take a $1,000 or so fling on media stocks.

Most major media companies are traded on the New York Stock Exchange or American Stock Exchange and are owned by thousands of shareholders. In 1993, for example, Knight-Ridder had 10,400 shareholders in all 50 states holding the company's 55 million shares.

When they went public, most family-owned media companies established two tiers of stock. Controlling stock largely was kept by family members; outside investors were permitted to buy stock with limited or no voting rights.

Figure 8–1
Leading media companies

LEADING MEDIA COMPANIES

Rank	Total Media Revenue (millions)
1. Time Warner	$5,559.4
2. Capital Cities/ABC	4,963.9
3. CBS	3,301.1
4. Tele-Communications	3,500.0
5. General Electric	3,363.0
6. Gannett	3,503.0
7. Advance Publications	3,257.2
8. Times Mirror	2,767.5
9. News Corp	2,455.8
10. Knight-Ridder	2,050.0
11. Hearst	1,973.5
12. Cox Enterprises	1,836.4
13. New York Times Co.	1,783.8
14. Tribune Co.	1,706.8
15. Viacom International	1,638.8

(Figures for 1992. Source: *Advertising Age*.)

HOW THE BIG GOT BIG

1. Time Warner Merger of Time Inc.'s magazine and cable-TV empire with the cable and entertainment businesses of Warner pushed Time Warner to the top in total revenue. Cable TV now outstrips magazines 3 to 1 in revenue. One of America's premier publishing houses now is run at the top by entertainment-oriented executives.

2. Capital Cities/ABC Holdings include ABC radio and television networks, TV and radio stations, cable, daily newspapers and nondailies and a huge stable of consumer magazines. Capital Cities is known for high profit margins and cutting costs to the bone.

3. CBS In addition to television and radio networks, CBS owns stations in major cities across the country. It sold companies dealing in consumer magazines, book publishing, records, music and video. Starting with Edward R. Murrow during World War II and continuing through Walter Cronkite and Dan Rather, CBS built a reputation for journalism that is solid, responsible and profitable as well. Numerous outside attempts to take over CBS forced management into extremely expensive defensive moves. CBS carried heavy debt—and slashed costs in its news division to help pay it off.

4. Tele-Communications Inc. (TCI) A dynamic Denver-based cable-TV company with no traditional print or broadcast media holdings. The company is trying to construct alliances with collaborators to help it move along the envisaged electronic highway and into American homes with two-way interactive circuits offering entertainment, advertising, information and other services.

5. General Electric Yes, this manufacturer of refrigerators, aircraft engines and other hard industrial products also is in the media. GE has well over $3.3 billion in TV and cable TV revenue, and owns NBC.

6. Gannett Owns 81 newspapers and in newspaper revenue, Gannett is the largest. In 20 years, the company exploded from a handful of upstate New York dailies into an international giant in television, radio, outdoor advertising and many other media-related areas. Gannett first acquired small and medium-size newspapers without head-on competition from other papers, a recipe for maximum profits. In the 1980s, the company began acquiring big-city newspapers—the *Des Moines Register & Tribune*, *Detroit News* and the *Louisville Courier-Journal* and *Times*. And it launched *USA Today*, a highly innovative national newspaper, but huge money loser until it turned profitable in 1993. Gannett entered the 1990s known for solid but unspectacular journalism carefully tuned to produce sound community newspapers and high profits.

7. Advance Publications This is the nation's largest *privately* owned media company, run by S. I. Newhouse, Jr., and Donald Newhouse, sons of founder S. I. Newhouse. Company revenue is estimated substantially in excess of $3.2 billion annually from daily newspapers in 10 states (largest, at 414,000 daily circulation, is the *Cleveland Plain Dealer*), magazines (*Mademoiselle*, *Bride's*, *Glamour*, *New Yorker*, *Parade* and others), book publishing (Random House, Alfred A. Knopf, Ballantine, Vintage, and Modern Library) and other holdings. The company regards cable TV as the wave of the electronic future. The group's newspapers are profit-oriented and generally undistinguished journalistically, although its *Plain Dealer*, *Newark (N.J.) Star-Ledger* (483,000 daily circulation), and *Portland Oregonian* (342,000) occasionally rise above modest heights.

8. Times Mirror Corp. A truly distinguished media company. It is professionally managed, profitable and a producer of high-quality, responsible journalism with its *Los Angeles Times*, *Newsday*, *Baltimore Sun* and other newspapers. After decades of nearly unbroken success, Times Mirror failed in a big way when its *Dallas Times Herald* was unable to overtake A. H. Belo Corp.'s *Dallas Morning News*. Times Mirror sold the paper in 1986. It also sold its *Denver Post*, which was unable to conquer its crosstown rival, Scripps-Howard's *Rocky Mountain News*. Company is widely diversified.

9. News Corp. This internationally diversified company is controlled by Australian-born Rupert Murdoch, who cut a swath through the media world Down Under before he was 40, turned Britain's Fleet Street on its ear, then set course for the New World and its media riches. Aggressive acquisitions and low-brow newspapering firmly established News Corp. as a multibillion dollar company. Murdoch's strategy: produce sensationalistic newspapers for readers left behind by elitist papers driving upscale in search of affluent subscribers. He produced huge circulations in a hurry—as high as 960,000 for the *New York Post*, 630,000 for the *Chicago Sun-Times*, and 360,000 for the *Boston Herald*. But Murdoch's readers were unattractive to advertisers, and the *Post* for years lost an estimated $1 million monthly; the *Herald* swam in red; and the *Sun-Times* didn't flourish. By 1986, Murdoch had sold out in Chicago and New York—and was redeploying assets into television, magazines, movies and his Fox TV network. In 1985, Murdoch became a naturalized American, which enabled him to meet federal regulations that only citizens may own more than 25 percent of a television station. In 1993, he negotiated to repurchase the *New York Post*, then in dire financial condition. Continuing his search for a profitable mix of properties, Murdoch agreed in 1994 to sell the *Boston Herald.*

10. Knight-Ridder, Inc. No company consistently produces more first-rate journalism than Knight-Ridder. Its executives seldom mention profit without insisting that high-quality journalism and community service are the way to achieve it. That spirit pervades the company, notably at the highly respected *Philadelphia Inquirer*, *Miami Herald*, *Detroit Free Press*, and *San Jose (Calif.) Mercury News*. A career journalist, James K. Batten, is chairman. He promoted other highly regarded news executives, thus ensuring continued commitment in top ranks to journalistic principle and quality.

Figure 8–1, continued

11. Hearst Corp. This private company, whose holdings include gold mines and other commercial activities, never publishes its financial figures. The media division is strongest in magazines but also owns newspapers, TV, radio and cable. In journalistic impact, the company is just a shadow of the company William Randolph Hearst put together. His strategy of operating big-city newspapers, a winner at the time, proved disastrous when socioeconomic decline in core cities caused affluent residents to flee to the suburbs. One by one, the influential (but never great) Hearst papers died. In the 1980s, the company closed its *Baltimore News-American* and *Los Angeles Herald-Examiner*. Hearst's *San Francisco Examiner* and *Seattle Post-Intelligence* are both number two papers in their markets. The company owns *Cosmopolitan*, *Good Housekeeping*, *Harper's Bazaar* and many other magazines; Arbor House, Avon, William Morrow and other book publishers and one of the country's leading syndicates, King.

12. Cox Enterprises Of the largest media companies, none has expanded so widely while remaining so unknown to the public. This privately owned company has properties in 21 states. The flagship is the *Atlanta Journal and Constitution*, which, under new young leadership, became one of the few success stories in big city newspapering in the 1990s. The Cox papers forced a costly retreat by New York Times Co., which brought a suburban paper, the *Gwinnett Daily News*, in an effort to exploit metropolitan Atlanta's rapid growth. The *News* folded in 1992.[2]

13. New York Times Co. This company's emergence as a profitable conglomerate is classic. Though its *New York Times* was the single-most influential paper in the country and, at the time, best journalistically by a wide margin, the company itself was in trouble in the 1960s. Profits were marginal and the company's most important—virtually its only—market, New York City, was in socioeconomic decline. While maintaining—in fact, enhancing—the journalistic quality of the *Times*, company executives under Chairman Arthur Ochs ("Punch") Sulzberger launched the expansion/diversification effort that in the 1980s made the company a nationwide media powerhouse. The company added commu-

So, obviously, not all shareholders are equal. The Grahams still tightly control their public Washington Post Co.; the Sulzberger family controls New York Times Co.

Major investors with considerable corporate clout include banks, mutual funds and other institutional investors, in addition to individuals with large holdings.

THE POLICY-SETTING APPARATUS

In theory, the policy-making apparatus of any publicly owned media company is a board of directors drawn from both inside and outside corporate ranks with the mission of guiding management and representing shareholder interests.

And, again in theory, the owner of even a single share can rise at the company's annual meeting, open by law to all shareholders, to nominate someone to the board or ask questions or demand action and thus influence company affairs.

In fact, those who own the shares have the votes, so directors often are selected to include holders of large numbers of shares (even if they possess no particular journalistic or managerial expertise) or individuals they nominate.

nity papers in Sun Belt states, television and radio stations, magazines (*Family Circle*, *Golf Digest* and others), and a large cable TV operation. In 1993, Times Co. acquired the *Boston Globe* for $1.1 billion. For thousands of important figures in government, finance, commerce and industry throughout the world, the *Times* is *the* source of important news and informed opinion. Further, for many editors, news becomes news when the *Times* says it's news. The paper thus has substantial influence on worldwide news-gathering habits.

14. Tribune Co. One of the nation's premier communications companies in journalistic excellence and profit. Two papers—the *Chicago Tribune* and *Orlando Sentinel*—are on most lists of the 10 best dailies. Tribune's WGN-TV in Chicago is first-rate. Tribune illustrates how widely diversified modern communications conglomerates have become. Holdings include dailies in California, Virginia and Florida; weeklies in Illinois, Florida and Oklahoma; television stations in Illinois, New York, Colorado, Louisiana, Georgia and California; radio stations in Illinois, New York, Connecticut and California; a cable television company based in New Jersey; a nationwide news and feature syndicate; a marketing company operating out of Chicago; newsprint mills and forest products holdings in four Canadian towns, plus 60 percent of a power company in Quebec; Tribune Entertainment Company; an independent TV news network—and the Chicago Cubs plus minor league baseball teams in Orlando, Fla., and Rockford, Ill.! By 1994, just 62 percent of Tribune's total revenue came from newspapers, the rest from entertainment and broadcasting.

15. Viacom International This company is a major player (more than $1.5 billion annual revenue) in cable TV and broadcasting—and is certain to be more influential in the future. Expansion in entertainment and new electronic services is in the offing. In 1994, Viacom acquired a huge Hollywood studio, Paramount, for about $10 billion.

Now, who manages such influential companies? Who controls what tens of millions of Americans read and view? Who, for better or worse, sets the ethical tone for the nation's leading media companies?

The selection process itself and policy guidelines issued by the board are influenced heavily by the very men and women they are meant to direct—the professional managers.

A professional manager can have strong influence—control, even—over the board. How much relates directly to his or her track record and strength of personality.

WHO REALLY RUNS THE GIANTS?

The key to who really runs the nation's largest media companies—and how—lies in the relationship between boards of directors and professional managers.

There is no typical board of directors, no typical flow of policy-making authority. But the men and women who make policy for hundreds of newspapers and television stations are drawn principally from predictable sources: inside managers and family members with large stock holdings, and outside members of what, for lack of a better word, can be called the establishment.

Let's look, for example, at Knight-Ridder's board in 1993:

"Inside" Directors	"Outside" Directors	Family Directors
James K. Batten, 57, chairman/CEO, former editor	C. Peter McColough, 70, former CEO, Xerox Corp.	Joan Ridder Challinor, 65
Alvah H. Chapman, Jr., 71, retired chairman/CEO	Jesse Hill Jr.,66, chairman/CEO Atlanta Life Insurance Co.	Eric Ridder, 74, retired publisher of Knight-Ridder's *Journal of Commerce*
P. Anthony Ridder, 52, president	Thomas L. Phillips, 68, retired chairman/Raytheon Co.	Barbara Knight Toomey, 55
Bernard H. Ridder, Jr., 76, retired chairman/CEO	Barbara Barnes Hauptfuhrer, 64, director of several companies	
Robert F. Singleton, 62, chief financial officer	Gonzalo F. Valdes-Fauli, 46, regional CEO of Barclays Bank PLC	
	Ben R. Morris, 70, former president of *Columbia (S.C.) State-Record*, which Knight-Ridder acquired	
	John L. Weinberg, 68, senior chairman of Goldman, Sachs & Co.	
	Peter C. Goldmark, Jr., 52, president of Rockefeller Foundation	
	William S. Lee, 63, chairman of Duke Power	

Knight-Ridder's board, then, is drawn heavily from inside company executives and members of the Knight and Ridder families who control huge blocs of stock and, thus, control the company.

Outside directors have varied backgrounds—industry, commercial banking, investment banking, Duke Power and so forth. Their expertise is helpful to management.

Note the board includes three women, a black (Hill) and a Hispanic (Gonzalo Valdes-Fauli)—an obvious attempt to build gender and ethnic diversity into the board. Nevertheless, all directors are very much establishment types, representing wealth and influence. They average 63.4 years of age.[6]

Seldom do career journalists gain significant power, as reporters or editors, on media boards of directors. Some, however, make mid-career moves into man-

CASE STUDY

The Monks and Gannett

In a classic display of corporate democracy, monks of the Capuchin Order in Milwaukee stepped forward as owners of 190 shares of Gannett stock and insisted the company consider refusing tobacco advertising.

In an equally classic display of corporate power, Gannett's board of directors and management, controlling huge blocs of the company's 146,581,806 shares outstanding, told shareholders at the 1993 annual meeting: "The Company is acting in a socially responsible manner concerning the advertising of tobacco products . . ."

The monks lost.[7]

agement, climb the corporate ranks to become top operating officers and then join boards in that managerial capacity. Jim Batten, chairman of Knight-Ridder, is an example, as is Peter Kann, a Pulitzer prize-winning foreign correspondent for the *Wall Street Journal* and now chairman and chief executive officer of the parent Dow Jones & Co.

So, boards of directors—or the insiders who control them—set policy for our largest media conglomerates. But who are the professional managers important to that policy? Where, how—by whom—is media policy actually executed?

THE TRUE "POWER CLIQUE"

The true power clique in American media companies is in the elite ranks of top management, in the executive committee or management committee chaired by the chief executive officer. Here, at a level just below the board of directors, are made truly crucial decisions on how the nation's newspapers and television stations are operated.

Large shareholder interests and family fortunes often are represented on these operating committees, but they largely are composed of men and women who fought to the top by proving they were better managers than others.

At Knight-Ridder, a six-man Executive Committee makes daily decisions affecting more than 20,000 men and women employed throughout the world by the company. Working directly for them are 18 corporate officers, mostly vice presidents, who are specialists in news, human resources, research, minority affairs, corporate relations, finance, technology, marketing and general operations.

If you read newspapers in Akron, Ohio; Duluth, Minn.; Macon, Ga., Tallahassee, Fla., or 24 other U.S. cities, Clark Hoyt and Marty Claus have much to say about what you see and don't see. Hoyt and Claus—hardly household names in Akron or Duluth—are vice presidents/news, carrying out the Executive Committee's directions.

If you subscribe to TKR Cable Co., or are a commodities trader in Chicago or a stock broker in Tokyo, you probably are influenced every day by decisions made by Knight-Ridder executives. For Knight-Ridder is part owner of TKR, operates one of the world's largest commodities news services and has international financial services reaching many countries.

In sum, this small group of Miami-based executives runs an information company that says it reaches "more than 100 million people in 100 countries."

There is careful cross-pollination between Knight-Ridder's powerful policy-making and operational bodies that implement policy. Of the six men on the Executive Committee, five also serve on the board of directors. Two are members of the Ridder family, which merged its properties with the Knight's in 1974, creating today's powerhouse conglomerate. All Executive Committee members have substantial stock holdings in Knight-Ridder.

Vice presidents (they're mostly in their 40s and 50s) are selected carefully to ensure they fit well into the company's philosophical and operational ethos. Promising young people are spotted early in their careers, then methodically exposed to company operations and training programs before being promoted to corporate headquarters.[8]

The result: A tight-knit group of people who, though individually strong-willed and professional, arrive at the top believing roughly the same things about corporate social responsibility and how newspapers should serve society, readers and advertisers.

Simply, *you believe as the others believe or you don't reach the top.*

Now, you might regard that as akin to intellectual incest, sure to deliver consensus, not imaginative thinking. And that is a true danger in the corporate world, where believing together is considered teamwork, cohesiveness—the organizational focus needed to get things done.

But, how does all this influence a worldwide company of more than 20,000 persons? How does a small group of believers at the top make believers of everybody down the line?

HOW CORPORATE PHILOSOPHY IS ENFORCED

Top managers of media conglomerates have powerful influence over their far-flung empires and, thus, what American news consumers see and read. Two devices are most important:

First, corporate managers appoint local managers and editors, the men and women who decide what will be on the front pages tomorrow in Akron and Duluth. And, in Knight-Ridder, if those local executives buck Miami, they're out.

Second, more indirectly but just as importantly, top executives at all groups, responding to shareholder profit expectations, approve—or disapprove—financial budgets and operating plans submitted by local newspaper, TV and news service managers. In this process, it's quite possible that a local executive's best intentions to, say, spend more to improve journalistic quality will wither before corporate's profit demands.

In just that manner, the distant, anonymous shareholder—who maybe never has been in Akron or who doesn't know where Duluth is—can influence the quality of journalism provided in those cities.

Most top group executives—particularly those at Knight- Ridder—would bristle at suggestions they promote those junior managers closest to their own personalities and operating styles, or use budgets and operating plans to force conformity at group newspapers.

But the plain fact is that executives all hired in accordance with the same corporate specifications, all trained at the same company seminars, all guided by the same top-level corporate philosophy, all following identical budget procedures tend to talk the same, think the same, act the same.

Even the media's worst critics cannot reasonably call this a sinister, centrally directed plot to distort or manage the news and unethically sway the hearts and minds of millions of readers or viewers. But unquestionably, a great deal of dull, look-alike journalism flows from it. Many group newspapers look alike, and in local TV newscasts you can see the handiwork of a group TV news doctor sent in to boost ratings with the "action-news" format of screaming sirens and whirling red lights, just like the sirens and red lights last night, in another town.

Believe top executives of most profit-driven groups who swear they don't interfere in local news coverage. But also believe that they slash the budget of any local manager who dares propose spending above group-approved levels to achieve journalistic excellence.

In a rare public break with industry colleagues, one group executive says group ownership is dragging down journalistic quality of many newspapers.

James H. Ottaway, Jr., president of Ottaway Newspapers, Inc., and a vice president of its parent, Dow Jones, says Thomson and Donrey are groups with "some of the highest profit-margin, lowest-quality newspapers in America today." He says it is "materialistic management philosophy, not public stockholder pressure, that pushes the men who manage these groups to run their newspapers for maximum short-term profit."

Ottaway, whose family built a nationwide group before merging with Dow Jones, says group ownership does not always mean reduction in quality:

> Many well-run groups greatly improve the newspapers they buy. I think we [Dow Jones] have. But too often in recent years, some groups, public and private, have paid prices that were so high, with multiples of revenue or net profits that were so high that severe cost-cutting, gradual or immediate reductions of staff, newshole, local coverage, news quality and reader service, have been required for the purchaser to make a reasonable return on such expensive investments.

THE NEW WEALTHY ELITE

Life at the top in the media world is tough, highly competitive and fast-moving. And, it can be golden.

VIEWPOINT

The Double Standard on Disclosure

"The double standard—the press's claimed rights to examine everything and everyone in the public eye, and its own resistance to having its own work and conduct placed under equal scrutiny—is one of the root causes of the huge loss of journalism's credibility with its audiences."

Norman E. Issacs, editor, educator, media critic

A new class of wealthy elite has developed out of the men and women who run the largest media companies. Examples:

In 1992, Charles T. Brumback, president and CEO of Tribune Co., was paid $668,000 in salary, $308,000 in bonus, $36,465 in other compensation. An additional $240,692 was paid to his long-term compensation plans, and Brumback received options to purchase 131,907 shares of Tribune stock (then trading around $45 to $55 a share). Stanton R. Cook, chairman, received $1,512,461 in annual and long-term compensation that year, plus options on 110,260 shares.

At Times Mirror, Robert F. Erburu, chairman and CEO, received $879,365 plus stock options. Times Mirror's lowest-paid group vice president came in at $513,980 plus options.[9]

SO, WHAT'S AHEAD?

Change in the decade ahead will transform how news is delivered—and the media conglomerates that deliver it.

New technology—the electronic highway—will lead the change. Traditional media, particularly newspapers, will need to change to meet new electronic competitive threats.

Amid the change will be one constant: Large media groups will get larger, competing fiercely to acquire the remaining independent newspapers and broadcast operations—then, when those are all gone, trying to swallow each other.

For shareholders addicted to huge leaps forward, incremental addition of a nice little community newspaper with $10 million annual revenue or so, or a TV station with $12 million, won't do it anymore. To add dramatically to the bottom line that must be displayed to shareholders will take big—really big—acquisitions.

How big? Well, there is the example of Warner and Time Inc., which merged, in a $14 billion deal, to create, overnight, the nation's largest media conglomerate, with well over $5 billion in revenue. In 1994, Viacom, Inc., acquired Paramount Communications for about $10 billion. In the past, Gannett talked friendly merger with both Time Inc. and CBS.

VIEWPOINT

Profits and the Public Trust

"The Bancroft family, which owns 56 percent of Dow Jones and has controlled the company since 1902, has for generations regarded the [*Wall Street*] *Journal* as a quasi-public trust and has encouraged journalistic independence and investment for the long term. . . . Our economic success hinges on that."

Then-chairman Warren Phillips, explaining Dow Jones Co., was instituting antitakeover steps to ensure continued Bancroft control of company

It will be difficult to pull off big coups through hostile takeover of another company—that is, by buying stock on the open market, then walking into corporate headquarters one day and introducing yourself as the new boss.

Media companies erect defenses against such tactics. They take on debt to make themselves unattractive or stagger terms of their directors so no raider easily can create a power base on the board, regardless of number of shares owned. Or, they change their bylaws to force raiders to buy all outstanding shares at the same price, which makes takeover too expensive.

Such antitakeover barriers always are erected in the name of good and right. Dow Jones and New York Times Co., for example, announced theirs as designed to ensure control remains in the hands of enlightened founding families and managers who supervised the growth to greatness of both companies. And it is true that in both cases socially responsible family members invested heavily in journalistic quality. For decades, the Sulzberger family insisted the *New York Times* maintain its quality even when that drained profits.

However, some antitakeover measures are ramrodded through by professional managers anxious to protect their own cushy jobs and prerogatives. Managers know that if they permit takeover by Capital Cities, Newhouse or other similarly profit-minded companies they can kiss good-bye the private jet, limo and other perks.

Now, all this is of considerable importance to Mr. and Mrs. Average Investor with their $1,000 worth of stock. In any hostile takeover attempt bidding for stock can drive up the per-share value 40 percent, 50 percent or more, and that $1,000 suddenly can grow into the price of a new car or Caribbean vacation. However, such hostile bidding contests, which can create wealth for thousands of shareholders, are precluded by antitakeover measures.

Antitakeover measures can solidify for a relative few individuals complete control of even those media companies whose stock is widely held by thousands of investors.

The Federal Securities and Exchange Commission (SEC) signaled in 1986 it feels one antitakeover measure—issuing stock with different classes of voting rights—undermines corporate democracy by giving inordinate power to a few persons. The SEC said, "If we abandon one-share, one vote, to whom will management be accountable for its actions?"

One tactic certain to be used in the future is taking private companies public by selling shares on the open market—but selling just enough to raise substantial capital, not enough to force the owner to relinquish control to anyone. Park Communications did this in 1983 by selling a shade over 10 percent of its stock. The rest—along with complete control of the company—stayed where it was, in the hands of Roy H. Park, founder of the company and, according to *Forbes,* a man worth at least half a billion dollars from newspapers and broadcast stations when he died in 1993.

Using this tactic, small companies unknown nationally today to the reading or viewing public will move into view as media growth companies in the next decade. And, the men and women who own and run them, equally unknown today, will assume new importance in American society.

NOW, *YOU* MAKE THE CALL

Should society—should you—be concerned about concentration of media power, about the focused influence of a handful of executives on the nation's news and information agenda?

Reflect on the societal values and journalistic principles we've applied to individual journalists throughout this book. Should—can—media companies and executives be measured against those same values and principles?

For example, John Rawls (Chapter 1, Box 1–1) would suggest reporters step behind a "veil of ignorance" and imagine themselves in the same socioeconomic circumstances of those they cover. Rawls would say that helps ensure equal and fair coverage of poor as well as rich, the anonymous as well as the famous. Do you think group executives who direct many newspapers or TV stations also should step behind the veil of ignorance? If so, do you think executives earning over $1 million a year and traveling by private jet and limo could, by any stretch of the imagination, really put themselves in the shoes of the less fortunate?

Has the profit-driven move upscale after affluent audiences caused groups to lose sight of the first journalistic principle—serve the public? Or, is the high-quality journalism produced by some groups possible only because they are financially successful?

Other questions to ponder:

Does a community suffer when control of its local news media passes from hands-on, hometown owners to distant group executives? Should society prevent that? If so, why not prevent sale of, say, a local hardware store to a chain? Does society have a bigger stake in the sale of news and information than in sale of hammers and screwdrivers?

With the groups swelling—21 have over $1 billion annual revenue each—an entirely new layer of media management is being created of accountants, lawyers and others skilled in handling money and expert in management science. But many are nonjournalists removed both geographically and psychologically from the communities their newspapers and television stations serve and, indeed, from news work itself. What are the societal implications of concentrating media power in nonnews, absentee hands?

Should society determine how big is big enough? Society already limits the number of broadcast stations any individual owner can possess and the percentage of total audience a single owner can reach. Should it similarly limit newspaper owners? If so, how would that square with the First Amendment guarantee of a free press?

Companies with newspaper or television roots are tucking strange bedfellows beneath their "communications" roofs. For example, the Chicago Cubs baseball team is owned by Tribune Company, and Grand Ole Opry by Oklahoma Publishing. Should communications companies own other companies their reporters cover?

The policy-setting apparatus of some large media companies is controlled by a few wealthy families and individuals. Some have interlocking relationships with other media firms that expand considerably their influence. For example, leading newspaper and broadcast group executives serve concurrently on the board of directors of the Associated Press, the world's largest general news agency. Should society demand such media giants have boards of directors and management truly representative of the communities they serve? Should it insist, for example, on ethnic, gender or racial balance in the policy-setting apparatus of any company so influential in how this country is run?

It can be argued that an executive's income and personal affairs are of no concern to the public, students of ethics—or authors. This author would agree if the executive were running a nuts and bolts factory or a dairy farm.

But we deal in Chapter 8 with men and women enormously influential in every sector of our society—executives who run some of America's most important institutions. Is that power argument for closer public examination of media executives, who they are, what they think, how they operate?

Should executives who operate news and information services reaching more than 100 million people in 100 countries be open to the same public scrutiny we routinely accord, say, a smalltown mayor or the youngest first-year congressperson?

Should the financial disclosure demanded of obscure government employees be demanded of, say, Gannett executives who operate 81 newspapers throughout the United States, plus *USA Today* and TV and radio stations?

Should individuals with power to influence tens of millions of readers and viewers—power to sway the affairs of state—live fully public lives? Should their personal ideologies and ethical codes be open to public scrutiny?

Finally, cable companies, regional Bell operating companies and AT&T are edging into transmission of news. Those companies have no tradition of journalism. They employ no large staffs of trained, dedicated reporters and editors. Does it concern you that the electronic highway may be controlled by technocrats, not journalists? Do you think society should insist that Ma Bell toe the line on the same societal values, journalistic principles and loyalties we require of newspapers and TV stations?

Summary

Widely diversified media groups own 76 percent of all daily newspapers and most attractive television stations.

The trend toward bigness will continue. It's corporate profit and personal prestige, not ideology or proselytism, that motivate media empire builders. On the seller's part, extraordinarily high inheritance taxes on media properties force many sales.

Of the 15 largest media companies, measured in total revenue, three are privately owned—Advance publications, Hearst Corp., and Cox Enterprises. Among those publicly held, Times Mirror, Gannett, Tribune Co., are strongly positioned to grow even larger in the 1990s.

Great fortunes are built in owning the media. Millions are made buying and selling media stocks.

The policy-setting apparatus of any publicly owned media company is, theoretically, its board of directors. Boards sometimes are controlled by heirs of founding families or strong-willed professional managers who get their way because they increase profits.

Power cliques in media companies are the elite ranks of top management in the executive committee that makes daily operating decisions. Their power flows from the ability to appoint—or fire—local managers and editors of group newspapers and TV stations throughout the country and in their absolute control at group level of operating plans and budgets drawn up by local managers.

Huge salaries—sometimes millions annually—are paid key media managers, some of whom consequently have become a wealthy new elite in the media world.

In decades ahead, the operating philosophy of the most influential media conglomerates likely will not change. Many are instituting antitakeover measures to solidify control in the hands of leading shareholders or carefully selected professional managers as insurance against such change. They also are planning more growth, perhaps by swallowing each other, merging or otherwise combining to create the financial, technological and managerial strength to exploit the electronic highway that promises new ways of delivering news, information and entertainment.

Notes

1. Daily Groups Slip to 132," *presstime,* quoting John Morton Newspaper Research, July 1993, p. 83.
2. I discuss the acquisition phenomenon more fully in Conrad Fink, *Strategic Newspaper Management* (New York: Random House, 1988).

3. A variety of sources yield insights into individual companies. Annual and quarterly reports plus letters to shareholders, obtainable from the secretary of each corporation, are prime sources, as are 10-K Reports, also obtainable from corporate secretaries or the Securities and Exchange Commission. Among trade publications, *Advertising Age* does superb wrap-ups on media activity. Its annual, "100 Leading Media Companies," is highly informative. The author finds one investment analyst particularly insightful—John Morton of Lynch, Jones & Ryan, 1037 Thirtieth St., N.W., Washington, D.C. 20007. *Forbes* magazine gives valuable details on revenues and profits.
4. Each year, *Forbes* publishes a special edition, "The *Forbes* Four Hundred," which gives details of fortunes in the media and elsewhere. My figures are from "The 100 Greatest Fortunes in the World," *Forbes,* July 5, 1993, p. 68.
5. "The *Forbes* Four Hundred," *Forbes* Special Edition, 1985.
6. Knight-Ridder, Inc., 1992 Annual Report, p. 72, et seq.
7. Gannett Notice of Annual Meeting of Shareholders, March 19, 1993, p. 16.
8. Ibid.
9. My figures are from 1993 notices of annual meetings issued by the respective companies. Separately, *NewsInc* employed a management consultant to study materials issued by publicly owned media groups and found that, "[l]ike most corporations, newspaper companies bury information on executive pay in obtuse paragraphs scattered throughout proxy reports . . ." As a result of its study, *NewsInc* put total 1990 compensation for John Curley, chairman and CEO of Gannett, at *$3,011,830*; at Knight-Ridder, James Batten's total take was $1,379,350. Figures covered salary, bonus, stock options, supplemental insurance and other goodies. In 1991, a bad year for media group profits, Arthur Ochs Sulzberger of New York Times Co. pulled $1,541,602, and Charles Brumback of Tribune Co., a whopping $3,825,105, *NewsInc* said. See "The Bottom Line," *NewsInc,* March 1992, p. 24, and "Sharing the Wealth," May 1992, p. 10.

PART 4

THE MEDIA INSTITUTION AND SOCIETY

Our study of ethics now turns to a broader view: the relationship of the media as an institution to other institutions in our society.

We must take this wider view because we won't truly understand ethical influences on individual journalists unless we proceed beyond what we've studied so far in this book—the history of ethical thought, societal and professional values and principles, the profit-driven character of media groups.

In Chapter 9, we look at whether the evolution of individually owned media into diversified conglomerates—a media institution with enormous power—might lead society to redefine the ground rules under which the media operate. Do societal and Constitutional standards laid down long ago, under quite different circumstances, still apply in the same way?

In Chapter 10, we examine critical problem areas in news coverage that affect institutional relationships between the media and other forces in society.

CHAPTER 9

NEW CORPORATE CHARACTER, NEW SOCIETAL STATUS?

Societal attitudes change toward major American institutions—Big Government, Big Business, Big Church—as political and economic circumstances change.

Add Big Media to the institutions undergoing rigorous societal examination and whose fortunes periodically rise or fall in public esteem and trust.

Because Big Media ranks so high among institutions having impact on society, are newspapers, magazines and broadcasters in for specially harsh treatment?

Will the huge, diversified media conglomerates of today—and tomorrow's even larger ones—be accorded the same special status that the independently owned newspaper, magazine and broadcast station enjoyed in the past?

Big Business increasingly is forced to reveal its innermost secrets—not only what profits were made but how they were made, whether skies were polluted in the making of chemicals or whether cheap foreign labor was exploited in manufacturing.

Big Church, whether of Rome or an evangelistic television studio in the Bible Belt, now must endure outsiders pawing through its financial affairs with iconoclastic fervor.

Is such intense scrutiny ahead for Big Media?

FROM THE BEGINNING: SPECIAL STATUS

Newspapers and magazines won special status early in America because of our predecessors' reverence for free dissemination of information. They held free speech essential in our democracy, and for 200 years a special niche in our society has been granted those who deal in ideas, news and opinion.

VIEWPOINT

Just Another Power Struggle

"We investigate conflict of interest on the part of public officials. Yet too many media executives are reluctant to acknowledge their own conflict of interest when they take editorial positions on legislation or community projects that can affect their own company's earnings. . . . Until we are as open as we expect others to be, the public will continue to regard us as one powerful institution doing battle with other powerful institutions—and also as having a dubious advantage because of our unique Constitutional protections."

Tom Johnson, then publisher of the *Los Angeles Times* and now president of CNN

Gradually, however, the print media edged many commercial as well as news activities into that protective niche and now argue, for example, that commercial speech—tobacco advertising, say—merits the same Constitutional protection given other forms of free speech.

The media also argue that the First Amendment guarantees much more than free speech, that it covers, for example, the right to put a newspaper coin box on a public sidewalk—a business consideration—even if it does block pedestrians.

The media's special niche has been expanded to include the right (indeed the duty) to investigate the affairs and finances of other institutions. Nevertheless, the media insist on being free of any similar outside scrutiny in return.

If two newspapers in the same city can prove one is in financial jeopardy they can win special exemption from antitrust laws and combine certain business operations—a privilege accorded no other type of business in our society.

And, from the days when Benjamin Franklin was the first postmaster general, newspapers and magazines have enjoyed preferential postal rates. Society even granted newspapers exemption from some child labor laws, permitting use of boys and girls as carriers.

Then came invention of the television money machine and rapid consolidation of broadcast and newspapers into huge diversified institutions of corporate character and philosophy far removed from the venerated political pamphleteer of revolutionary lore.[1]

All this inevitably blurs whatever distinction exists between newspaper and television companies and, say, banks, railroads, steel companies or any other similarly profit-driven firms. And, it can lead to society demanding that the media institution now submit to public examination on how it meets society's expectations.

Certainly, new questions are injected into the public dialogue by Big Media's character change. For example:

Can profit-oriented companies that diversify into nonmedia enterprises still expect to position themselves in society as newspaper and television companies?

VIEWPOINT

Newspapers Abandoning Their Status?

"One day before long, a judge will hand down a ruling favoring the plaintiff in a libel suit. The reasoning will likely be convoluted, but it will boil down to this: A newspaper which is operated solely for profit, and which bases its editorial decisions on the same motive, will be found to have abandoned its status as an entity which operates for the public good.

"The situation is analogous to . . . hospitals . . . in Pennsylvania which are having their tax-exempt status revoked because they have been found by the courts to have abandoned their charity care and public service functions in favor of profits . . ."

Letter to the Editor of *Editor & Publisher Magazine.*[2]

Should Tribune Company, owner of the Chicago Cubs baseball team and a major investor in Ontario newsprint mills, as well as owner of the *Chicago Tribune,* classify itself, as it does, as a "diversified media company"?

Is Oklahoma Publishing, owner of Grand Ole Opry, as well as newspapers and broadcast stations, truly a media company?

How about NBC News, now a relatively small division of huge RCA, which, in turn, is a subsidiary of multibillion dollar General Electric Co., maker of refrigerators and jet engines?

Does the character of a media conglomerate change—and will society's attitude toward it thus change also—depending on who owns that company? Is Time Warner, the nation's largest media company, still truly a media enterprise, now that Seagram Co., a liquor company, acquired a 5.7 percent stake in it for $702 million in 1993? Is Time Warner's status further changed by a $2.5 billion investment in it that same year by US West, one of America's huge regional Bell telephone companies?[3]

Should the special exemption from antitrust laws extended some unprofitable newspapers be claimed, as it is for some of their papers, by enormously profitable Gannett or Knight-Ridder?

Simply put, is the media institution in danger of expanding and diversifying itself right out from beneath the First Amendment tent, where, when composed of strictly communications companies, it sat so comfortably for so long, enjoying special legal benefits and societal status?

Opinion surveys reveal growing feeling among readers and viewers that the media's size and power call for new ground rules.

Note seemingly contradictory public attitudes: a fundamental belief in free speech and even appreciation of the media's watchdog role but, just as clearly, a fear that the media are too big, too powerful—an irreverent, irresponsible cannon loose on a pitching deck that must be snubbed down before it punches a hole in the ship of state.[4]

VIEWPOINT

The Press and Suspicion of Power

" . . . Americans are suspicious of power wherever they see it. The press believes, in my view correctly, that whatever power it has is necessary to combat a government that has grown incomparably more powerful. But the public evidently sees big press corporations as among the social institutions that have to be kept in check."

Anthony Lewis, veteran columnist, *New York Times*

Does it all portend escalating attacks on the media and their special status? Hard to say. However, the media institution has marshaled powerful forces to protect its interests.

THE MEDIA LOBBY GATHERS STRENGTH

The public doesn't know much about them, but two media lobby groups have strong political clout in Washington.

They are the Newspaper Association of America (NAA), which represents (1993) 1,450 newspapers accounting for 90 percent of daily circulation in the United States, and the National Association of Broadcasters (NAB), which represents the networks and 90 percent of all TV stations and about half of all radio stations.

What must a U.S. senator or representative think when an NAA or NAB representative comes through the front door! Perhaps something like, "Here comes a person speaking for virtually all significant newspapers (or broadcast stations) in the country." Now, that's clout!

NAA, with an annual budget approaching $35 million, and NAB, which spends about $17 million annually, are only two of many effective pressure groups the media institution has organized.[5]

Additional millions for lobbying are spent by national groups for weekly publishers, suburban newspapers, the black press and others. There are powerful regional publishers associations, including the Southern Newspaper Publishers Association and New England Daily Newspaper Association, plus newspaper groups in each state.

Behind NAB are the Television Information Bureau, Radio Advertising Bureau and regional and state broadcaster groups.

These deal primarily with the media's business interests. Each industry also has national and state groups dealing with news matters, among them the influential American Society of Newspaper Editors, Associated Press Managing Editors and Radio-TV News Directors Association.

VIEWPOINT

Power or Cliché?

"It is a cliché that the American press has great power. That's one of the few contentions shared by the most far-out liberals and the most rock-ribbed conservatives—though, of course, both look under each other's bed for the villain.

"The truth is that the American press, as an industry, has been ineffective in debates on public policy that impact our business.

"Why?

"Largely, because we take so much of our nourishment from individuality. We are, by and large, fiercely dedicated to constitutional liberty. By and large, we detest collectivism, in terms of government power or industrial monopoly. That makes us lousy candidates for collective action—even in our own defense."

Charles T. Brumback, president and chief executive officer, Tribune Co.[6]

There is extremely close cross-pollination between these lobbying groups and the newspaper, TV and cable conglomerates we discussed in Chapter 8. For example, NAA's board of directors always includes top executives from the largest media companies. In 1993, Donald Newhouse, co-owner of Advance Publications, the nation's largest privately owned media company, became NAA chairman. He succeeded Frank Bennack, chief executive officer of Hearst, a multibillion dollar conglomerate.

Conglomerate executives also increase dramatically their impact on our society by serving on the policy-setting board of directors of the Associated Press, the principal source of international and national news for (in 1993) 1,559 U.S. daily and weekly newspapers and 5,900 broadcast stations (and thousands overseas, as well).

Of course, the media institution is not solely preoccupied with influencing public policy in its own selfish self-interest.

NAA, for example, broadly states that its primary mission is " . . . to advance the cause of a free press, and to ensure that newspapers maintain the economic strength essential to serve the American people."[7] NAA does highly regarded research in equipment, newsprint, circulation, advertising and other operating sectors essential to a newspaper's business success. NAB provides advisory services crucial to television and radio operations.

But the media institution often dons lobbyist gloves in Washington, and when it does, it's not always out to protect the First Amendment or the people's right to know—it's often naked self-interest.

WHOSE INTERESTS ARE AT STAKE?

NAB lobbies hard for three broad goals: generally reducing federal regulation of broadcasting, resisting federal or state intervention in advertising (fighting bans

VIEWPOINT

Pork Bellies versus Public Service

"Are TV and radio stations becoming, like pork bellies, a commodity to be bought and sold by fast-moving traders? Does the licensee's fitness to serve the public have any meaning today, or are stations to be sold to the highest bidder? Are the public's airwaves to be used as tax shelters for the wealthy? Is there a future for the more responsible station owners—those with a sense of tradition and pride in being assigned those rights—in such a setting?"

Advertising Age, editorial attacking "fast-buck artists" who ignore public service responsibilities of broadcast ownership

on beer and wine commercials is a major effort) and gaining full First Amendment rights for radio and TV. NAB has the Newspaper Association's backing in fighting for relaxation of Federal Communications Commission regulation of broadcast.[8] Newspaper groups, of course, own broadcast stations.

Under the Reagan administration, the two groups made considerable progress. For example, the Federal Communications Commission dropped requirements that AM radio stations devote 8 percent of airtime (and FM stations 6 percent) to nonentertainment. Also dropped were restrictions on the number of minutes that could be devoted to commercials in an hour and a requirement that stations keep detailed program logs open to public inspection.

NAB mustered strong support to pressure the FCC to require cable television systems to carry local TV stations. With well over half of U.S. television homes wired for cable, TV station owners fear they will lose audience unless their signals are carried on cable. The NAB says it recruited about 1,000 broadcasters to press members of Congress for action; it estimates 120 Congress members then wrote the FCC supporting "must-carry" rules forcing cable operators to carry local TV stations.[9]

NAB also claims its lobbying beat back in Congress an effort to impose mandatory warnings in broadcast advertising that aspirin might trigger in children a serious illness called Reye's syndrome.[10]

In a victory for Big Media that wants to get bigger, the FCC in 1985 raised limits on number of broadcast licenses any single owner can hold. And broadcasters no longer must own stations for three years before reselling—great news for many who deal in radio and TV properties as they would any commodity, buying and reselling for often enormous short-term capital gain without the slightest concern for serving the public interest in communities where they made those gains.

A significant win came in 1985 with an FCC statement that the fairness doctrine is contrary to public interest. In 1987, the FCC said the doctrine no longer was FCC policy. Since 1949, this doctrine had required broadcasters to provide balanced coverage and to give opposing sides in any controversy reasonable opportunity to respond—but under such cumbersome, time-consuming conditions that broadcast journalists often simply avoided controversial issues.[11]

In general, the broadcast and newspaper associations argue that new technology, particularly cable TV, militates for relaxed regulatory policy. The FCC's founding principle was that airwaves were finite, were public property and that the relative scarcity of broadcast opportunities required regulation and licensing of the entire industry in the public interest. In these days of proliferating cable TV and other broadcast options, the NAB and NAA argue diversity in a competitive marketplace will work it all out But neither has the temerity to suggest that letting marketplace factors rule will yield for the American viewer or listener higher quality, more principled news or entertainment programming.

A FREE PRESS FIGHTS FREE COMPETITION

Although favoring a competitive broadcasting marketplace open to all, The Newspaper Association of America is far less charitable when it comes to a telephone company offering information services that might threaten newspapers. Here, naked self-interest has triumphed in a revealing illustration of how a free press supposedly dedicated to free exchange of ideas can forget all that when money is at stake.

To explain:

For decades, bringing in raw newsprint by the expensive ton, then sending it out as finished newspapers for delivery, in part by teenagers on bicycles, caused many publishers to wonder if there was a better way. That same wonder led other communications experts, notably at telephone companies, to develop technology that electronically can deliver huge amounts of information to individual homes.

AT&T, for example, engineered telephone circuits that speedily can deliver shopping information, household hints, banking services and scores of other information services. Newspapers came under obvious threat: news and advertising could flow over new fiber optics circuits and into desktop terminals in kitchens or dens all over America for use by increasingly computer-skilled householders. A nightmare for publishers: electronic Yellow Pages, with prices updated minute by minute, or electronic classified advertising available through telephone not newspaper facilities.

The newspaper institution reacted generally in two ways:

First, many companies, including Washington Post Co., launched their own infant electronic systems, using cable TV or telephone company facilities to exploit the new technology. Some invested heavily in cellular or mobile telephone systems.

Second, in what probably was the worst, most blatantly selfish strategic move—and error—in the history of American newspapering, publishers unleashed their association (then the American Newspaper Publishers Association) in an unprecedently vigorous lobbying effort to keep telephone companies out of information services.

VIEWPOINT

Free Press Fat Cats

"It was a disaster, a complete disaster . . . we come on as fat-cat heavies trying to protect our turf."

Scott Low, publisher of the *Quincy (Mass.) Patriot-Ledger,* recalling lobbying efforts in Congress against telephone company services that compete with newspapers

Newspapers thus positioned themselves in public perception as some sort of 20th Century Luddites—determined, in their own self-interest, to prevent new technology and new competitors from entering the information marketplace.

Although history yields no example of superior technology being kept out of the marketplace, newspaper lobbyists, including Katharine Graham, then chairman of both the Washington Post Co., and the newspaper association, hurried to Congress with the argument, somewhat embarrassing even to publishers in the rereading, that telephone companies must be kept out of the information business—but that this is not, gracious, as it must seem, anticompetitive.

It in fact is a defense of the First Amendment, newspaper lobbyists said, because if telephone companies are permitted to both generate and transmit information they might be able to use their enormous resources to gain monopoly control over the free flow of information.

Said Barry Bingham, then publisher of the *Louisville Courier-Journal*: "I break ranks with the publishers' group when they say in the name of the First Amendment they're going to abbreviate Bell's right to publish."[12] (Washington Post Company's telephone business flourished—"fulfilling the optimistic expectations we held upon entering this new field," Katharine Graham said in her 1986 annual report to shareholders; telephone companies, on the other hand, still were not in the information business.)

Newspapers generally found consumers not eager for the early electronic services they launched by themselves. Knight-Ridder and Times Mirror each lost tens of millions of dollars before scrapping efforts to sell electronic delivery systems to householders. However, the computer-driven technology worked brilliantly, and by 1994 there was the reality—or, depending on your view, the specter—of telephone companies throwing their resources, which dwarf those of even the largest media companies, into developing new electronic ways of reaching desired household targets.

It remains Newspaper Association of America dogma: "A telephone company that provides a conduit for information as a common carrier should not also be a competing information carrier over the same lines or conduits which the carrier controls."[13]

But the publishers' solid front is broken and individual companies are scrambling to sign collaborative deals with telephone companies and other players in electronic communications.

NEWSPAPERS VERSUS DIRECT MAIL

NAA vigorously fights another competitor, also in defense of newspaper advertising revenue: direct-mail companies.

Not needing expensive news-gathering staffs, these competitors offer advertisers relatively low-cost service and, with relative ease do two things paid-circulation newspapers can accomplish only at high costs and with operational difficulty—reach nearly all households in a market or, alternatively, single out for target marketing only those households geographically or demographically attractive to advertisers.

Direct-mail companies depend on efficient, speedy and affordable performance by the U.S. Postal Service—and that is where NAA focuses its attack on "junk mail." This requires delicate handling, of course, because (1) newspapers themselves from colonial days have enjoyed highly preferential postal rates and (2) many today operate their own direct-mail services.

NAA's tactic is to lobby for lowest possible second-class rates, under which newspapers are mailed; to demand expeditious handling of matter mailed by newspapers—and to attack vigorously, in public and before the U.S. Postal Rate Commission, the slightest hint of favoritism for direct mailers. Direct mailers are heavy users of third-class rates, and NAA claims those rates are subsidized by first-class rates, unfairly pegged up to nine times higher.

Jack Valentine, president of Advo-Systems, Inc., the nation's largest direct-mail company, responded in a speech to NAA: "People are not being fooled by canned editorials about junk mail and subsidized rates. . . . You really are only seeking higher rates in order to protect your monopolies in local print advertising."[14]

A SAFETY NET FOR RICH AND POOR

As far back as the 1930s, Congress helped maintain separate editorial voices in some cities by making it possible for financially ailing newspapers to gain exemption from certain antitrust laws. In 1970, this became the Newspaper Preservation Act, a safety net into which some of the largest, most profitable media conglomerates have pushed a few of their failures.

In sum, if a newspaper is provably failing financially and in danger of being shut down, it can combine with another, stronger paper in all but news functions, with the U.S. attorney general's approval, and do so free of antitrust restrictions.

That permits combining all production and business activities in a joint operating agreement (JOA), housing both newspapers in the same building, selling advertising and circulation with the same sales crew and using the same accounting, transportation, production staffs.

Table 9–1
Joint operating agreements*

City	Year Began	Partners
Albuquerque	1933	Scripps, independent
El Paso	1936	Scripps, Gannett
Nashville	1937	Gannett, independent
Evansville, Ind.	1938	Scripps, independent
Tucson	1940	Pulitzer, Gannett
Chattanooga (dissolved 1966, renewed 1980)	1942	Two independents
Madison, Wis.	1948	Lee, independent
Fort Wayne, Ind.	1950	Knight-Ridder, independent
Birmingham, Ala.	1950	Scripps, Newhouse
Lincoln, Neb.	1950	Lee, independent
Salt Lake City	1952	Two independents
Shreveport	1953	Gannett, independent
Knoxville	1957	Scripps, independent
Charleston, W. Va.	1958	Thomson, independent
Honolulu	1962	Gannett, independent
San Francisco	1965	Hearst, independent
Cincinnati	1979	Scripps, Gannett
Seattle	1983	Hearst, independent
Detroit	1988	Gannett, Knight-Ridder

*Cities in which two newspapers share all but news and editorial facilities under joint operating agreements. The U.S. Justice Department permits such arrangements free of antitrust considerations if one of the cooperating newspapers can prove it otherwise would fail financially.

In any other industry, even a hint that two competing companies were discussing such a combination would arouse the Justice Department's antitrust division. The rationale behind the Newspaper Preservation Act, of course, is that greater societal good is served if newspapers, separate in at least news and editorial functions, survive in cities where they otherwise would fail (see Table 9–1).

In yet another special favor for newspapers, then, society constructed a safety net for weak publications. Generally, JOAs increase profits enormously.

In the 19 JOAs (see Table 9–1), groups outnumber independents 22 to 14. Gannett, with revenue well over $3.3 billion, has six newspapers in JOAs. Knight-Ridder and Hearst, both multibillion dollar corporations, have two each.

JOAS ARE CRITICIZED

Some advertisers complain JOAs create monopolies under which ad rates are forced to unfair heights. Competitors—including television, radio and suburban newspapers—claim JOAs create an artificially low cost base for the participating papers, giving them unfair advantage over other advertising media.

Unions complain JOAs permit newspapers to unfairly fire large numbers of employees displaced when production and business departments are merged.

Some argue readers suffer. Coleman Young, then Detroit's mayor, noting that in pre-JOA days the *Free Press* was selling for .25 cents, the *News* for .15 cents, commented:

> They're creating a monopoly . . . and I'll bet you 24 hours after they approve that JOA the . . . papers cost .30 cents each. If they would do that right now, they wouldn't need a JOA, because the *Free Press* couldn't say they were losing money. They'd both be making money.[15]

Coleman was a bit off on his timing, but both Detroit papers did raise daily prices to .35 cents (and to $1.25 for their jointly produced Sunday edition). Still, at .35 cents the two papers, both strong journalistically, were real bargains—and priced in line with other dailies. In 1993, 703 U.S. dailies were at .35 cents, 522, at .50 cents.

Other objections to JOAs arise from structural changes in media companies. For example, Congress's intent clearly was to protect diversity of news and editorial voices. Yet, JOA partners today engage in many nonnews activities, such as operating free-circulation shoppers with no news and direct-mail services that hardly add to the diversity of voices and opinions.

Clearly, however, the alternative to JOAs is a rising number of dead newspapers.

For complex reasons of newspaper economics fewer than 20 U.S. cities today support two or more competing metro dailies of like size and characteristics. And, pressed by the Rising Tide of Shareholder Expectation, publicly owned media companies will not—cannot—pump unlimited funds into a losing newspaper to subsidize it indefinitely. Al Neuharth, then chairman of Gannett, commented: "The fact is that the Detroit newspaper issue is very simple. Shall there be one daily newspaper or two?"[16]

Still, questions remain:

When, in 1933, it began to succor failing newspapers, Congress didn't have to worry that television competitors would suffer if core city metros were aided. TV hadn't been launched yet. There was virtually no significant radio or suburban newspaper competition, either. Has the newspaper competitive environment changed so radically that the end result of Congress's good intentions is changed?

Did Congress envisage huge, highly profitable groups enjoying JOAs? When, in 1937, it permitted the *Nashville Banner* and the *Tennessean*—both then independently owned—to form a JOA, did Congress intend to create a situation that in the 1990s would add handsomely to the coffers of multibillion dollar Gannett?

NEWSPAPERS GET OTHER GOOD DEALS

In other areas of business, the newspaper institution seeks special treatment due to its unique status in our society.

NAA, for example, resists—most often successfully—attempts to tax newsprint and ink purchases or institute sales tax on circulation and advertising sales.

NAA resists proposals that would deny tax deductions to companies for their advertising expenditures, which certainly would reduce newspaper revenue. NAA says "valid commercial speech concerns" are raised by such proposals. NAA also supports the "historic principle of duty-free importation of newsprint"—historic principle importers of most other commodities would search for in vain.[17]

Newspapers seek Labor Department recognition for reporters as professionals, which would eliminate a Fair Labor Standards Act requirement that they be paid overtime for hours worked beyond a normal workweek.[18]

NOW, *YOU* MAKE THE CALL

So, the media stand revealed as Big Business and preoccupied with profit and self-interest, as are other businesses.

But, after all, is that a damning indictment? And, really, do you have a better alternative to free-enterprise media that are uniquely independent financially as well as Constitutionally?[19]

Viable alternatives are extremely limited:

Narrowly partisan journalism. This would involve political, economic, religious or other groups owning the media to insure news coverage and editorial opinion are to their liking. Aside from being incredibly anachronistic in contemporary American society, media owned by railroads, labor unions or other special interest groups would be impossible economically. There isn't enough special-interest funding to support today's metro dailies, the multibillion dollar broadcasting industry or the hundreds of small-town papers scattered across the nation.

Nonprofit journalism. Absent the tradition of Britain's independent, nonprofit (but government-supported) British Broadcasting Corp., U.S. publicly supported, nonprofit radio and television have unending financial problems even though they operate on a comparatively limited scale. Public broadcasting in America, like its free enterprise brethren, increasingly seeks commercial support from business and industry.

Government sponsorship (plus its concomitant control). Look at authoritarian systems around the world and see the disasters that befall any society submitting to government control of the media. This alternative is unacceptable in our society.

Is it, then, to be continuation of a media institution operating under a free enterprise system, with its inherent weaknesses and dangers, as well as strengths? Even in those opinion polls revealing public unease about the media, the answer overwhelmingly is yes, that there is no acceptable alternative.

Yet, media supporters and critics alike see problems developing between the free-enterprise newspaper and broadcasting industries and other institutions in our society. The problems likely will become more severe due to changes under way in corporate character and philosophy and in societal attitudes. But, if there are to be changes, what shall they be and who shall make them?

Anyway, isn't it possible for the media as an institution to be profit-oriented and good citizens? Can't an enlightened media institution subscribe to values our society cherishes? Indeed, isn't it good business to do so?

VIEWPOINT

The Private Enterprise Media

"Private enterprise [media] will not only be with us for a long time, but so far as most of us can see, it will be the best system for producing the general run of news and views.

"Once we have acknowledged that a business enterprise, organized to make a profit, is the optimum basis for our news institutions, we need not ignore serious problems within that system. Keeping our news as honest and as competent as possible is not a luxury; it is not merely the simple elegance of purity. In our society, it is closely related to the survival of democracy."

Ben H. Bagdikian, editor, media critic, teacher

Do you see a contradiction in the media fighting to retain their favored niche in our society and simultaneously lobbying, vigorously and nakedly, in their own business self-interest? Is that misuse of the First Amendment protection and media power? Or, do you think the media institution should be permitted to lobby in its own self-interest, just like any other business or special-interest bloc?

Do you agree society has a stake in maintaining separate news and editorial voices in U.S. cities and thus should extend JOA protection to failing newspapers? If so, should that protection be extended to newspapers owned by enormously profitable media groups such as Knight-Ridder and Gannett? Should similar protection against financial failure be extended to, say, hotdog stands? After all, wouldn't there be direct societal benefit—wouldn't more hotdog stands competing for your business mean better service and lower prices?

Now, really back off and consider: To offer no JOA protection or preferential postal rates and other privileges would cause some newspapers to die and perhaps substantially reduce the effectiveness of others. Our society has decided (as reflected in the Newspaper Preservation Act) to support diversity of voices. Has our society in fact reached a Golden Mean solution?

You make the call—but don't expect unanimous answers from media critics or the media themselves. On those questions, even the media are split.

THE MEDIA BLOC THAT ISN'T

In the McCarthy era, an ethical Dark Age for both American politics and journalism compressed mostly into one decade, the 1950s, there arose the media conspiracy theory.

For a journalist, the price of attendance at a cocktail party could be the question, "Who really tells you what to write?"

For media owners, the times gave rise to a suspicion, later refined in the Nixon-Agnew era, when ethical lights went out again in some halls of govern-

VIEWPOINT

Conspiracy or Stupidity?

" . . . the more time I've spent covering the media, the more I've come to realize that a great deal of what appears to outsiders—and indeed to many insiders—to be the product of calculation, conspiracy, collusion, and/or personal, political, social or financial interest on the part of some editor or publisher has actually come about because of stupidity, vanity, carelessness, inefficiency, insecurity, competitive zeal, personal weakness, institutional idiosyncrasy or even . . . coincidence.

"Time and again I have been told of high-ranking editors having stories killed, eviscerated, buried or bannered, either out of cowardice or vested interest, and time and again my reporting has disclosed a far less sinister (if no less damning) explanation for what had happened."

David Shaw, noted media critic, *Los Angeles Times*[20]

ment, that somewhere, somehow, a small but sinister band, often characterized as eastern intellectuals, were conspiring over what news the nation would, and wouldn't, read or view.

It left me, for one, slightly bemused—laboring in frenetic newsrooms where clearly nobody was remotely capable of efficiently handling, let alone controlling, the unending torrent of news, then hearing the suspicion that somebody must be telling everybody else how to slant it. Newsrooms in fact were not overburdened with easterners or, certainly, intellectuals of the think-alike type or any other kind.

The point was—and is—undeniable: The media institution is big, powerful and does hold certain selfish philosophical and business interests, and is organized to lobby to protect them. But, there is no "the media"—if that connotes group-think on the media's role in society, if it means united response to external criticism or that newspaper and television executives are moving lock-step toward jointly creating a new institutional relationship with society.

Journalists cannot even agree on whether newspapers and television truly have a serious problem with society, let alone what to do if there is one.

One group within the media is gloomily pessimistic. Norman Isaacs, following a distinguished career as editor at some of the nation's great newspapers, sees a gathering storm ahead. He warns in his excellent *Untended Gate* (New York: Columbia University Press, 1986) of " . . . the next ten to twenty years as possibly being the most crucial for journalism to survive as a free-standing entity." Isaacs fears enemies of free speech undermining the First Amendment—perhaps in a constitutional convention—by using as leverage the public's currently low esteem for the media. Isaacs and others warn that the media have let slip their journalistic quality, their dedication to accuracy, balance, fairness, compassion and ethical performance. There is call for accountability—to a sense of professionalism and to the public—and all under some type of formalized auditing or monitoring, preferably by an independent, nongovernment body.

A second media group sees the "credibility gap" simply as more of the ups and downs in public esteem that journalists must endure. Ben Bradlee, as *Washington Post* executive editor, counseled his colleagues to just do the best journalistic job possible and not worry about being liked. This group, which includes some of the country's most influential editors and publishers, strongly resists any formalized monitoring of the media, either from within or by outside critics.

A third group: journalists of self-doubt, practice ethical-reactive journalism, displaying Pavlovian response to whatever the latest poll indicates the public wants on the front page or on the evening news.

It's a far cry from media conspiracy. Indeed, opinions within the media institution are so deeply divided that newspapers and television generally unite only to reject any systematic appraisal other than that of the individual reader or viewer making the daily marketplace decision on what to read and what to view.

THE NEWS COUNCIL AND OTHER FAILURES

The most ambitious effort to independently monitor the media institution's performance was made by the National News Council. It struggled 11 years for support, then died in 1984, generally unknown to the public and mostly ignored or actively resisted by the media.

The council was sponsored by the Twentieth Century Fund (but independently financed) and took the mission of investigating public complaints about media performance. Participation by newspapers and broadcast organizations was voluntary and the council had no enforcement powers. The council considered 242 complaints against the media, found 120 unwarranted, 64 warranted, 18 partially warranted and dismissed 37. Three were withdrawn. Council presidents included a former chief justice of the California Supreme Court, a former chief judge of the New York State Court of Appeals, Norman Isaacs, Edward Barrett (former dean of Columbia University's Graduate School of Journalism) and Richard Salant (former president of CBS News).[21]

The council was not antimedia; in fact, it found for the media more than against them. And, council members generally were widely respected.

Why, then, did the council fail? Postmortems reveal not only why, but also why similar efforts to monitor the media fail at state and national levels.

First, the council did not establish a public constituency. It did not convince the media it critiqued to publish or broadcast its findings. Neither did the council devise public relations means of end-running the media and reaching the public directly to build support or, even, public awareness.

Second, the council failed to win support from some of the nation's most influential newspapers and journalists. For example, publisher Arthur Ochs Sulzberger announced early that the *New York Times* opposed the concept and would not respond to council findings. As in many matters journalistic, the *Times* was watched for guidance by hundreds of newspaper and television journalists.

Third, and most importantly, the council failed to quiet the fears of many responsible, respected journalists that the council could be the first step toward compulsory auditing or, even, licensing by government. These critics feared any

VIEWPOINT

National News Council: Three Views

"A lot of people should miss it and nobody does."

Richard Salant, last president of now-defunct National News Council

"Basically, a newspaper is responsible to its readers and not to a bunch of self-appointed busybodies with time on their hands. Beyond that, it's dangerous in that it creates the notion in some minds that there is such a thing as a code or standards you can edit newspapers by and anybody who deviates from those is not playing by the rules."

Creed Black, then publisher of the *Lexington (Ky.) Herald-Leader*

"The death of the National News Council should not mean the death of the concept. Failure to renew these efforts may exacerbate our perilous state. If we don't do it someone may do it for us."

Peter Stone, vice president and general counsel of Dow Jones' Ottaway Newspapers subsidiary

widespread support for the council could turn into demands for government control of the media. At minimum, they saw the council lending credence to special-interest pressure groups trying to influence news coverage.

For roughly the same reasons, the media institution generally ignores or resists other outside efforts to judge its performance. Even groups allied with the media are ineffective in critiquing them and getting the right people to listen. That includes most journalism schools and journalists' associations.

The Society of Professional Journalists, for example, flirted with encouraging its chapters nationwide to judge local media performance and even talked of expelling ethical transgressors from the fraternity. The idea didn't catch on.

In 1985, the Kentucky Press Association voted against establishing a state news council, leaving Minnesota and Hawaii as the only states with their own councils.

A substantial number of partisan political, economic and religious groups monitor the media and a few watch over business interests. None, however, has widespread public support.[22]

So, you ask, who watches the watchdog? Well, this watchdog reserves the right to watch itself. But, does it bark at itself, too?

THE STORY THAT'S COVERED EVER SO GENTLY

If there is a foul-up in U.S. foreign policy, it will be on the news tonight and front pages tomorrow.

Business writers will leap all over falling profits at IBM or GM.

If the city council flubs a zoning decision or a quarterback goofs on a crucial play, readers or viewers know where to turn for penetrating, no-holds-barred details.

But where do they turn if interested in whether local TV covered the zoning debate fairly or how accurately the local paper covered the football game? And, if interested in media investments, where do they turn for detailed—and dispassionate— information on how well Knight-Ridder, say, or Gannett are being run?

The plain fact is that for that kind of behind-the-scenes information Americans cannot turn with confidence to their newspapers or television. The media story is a story covered ever so gently, without the hard-hitting, methodical regularity that characterizes coverage of nonmedia stories.

There are exceptions. Some newspapers have at least one staffer who produces excellent media coverage—*New York Times, Los Angeles Times,* the *Washington Post* and the *Wall Street Journal* are examples. And, of course, any self-respecting newspaper has a critic regularly slamming away at TV. Network TV offers, albeit rarely, some media coverage.

But, anyone seriously interested in investment information on media companies turns to Wall Street analysts, not newspapers or television. And, for those interested in how accurately or fairly the local newspaper or TV station is performing, there is no readily available third-party source of detailed, dispassionate information.

It is not enough to say, as some do, that proliferating information sources—magazines, cable TV and suburban weeklies—serve as counterbalance, offering wider coverage and alternate views so readers or viewers somehow can assemble the facts and put them together in an understandable, accurate fashion.

First, general circulation magazines, cable TV and weeklies don't cover the media institution with any perceptive regularity, particularly on a local level.

Second, the average reader or viewer doesn't have the reportorial training, time or inclination to go much beyond the 26 minutes or so devoted on average to reading a single daily paper, or the 22 minutes (30 minutes minus commercials) allocated for watching an evening anchor.

It comes down to whether the media institution—our society's watchdog—barks at itself, whether it honestly, fairly levels with readers or viewers on how well it is doing its job.

There are splendid examples of honest newspapers overcoming the understandable instinct to hide their own mistakes—the *Washington Post* agonizing in a published explanation to readers of how it was hoaxed by a staffer who wrote a phony story about a nonexistent child heroin addict; the *New York Times* using both its front and editorial pages to explain (under the headline, "A Lie in the *Times*") how it was hoaxed by a free-lance writer who never visited Cambodia, about which he wrote a first-person account; the *Wall Street Journal* eviscerating itself in print because a columnist betrayed newspaper and reader alike by misusing inside information; NBC News eventually coming clean on how it faked pickup truck explosions for a story on vehicle safety.[23]

CASE STUDY

Coming Clean With Your Readers

You are editor of a top newspaper known for hard-hitting, investigative reporting, and you've scored again!

A new young reporter (her résumé lists Vassar, magna cum laude; University of Toledo, master's degree; studies at the Sorbonne in Paris; four languages) has developed, while working alone, a terrific series on "Jimmy," an 8-year-old heroin addict "turned on" by his mother's lover.

Police want to rescue the child but your reporter warns her life will be endangered if she identifies "Jimmy," even to you. The story gets national attention.

Then comes a coveted Pulitzer Prize—and startling revelations: The reporter's résumé is full of lies, and there is no 8-year-old heroin addict. The story is fake.

What do you do?

Ben Bradlee, then executive editor of the *Washington Post,* where it happened, returned the Pulitzer and directed his ombudsman, Bill Green, to tell all to *Post* readers. Green wrote that there was a "complete systems failure" in the high-tension *Post* newsroom, and not only by Janet Cooke, who wrote "this journalistic felony." Cooke had been hired without background check. Bradlee and other editors failed to control her work and ask tough questions about her story, which simply was too dramatic to be believed.

"This business of trusting reporters absolutely goes too far," Green said.

Impatient young reporters already are too anxious for more Watergate exposés, and pressuring them to break big stories "is a high-risk undertaking." "The scramble for journalistic prizes is poisonous."

"If the reporter can't support the integrity of his story by revealing the [source's] name to his editor, the story shouldn't be published."

Now, *You* Make the Call

Shouldn't each journalist who saw the "Jimmy" story in preparation—or competing journalists who saw the published version—have immediately dropped everything and rushed to rescue the child?

Wasn't failure to do that the *first* moral breakdown at the *Post*? Wasn't the societal value of humaneness ignored?

Which societal values and journalistic principles were violated by the writer?

Did the lure of a prize-winning story—the judgment of professional peers—blind *Post* editors who edited her story?

In unleashing the ombudsman for no-holds-barred revelations about the *Post*'s failures, did Ben Bradlee subscribe to societal values, journalistic principles and loyalties we discussed in Chapter 1? If so, which ones?

But pride and the survival instinct are powerful forces preventing newspapers and television universally from being frank on their shortcomings as well as triumphs (compare the number of full-page ads you've seen recently in which newspapers apologize for errors or unfair coverage as contrasted with those boasting about Pulitzer Prizes or exclusive stories).

WHAT CAN BE DONE?

Given the media institution's demonstrated refusal to submit to outside monitoring, what can be done to build a bridge of trust with other institutions in society?

We return to where we started in this book: to the importance of individual journalists exercising their personal sense of ethics and social responsibility to influence the conduct of their newspapers and television news operations.

This, of course, is highly unsatisfactory to those critics firmly convinced the media must be brought to heel and made more responsive. Critics of the media see self-improvement pledges depending, in the final analysis, on the moral character of individual journalists and leaving the media as the only major institution in the nation without some sort of external control or formal counterbalancing mechanism.

If the media do not respond to problems perceived by the public, there is danger of society becoming impatient and using other means to achieve change—through government intervention or the courts, much as libel law is used today by many who are offended by the media and feel they have no other recourse.

But for anyone seriously interested in protecting free speech in America there seems no alternative to leaving responsibility for change with the media themselves and with readers and viewers free to exert marketplace pressure by deciding what is good or bad, right or wrong about how newspapers and television conduct themselves.

David Shaw, widely respected media reporter for the *Los Angeles Times,* says he frequently is asked, "Who watches the watchers?" His response: "No one. We have a free press in this country. That's the way the First Amendment says it should be, and that's the way it is." Shaw, however, acknowledges he has "never been altogether comfortable with that answer," adding:

> If, as we frequently argue, a free, vigilant press helps keep our other institutions honest, just what does keep *us* honest? Our professionalism? Our sense of duty? Our innate goodness? Does the decision to become a journalist automatically render one immune to such otherwise human failings as carelessness, irresponsibility, avarice and egotism? Obviously not. The First Amendment gives us a special privilege and a special responsibility, but it does not guarantee us infallibility . . .[24]

WHAT THE MEDIA CAN DO

Many editors and publishers share Shaw's uncomfortable feeling that society requires—and quickly—answers to questions about the media. These broad avenues are available for a response:

VIEWPOINT

Media: Judge Yourselves

"It is very seldom that I read in any of your papers. . . . 'Our colleagues over there on that other sheet are talking nonsense. The real truth is the following' . . . In my judgment as a citizen, you have an obligation to monitor each other, to debate each other, directly and forthrightly, if the American people are going to be the full beneficiaries of this precious right called the freedom of the press. I do not think I am in favor of codes of ethics in the field of journalism. I do not like rules which tend to inhibit the unrestricted freedom of opinion through the written media."

Dean Rusk, former U.S. secretary of state, in speech to American Society of Newspaper Editors

First, the media should cover the media story. Newspaper and television journalists should cover each other just as critically as they cover any other story. This should include day-by-day examination of how news is covered and, importantly, how the huge media conglomerates dominating the industry conduct their business, financial and shareholder affairs. Coverage should be straight and hard-hitting, without the undercurrent of personal feuding that characterizes some coverage today—without columnists or editorial writers undercutting each other in terms so subtle that only fraternal insiders catch the message. (Watch *New York Times* and *Wall Street Journal* editorial writers taking shots at each other in print, for example.) Whether measured for economic impact or the role their news and comment play in our society, the media are an important story. To see them covered penetratingly would reassure many readers and viewers who now feel the media institution is free to do as it pleases without fear of meaningful criticism.

Second, newspapers and television should create a compact of openness with readers and viewers. Done correctly, this is agonizing for it requires brutal, ego-damaging frankness—a journalistic version of a surgeon acknowledging there was a slight slip of the scalpel back there in the operating room or a lawyer admitting it was his fault as the client heads for prison (and, how often have you heard anything resembling that?). Fewer than 35 newspapers do this by employing full-time reader advocates or ombudsmen to go into print regularly on behalf of readers and critique newsroom performance.

Many editors are uncomfortable with the thought of unleashing even a staff member to barge around behind the scenes, then tell all. Some editors say it's their duty to do that by periodically writing a column explaining how—and why—the news is covered. But no Pulitzer Prizes have been handed out to editors for hard-hitting, investigative reporting on themselves (although I think the *Washington Post* deserves some prize for telling all on the Janet Cooke hoax).

As limited as it is, print journalism's self-examination is unmatched in television. Neither at network nor local level does television spend much time dissecting its own performance.

VIEWPOINT

Second Thoughts on Ombudsmen

"For years, I argued that to hire an ombudsman would be to abdicate the editor's responsibility and, in fact, to diminish the responsibility of all the people who work for us. Fundamental to my philosophy—then, and now—is the strong sense that everyone who works for us is a 'reader's representative' . . . that the way an assistant editor handles the phone can leave a permanent impression—positive or negative—with a reader . . . that how a circulator handles a complaint can make all the difference in the world as to how the customer feels about us, or even whether we have that customer any more . . . that our credibility is directly related to every contact we have with readers and potential readers . . . that no one should get in the way of a collective and individual effort to build real relationships with readers.

"But maybe I have been missing something important—perhaps an ombudsman could complement, and contribute to, our total efforts toward a newspaper of heightened credibility."

David Lawrence Jr., then publisher and chairman, *Detroit Free Press*

In recent years, newspapers have become much more open about publishing corrections or explanations of what appeared in print. Many newspapers regularly position corrections in the same spot each day. There also is noticeable increase in newspapers explaining within the body of stories any special circumstances or background affecting coverage—why they granted anonymity to sources or why an individual mentioned in the story was unavailable for comment.

Making letters columns and op-ed pages easily accessible to readers or guest editorial spots open to viewers are other ways links are established with the public.

On the local level, newspapers and television stations can do much more to invite the public for tours and get-acquainted chats with newsroom staffers. Newspapers should run house ads describing the people who write and edit the news (public opinion surveys repeatedly show readers want to know who puts out the papers—and that they don't fully trust people they don't know).[25] Just answering the mail quickly and the telephone politely would help remove the patina of cold, distant arrogance that covers so many things journalistic.

Third, however, the media simply must do better in explaining to the public how a great many sincerely dedicated journalists and media managers try very hard to do an ethical, socially responsible job. The media institution has a much better story in that respect than it tells.

Few industries spend so much time in severely critical self-examination as do newspapers and television. In news, highly professional, hard-hitting critiques are run by the American Society of Newspaper Editors, Associated Press Managing Editors Association and the Radio and Television News Directors Association. *But it's all done for insiders, people essentially already in the know, and not the bemused (or befuddled) public watching from the outside.* Journalism reviews and professional magazines sometimes do excellent critiques but also play to small, insider audiences.

Too often, when the newspaper or magazine story is told it is cloaked in so much self-promotional hocus-pocus that the story of news and how it's covered is lost, and the public is turned off. Television often is just plain embarrassing in its shallow promotion, stressing not worldwide news-gathering bureaus, splendid technology or reporting but, rather, the cult of personality—bush jackets and palm trees for the newest expert in foreign news and the White House lawn for political analysts.

The media institution must reach the public with meaningful, high-quality promotion. Suggested themes for starters:

The First Amendment belongs to the people and we, the media, are defending your rights when we stand up for ours.

We offer hard news, the facts, on health, science, technology, diet and nutrition, child-rearing—all the subjects you must know to cope with daily life. And, we offer it at bargain prices—free on television, about .35 cents to .50 cents on newsprint.

Every effort is made to present fair and unbiased news and to allocate space and time to all our constituents.

Our job is reporting news and presenting informed opinion, not manipulating you, the reader or viewer.

(Each suggested promotional theme above responds directly to negative views of the media uncovered by researcher Ruth Clark in a study of public attitudes commissioned by ASNE.)[26]

Obviously, it's simplistic to suggest the media institution can construct a new relationship with society just by answering the telephone more politely or cranking off a few promotional ads. Indeed, there are fundamentally serious roadblocks between media and society and unless the media can remove them, there may be, as Norman Isaacs warns, a gathering storm ahead. We look at those roadblocks in Chapter 10.

Summary

Big Media must submit to critical examination by society as do Big Government, Big Business and Big Church. One question is whether the changing corporate character of the media, from essentially vehicles of news and advertising to diversified conglomerates, will lead society to reassess the media as just another profit-oriented industry.

After all, can Tribune Co., for example, position itself before society as a newspaper and television company now that it owns the Chicago Cubs baseball team and newsprint mill investments in Ontario?

To defend its business as well as news interests, the media institution has organized giant lobbying efforts with strong clout in Washington. Television fights for less government regulation, less interference in advertising and other changes—all likely to enhance its business interests. Newspapers lobby strongly against telephone companies becoming competitors and for special exemption from antitrust laws and some taxes.

Despite obvious problems stemming from the profit-oriented, free-enterprise nature of our media, anyone seriously interested in protecting free speech in America will be hard pressed to suggest viable alternatives.

A journalism owned and operated by narrowly partisan groups is unattractive (and probably unworkable); there is no tradition (and little chance of one developing) for nonprofit journalism (as with Britain's BBC), and government-sponsored (and, thus controlled) journalism is unacceptable in any free society.

The media should cover each other just as penetratingly as they cover other stories. Newspapers and television must create a compact of openness with readers and viewers. And, the media institution as a whole must better explain to the public just how hard it tries to do the job well.

At the end of Chapter 9 we are where this book started—with a need for each journalist to help create honest, ethical and socially responsible journalism at his or her newspaper or television station.

Notes

1. American Newspaper Publishers Association (now NAA), The Newspaper Center, Box 17407, Dulles Airport, Washington, D.C., 20041, illustrates an expanded view of First Amendment and newspaper rights in two documents: "An Overview of Current Issues," a March 1986 publication, and "ANPA Highlights '86," a summary of association activities.
2. Allan J. Bassler, "Missed the Point," *Editor & Publisher,* Feb. 27, 1993, p. 7.
3. "Seagram Buys into Time Warner," *Advertising Age,* May 31, 1993, p. 2; also, "The Mogul on The Line," *The Economist,* May 22, 1993, p. 67.
4. Particularly revealing surveys include, "Relating to Readers in the '80s," commissioned by ASNE and conducted by Clark, Martire & Bartolomeo, Inc., May 1984; "Changing Needs of Changing Readers," sponsored by ASNE in 1978; "Credibility," a 1984 survey by Associated Press Managing Editors Association; "The People & The Press," a 1986 study sponsored by Times Mirror Corp. Major work in reader attitudes has been done also by Belden Associates, 2900 Turtle Creek Plaza, Dallas, Tex., 74219.
5. NAA figures from Walt Potter, "ANPA and NAP Plan to Merge," *presstime,* February 1992, p. 6. NAB figures from "NAB Board Adopts $16.6 Million Budget," *Broadcasting,* Jan. 22, 1990, p. 42.
6. Charles T. Brumback, "Priority One: The Bell Ringer," speech to Inland Press Association, Chicago, Oct. 21, 1991.
7. ANPA's "Overview of Current Issues," op. cit.
8. NAB discusses each year's lobbying efforts in its annual report, issued to association members from the Washington headquarters.
9. Bob Davis, "Cable TV Operators May Be Required to Carry Some Local Broadcast Station," *Wall Street Journal,* July 23, 1986, p. 4.

10. NAB "Annual Report 1985," p. 2–3.
11. Ibid.
12. Margaret Garrard Warner, "Newspaper Publishers Lobby to Keep AT&T from Role They Covet," *Wall Street Journal,* July 9, 1982, p. 1.
13. ANPA, "An Overview of Current Issues," op. cit.
14. Andrew Radolf, "Detached Labeler Fights Back," *Editor & Publisher,* June 16, 1984, p. 9; also see, "Valentine: ANPA Trying to Kill Advo," *presstime,* June 1984, p. 35.
15. Mark Fitzgerald, "Detroit JOA Sparks Protests, Request for Hearing," *Editor & Publisher,* June 7, 1986, p. 20.
16. This quote and other details of the JOA were revealed by Chairman Al Neuharth of Gannett in a number of ways, including his speech to the Detroit Chamber of Commerce Legislative Agenda Conference, Mackinac Island, Mich., May 30, 1986. Also note "Mackinac Straight Talk: How Dailies Survive," *Detroit News,* June 1, 1986, p. 23-A.
17. ANPA, "An Overview of Current Issues," op. cit.
18. A superb treatment of this issue is, "Suit Studies the Wages of Journalism," *New York Times,* July 20, 1986, p. 26.
19. Ben H. Bagdikian, editor, media critic and teacher, is thoughtful on this. See particularly his *The Information Machines* (New York: Harper & Row, 1971) and his speech to the University of Minnesota Journalism Center, March 3, 1984, reproduced in Michael Emery and Ted Curtis Smythe, *Readings in Mass Communications* (Dubuque, Iowa: Wm. C. Brown Publishers, 1986).
20. David Shaw, "Of Isms and Prisms," *Columbia Journalism Review,* January/February 1991, p. 55.
21. See particularly Richard P. Cunningham's report on his work with the council, "Why The News Council Failed," in "1984–85 Journalism Ethics Report," Society of Professional Journalists, Sigma Delta Chi, p. 4; also, Marcia Ruth, "Does Anyone Miss the News Council?"' *presstime,* March 1985, p. 32.
22. For penetrating observations on the wider issues of business and social responsibility and licensing in the free enterprise system see Milton Friedman, *Capitalism and Freedom* (Chicago: University of Chicago Press, 1962).
23. "A Lie in the *Times,*" an editorial, *New York Times,* Feb. 23, 1982, p. A-22.
24. David Shaw, "Watching the Watchers," *The Quill,* December 1981, p. 12.
25. See particularly Ruth Clark's "Relating to Readers in the '80s," a study commissioned in 1984 by ASNE.
26. Ibid.

CHAPTER 10

SPECIAL PROBLEM AREAS

We now turn to problems of special importance in our study of ethical relationships between the media as an institution and other institutions in society.

As a journalist reporting in these problem areas, you'll find that sorting out right from wrong often is extraordinarily difficult. And, you'll encounter public doubt—suspicion, often—about how you and the media in general do things.

We concentrate on these areas:

- The media and the presidency. The institutional relationship between the media and America's wider political structure is extremely important, of course. But that's a book (or books) in itself, far beyond the scope of our discussion. So, we look at the media and the power center of that political structure, the presidency.
- The media and coverage of crime, AIDS and homosexual outing. Hugely complicated questions of ethics and social responsibility arise here.
- The media and "political correctness." Your challenge: Respect each group demanding a place in the sun in our society, but report fully, accurately and honestly for your wider audience.

We also look briefly at the media and their responsibilities in the fight for freedom of information.

THE MEDIA AND THE PRESIDENCY

Was it "journalistic cannibalism," as a *New York Times* columnist termed it? Or, did reporters not only have the right but also the obligation to dig into Bill Clinton's past sex life?[1]

VIEWPOINT

Oldest Game in Town

"Managing the news, of course, is the oldest game in town [Washington]. Franklin Roosevelt was a master at it. The leaders of all institutions try to manage the news in the sense of emphasizing their virtues and minimizing or suppressing their failures. Even newspaper owners have been known to fiddle with the facts."

James Reston, the *New York Times* columnist

"All presidents seek to manage the news and all are successful to a degree."

George Reedy, White House press secretary for President Lyndon Johnson, 1964–1965

"[L]et's face it. Presidents want the press to be their press agents."

Helen Thomas, longtime UPI White House correspondent

"I need your help . . . [But] if you want to play it the other way . . . I know how to cut off the flow of news except in handouts. . . . If you help me, I'll help you. I'll make you-all big men in your profession."

President Johnson to reporters

Whichever, during the run-up to Clinton's election as U.S. President, the media dug deeply, and largely unashamedly, into his past. The justification: Voters couldn't properly assess Clinton's candidacy for the nation's highest office unless they knew whether he had extramarital affairs, smoked marijuana as a young man or dodged military service during the Vietnam War.

It wasn't the first time ugly details of a politician's personal life surfaced in the media, of course. Way back in the 1700s, Thomas Jefferson was said to have sired children by one of his slaves, and rumor and innuendo have touched virtually every major American political candidate since his time.

What seemed different in coverage of Clinton was how readily the media accepted the character issue as now a routine element in covering presidential politics. There was virtual institutionalization of the concept that nothing—literally nothing—about presidential candidates should remain hidden. The single test of relevancy seemed to be whether past conduct, by even the longest stretch of imagination, could be deemed essential to understanding the character of candidates or the leadership and policies that would emerge once the White House was won.

PERMANENT STRUGGLE AND FRICTION?

Probing and very personal coverage cause permanent friction between the media and the presidency, two institutions that dominate the shape and tone of news emanating from Washington, the world's most important power center.

VIEWPOINT

These People *Bleed*

"Let's not kid ourselves about the potential harm here. People who seek public office are human beings. They bleed. They cry. They hurt for themselves and their children. Most of them live with the constant fear that something like what the Clintons are going through will happen to them. And they know that there is nothing that can be done to prevent it and precious little to stop it once it starts—because truth may have little to do with it."

Jody Powell, former press secretary to President Carter, commenting on coverage of Bill Clinton's sex life[2]

The struggle between these two institutions is over any president's single-most important political concern—his relationship with the voting public and how and by whom that relationship will be portrayed.

Arrayed against a handful of presidential image makers at any given time are about 10,000 reporters, editors, writers, columnists, correspondents, free-lancers and others who make up the Washington Press Corps. More than 4,000 are accredited to Congress, 1,500 or so to the White House.

Despite disparity in opposing numbers, the contest is weighted in favor of the image makers. They, after all, control what President Reagan's adviser, Michael Deaver, called the "talent." But the media are the main conduits any president must use to reach the public, despite efforts by Clinton and other presidents to end-run reporters by reaching out directly through televised town meetings and similar techniques. So, the contest is not only spirited, but almost Machiavellian in its complexity.

For example, to properly market their talent, the image makers control not only what presidents say, but how it is said, where and when. Deaver worried about the smallest details, even the color of drapes on windows behind the President as he spoke on television.

The public—ultimate target of both the media and President—displays wide mood swings over how deeply reporters should probe into a candidate's personal past.

Unquestionably, coverage of intimate (and titillating) details is followed closely. Clinton's extramarital past was first explored in a big way publicly by the *Star*, a supermarket tabloid. It soon was on front pages and newscasts coast to coast, every day.

Yet, opinion polls revealed public unease—disgust, at times—over such coverage. Shortly after major news organizations reported the *Star*'s still-unsubstantiated allegations about extramarital affairs, a *Time*-CNN poll showed 70 percent of respondents agreed the media should respect a candidate's privacy and not report private behavior, including extramarital affairs.[3] And, of course, by electing

CASE STUDY

Reporter to "Spin Doctor" and Back

One day, David Gergen was a widely recognized and popular magazine editor who appeared regularly on television as a political commentator.

The next day, he was still on TV—but this time, he was standing beside President Clinton as the White House's newest "spin doctor," appointed to manage (not to say, manipulate) the presidential image.

His popularity dropping in 1993 and his own staff fumbling, Clinton named Gergen, *U.S. News and World Report's* editor at large, to put things right.[4]

It wasn't the first time a president reached into the press corps for expertise to deal with reporters and shape image and policy for public consumption. Many presidential press secretaries and advisers came from the press corps. Some were given—or assumed—extraordinary powers. James Haggerty, a former *New York Times* political writer, for years was one of the most influential advisers to President Eisenhower—and not only on press affairs.

However, unlike previous White House communications advisers, Gergen had no political alignment with the man in the Oval Office. In fact, Gergen previously served three Republican presidents and was particularly prominent in the Reagan and Bush administrations, against whose policies Democrat Clinton had run!

Clinton clearly was reaching for a man who, ideology aside, knew the techniques of "handling" the press corps and public opinion. Gergen, obviously delighted to be back in the Washington power game, put his own spin on the appointment: When the commander in chief summons, he said, you go—whoever you are.

Lust for power or, simply, desire for change leads many reporters into government ranks. Fair enough. No ethical problems there if reporters who cross over drop all pretense of being dispassionate, and openly become advocates.

But what about ex-reporters who go the other way, from government advocacy back into the media?

Pete Williams, Pentagon spokesman during the Gulf War and thus immediately recognizable to millions as a supporter of the Bush administration, joined NBC television as

Clinton, voters showed that although they avidly view and read the coverage, they can ignore it and independently judge a candidate.

The public seems to (1) downplay or even disregard what some candidates did in the past but, however, (2) pay close attention to how candidates respond to reporters' questions about their past. Polls showed clearly that a majority of respondents thought that if Clinton didn't tell the truth about the past, he should step aside. (Gary Hart's earlier attempt to cover up an extramarital liaison created such negative public reaction that he quit his race for the Democrats' presidential nomination.)

a presumably neutral reporter covering the Clinton Justice Department. Bill Moyers moved to TV fame after serving as President Lyndon Johnson's press secretary.

William Safire, a high-profile *New York Times* columnist, was a speech writer for President Nixon. Pat Buchanan went from newspaper editorial writer (St. Louis *Globe-Democrat*) to Nixon aide to newspaper columnist and TV commentator to the Reagan White House, then to television once more, then to being a presidential candidate himself—and back to TV (on CNN's "Crossfire").

Leslie Gelb left the *New York Times* for a high-ranking job in the Carter administration's State Department, then went back to the *Times*—to cover the State Department.

Now, *You* Make the Call

- Do newspapers and television ignore an important social responsibility—to be independent and objective—when they permit men and women who publicly commit themselves to partisan politics to resume careers as ostensibly objective reporters? But why shouldn't political writers use expertise gained in government as, say, sports writers use expertise gained in playing baseball?
- Should columnists and commentators be permitted to move from government into opinion-making? If so, are they ethically bound to divulge to readers or viewers any previous political or governmental ties? Should they avoid covering political parties or governments that previously employed them?
- If you think journalists should reveal any previous political affiliation, where would you stop such mandatory labeling? Should a reporter or columnist be required to reveal previous membership in, say, the Boy Scouts of America or affiliation with the Catholic Church? Both often are in the news and must be reported on as objectively and dispassionately as possible.
- Even if newspapers and TV networks are satisfied that individuals can safely make the switch from spin doctor to dispassionate journalist, what do you believe is the public perception of such switches?

NOW, *YOU* MAKE THE CALL

Is a candidate's personal past truly indicative of future official conduct in the Oval Office and should the past therefore be covered? Consider societal values discussed in Chapter 1. Are truth-telling and humaneness operative here? How about the journalistic principles of serve the public and monitor the powerful? Do they, in this instance, conflict with be compassionate?

Perhaps your decision-making process will be aided by learning how reporters answer such questions.

Many journalists opt for full and detailed coverage, justifying their position this way:

- A candidate's character is important because voters must have full information for this evaluation: Is the candidate trustworthy? Does the candidate share my personal principles and values? Thus, whether a candidate is loyal to, say, marital vows is relevant to voter judgment on whether he or she will be loyal to vows given the American public.
- A pattern of personal behavior is a strong indicator of what official behavior would be in the White House. The reasoning here is that a single infidelity, as contrasted with a pattern of infidelity, wouldn't warrant the full coverage given allegations that Clinton had a 12-year extramarital affair.
- Serious political candidates know the rules, and infidelity and dishonesty during a campaign indicate lack of character and judgment—and voters need to know of such conduct.
- Voters have shown repeatedly they can assess such information about candidates, then make decisions based principally on more crucial issues. Therefore, some reporters say they should provide all the information about candidates and let voters decide what is important.
- Leading public officials—especially presidents—implicitly agree to be role models for the entire nation, particularly young people. If candidates' personal conduct fails to meet generally accepted societal standards of behavior they fail in the test for high office.

Conversely, strong arguments are made for restrictions—mostly self-imposed—on how the media cover candidates' private lives. Principal arguments:

- A candidate's sex life has no relevance to ability to govern and lead. Before telling all, reporters should consider whether all truly is indicative of ability to perform in the White House.
- Media ethics should reflect societal standards—and standards are changing. Being divorced once was a death sentence in American politics; it's not anymore. The public is increasingly lenient in judging the personal morality of candidates and the media are holding candidates to higher standards than the voters require of anyone (including themselves). Nobody's perfect, the argument goes, and voters know it.
- Focusing on private lives can overshadow coverage of truly important social and economic issues and, indeed, can eliminate from public life men and women superbly equipped to help govern the nation.
- Too often, herd instinct takes over when private scandal is published and the media stampede to repeat it without substantiation. (Many reported the *Star*'s allegations about Clinton without first-hand verification.) This leaves the media open to manipulation by persons anonymously leaking tantalizing tidbits of scandal to attack their enemies.

VIEWPOINT

Press Open to Exploitation?

"The press is constantly vulnerable to exploitation of its worst instincts because it has taken on the culture of entertainment television. The 'best' stories now concern the same subjects as prime-time programming—the sexual, the comedic, the criminal or the perverse . . .

"In the competitive rush to entertain its audience, both the obligation of the press to educate the public and its ability to do so are being trampled. Where it once examined the total character of a political candidate, it is concerned now mainly with character flaws. Yet the power to focus the entire political debate on the private life of a candidate simply does not extend to forcing the candidates to debate the economy. The press has become a one-trick pony."

James D. Squires, former *Chicago Tribune* editor who became spokesperson for Ross Perot, Texas billionaire and 1992 candidate for president[5]

- All other factors aside, the media should recognize a zone of privacy around all persons, including public officials, and common decency should prohibit invading it. Besides, some critics say, fair play requires that editors who cover the sex lives of others should reveal details of their own bedtime habits!

Is either side completely right in this controversy? Is a Golden Mean solution possible?

You make the call.

PRESIDENTIAL NEWS MANAGEMENT

Many are the techniques used by presidents and their advisers to manage the news and create a favorable image for the White House.

Two techniques are most effective: controlling access to the principal newsmaker, the president, and selectively using news leaks to manage the flow of news.

CONTROLLING ACCESS TO THE PRESIDENT

The president is news. So is what he says, how he looks and even what he eats. Reporters often are kept at bay (and in the dark) until the president has good news to report and looks splendid (usually while jogging or relaxing).

Cabinet members often are delegated to announce bad news; the White House releases good news.

Television and radio are used so the president can get his message directly to the people without pesky print reporters asking probing questions. Press conferences are tightly managed, with advisers carefully briefing the president in advance on difficult questions that will be asked—and which reporters (friendly or unfriendly) likely will ask them.

Exclusive interviews often are granted friendly reporters and those who signal in advance they are likely to do positive stories. The forum and timing for speeches are selected carefully—for example, schools for announcements on aid to education (schools are particularly effective because of all those teenagers jumping up and down on camera and screaming their presidential adoration). Veterans of Foreign Wars conventions are chosen for announcements on increased defense spending or warlike warnings to upstart foreign countries threatening U.S. interests.

Photo ops are used to admit photographers and a few reporters (who are supposed to only watch) to the inner circle when a president has a friendly guest who, while seated before a cozy fireplace, can be counted on to smile and say nice things. (Listen carefully next time you see a photo op on television and you'll hear a few off-camera reporters shouting serious questions over the click of the shutters, trying to develop news out of what is designed to be a PR event.)

Perhaps the most unlikely (and successful) photo op was one designed to show President Gerald Ford had the common touch: Photographers were permitted to click away as Ford arose early in the White House and, without help from servants, toasted his own breakfast muffin! On occasion, presidents slip their advisers' leash and photo ops turn into PR disaster—as when President Johnson displayed his technique for picking up Beagle puppies by their ears (enraging dog lovers) and hoisting his shirt to display a surgical scar on his, shall we say, ample abdomen (literally turning stomachs worldwide).

With presidential exposure limited, White House advisers can strongly influence the day's news agenda. After leaving government, a number of press secretaries acknowledged, with great amusement, that they and the presidents they served had agreed each day on which single important story would be released to achieve major impact for the administration's viewpoint.

USING NEWS LEAKS

" . . . it was learned today."

That sourcing appears often in newspaper dispatches from the White House and frequently is used by TV correspondents in stand-up reports on the lawn outside the Oval Office.

Many things are wrong journalistically with anonymous sourcing. But it raises important ethical issues, too. For one thing, it forces readers and viewers to accept on faith information from sources whose identity, credentials and authoritativeness they have a right to know. Recall from Chapter 1 that the societal value of truth-telling requires reporters to reveal all the pertinent facts.

Perhaps most important, however, is that when "it was learned" is used readers and viewers don't know whether journalists diligently reported the information being passed along (required under the journalistic principle of serve the public) or whether the reporters were spoon-fed by a political image maker involved in surreptitious media manipulation.

The inability of readers and viewers to distinguish between what a correspondent is writing and what the White House is originating is, of course, why the news leak is any news manager's most effective device.

For journalists (and their readers and viewers) the danger is three-fold:

First, the media can be used for trial balloons. A president unsure of a new policy or appointment can leak word to test public reaction before any formal announcement.

Second, the media can be used to send messages that the president doesn't want to send openly himself. An it-was-learned dispatch on, say, White House "unease" over performance of a federal official is a clear signal that the official should resign. A dispatch on White House "concern" over Iraq may be aimed more at Iraq's leaders than American readers and viewers.

Third, a leak to the right reporter—particularly from the trend-setting *New York Times, Washington Post* or *Wall Street Journal*—can shape a news development in a form desired by the White House. Rather than let many reporters speculate on the meaning of a story, the White House can leak it to one or two in a form most advantageous to the president. Other media often follow the lead of print's big boys.

Leaks can be misleading particularly when the originating official insists they can be used as deep background. In Washington parlance that means reporters must use information as their own thoughts, not tied to any informed source or high-ranking official or other sourcing subterfuges so widely used. Presidents themselves use deep background, leaving reporters with the agonizing choice of using the president's party line as their own or risk getting scooped by competitors not so choosy. Give five competitive political reporters a high-level briefing in the White House and the herd instinct likely will drive all five to report, on their own authority, the presidential line handed out in deep background.

However, leaks can be dangerous for leakers, too. During the Clinton presidency's early days, the White House leaked uncontrollably—often to its own embarrassment. For example, the *New York Times* reported a leak that Kimba M. Wood, a U.S. district judge, was Clinton's choice for attorney general. When a subsequent check of her background proved unsatisfactory, the White House had to announce she was not a candidate, and Wood was publicly humiliated—raising charges that Clinton was insensitive to candidates considered in his nominating process.[6]

CONTROL OF NEWS ISN'T ALL BAD?

It is a president's public popularity that establishes the basic relationship between media and the White House. In times of relatively weak presidents, when lack of substantive policy and leadership become apparent, the media assume a strong hand; confronted by a president shrewd in image building and strong in the polls, the media's influence wanes.

However, for their own purposes, the media invite some control of the news flow. George Reedy, White House press secretary under President Lyndon Johnson from 1964 to 1965, says reporters know there would be chaos if there were an end to daily press briefings, pools, prearranged travel and other physical arrangements in place since Franklin Delano Roosevelt's day. Reedy recalls President Johnson unexpectedly holding Saturday morning news conferences—and Washington bureau chiefs pleading the practice be stopped. Printers had to be called in to work at overtime rates, and everybody's work week simply was being disrupted. Says Reedy:

> This may well account for the indifference of the public to the periodic campaigns [by the media] against news management. Even to an unsophisticated audience it is apparent that journalists are not objecting to news management per se but only to the kind of news management that makes their professional lives more difficult. However it may look in Washington, at a distance the issue appears as a dispute over control of the news for the convenience of the President or for the convenience of the press. In such a situation, Americans tend to come down on the side of the President. Of course, if the President is caught in an outright lie—a lie about something in which the public is really concerned—the public will mobilize against him swiftly. But many charges of news management are directed at statements that Americans do not regard as outright lies. Americans have become too accustomed to the kind of exaggeration and misleading facts that are used to sell products on nightly television that a little White House puffery seems quite natural.[7]

CRIME AND REPORTER ETHICS

Delicate ethical issues of balance and social responsibility arise in crime coverage. Broadly, two issues are of compelling importance to our discussion:

First, when does society's right (or need) to know outweigh the rights of individuals who commit crime, are accused of committing crime—or are its victims?

Second, how can the media cover crime, cops and, particularly, terrorists without interfering with ongoing official investigations and, in other words, becoming part of the problem, not its solution?

A DILEMMA: RAPE COVERAGE

Society regards rape as a particularly heinous crime that, unfortunately, can attach stigma to the victim. Consequently, most media withhold identification of rape victims.

However, despite the obvious stigma that also attaches to being named as a rapist, most media identify men accused—without substantiation, before trial—of committing rape.

A double standard? Yes, and there are stirrings of change in how rape is covered.

For example, Geneva Overholser, editor of the *Des Moines Register,* says editors may think they are protecting a rape victim from stigma by withholding her name but they really are compounding—perpetuating—the stigma by treating rape differently from other crimes.

Overholser wrote in a column: "As long as rape is deemed unspeakable—and is therefore not fully and honestly spoken of—the public outrage will be muted as well."

That column led one Iowa woman to volunteer to tell her story of being raped and to be identified. The *Register*'s subsequent Pulitzer Prize-winning series in 1990 named the victim, mentioned the attacker's penis, that he ejaculated, that he was black and the woman white.[8]

A year later, some media identified—without her permission—a woman who said she was raped by a nephew of U.S. Sen. Edward Kennedy, in the Kennedy mansion in Palm Beach, Fla. A foreign newspaper, the *Sunday Mirror* in London, was first to identify her; the supermarket tabloid, the *Globe,* followed. NBC News then aired her identity, explaining. " . . . the more we tell our viewers, the better informed they will be in making up their own minds about the issues involved . . ." *New York Times* editors published the woman's name, saying NBC's nationwide broadcast had taken the matter of her privacy out of their hands.

NOW, *YOU* MAKE THE CALL

- Should the media treat rape as just another crime and identify victims as they identify victims of, say, bank robbery? Should alleged rapists be identified? Before they're officially charged or only after?
- Should I have identified the Iowa rape victim for you? Or, do you agree with me that now, after so much time elapsed, that her name is irrelevant to our discussion? Should such a test of relevancy be the guideline for deciding whether to identify rape victims? Is it relevant for readers and viewers in, say, Memphis to know the name of a rape victim in Miami? Is there societal need to know names?
- Should I have identified the alleged victim (she later went public voluntarily) and the alleged rapist (he was acquitted) at the "Kennedy compound"? I used Sen. Kennedy's name and Kennedy compound to help you identify the case. The Kennedy link, after all, made the case "news." Was I, along with probably every newspaper and TV station in the country, wrong in bringing the Kennedy name into my narrative? Did the way I wrote about the case create more victims?
- Is naming a rape victim in fact raping her a second time?
- Many editors publish names of women who seek damages by bringing civil lawsuits against alleged attackers. Is there valid distinction between printing names in criminal and civil proceedings?
- Finally, were *New York Times* editors on morally sound ground in saying the NBC identification of the woman in the Florida case took the matter of her privacy out of their hands? Or, is each medium—each journalist—obliged to decide such ethical questions independently, regardless of what the rest of the herd does?

Here, to help you make your call on these difficult questions, are views of others:

A television trade magazine, *Electronic Media,* commented editorially that NBC's decision "was correct because it is time to start treating rape the same way that any other crime of violence is treated. To do otherwise is to reinforce and perpetuate the archaic, sexist notion that rape carries a special stigma."[9]

Most media, however, forbid use of rape victims' names unless highly unusual circumstances exist. The *Philadelphia Inquirer*'s "Ethical Goals and Guidelines" puts it this way: "The name of a rape victim generally is not published except as determined by the executive editor or managing editor or, in their absence, by the editor in charge."

The *Wall Street Journal* let a guest columnist—a rape victim whom it would not identify—speak for the policy of no identification. She wrote:

> Rape remains the most profound of assaults because it violates a woman's very being, her sexual identity. Publishing a rape victim's name is tantamount to raping her again—because publishing her name means also publishing her life story, her photograph, her sexual proclivities, and the incident of the rape in as much lurid details as possible.[10]

David H. Bludworth, state attorney in Palm Beach County, Florida, where the Kennedy compound is located: "The chilling effect of printing, publishing and broadcasting the victim's name causes many [women] not to report this type of crime."

Richard M. Schmidt, Jr., general counsel for the American Society of Newspaper Editors, commented on proposed state laws that would ban victim identification: " . . . a very bad idea. . . . This is clearly a violation of the First Amendment. . . ."

Gov. John Ashcroft of Missouri vetoed a bill passed by the state legislature that would have made it illegal for news organizations to publish names of victims of sexual abuse. Ashcroft said, "While the intent of the provision to protect victims of sexual offenses from unwanted publicity is well meaning, the bill appears to be an unconstitutional violation of the First Amendment."[11]

But, just because it's legal to identify an alleged rape victim, is it ethical?

OTHER PROBLEM AREAS IN CRIME COVERAGE

Ethical problems abound in other types of crime coverage. Here are some of the most troubling.

IDENTIFICATION OF JUVENILES

Few editors quarrel with the accepted practice of shielding underage victims of crime from public identification. There, however, is divided opinion when (1) alleged juvenile victims (of, say, child molestation) make unsubstantiated charges that could destroy the reputations (virtually, the lives) of adults, and (2) when juveniles commit especially violent crimes.

You've seen it many times: newspaper or television pictures of downcast men and women, often in handcuffs, being led into court to face charges of child molestation. They certainly look guilty, don't they?

Yet, child molestation is extremely difficult to prove and several sensational cases of alleged molestation at day care centers dragged on for years without clear-cut resolution. Additionally, defense attorneys raised the question of whether overzealous prosecutors and child psychologists, through suggestive questioning, created allegations of molestation in children's minds.

As in reporting rape cases, editors often withhold identification of alleged molesters unless official charges are lodged. Stories then quote not children but, rather, adult officials whose investigations presumably show abuse did occur.

Historically, most media withheld names of underage juveniles—usually under 18—who committed crimes. That's changing. Here is how the *Philadelphia Inquirer* states its policy:

> Because *The Inquirer* customarily covers only crimes of special importance or unusual violence, it is important that the public be informed of the identity of the accused, *regardless of age* [emphasis added]. In crimes of this nature, the service to the community of full coverage far outweighs any realistic expectation that not naming the accused would assist in his or her eventual rehabilitation. Therefore, the name of a person under 18 accused of a crime is to be published except as determined by the executive editor or managing editor or, in their absence, the editor in charge.
>
> Care should be exercised in deciding whether to identify a juvenile victim. It is useful to bear in mind that in coverage of family crime or violence—such as child abuse—identification of an adult could effectively identify a juvenile victim who is related to the adult.

Note the *Inquirer* distinguishes between crimes of "special importance or unusual violence" and misdemeanors published in "Neighbors"—its special sections devoted to local community news. A 10-year-old apprehended for shoplifting a candy bar won't be named in the *Inquirer*.

Still, are you uneasy about naming a juvenile who commits a crime of even special importance?

New York Times editors were when a two-day-old baby was discovered (still alive) in a trash compactor. Their reporters found the mother was 12 years old, an orphan, a rape victim and a slow learner in school who lived in a neighborhood torn by drug and alcohol abuse.

The *Times* told readers of its front-page story: "The *New York Times* is not printing the girl's name. Along with many newspapers, the *Times* ordinarily omits the names of sex-crime victims and juvenile suspects."

What do you think? Should media crime coverage include background on such socioeconomic causes of crime? (A neighbor of the 12-year-old rape victim-mother told the *Times*: "She never had no chance.")[12]

If you believe coverage routinely should explore possible causes for crimes—that is, place mitigating circumstances before readers and viewers—how far should journalists go in being judges and juries, as well as reporters? Would you, for example, agree that the 12-year-old's tragic background is reason for shielding her identity? If so, where would you draw the line? At 14 years of age? Or, 15, 16, 18, 28?

If you agree her background of being raped and orphaned is good reason to be sympathetic toward her, would you feel similarly sensitive toward a young woman who suffered from, say, verbal abuse from an alcoholic father or rejection by schoolmates? If you are going to apply the journalistic principle of compassion to your reporting, at what level of abuse would you apply it?

See the difficulty of taking situational approaches to the values and principles we apply to decision making in ethics?

If it's of any comfort to you, many editors do take situational approaches. They (1) have a general policy of not identifying juveniles but (2) depart from that policy under certain circumstances and after careful consideration.

Aren't we discussing here total rejection of Immanuel Kant's absolutism and adoption, instead of flexible, situational ethics in which good judgment is substituted for rigid guidelines? But, look at those sitting around you in class. Is their good judgment the same as yours? Can we base ethical decision making on such personal, subjective variables?

Note the National Victim Center's suggested media code, which is found in Appendix J. Do you agree with the code's central thrust—that media coverage must be more sensitive toward victims?

Now try these questions.

RACIAL AND ETHNIC IDENTIFICATION

Should crime coverage include racial or ethnic identifications? No? That just reinforces stereotypes about criminals? Well, what if a serial killer is on the loose? Are the media responsible for giving readers and viewers all information—whether the suspect is white, black, Asian or Hispanic, in addition to height, weight, age and so forth?

As a reporter, where does your principal responsibility lie? With (1) doing all possible to avoid racial stereotypes in reporting crime? Or, (2) giving your readers or viewers information they need to ensure their own safety? (Many newspapers include race or ethnicity when a killer is on the loose or a police search under way.)

PRESERVING PRESUMPTION OF INNOCENCE

Does the sheer weight of front-page coverage and television news tend to convict alleged perpetrators in reader and viewer minds? Recall those photos of alleged child molesters. Don't readers and viewers think, "Those men and women wouldn't look so downcast, so guilty, if they weren't guilty"?

Do you favor legal restrictions on pretrial or, even, preconviction coverage? If so, how does that square with the First Amendment's guarantee of a free press, and the public's right to know?

If you favor no restrictions, how does your viewpoint square with our judicial system's presumption of innocence until proved guilty? Is that legal presumption an ethical responsibility for journalists, as well?

RELEVANCE OF BACKGROUND

How much background on an accused person is too much? Is a man's record of, say, teenage shoplifting relevant to coverage of his arrest 20 years later on a charge of rape? No? What if his teenage record two decades earlier included a charge of rape?

If reporters uncover even a whiff of sexual scandal in the background of, say, a childcare worker or priest, is the societal responsibility to protect children so great that the background should be brought to light?

How about revealing the background of accusers? In covering the Florida rape case, the *New York Times* reported: "The accuser has a 2-year-old child born out of wedlock and is said by friends and bartenders, among others, to be a regular patron of Palm Beach bars." Was that background relevant for readers? Did it cast doubt on the woman's claim she had been raped? The *Times* mentioned the background obliquely, in discussing whether, under Florida law, such facts could be introduced in court to help the jury decide if the woman's actions during the alleged incident fit a pattern of her previous behavior. Did the *Times* act ethically? Would information in a national newspaper improperly influence a local jury?[13] Did society at large need to know? Was there utilitarian value in publishing that information?

COVERING ONGOING INVESTIGATIONS AND TERRORISM

Two scenarios:

You're covering the brutal slaying of a 20-year-old woman in Texas. You learn police plan to search the apartment of a jailed suspect. Should you include that fact in your story?

You're covering a terrorist bombing and you learn officials have traced a van used in the attack. Should you report it?

In both (true) scenarios, reporters published those facts, ostensibly serving their readers' right (if not, need) to know—but also enormously complicating ongoing investigations.

In Texas, the mother of the slain woman commented:

> A so-called 'scoop' is not really worth letting a criminal go free. In my case, the press printed a story relating police intentions to search a jailed rapist-murder suspect's apartment to find more evidence. The result? By the time they searched the apartment, it had been sterilized of all evidence.[14]

The report on the terrorists' van—used in bombing New York City's World Trade Center in 1993—was in *Newsday* and, well, I'll let the *New York Times* comment:

> . . . City law-enforcement officials . . . said a *New York Newsday* report yesterday tracing the van to a rental agency in Jersey City had forced a premature arrest of a sus-

CASE STUDY

Reporter or Cop?

A huge bomb explosion rips through a building in your city. Six persons are killed and 1,000 are injured. Fear of terrorism is everywhere.

Four days after the bombing, a news clerk in your newsroom opens a large manila envelope addressed to your newspaper. The letter is signed by the "Liberation Army Fifth Battalion" and takes responsibility for the bombing.

The news clerk gives the letter to your assistant metropolitan editor who is coordinating coverage of the bombing.

The letter is faxed to one of your police reporters, who is instructed to give it to the police department. The police request and receive the original letter.

Then, you receive a Federal subpoena demanding documents to show who in your newspaper came into contact with the letter. Presumably, fingerprints would be checked.

At this point, you wonder: Are your staffers reporters or cops? How far should you go in lending direct assistance to officialdom?

It happened in March 1993 at the *New York Times,* which received a subpoena from a Federal grand jury in Manhattan that was investigating the World Trade Center bombing earlier that year.

News organizations often are subpoenaed for—and, under the law, must deliver—reporters' notes, videotape and photographs for use in both civil lawsuits and criminal tri-

pect who was being followed, dashing all hopes that he might lead them to other collaborators. There was no indication that the newspaper was asked to withhold the article.[15]

In 1994, the FBI said it *did* ask a newspaper, the *Portland (Ore.) Oregonian,* to withhold for 24 hours an exclusive story it had on an attack on Olympic skater Nancy Kerrigan by supporters of her rival, Tonya Harding. The story was published and, the FBI said, important evidence may have been destroyed before agents could seize it.

Questions:

Can there be reporter objectivity in the battle between good and evil? Can a reporter be dispassionate as good guys try to hunt down bad guys?

If your reporting uncovered facts you knew would lead police to, say, a killer, would you tell authorities before publishing a story? Every reporter is a citizen and every citizen has a duty to help justice prevail—right? But wouldn't that make you an undercover investigator, not a reporter?

Would you ask authorities to read your story in advance of publication to judge whether it contains information damaging to their investigation?

als. (In 1993, the Reporters Committee for Freedom of the Press concluded a study showing that 3,281 subpoenas were served on 1,010 news organizations in 1991. That was down from 4,408 subpoenas served on 1,042 organizations in 1989.)

Now, *You* Make the Call

Where does the journalist's first loyalty lie—in protection of the news-collection process and news sources, or in cooperating with participants in lawsuits, criminal trials and police investigations?

Should a journalist willingly turn over notes or cooperate if that means betraying a news source?

If a judge or grand jury says a journalist's cooperation is essential in, say, a murder trial or criminal investigation, which comes first, the journalistic obligation to sources? Or a citizen-journalist's responsibility to aid justice?

If it becomes known that journalists cooperate with officials, will any confidential source ever trust journalists?

If the *New York Times* turned over documents in the World Trade Center bombing case, would it compromise its news-collection mechanism? Is the press—the Fourth Estate—truly a separate entity? Can it stand aside from such things as bomb investigations, restricting itself to monitoring and reporting but avoiding cooperation?

The *New York Times'* solution: It declined to turn over documents but offered to permit police to interview the news clerk and editor involved. The *Times* said through its lawyer that "the newspaper had agreed to the interviews because they would not concern any newsgathering activity or compromise any sources."

Would you withhold certain details of, say, a sex killing if police say publication might trigger copy-cat psychos nationwide? Is what might happen half a continent away your responsibility? Or is your responsibility to your own readers or viewers? And, don't they deserve to know details of what's happening in their own city? (In a unique twist on the copy-cat theme, San Diego officials complained in 1993 that media coverage of gangs—even their brutality—was glorifying their lifestyles. One official said, "Gang members are going out with these stories and saying to the kids, 'See we're the right gang for you.'")[16]

WHEN PUBLICITY IS TERRORISM'S GOAL

It is axiomatic that ethical and responsible journalists provide equal access to the media for all participants in a controversy.

But what if some participants kidnap and kill for the sole purpose of gaining such access?

What should editors do when terrorists wave pistols and grenades over cowering hostages and demand, in return for their lives, front-page space or a television interview?

THE CASE OF FLIGHT 847

Arab terrorists on June 14, 1985, found weaknesses in how that 20th century electronic marvel, television, is used. For the next 16 days, they manipulated the medium as if they owned it.[17]

It all started when two terrorists armed with pistols and grenades hijacked TWA Flight 847 from Athens and forced the pilot to land in Beirut. One American serviceman in the plane was slain. Television journalists jumped on the story, showing up with lights, cameras and sound crews each time the terrorists paraded their frightened hostages, each time they shouted yet another demand, each time they created another gun-waving spectacle.

Television produced saturation coverage around the clock. Network programming in the United States was interrupted repeatedly with the latest tidbit from Beirut (CBS announced at one point the copilot had an infected spider bite); star anchors interrogated news sources live 5,000 miles from their New York City studios; news shows were given over to the story without reservation.

The terrorists thus were given the opportunity to tell their story directly to the American people, which of course was the object of the whole exercise. Heretofore unknown Arabs, espousing slogans and causes not entirely clear even to this day, gained an unprecedented international forum and exerted enormous pressure on the White House. In effect, terrorists used network anchors as intermediaries to open public negotiations with the U.S. government, which at the time was trying to sort things out privately and behind the scenes.

Manipulating the media didn't start with Arab terrorism, of course. It's been tried since the invention of movable type. But the Beirut incident showed that anyone shrewd—and brutal—enough could exploit television's need for a visual story (the more dramatic the better) and the scoop mentality that entices competing networks to rush stories on the air without adequate explanatory background or editing.

Above all, Beirut showed television's sense of journalistic caution and discipline could break down and give a handful of screaming gunmen instantaneous links via satellite to living rooms throughout the world. Beirut showed television's extraordinary technology and its ability to span the world with live broadcasts could outrun its masters' ability to use it ethically and responsibly when they strive for even the slightest competitive advantage over other networks and media.

Intense criticism followed. Then British Prime Minister Margaret Thatcher told the American Bar Association, "We must try to find ways to starve the terrorists and the hijacker of the oxygen of publicity on which they depend." U.S. Attorney General Edwin Meese III floated the idea of the Justice Department asking the media to adopt voluntary guidelines on covering terrorism.

Predictably, there were calls for government regulation of news during any hostage situation. Just as predictably, the media united in opposition to even voluntary guidelines, let alone any imposed by government. John Corry, respected *New York Times* TV critic, said a voluntary code wouldn't work and "it is chilling" to think of government enforcing one.

VIEWPOINT

Networks War over News

"It's trench warfare. There's everything out there but mustard gas."

Van Gordon Sauter, describing news competition between networks when he was president of CBS News

Corry said that in Beirut television asserted "journalism's prerogatives without meeting its responsibilities" and "surrendered journalistic sovereignty by showing whatever it could whenever it could. . . . Valid criticism of television would disappear if it practiced responsible journalism in the first place."[18]

Publicity isn't always terrorism's goal, of course. But it was when terrorists in Lebanon hanged a hostage U.S. Marine colonel and distributed a videotape of his death throes. The accompanying message: Israel must release a captured Muslim cleric or another American hostage would be killed. CBS, NBC and CNN showed short sections of the videotape; ABC used only still photos on grounds it would demean the colonel to show him swinging at the end of a rope. A still photo was front-paged by the *New York Times* and other papers.

In 1993, a religious cult leader in Waco, Tex., under siege by Federal agents, signaled he would surrender if given a live interview on CNN. He got it—and was quoted in broadcast and print coverage nationwide. At one point, cult members hung out a banner: "God Help Us We Want the Press." (There was no surrender. Four federal agents and at least 10 cult members died in a shootout.)

Television obviously isn't alone in its vulnerability to manipulation by terrorists. They can establish the news agenda for newspapers, as well.

But there is a difference: It relates to television's technical capabilities, its immediacy, its tendency to run stories for visual effect without tight editorial control and editing—thus offering terrorists direct access to the audience they seek. It is television's sight-and-sound high drama the terrorists want to employ.

And that high drama—guns held to hostage heads, threats of assassinations—can create such widespread public pressure that governments have difficulty pursuing broader policies, such as refusing to negotiate with terrorists.

NOW, *YOU* MAKE THE CALL

What general guidelines would you lay down for covering terrorists if you were a newspaper or magazine editor or TV news director?

Despite the media's inability (or unwillingness) to agree on a firm code for covering terrorism, there is general agreement on some points. Perhaps these will aid your decision-making process:

VIEWPOINT

Terrorism Live and Unedited

"Three miracles—the jet airplane, the television and the satellite—have made it possible for a few anarchists or murders to take the laws of civilization and the attention of the world into their own hands. When they succeed, we are all hostages, not just the passengers on the jet, but all of us and especially the president of the United States and television. And it is the television spotlight that is the real ransom the terrorists demand and get. . . . Live interviews—unedited—with terrorists is unconscionable. It is like handing over the front page to one side and saying, 'Fill in the headline.'"

Fred Friendly, former CBS News executive

"[I] hear that TV has become the terrorists' ultimate tool. This is a daffy and irresponsible charge. The competitive zeal with which the networks chased after the story of the [TWA Flight 847 hostages in Beirut] should be celebrated as an example of what's right about the democratic system, not what's wrong with it. There were, to be sure, some unruly and odious excesses. But I believe that such indiscretions are a worthwhile price to pay for a precious freedom that does not exist for more than 80 percent of the world's citizens."

Morton Dean, veteran TV newsman

"TV news cameras and political agitators have had a much-discussed symbiotic relationship from the very beginning of TV. TV producers like action and the agitators like attention. But political atrocities did not begin with the television age, any careful reading of the exploits of Joe Stalin, Adolf Hitler or Genghis Kahn will attest. Today's political extremists may enjoy the camera's attention, but they do not necessarily 'thrive' on it."

Wall Street Journal editorial arguing against even voluntary codes for television coverage in hostage situations

Terrorism is news and must be covered. But the media must not indiscriminately provide the terrorists with a platform and audience. Avoid giving terrorists incentive to seek more exposure by striking again.

The media must reexamine objectivity. It is foolishness, not objectivity, to treat hijackers and the hijacked as equals. By any civilized standard, it is wrong for a person to hold a gun at the head of an innocent. It also is wrong for journalists to describe such an act as a justifiable political statement.

TV journalists should take guidance from ABC News' internal guidelines: avoid sensationalizing any terrorist act, do nothing to jeopardize hostages' lives or interfere with police efforts, broadcast no incident live except in the most compelling circumstances—and report terrorists' demands only with explanatory background. NBC has good advice, too, for its reporters: keep a low profile, limit use of lights, locate cameras and mikes as inconspicuously as possible.[19]

The media must avoid participating in negotiations with terrorists. Television anchors in New York City in effect bargained directly with terrorists 5,000 miles away, asking—with the court of American public opinion watching—what their

CASE STUDY

Quick! You Decide

You are news director of an ABC television affiliate. A convict being treated at a local hospital escapes, obtains a gun and holds hostages in the hospital. He warns he will kill his prisoners unless his grievances are broadcast by television. Police want you to broadcast the statement verbatim. Obviously concerned that the killing could start momentarily, police ask you to decide immediately.

ABC News policy gives you this guidance:

"We must guard against efforts by terrorists to use or manipulate us for their own ends. . . . [N]o such incident should be broadcast live except in the most compelling circumstances. . . . Demands of the terrorist should be reported as an essential ingredient of the story. But we must avoid becoming a platform for propaganda and rhetoric. In most cases, this means we will condense, edit or paraphrase the demands and explain the background against which they were made."

Confronted by this problem, WABC-TV, New York City, agreed to broadcast the gunman's statement. Said the station's Cliff Abromats: "We didn't have time to sit down and debate the philosophic and ethical aspects of the request. We had two minutes."

Afterward, the *New York Daily News* commented in an editorial:

"There's something wrong when a guy who was just a number in Attica [a New York State prison] a few days ago can commandeer the spotlight like that. We in the news business must draw the line against being twisted so easily."

Was WABC-TV right to assist police, turning over its facilities to a gunman?

Did the station let a criminal "commandeer the spotlight," as the *Daily News* charged?

(Postscript: The incident ended without bloodshed.)

demands were and whether they had any word for the U.S. president. That was an impressive display of technological prowess, but it amounted to journalistic stunting, not reporting. Calm, professional editing must be inserted between the sight and sound of terrorism and what hits the screen or front page.

The media must avoid publishing information that might preempt action to free hostages. For example, the *Atlanta Constitution,* covering the hijacking of an EgyptAir jet, reported on its front page "[T]he pilot punched the button of the emergency transponder, silently notifying the Athens tower that a hijacking had begun." That undoubtedly revealed a great many people, prospective terrorists included, there was such a thing as an "emergency transponder."[20] The *New York Times* published a detailed story, complete with diagrams, on how airport security devices detect terrorists' bombs in luggage—and, for any alert terrorist, how such security measures can be evaded.[21]

AIDS, PRIVACY AND THE PUBLIC

We discussed in Chapter 2 how the media generally mishandled reporting of AIDS when it first broke into public view. In misguided attempts to write in good taste, many journalists avoided frank discussion of how AIDS can be transmitted through sexual contact. Result: A near health panic as the public mistakenly concluded AIDS could be transmitted through a handshake or the air we breathe.

Let's now approach ethical problems in another dimension of AIDS coverage. We'll use a case study. Recall the five-step process of decision making in ethics: Assemble all the facts, identify the ethical issues(s), consider alternative solutions, then decide and act. Reflect on the societal values, journalistic principles and loyalties identified in Chapter 1.

Now, you make the call:

You learn an internationally renowned tennis star has AIDS. You have this story *exclusively.*

Though retired, the wealthy tennis star still is in the public eye, as a television commentator and columnist.

The star knows that having AIDS, like being raped, carries social stigma. He pleads with you not to publish the story, saying he contracted the disease through blood transfusions after heart surgery. He points out that he is married and a father.

Will you publish this story?

USA Today faced this question when one of its reporters was tipped by a source in 1992 that Arthur Ashe, one-time Wimbledon and U.S. Open champion, had AIDS.

Ashe said *USA Today*'s inquiries forced him to divulge news of his illness on a media time schedule, not his own—and he held a press conference, confirming he tested positive more than three years earlier and that friends, including journalists, had kept his secret.

"I am angry," he said, "that I was put in the unenviable position of having to lie if I was to protect my privacy. After all, I am not running for some office of public trust, nor do I have stockholders to account to. It was only that I fall under the dubious umbrella of 'public figure.'"

Ashe broke down in tears and his wife had to finish reading his statement. It said the couple had to break the news to their 5-year-old daughter and "teach her how to react to new, different and sometimes cruel comments that have very little to do with her reality."

Now, confront your reality: As a journalist you sometimes hurt people with judgment calls in ethics. Ashe was visibly shaken at having to tell his daughter that her daddy had a fatal illness.

Here is how Gene Policinski, *USA Today*'s managing editor/sports, answers two obvious questions:

Q. Why did *USA Today* pursue the Ashe story?

A. The very simple fact that it's news. Clearly this was a person who by all estimations was a public person—a person of great interest to people. We make decisions every day: "This is news and that is not news." I felt we handled it according to our guidelines; we did not publish Wednesday morning prior to his press conference. [The story] had to have a confirmed source and a primary source—someone who was in the position to back it up. Those are guidelines we act upon everyday. They applied to this story just as any story.

Q. Was this an issue of privacy infringement?

A. What we're talking about here is not really privacy. What we have here is a person whose disease was known widely about by friends, colleagues and medical persons. [This is about] the right of someone who has spent many years perfecting and fleshing out a public image to protect that image from harm. We're talking about economics. His privacy hasn't been violated. The private details of how he's dealing with AIDS have not been published.

AIDS indeed is news, of course, and Ashe's sports stardom doubled the impact. A year earlier, a basketball super star, Magic Johnson, revealed he had tested positive for the HIV virus that causes AIDS. Johnson acknowledged he caught the virus through sexual promiscuity.

The Ashe story was front-page news. His news conference was televised live. Few editors held back: The story won *big* display.

The *New York Times* commented editorially that Ashe "aimed his barbs at the wrong target when he complained about the person who 'ratted' on him to a newspaper. The real villainy lies in the cruel and benighted public attitudes that compelled Mr. Ashe to keep his disease secret for three years." The *Times* pleaded with Ashe to become an advocate for AIDS victims and "help change the ignorant attitudes that forced him underground."

Yet, there were dissenters. *Forbes* magazine said in an editorial: "What was the purpose of this invasion of privacy? Ashe is retired. He wasn't up for a Cabinet post. He wasn't running for public office. What right did the public have to know of his current condition if he did not wish to make it public?"

Now answer these questions:

Was Ashe (who subsequently died of AIDS-related illness) a public figure or private person? Should that make a difference to journalists?

Can persons who become famous and wealthy as public figures suddenly and unilaterally declare themselves to be private persons?

Does contracting a fatal disease in itself make a public figure out of a person who wants a private life?

Postscript: At almost the same time the Ashe story broke, police in Philadelphia arrested a man with AIDS who acknowledged paying for sex with several hundred male teenagers over the previous several years.

The district attorney refused to identify the man, saying Pennsylvania law prohibited naming persons with AIDS. The official said the man agreed to being identified only as "Uncle Ed" to alert boys who may have had sex with him.

The Associated Press learned—and published—the man's name, age and where he lived.

Was AP right to break the law? What would Immanuel Kant say?[22]

ETHICS AND HOMOSEXUAL "OUTING"

Many ethical dilemmas arise for editors as gay rights groups become increasingly open and aggressive in the 1990s.

But no dilemma is more difficult than what to do when some gay magazines "out" prominent American gays—identifying them publicly, even against their wishes.

Gay advocacy magazines say they are trying to liberalize public attitudes toward homosexuals by openly discussing sexual orientation. And, they say, disclosing the homosexuality of people of fame and fortune will encourage other gays to emerge from the "closet" and publicly take gay identities.

One high-ranking Pentagon official, familiar to millions of TV viewers and newspaper readers, was among those outed by gay publications. Then, mainstream columnist Jack Anderson reported it. Anderson said the man's homosexuality was news because he was a public official serving the armed forces, which then had a strict policy of locating and expelling gays from the ranks. That, Anderson said, was a contradiction that had to be reported.

"It was not our intention to out him," wrote Anderson and the co-author of his column, Dale Van Atta. "The gay media and others had already done that. Our purpose was to out the Pentagon policy from the closet of bigotry and paranoia. . . . We're genuinely pleased that he still has his job. The thousands of people bounced from the military during nearly 50 years of homophobia at the Defense Department should be able to say the same."[23]

You make the call:

Did the public have a right (need) to know the sexual orientation of the Pentagon official? Was there utilitarian value in covering this story that overrode the societal value of humaneness and the journalistic principle of compassion?

The mainstream media decided the character issue was important in covering presidential politics and reported Bill Clinton's alleged heterosexual past. Was the character issue also important in covering the homosexual in the Pentagon?

In covering the alleged rape in Florida discussed earlier in this chapter, *New York Times* editors identified the alleged victim, saying NBC earlier identified her and, thus, the issue was out of their hands. Since the Pentagon official already had been outed in a gay magazine, should the mainstream media have felt free to follow suit?

Tough questions, right? It might help your decision making to know that in the Pentagon case the herd instinct didn't stampede the media into following the lead of the gay magazine or Jack Anderson. The story wasn't aired or published generally. In fact, some newspapers that normally carry Anderson's column decided not to run the one on the Pentagon gay. (Incidentally, the Pentagon official now is a journalist himself. I am not naming him here because I see no journalistic relevance in doing so. Is there, these years later, a people's right—need—to know? Isn't compassion the operative journalistic principle, absent any need for the public to know?)

YOU AND POLITICAL CORRECTNESS

Pop quiz: If you refuse on principle to use "indians" when writing about the Cleveland Indians baseball team are you being:

1. sensitive to the feelings of Native Americans?
2. ethnically aware, socially inclusive and a proponent of diversity in America, or
3. ridiculous?

Take your pick—and welcome to the discussion—nay, quarrel—over what, for lack of a better term, is called *political correctness (PC).*

Broadly, PC is a term given the effort to ensure our society—particularly our language in print and broadcast—treats fairly all groups, regardless of race, gender, age, ethnicity, sexual orientation and so forth.

Actually, PC isn't new. In multicultural, diverse America different groups always have struggled for even-handed treatment—particularly minorities and those historically disenfranchised politically, economically or socially. And, persuading both the media and public to use appropriate language in discussing those groups has been part of that struggle because lasting stereotypes and vicious prejudices are created—and perpetuated—by language.

Among journalists the current PC debate undeniably is hotter than ever before, due particularly to two factors: First, a societal revolution is under way in America, with minorities and groups of all kinds demanding their fair share, their place in the sun, and second, the media generally are making great effort to be sensitive to those groups, to reflect their values and assist their battle for fairness. Some of this is quite new.

Witness, for example, the snap quiz that opened this discussion. It would have been unthinkable as recently as, say, 1972 for the media to even consider whether "Cleveland *Indians*" was inappropriate language. Yet, in 1992, the *Portland Oregonian* announced it would stop publishing Indian-related names of sports teams because they

> tend to perpetuate stereotypes that damage the dignity and self-respect of many people in our society and that this harm far transcends any innocent entertainment or promotional values those names may have . . . the *Oregonian* is sensitive to the feelings of those in our society who are rightly offended today by names and nicknames that came into being when a majority in this country was insensitive to minority concerns.[24]

The *Oregonian*'s policy is not catching on. Other journalists ask, What are we to call the people involved? "Indians"? "Native Americans"? "American Indians"? "Native American Indians"? Anyway, critics ask, how can any single term be used to cover all tribes or aboriginal nations, some of which fought each other in times bygone and which still don't like to be considered identical?

This confusion over preferences and terms springs up elsewhere. Some media use *blacks,* others *African-Americans*—and a 1991 survey by the Joint Center for Political and Economic Studies shows divided preferences among black people themselves: Of 759 respondents, 72 percent preferred *black*; 15 percent, *African-American*; 3 percent, *Afro-American*; 2 percent *negro*; 8 percent had no opinion or preferred some other term.

A 1993 survey by The Associated Press Managing Editors Association showed that of 99 newspapers responding, 61 followed AP's style of using "black"; 5 used "African-American." By an overwhelming margin, "Hispanic" was favored over "Latino." "American Indian" was used by 45 newspapers, "Native American" by 34; other papers used both, or other designations.[25]

Among homosexuals, preferences include *gay, gay* and *lesbian,* and *gay, lesbian* and *bisexual.* But, in their drive for social acceptance and equality, some homosexual activists use—proudly and affirmatively—labels long ago classified as unacceptable: *queer, fag, homo.*

Obviously, such terms can have extraordinary connotations for readers and viewers.

Consider, for example, the different impact of *pro-life* and *anti-abortion* or the difference between *free choice* and *pro-abortion.* Each term drips with political and social nuances that are highly emotional in one of the most heated national debates in America today.

Or, consider the warning of the Hawaii chapter of the Asian American Journalists Association, which felt it necessary to issue a guide for journalists covering the 50th anniversary of Japan's attack on Pearl Harbor: " . . . stereotypes and reporting biased against one group—even a foreign nation—can affect all Asian Pacific Americans, because the public often views all Asian Pacific Americans as alike . . ."[26]

All to say that as a journalist in this contentious PC era you'll build your personal code of ethics on shifting societal sands and evolving journalistic principles. If nothing else, PC means change—constant, important change.

An example of change leading to unusual situations: Today, individuals in the news often are given a choice of how they will be identified. Many editors let women choose between *Miss, Mrs.* or *Ms.*

When Bill Clinton's marital relations became an issue during his presidential campaign, his spouse preferred "Hillary Clinton," loyal wife of the candidate. When he was elected, she switched to "Hillary Rodham Clinton," inserting her maiden name—still a spouse but also a successful attorney and political activist in her own right.

Each time, the media generally switched usage in conformity with her desire.

THE DANGERS OF PC EXTREMES

There are dangers for you, as a journalist, on many PC issues.

First, there is the risk of unthinkingly using language that's unnecessarily offensive to groups or that tends to build stereotypes about them. This can have divisive effect in our society, which badly needs unity, and exclude people and groups from the even-handed treatment and fair share they deserve.

Second, there is danger of being so sensitive that you'll allow the desires—demands—of groups to color, restrict or, indeed, censor your reporting and writing. This can have the effect of denying your wider audience—your first responsibility—the honest journalism it deserves.

Prepare to take some heat over all this.

Andy Rooney, CBS humorist, acknowledges he "pulled back some" on controversial stories because he didn't want to be branded a racist. CBS suspended him briefly in 1990 for comments (which he denied making) attributed to him in a magazine for gays. That, he says, was a "chilling experience."[27]

Howard Kurtz, media reporter for the *Washington Post,* writes of journalists who avoid "touchy" stories, asking,

> Is it still possible to candidly explore the treacherous terrain of race, crime, poverty, abortion or homosexuality without triggering a firestorm of protest? Or is the journalism of the 1990s destined to be a bland form of discourse that tiptoes around the sensitive subjects that people are thrashing out in private?

Kurtz applauds any group's right to protest its treatment in the media but asks whether even "insensitive, muddled or just plain wrongheaded" remarks warrant boycotts, protests and "journalistic excommunication." He asks, "Do the thought police have to make an arrest for every real or imagined transgression?"

Kurtz continues:

> The larger problem with such gale-force protests is that any attempt at rational discourse is swept away. Modern life, after all, is filled with unpleasant facts: Most prison inmates are black and Hispanic. Many poor women are having children that they are unable to care for adequately even with welfare assistance. The prevalence of AIDS is far greater in the homosexual community, particularly among gays who are promiscuous and do not take precautions. The drug problem was not treated as a national crisis until it spread from slum areas to white middle-class neighborhoods. Yet to delve into these subjects is to risk charges of racism or sexism or homophobia.[28]

So, what can you do as a journalist? Is an Aristotelian Golden Mean available?

SOME SUGGESTIONS

A study of what principled editors across the nation say about PC reveals these suggestions:

- At all cost, resist censorship or any effort by any group to shut down reasoned discourse.
- Resist revisionism, the effort to rewrite what was. There should have been Founding Mothers present when the U.S. Constitution was written. There weren't.
- But be sensible and avoid sexual bias. To harp constantly on achievements of the Founding Fathers is insensitive to women who feel themselves only now

emerging from male-dominated history. Use asexual words when appropriate: work hours, not man hours; synthetic, not man-made. But a male is a spokes*man*; a female, a spokes*woman.*

- Avoid obvious stereotypes—the arrogant white policeman, the shiftless black, the proud and stoic Native American.
- Avoid implied stereotypes. The "black computer whiz" implies this black is an exception and that other blacks can't be computer whizzes, too.
- Use racial and ethnic identification only when necessary. No need to specify that a "black" or "white" passerby spotted the fire and dialed 911. But do get specific when describing a rapist who is on the loose in the neighborhood.
- Avoid cliches and what they often imply. For example: "Hard-working, church-going suburbanites" (implication: white). "Unemployed, inner-city drug addicts (means blacks to many).
- Seek diversity in your reporting. You simply haven't done a responsible job unless your story reflects the diversity of our society. (Which is why media organizations strive to create in their newsrooms a racial, ethnic and gender balance that reflects their marketplaces.)
- Use journalistic devices to get into print or on the air with what must be said but said with sensitivity. For example, the most spectacular trial of 1993 was that of white policemen videotaped while beating a black Los Angeles motorist, Rodney King. It was essential to report King's testimony about what he was told while being beaten. The *Atlanta Constitution* sensibly held for deep in the story, on page A12, King's most inflammatory quote: King said his attackers shouted, "We're going to kill you nigger; run!" On its front page, in the lead paragraph, *Constitution* editors used accurate but less inflammatory language—that King said the policemen "screamed racial insults" at him. The *Constitution* met the requirements of truth-telling and responsible journalism that day.[29]

However, when there is compelling journalistic need to say it straight, do just that and forget the journalistic devices. In 1991, when law professor Anita F. Hill charged sexual harassment by Clarence Thomas, a nominee to the U.S. Supreme Court, newspapers fronted no-holds-barred coverage. A *New York Times* page-one headline: "Taboo Issues of Sex and Race Explode in Glare of Hearing." The *Times* fronted explicit testimony by Thomas before Congress about what he called bigoted "language about the sex organs of black men and the sizes, et cetera." Testimony by Thomas was central to his successful defense. Eliminating it out of a sense of good taste would have been misguided and a betrayal of the *Times'* compelling responsibility.[30]

THE MEDIA, FREEDOM OF INFORMATION AND THE LAW

Not long after Johann Gutenberg popularized movable type in the mid-1440s, the Western world's power structure realized he had created a monster: The printing press was a clear threat to established authority.

VIEWPOINT

Whose Government Is It Anyway?

"It's incongruous in a democracy for the government to know more about its people than the people know about their government. Yet this pattern has been established. I fear that news from the White House will continue to be manipulated and distorted as in a Hollywood script."

Thomas Winship, then editor of the *Boston Globe*

Ever since, the political, religious, economic and social establishment has understood—and feared and periodically restricted—the power that flows from rapid and widespread exchange of information among vast audiences.

This brings us to one of the most important influences on journalism ethics and media social responsibility—the desire of governments and special interest groups to license and censor the media or, simply, to refuse to reveal to the media and, thus, to the people, what the people have a right to know about the people's own business.

Worldwide, it's been a constant fight since Gutenberg's day to achieve free flow of information. In America, the media are in the forefront of the battle—and you and Gutenberg's other distant successors will have to continue the fight (which never is won) or you will fail the test of an important societal value—stewardship—and the journalistic principle of defending the First Amendment.

Consider, for example, the enormous bureaucratic structure that has mushroomed to handle (and control) information about the federal government—the presidency, state department, military.

Reflect on the reality that the obsession with secrecy permeates the lowest rungs of government—local school boards, city commissions—and even universities, those supposed citadels of free expression where information now is routinely withheld from student newspapers and, indeed, taxpayers.

Isn't it curious: The media today enjoy strong economic support in the marketplace. Advertisers spend well over $137 billion in the United States each year; nearly 60 million Americans vote for newspapers by buying them each day; millions more listen to radio and watch TV. Yet, societal regard for the media generally is low and perhaps slipping, whether you measure it in the judgments libel juries hand down or by the public's relative comfort with—or, indeed, participation in—media bashing.

THE FREEDOM OF INFORMATION ACT

In 1967, a law was passed giving U.S. citizens for the first time the right to see, within limits, what is in the files of many federal agencies. President Lyndon B. Johnson reluctantly signed the Freedom of Information Act (FOIA) under con-

VIEWPOINT

It Is The People's Amendment

"All the talk about the First Amendment rights of the press is not about special privileges for newspaper reporters and publishers, but about rights of the public—the right to be kept informed, the right of the governed to have a surrogate watching the governors. The First Amendment wasn't drafted for the publisher's benefit but for the public's."

Warren Phillips, then chairman, Dow Jones & Co., publisher, *Wall Street Journal*

gressional pressure and thus added substantial right of access to the right of free press established back in 1791, with the First Amendment.

It was a historic development, for there always had been—and still is—argument over whether the First Amendment implies a guaranteed right to gather news as well as print it. Some legal scholars say the Constitution means only what it says—and it doesn't say anything about the right of access to news; others say the Constitution means what the U.S. Supreme Court says it means, and that the law which has developed since the First Amendment was written clearly implies the right of access. Otherwise, they ask, how could we have a truly free press?

What the Constitution's drafters intended never will be known. They drafted the Constitution in secrecy.

In any event, FOIA, stiffened by amendments in 1974 and 1986, orders open all but highly sensitive records in many agencies. The agencies combined receive 250,000 to 300,000 requests annually for documents. The result is a huge flow into the public domain of information previously withheld.[31]

However, the federal government continues stamping secrecy classifications on millions of documents. One study in 1993 discovered that 5,793 persons in the federal government were authorized to use the "secret" stamp—and they classified 6,349,532 documents in fiscal year 1992. The study revealed that the National Archive alone has 325 million pages of classified documents. The Archive is just one of 80,000 repositories for the government's classified material.[32]

One problem is that when information is requested, an agency decides whether it falls within nine categories of documents that, under FOIA, legally can be withheld—documents classified to protect national security, records on personnel matters, business or trade secrets obtained from a business firm or person, law enforcement investigations, records kept in regulation of financial institutions, and geologic and other data on oil and gas wells. Thousands of requests are denied on these grounds.

Despite problems, FOIA brings to light much government information that otherwise never would be published or broadcast. In 1986 alone, three newspapers won Pulitzer prizes with information unlocked through FOIA.

However, the media, often on deadline and unable to wait for time-consuming file searches, actually are relatively minor users of FOIA. One estimate is that fewer than five percent of requests are from the media.[33] Some in the federal government want to restrict FOIA on grounds many requests are from business firms—foreign as well as American—seeking proprietary information from competitors, and from foreign governments, including some that find it an inexpensive form of espionage.

Iran's leader, the Ayatollah Khomeini, once employed an American law firm to ask the CIA through FOIA for all its information on the ousted Shah of Iran! The Secret Service reports a decline in the number of informants who fear their identities can become known to criminal elements through FOIA. (A sample letter for requesting information under FOIA can be found in Appendix H.)

Many state and local governments have sunshine laws requiring that the people's business be conducted openly, in full view of the media (and, thus, the people). However, these laws often are ignored at all levels of government. It is the responsibility of all journalists to raise the alarm when that happens.

SPECIAL INTEREST PRESSURE GROUPS

The media today are caught in the middle of arguments for or against the women's movement, school prayer, racial equality, homosexuality, abortion, pornography, capital punishment, arms control—and dozens more emotional issues.

Nothing new in that. America always has felt the tug and pull of opposing ideas, and first newspapers, then television as well, have been tugged and pulled in the process.

Now, however, some groups, particularly conservative religious and political elements, strike directly at media ownership and financial stability in intimidation campaigns to influence the flow of news and shape what is reported about them. Their techniques include organizing reader or viewer boycotts to frighten off advertisers and even attempting takeover of a company that, if only a bluff that fails, can destabilize its management. Consider CBS:

Throughout the mid-1980s, CBS's management was trying to run the network on a day-by-day basis and improve its long-range prospects while simultaneously fighting off repeated takeover attempts on one hand and, on the other, responding to conservative charges that it had unpatriotic reporters and anchors bent on giving the news a liberal twist.

At the 1986 CBS annual meeting, leaders of three special issue pressure groups dominated floor questions: Accuracy in Media charged that CBS "goes out of its way to undermine confidence in the United States," and attacked anchor Dan Rather; Fairness in Media, part of a conservative bloc supporting Sen. Jesse Helms (R–N.C.), rose to make sure CBS was aware of the threat from leftist insurgencies; and Rev. Jesse Jackson criticized lack of blacks in both management and anchor ranks at the network and local CBS stations.

It is ability to hit the media where it hurts—in their business affairs—that marks today's special issue pressure groups.

Helms, for example, announced he was leading an effort to buy CBS so conservatives could end the network's "liberal bias" and "become Dan Rather's boss." The move aroused enormous concern among investors on Wall Street, and Gene Jankowski, CBS/Broadcast Group president, said it seriously distracted him and others responsible for improving the network's faltering ratings.[34]

There were other efforts to take over CBS, one by Ted Turner, Atlanta entrepreneur and principal owner of CNN. He spoke of a combination of business and ideological motives. (Turner was quoted once as saying, "The greatest enemies America has ever had, posing a greater threat to our way of life than Nazi Germany or Tojo's Japan, are the three television networks.")[35]

Helms and Turner failed to gain control of the company but both helped destabilize it so badly that CBS never will be the same again.

To fight the takeover, CBS management made defensive maneuvers, including purchase of the company's own stock on the open market, which cost nearly $1 billion. That, in turn, forced an expense reduction program that, among other things, led to elimination of more than 700 jobs, well over 100 in the news division alone.

Before the dust settled, Loew's Corp. bought 24.9 percent of CBS's common stock, becoming the largest shareholder, and Loew's chairman, Laurence Tisch, became CBS's president and chief executive officer.

Those were tangible effects of destabilization. Were there others, more intangible? Did conservative attacks chill the CBS newsroom? Did reporters, even subconsciously, cautiously rethink how they would cover the news? Did knowing his every word, every gesture, was being monitored by conservative groups change the way Dan Rather viewed the news?

ARE THE MEDIA "LIBERAL"?

Conservative groups frequently seek ammunition in studies reporting that many journalists term themselves liberal and vote Democratic in presidential elections. That leads to charges that journalists are, among other things, hostile to business and religion, are supportive of homosexuality and generally are left-wing in attitudes.

Such attacks aren't universally accepted, of course. Albert Hunt, *Wall Street Journal* Washington bureau chief, says careful analysis of reporting on the national level would show some bad journalism is practiced and that the media "sometimes lack discipline and are swept away by the passions of the moment," but that journalists as a group are not ideologically biased or unpatriotic.[36]

Despite many such pressures, journalists are far more worried about what is happening in U.S. courtrooms and its impact on free flow of information.

THE MEDIA AND THE LAW

Restrictions on free flow of information can stem from attempts to restrain the media prior to publication and from use of libel law to chill the media with threat of heavy financial penalties after publication.

VIEWPOINT

Attacks from Right and Left

"The New Right and the New Left, the pro-nukes and the anti-nukes, the National Conservative Political Action committee and the National Abortion Rights Action League have found a common enemy. It is us—the press."

Fred Barnes, national political correspondent, *Baltimore Sun,* writing in *Washington Journalism Review*

PRIOR RESTRAINT

Although the U.S. Supreme Court has held that the Constitution forbids prepublication licensing or censorship, there have been numerous attempts to accomplish just that, particularly by the government in national security cases.

In one of many battles over the issue, the U.S. Supreme Court strongly affirmed the freedom to publish, under all but highly unusual circumstances, without prior restraint in a 1931 landmark case, *Near v. Minnesota.*

In 1971, in the Pentagon papers case, the Nixon administration won in a lower court a temporary order restraining the *New York Times* from publishing stories on a confidential government study of the Vietnam War. On appeal, the Supreme Court continued the temporary order; *Times* lawyers sidestepped a direct confrontation on what many experts felt was the court's serious dilution of the First Amendment. The lawyers argued instead the government could not prove publication would harm national security, and the *Times* was permitted to proceed with the series.

The court stated, "Any system of prior restraint of expression comes to this court bearing a heavy presumption against its constitutional validity." But the ruling, nevertheless, widely was interpreted as meaning the government might be able to argue successfully for prior restraint in some future case. The battle over such censorship clearly is not finished.

THE CHILLING EFFECT

Another major impediment to free flow of information, the chilling effect, is extremely complicated.

Although the Constitution establishes the right to speak and write as we please without prior restraint, the law of course leaves everyone who does so subject to punishment after the fact for what they say or write. For that purpose, society devised libel laws covering those who harm the reputation of an individual or corporation by publishing or broadcasting a falsehood.

Society also has laws to punish those who offend it in other ways, by publishing obscenity, for example, or seditious material. But libel law is of particular concern because Americans are using it with unprecedented vigor, sometimes frivolously, sometimes harshly and openly threatening—and often successfully chilling coverage.

Consider the following:

- A Dallas jury awards a district attorney $58 million in 1991 for a television station's story that he was taking payments to quash drunken driving cases. A Philadelphia jury grants a $34 million libel award against the *Philadelphia Inquirer* for its story suggesting a former prosecutor quashed a homicide inquiry as a favor to a friend.
- Frank Sinatra's attorneys ask Universal Press Syndicate for the names of newspapers that published its "Doonesbury" comic strip satirizing him. They just asked, mind you—but get the point? Editors all over the country are looking at comic strips just a little more carefully. (Universal says 30 newspapers did not print all or part of the Sinatra series; two papers canceled the popular strip altogether.)[37]
- An indian tribe sues Gannett's *Santa Fe (N.M.) New Mexican* for $3.6 million because it published two photos of a private tribal dance. To settle, the *New Mexican* makes two apologies, and, when both are rejected as inadequate, makes a third—and promises $20,000 for a tribal college scholarship fund, internships for tribal students, free advertising for some tribal enterprises and assigns a reporter to cover indian affairs.[38]
- Gen. William C. Westmoreland sues CBS for $120 million on grounds a documentary defamed him by accusing his command in Vietnam of engaging in a conspiracy to understate enemy capabilities in reports to Washington. Before settling, Westmoreland and supporters spend about $3.25 million pursuing the case; CBS, $5 million.[39]
- Gen. Ariel Sharon, former defense minister of Israel, sues *Time* magazine for $50 million on grounds a story about Lebanon contained a paragraph that defamed him by falsely accusing him of encouraging a massacre. After a legal battle costing more than $3 million, a jury says *Time* was "negligently and carelessly" wrong but didn't libel Sharon because it didn't publish the information with "serious doubts as to its truth." Both *Time* and Sharon claim victory.[40]

What's happening here? It is this:

Many Americans regard the media as negligent and insensitive, cold and distant and offering no self-correcting mechanism under which offended individuals can have access to the media for their side of the story.

The public has no legal right of access to newspapers, and what do many newspapers offer those who feel harmed by coverage? A letter to the editor, perhaps, or if pressed, a correction buried on an inside page. Television only rarely offers even those limited remedies.

For many persons, the courtroom is their only forum, the law their only weapon for restoring reputation and punishing the media they feel harmed them.

For the media, enormous legal costs and potentially crippling damage awards are real dangers in everyday journalism.

For society, as well as the media, a major question is how expensive litigation—or merely its threat—is chilling news coverage and slowing the free flow of information.

Conservative groups monitoring the media say complaints about legal costs are a smokescreen; most citizens, they say, are less able to afford litigation than newspapers or television networks. Reed Irvine, then chairman of Accuracy in Media, added:

> What is wrong with chilling any propensity of journalists to defame with reckless disregard of the truth? Isn't that supposed to be what professional journalists are taught to avoid doing? Isn't that what editors are supposed to do? If journalists fail to observe the ethical codes of their profession, and if editors fail to do their job, why shouldn't there be a penalty for malpractice in a possible libel judgment?[41]

WOULD ADMISSION OF ERROR HELP?

Commenting on the Sharon case, Richard Clurman, former chief of correspondents for *Time* and *Life,* noted *Time* declared itself the winner even though found "negligently and carelessly" wrong in its reporting. Clurman continued:

> In journalism, there is only one sin worse than being found wrong: an unwillingness to admit it. . . . We do not need to revise our laws or tamper with First Amendment principles. But the press must change many of its ways. For example, if the media make a serious factual charge against a public figure, they had better be able to offer proof that it is true. If they cannot—as *Time* could not—whether they believe it or not, they should retract the charge. And then if a Sharon—or other officials—still choose to sue, let them face the weight of the press's vital constitutional protection.[42]

Sharon insists it was a retraction, not financial award, he sought from *Time.* Westmoreland says he had no place but the courtroom to go.

Many libel cases are instituted by people who, like Sharon and Westmoreland, feel harmed not financially but emotionally. A study by the University of Iowa Libel Research Project finds plaintiffs sue not for financial reward, but "to restore their reputation or punish the media."

A famous trial lawyer, Harvard Prof. Alan Dershowitz, insisting he doesn't suggest control by government or any other group, proposes "that the journalism profession establish an internal court of corrections, something to which aggrieved consumers of the media can go to see errors corrected on the basis of peer appraisal."[43]

Unquestionably, many Americans are sympathetic to people who claim damage by the media—and prove that sympathy as jurors in libel cases.

The Libel Defense Resource Center reports that in 1992 and 1993, the average jury award to libel plaintiffs was about $1.1 million.[44]

About 90 percent of all libel suits are dropped, settled or dismissed before trial. But when they get before juries, the media lose most of the time. From

1990 to 1991, the media lost 72.4 percent of libel suits decided by juries—but only 32 percent of suits decided by judges.

Judges rule on the law; clearly, juries often reflect deeper societal anger about the conduct of newspapers, magazines and television. Howard B. Cohen, a lawyer who won an $18.5 million award against Capital Cities Communications in 1992, said, "People are tired of letting the media stand behind the First Amendment when they've acted with reckless disregard" of the truth.[45]

So, we end this chapter with media ethics and media law overlapping. It's worth emphasizing: If an institution loses favor with society laws inevitably are enacted to control that institution or modify its behavior. Our society doesn't want steel companies polluting the skies or manufacturing firms mistreating employees—and absent voluntary compliance, it has laws aimed at preventing that from happening.

Is the vigorous use of libel law against the media a societal signal to journalists? Are libel judgments, as well as opinion surveys, further signals of public attitudes?

Good reason, it seems, for every journalist to think deeply about ethics and social responsibility.

Summary

Was it journalistic cannibalism or were reporters obligated to dig into Bill Clinton's past sex life? Whichever, the character issue became routine in political coverage during Clinton's run-up to election as president.

Probing coverage of presidents creates permanent friction between the White House and Washington press corps. Reporters probe for news; presidents try to manage it.

Questions: Are a politicians' private life and past truly indicative of future official conduct and thus subjects that must be covered? Are reporters meeting their obligations to serve the public and monitor the powerful—or do reporter tactics conflict with the journalistic principle of be compassionate?

White House news managers have two enormously powerful techniques: control access to the president and use news leaks, which shape news coverage.

In covering crime, reporters face issues of compelling importance. When does society's right (or need) to know outweigh the rights of individuals in crime stories? How can crime be covered without interfering with ongoing investigations?

Covering rape is particularly troublesome because of a commonly accepted double standard: The alleged victims of rape normally are shielded by the media from public identification; yet, alleged rapists frequently are identified even before trial.

Other problems in crime coverage include whether to identify juveniles, when to include racial or ethnic identification and how to preserve the presumption of innocence for persons involved in the news.

Terrorists sometimes seek publicity, and kidnap and kill for that purpose. A dilemma for the media is how to cover terrorism without providing the publicity that will tempt other terrorists to strike.

For several years after he contracted AIDS, Arthur Ashe's secret was kept out of the media. Then, the story was published on grounds that the former tennis star was a public figure and, therefore, news. Should the media respect a zone of privacy around all individuals thrust into the news?

Political correctness—PC—is one of the most difficult issues confronting journalists today. The challenge is to deal sensitively with minorities and groups that feel disenfranchised, yet not let those groups censor rational discourse and honest journalism.

Since Johann Gutenberg popularized movable type, there has been a constant worldwide fight to achieve free exchange of information. Journalists today must continue that fight or fail the test of an important societal value—stewardship—and the journalistic principle of protecting the First Amendment.

Notes

1. Leslie H. Gelb, "Journalistic Cannibals," *New York Times,* national edition, Jan. 27, 1992, p. A-11.
2. Jody Powell, "Clinton Coverage Shames the Media," *The Atlanta Journal and Constitution,* Feb. 2, 1992, p. C-1.
3. Note particularly Debra Gersh, "How the Public Views the Clinton Coverage," *Editor & Publisher,* Feb. 8, 1992, p. 9, quoting the Times Mirror Center for the People and the Press, and the Time-CNN Poll results, released for use on Feb. 3, 1992, and summarized that day in "Don't Bare Private Life, 7 in 10 Say," *The Atlanta Constitution,* p. A-7.
4. Gergen's appointment was widely covered, of course. One available source is Gwen Ifill, "Ex-Reagan Adviser Appointed to Post in the White House," *New York Times,* national edition, May 30, 1993, p. 1.
5. James D. Squires, "Newspapers Have Lost Their Zeal to Educate the Public about the Real Issues," *ASNE Bulletin,* November 1992, p. 4.
6. New York Times News Service dispatch for morning papers of Feb. 5, 1993, published that day by *The Atlanta Constitution* under the headline, "Clinton Picks Female Judge to Lead Justice," p. A-1.
7. George E. Reedy, "There They Go Again," *Columbia Journalism Review,* May/June 1983, p. 35.
8. The *Register*'s rape series was widely covered in the general and trade press. One valuable overview is David Margolick, "A Name, a Face and a Rape: Iowa Victim Tells Her Story," *New York Times,* national edition, March 25, 1990, p. 1.
9. "Report Rape Victims' Names," an editorial, *Electronic Media,* April 29, 1991, p. 12. The case itself was widely reported. See particularly, William Glaberson, "Media Memo: *Times* Article Naming Rape Accuser Ignites Debate on Journalistic Values," *New York Times,* national edition, April 26, 1991, p. A-12.

10. "Respect Rape Victims' Privacy," *Wall Street Journal,* April 24, 1991, p. A-14.
11. Schmidt and Bludworth quotes are from "Media Say Rape-Name Bans Are Unconstitutional," *presstime,* June 1991, p. 69. For quotes from Ashcroft and other state officials see Traci Bauer, "When to Name Names," *The Quill,* October 1991, p. 21.
12. Chris Hedges, "A Child-Mother in the Jaws of New York," *New York Times,* national edition, March 29, 1991, p. A-1.
13. Fox Butterfield, "Rape Case Puzzles Palm Beach Police," *New York Times,* national edition, April 15, 1991, p. A-10.
14. Lavonne Griffin, "Crime Survivors Deserve as Much Protection as Those of Crime," *ASNE Bulletin,* November 1987, p. 42.
15. Alison Mitchell, "Suspect in Bombing Is Linked to Sect with a Violent Voice." *New York Times,* national edition, March 5, 1993, p. A-1.
16. M. L. Stein, "San Diego Mayor Discusses Gang Coverage with Media," *Editor & Publisher,* March 13, 1993, p. 29.
17. Coverage of this incident was widespread. Helpful: John Corry, "Must TV Be at the Mercy of Terrorists?" *New York Times,* July 21, 1985, p. H1; Margaret Genovese, "Terrorism," *presstime,* August 1986, p. 26; John Corry, "Critic's Notebook," *New York Times* editorial, July 22, 1985, p. C-14; "Taking the Cameras Hostage," *Wall Street Journal* editorial, July 12, 1985, p. 42; Morton Dean, "TV's Duty to Cover Terror," *New York Times,* July 12, 1985, p. A-27; Hodding Carter, "More Is Better But . . ." *Washington Journalism Review,* September 1985, p. 56; Fred W. Friendly, speech to Association for Education in Journalism and Mass Communications, reproduced in *AEJMC News,* October 1985, p. 3.
18. John Corry, "Must TV Be at the Mercy of Terrorists?" op. cit.
19. ABC News Policy Book, ABC News, 7 West 66th St., New York, N.Y., 10023; Larry Grossman, NBC News, 30 Rockefeller Plaza, New York, N.Y., 10112, memo to NBC News staff, July 24, 1985, p. 1.
20. Joseph Albright, "Survivors Recall Terror, Desperation of Hijack," *Atlanta Constitution,* Nov. 27, 1985, p. 1.
21. Carl H. Lavin, "New Machines Can Detect Terrorists' Bombs, Usually," *New York Times,* Sept. 12, 1989, p. C-1.
22. The Ashe/AIDS press conference story broke for morning papers of April 9, 1992, and spot news coverage was voluminous. Useful summaries are Christine Spolar, "Privacy for Public Figures?," *Washington Journalism Review,* June 1992, p. 20, and Alex S. Jones, "News Media Sharply Divided on When Right to Know Becomes Intrusion," *New York Times,* national edition, April 30, 1992, p. A-11. Quotes from Policinski of *USA Today* are in *Gannetteer,* September 1992, p. 25. The *Forbes* editorial is "Two Media Mistakes—And a Fabulous Success," May 11, 1992, p. 26. The *Times* editorial is "Why Arthur Ashe Kept It Secret," April 10, 1992, on p. A-18 in the national edition. For the "Uncle Ed" story see Michael deCourcy Hinds, "Philadelphian with AIDS Tells of Sex with Many Boys," *New York Times,* national edition, March 28, 1992, p. A-6.
23. Jack Anderson and Dale Van Atta, "Private Lives of Public Officials," a letter to *Time,* Sept. 9, 1991, p. 9.
24. This was widely covered in newspaper trade magazines. One excellent wrap-up is the Associated Press dispatch, from Portland, for morning papers of Feb. 16, 1992. It was on p. 17 of the *New York Times* national edition of that date.

25. The Joint Center's survey was reported in "Racial References," *USA Today,* Jan. 31, 1991, p. D-1. The APME survey was reported in Peter Bhatia, "Newsrooms Still Wrestle with Identifying Minorities," *APME Reports,* July–August–September 1993, p. 24.
26. See, "Air Raid Pearl Harbor," a guide published by the Hawaii chapter and distributed under Sept. 16, 1991, date by the Asian American Journalists Association, 1765 Sutter St., Room 1000, San Francisco, Calif. 94115.
27. See particularly The Associated Press dispatch, datelined Dallas, for Nov. 3, 1990. It was on p. 6-A of the *Athens (Ga.) Daily News and Banner-Herald* of that date.
28. Howard Kurtz, "Our Politically Correct Press," *The Washington Post,* Jan. 20, 1991, p. B-1.
29. The story was an Associated Press dispatch for morning papers of March 10, 1993; it started on p. A-1 of that day's *Constitution,* under the headline, "Rodney King: 'I Was Trying to Stay Alive'."
30. Richard L. Berke, "Thomas Backers Attack Hill; Judge, Vowing He Won't Quit, Says He is Victim of Race Stigma," *New York Times,* national edition, Oct. 13, 1991, p. A-1.
31. House Subcommittee on Government Information, quoted by David Burnham, "Assessing the Freedom of Information Act," *New York Times,* Aug. 29, 1985, p. B-10.
32. Paul McMasters, "The Dirty Little Secret of Our 'Open' Society," *ASNE Bulletin,* December 1993, p. 28.
33. Richard Huff, codirector of the Justice Department's Office of Information and Privacy, quoted by Margaret Genovese, "FOIA," *presstime,* July 1986, p. 22.
34. Peter Boyer, "Loew's Increase Its Stake in CBS," *New York Times,* Aug. 12, 1986, p. C-18.
35. John Corry, "Is TV Unpatriotic or Simply Unmindful?," *New York Times,* May 12, 1985, p. 1, Section 2.
36. Albert R. Hunt, "Media Bias Is in Eye of the Beholder," *Wall Street Journal,* July 23, 1985, p. 32.
37. The Sinatra incident, which quickly faded from public view, is summarized in *SNPA Bulletin,* July 3, 1985, p. 4.
38. This incident involved indians of the Santo Domingo Pueblo and extended over many months. Final settlement is recounted in "*New Mexican* Reaches Settlement with Indians," *Editor & Publisher,* Feb. 16, 1985, p. 23.
39. Coverage was voluminous; in publications of record generally available, note summaries: M. A. Farber, "A Joint Statement Ends Libel Action by Westmoreland," and Peter Kaplan, "'Best I Could Get,' General Asserts," *New York Times,* national edition, Feb. 19, 1985, p. 1; Karen Rothmayer, "Westmoreland v. CBS," *Columbia Journalism Review,* May/June 1985, p. 25; *USA Today* devoted its Feb. 21, 1985, editorial page to five differing views of the Westmoreland trial.
40. Note Stuart Elliott, "*Time* Fights 'Malice in Blunderland' Image," *Advertising Age,* Feb. 4, 1985, p. 4; Arnold Lubasch, "*Time* Cleared of Libeling Sharon but Jurors Criticize Its Reporting," *New York Times,* national edition, Jan. 25, 1985, p. 1; David Margolick, "Sharon Case and the Law," *New York Times,* national edition, Jan. 25, 1985, p. 13.
41. Reed Irvine, letter to editor, *New York Times,* Dec. 30, 1984, p. 12-E.

42. Richard M. Clurman, "Fallout from the Sharon Trial," *New York Times,* Jan. 30, 1985, p. 23.
43. Debra Gersh, "Resurrect the National News Council?," *Editor & Publisher,* May 8, 1993, p. 12.
44. "Update," *New York Law Journal,* Feb. 7, 1994, p. 1.
45. "Average Jury Libel Award Rises to $9 million," *New York Times,* national edition, Sept. 20, 1992.

PART 5

PUBLIC RELATIONS, THE MEDIA AND SOCIETY

You could argue that a discussion of public relations has no place in a book on media ethics. After all, PR practitioners, like their colleagues in advertising, are advocates, not reporters.

But, that advocacy role has a huge impact on both press and public—and that is precisely why we must turn now to public relations.

By some estimates, well over 100,000 persons nationwide work in public relations, creating and shaping, packaging or handling 40 percent or so of the daily news diet the American media serve their readers and viewers.[1]

For any student of media ethics, the multibillion dollar PR industry must be of compelling concern.[2] We look at it from three viewpoints:

1. The sense of ethics and personal conscience associated with conduct of individual PR practitioners.
2. Institutional or corporate attitudes toward socially responsible public relations and ethical conduct in the marketplace.
3. Public relations industry standards of integrity in relations with the media and public.

PUBLIC RELATIONS, THE MEDIA AND SOCIETY

CHAPTER 11

Public Relations: Ethics of Its Goals and Techniques

GOALS AND TECHNIQUES

Make no mistake about the goals of public relations practitioners: They are out to influence you, me, the public and the media on how to view governments and individuals, companies and products, ideas and causes.

With varying degrees of honesty and integrity, practitioners direct an enormous flow of information into the marketplace of ideas in a never-ending and highly competitive battle for the American mind.

Simultaneously, PR practitioners study the marketplace, retrieving from it research on media and public attitudes toward the governments, organizations and individuals they serve.

Without question, the two-way process is instrumental in the policies guiding some of this nation's most important institutions—and how the rest of us, the press and public, view them.

Scott M. Cutlip, a noted researcher in PR, describes public relations as an "organized calling . . . a management function that identifies, establishes and maintains mutually beneficial relationships between an organization and the various publics on whom its success or failure depends."[3]

Ethical choices arise in each major public relations function that practitioners perform as in-house employees, as members of outside PR agencies or in management:

VIEWPOINT

One-Sided Arguments

"In the public relations business we have learned how to work with the media to protect our clients' interests without compromising the public's need to know. We help corporations, interest groups and foreign governments communicate their story to the public. We must argue our side as forcefully as possible *and trust the news media will search out the opposing view* [author's emphasis]. We are rarely disappointed."

James McAvoy, executive vice president, Ruder Finn public relations agency in Washington[4]

- Publicity, or releasing to the news media information about a corporation or product, for example.
- Advertising, an allied function that involves paying the media to reach an audience and enhance reputation.
- Public affairs, attempting to influence or lobby the political process on behalf of, say, a corporation, the government, the military.
- Press-agentry, helping publicize individuals, such as movie stars, for example, or entertainment companies.
- Investor and financial community relations, such as representing a company in its dealings with shareholders, banks or Wall Street.
- Internal relations, such as recruiting or operating information systems for employees.

Practitioners face many ethical stresses in the employ of corporations, governments, educational systems, labor unions, trade associations, religious groups—every type of organization with a product or cause to push, a reputation to promote and enhance. Practitioners serve in management or as high-level public relations advisers to their clients or companies, a function that should carry a high degree of integrity, and on a lower level perform technical functions—writing and editing, contacting media, arranging special events such as press conferences or trade shows, producing annual reports or information booklets, conducting research, managing public relations efforts.

For individual practitioners, Cutlip acknowledges, a fundamental ethical problem is "how to maintain credibility . . . how to represent the client, yet stay separate and independent to tell the truth."[5]

For society, an ethical question, obviously, is how much of what pours out of a mammoth, often slick public relations effort is truthful, legitimate pleading on behalf of a client or employer, an idea or cause, and how much is designed—without truth, without principle—to cajole, wheedle or sell something in disguise.

For newspaper or broadcast journalists honest enough to acknowledge it, getting the paper out on time or the newscast on the air would be supremely difficult without assists from public relations practitioners (one analysis indicates 45 percent of 188 news items in a single edition of the *Wall Street Journal* came from public relations sources).[6]

Let's examine one practitioner's crisis of conscience in government public relations that illustrates some ethical questions individual practitioners confront.

THE PRACTITIONER AND PERSONAL ETHICS

Unusual quiet descended over the U.S. State Department auditorium as Bernard Kalb briefed assembled reporters. He had appeared before them many times, but this was high drama with international implications.

Kalb was publicly quitting as the nation's principal foreign policy spokesman in protest over a secret government program that he otherwise would be obliged to explain and defend before the media and American public.

It was obvious to every reporter in that room that Bernie Kalb sincerely desired to serve his country as a member of the administration. He had put aside a career of substantial renown as a journalist (the *New York Times,* CBS and NBC) to do so. But he made clear that to continue in the state department would force him to lie, and that he would not do.

It is an extraordinary example of a fundamental dilemma that can arise for public relations practitioners when their sense of personal integrity makes it impossible to believe in and thus wholeheartedly represent their client organization, idea or cause.

The Kalb affair also illustrates vividly how wrong a government effort can go when based on shaky ethical principles and without expert advice on possible public relations fallout. To explain:

On April 14, 1986, U.S. warplanes bombed Libya in retaliation for what the Reagan administration said was sponsorship of international terrorism by the regime of Col. Muammar el-Qaddafi. The United States tried to stoke worldwide condemnation of Qaddafi, and in early August, three months prior to the Kalb drama, U.S. diplomats began a secret campaign of deception—a disinformation program—against Libya. It was a campaign designed to confuse world public opinion and mislead the media. Word was put out that Qaddafi still was supporting terrorism and that the United States was about to move once more against him militarily.

On August 25, the *Wall Street Journal,* quoting intelligence officials, reported "The U.S. and Libya are on a collision course again." Then, ABC, NBC, CBS, the *Washington Post* and others picked up those reports and, as the disinformation experts had hoped, aired and published stories that helped focus worldwide pressure on Libya.

THOSE ANONYMOUS SOURCES AGAIN

As the story gained momentum, more than a dozen officials in Washington were quoted separately as saying—anonymously—that Qaddafi again was supporting terrorists. White House spokesman Larry Speakes, artfully choosing his words, said the *Journal* story was "authoritative but not authorized." When pressed, Speakes said—in a statement he insisted be attributed to "a senior White House official"—that there was "hard evidence" against Qaddafi.

That all this flowed into the media—and thus into living rooms across America—from a secret, tightly coordinated effort wasn't known publicly until October 2. On that day, the *Washington Post* published excerpts from what it said was a White House memorandum written by Vice Adm. John M. Poindexter, the President's national security adviser. The memo counseled a strategy that "combines real and illusionary events—through a disinformation program—with the basic goal of making Qaddafi think that there is a high degree of internal opposition to him within Libya, that his key trusted aides are disloyal, that the U.S. is about to move against him militarily."

In sum, the outcome was a public relations disaster: to protect his own integrity, the U.S. State Department's principal spokesman publicly—and, for the administration, embarrassingly—quit; the U.S. government and its wider information programs stood revealed to the American public and the world as untrustworthy; and journalists were furious at having been suckered by a secret disinformation program orchestrated internationally.[7]

Lesson No. 1: Aside from being revealed as unethical, a government (or corporation, group or cause) that engages in a Big Lie will—almost inevitably in our open society—end up with egg on its face. Too many willing leakers are inside any institution and too many probing reporters outside, for such things as worldwide disinformation programs to stay secret for long. Fabrication quite simply is bad policy for any institution.

Lesson No. 2: For the individual public relations practitioner, credibility is a most precious asset. Protecting personal credibility is not only the ethical thing to do, but it is essential to continued professional effectiveness. Kalb said, "I have been agonizing about this thing [the disinformation program]. I knew nothing about it. I was concerned with the impact of any such program on the credibility of the United States and the word of America and what the word of America means. And I was concerned about my own integrity. . . . I didn't want my own integrity to get scooped up in this controversy." On the other hand, spokesman Larry Speakes continued at the White House before stepping down in 1987, to join a Wall Street brokerage firm.

Lesson No. 3: Misleading or lying to the media and thus embarrassing them with their reading/viewing publics will draw furious media attack. The Qaddafi affair drew media criticism from across the land against the administration: "Despicable . . ." Roone Arledge, president of ABC News; "Deplorable . . ." Eugene Roberts, executive editor, *Philadelphia Inquirer*; and "Pretty disgusting . . ." William Thomas, editor of the *Los Angeles Times.* The *New York Times,* in an editorial, "Lies Wound America, Not Libya," hit hard: "However desirable it may

VIEWPOINT

Sunrise and the Rooster

"It's like trying to sneak sunrise past a rooster."

John Trattner, State Department official, on trying to sell the press a story it doesn't want to buy

be to get rid of this unstable, dangerous dictator [Qaddafi], the chosen technique was worthy of the K.G.B. [Soviet secret police]. To the Reagan administration's shame, the 'disinformation' worked all too well, but only here in the land of the free."[8] The American Society of Newspaper Editors telegraphed Reagan its "outrage and alarm" over "this calculated technique of falsehood. . . ."[9]

Lesson No. 4: When the game is up, come clean. The only ethical—and effective—public relations response to such a foul-up is to tell what happened and why. Early on, Washington actually had much public support for its anti-Qaddafi tactics. The April 14 bombing raid drew praise. But administration spokespersons failed to capitalize on that foundation of public support by forthrightly revealing details of what it regarded as justifiable U.S. aims. Wider damage resulted when officials fudged their explanations of the disinformation program. Secretary of State George Shultz didn't endear himself to the media by saying:

> If I were a private citizen . . . and I read that my government was trying to confuse somebody who was conducting terrorist acts and murdering Americans, I'd say, "Gee, I hope it's true." I know of no decision to go out and tell lies to the media. I think, however, that if there are ways in which we can make Qaddafi nervous, why shouldn't we? That is not deceiving you [reporters], but just using your predictable tendencies to report things that we try to keep secret, so we'll label it a big secret and you'll report it. We know that. The higher the classification, the quicker you'll report it. So you're predictable in that sense.

NOW, *YOU* MAKE THE CALL

Well, then, for the public relations practitioner—and the media and public—are the ethical conflicts in the Qaddafi affair neatly divided between right and wrong and good and bad? Are bad guys those who deceive and good guys those who uncover and publish?

Is misleading or lying ever justifiable? Should a practitioner ever deceive or lie on behalf of what he or she regards as a greater good? How about in time of war, when a nation's fate can hang in the balance? (Shultz said the United States was "pretty darn close" to war with Libya.)[10]

Before deciding, step way back and consider:

- Should societal values and journalistic principles we discussed in Chapter 1 even be raised in a discussion of PR practitioner techniques? After all, don't we all know that PR is different from journalism? Should we, therefore, establish different yardsticks for measuring the morality of PR?
- If you think (as I do) that PR practitioners must meet the same standards of morality we use in measuring journalists, which societal values do you identify at play in the Kalb affair? How do Kalb and the Reagan administration measure up on truth-telling, stewardship, promise keeping?
- Which loyalties discussed in Chapter 1 motivated Kalb? Loyalty to self and conscience? To society? Or, was he responding to what he knew would be applause from his professional peers (and he got plenty)?
- Would you put society—your country—above self and conscience? Would you lie for America? If our society condones—indeed, cheers—American soldiers who kill our enemies, why don't you cheer Poindexter, Schultz and other officials who said they were, after all, only lying to our enemies in America's best interests?

The question of whether lying ever is an ethical choice surfaced with international impact when Arthur Sylvester, Pentagon spokesman under the Kennedy and Johnson administrations, defended official management of news. It was during a period of enormous tension in 1962 between the United States and Soviet Union because Moscow had placed missiles in Cuba capable of hitting American targets.

Said Sylvester: "In the kind of world we live in, the generation of news by actions taken by the government becomes one weapon in a strained situation. The results justify the methods we used . . ." And then: "I think the inherent right of the government to lie—is basic, basic."

Would you resign if involved in such news management—lying?

Few press secretaries on the White House level either faced such matters of conscience—or felt compelled to publicly resign over them. Only three resigned on principle in the 13 years preceding the Qaddafi affair—Les Janka, deputy White House press secretary for foreign affairs, quit in 1983, to protest Reagan administration restrictions on the media during the Grenada invasion; Jerald F. terHorst resigned in 1974, as President Ford's press secretary on grounds he was misled by White House officials over the President's pardon of former President Nixon; Charles W. Bray 3d., deputy assistant secretary for state department press relations, quit in 1973, over appointment of Henry Kissinger as secretary of state (because, Bray said, Kissinger had ordered wiretapping of aides).[11]

Where do practitioners' loyalties lie in such situations? Do practitioners have a responsibility to the institution they represent to resign? Jerald terHorst says yes: "Whenever a spokesman reaches a conclusion that he is in a position in which he must defend or endorse or carry on policies or actions with which he personally disagrees or believes not to be truthful, *he owes it to his government to step down* [emphasis added]."

VIEWPOINT

Disinformation: Three Views

"[I] would dodge, not lie, in the national interest. . . . There are 10,000 ways to say 'no comment' and I have used 9,999. . . ."

Larry Speakes in interviews before his resignation in 1987 as President Reagan's press spokesman

"The whole question comes down to: 'Is deception going to be a tool that the government can use in combating a very significant national security problem,' and I think the answer . . . has to be yes."

John M. Poindexter, White House author of memo outlining disinformation program against Libya

"We suggest that the other news media grow up and get back to the business they're in and stop using their news columns to try to run the government. Disinformation is a fact of life."

Advertising Age, editorial following the Qaddafi affair

But, must practitioners always resign when their conscience conflicts with the message or goal of the employer? Or, can practitioners ethically continue to serve as messengers and take no moral responsibility for the message?

Courts have held messengers have legal responsibility for the message if, for example, it commits a libel. But lawyers serve even patently guilty clients and physicians treat condemned murderers. Should public relations practitioners be similarly nonjudgmental in representing employers or clients who dispense disinformation or who pollute the environment or who sell products, such as tobacco, that are harmful?

Should American practitioners be nonjudgmental toward representing foreign governments hostile to U.S. interests? What ethical questions arise if a practitioner represents, say, Iran, whose government declared the United States an enemy, the Great Satan?

Another question: How far should practitioners go in insisting that ethics be pivotal in their employers' decision-making process?

For example, should corporate practitioners attempt to veto proposed action by their company on grounds it is unethical or will be perceived negatively by the public? Some argue the most practitioners can expect of employers is that public relations factors be considered before a major decision is taken or policy formulated—but not that public relations considerations must be controlling factors. Cutlip argues there are times, in its own best interests, when an institution should ignore public opinion, and the practitioner's job then becomes one of explaining and justifying to gain public acceptance of the unpopular decision or action.

TerHorst says practitioners must step aside when in conflict with the client or mission. Would you step aside quietly and let a lie continue? Or, would you feel morally bound to blow the whistle, as Bernie Kalb did?

These are questions answerable only by individual practitioners who must construct their own personal codes of ethics. They must decide for themselves what is right or wrong in the practice of public relations, what they personally will do—and won't do—for the government, corporation, product or cause they represent.

INSTITUTIONAL PUBLIC RELATIONS ETHICS

For Johnson & Johnson, worldwide distributor of pharmaceuticals and other products, Sept. 30, 1982, was the precise date it was challenged to turn a public relations disaster into a business success—and do it with a high degree of institutional ethics and social responsibility.

Larry Foster, vice president–public relations, got first word. He was in his New Brunswick, New Jersey, office that day when a reporter telephoned from Chicago: Cyanide had been found in a bottle of Extra-Strength Tylenol, marketed by McNeil Consumer Products, a Johnson & Johnson subsidiary. People had died after taking the pain reliever.[12]

For Johnson & Johnson, the stakes were enormous. An estimated 100 million Americans used Tylenol; the product captured 37 percent of the market with $400 million annual sales and was highly profitable. Foster had to move quickly.

At such a moment in any public relations crisis, a corporation's options include evading the press, meeting reporters but stonewalling (saying nothing substantive), issuing vague we-are-looking-into-it statements—many are the devices to protect corporate image or product reputation and ignore any larger social responsibility the corporation might have.

Foster recalls Johnson & Johnson decided automatically how to proceed even without a meeting of executives:

> Since the extent of the contamination was not immediately known, there was grave concern for the safety of the estimated 100 million Americans who were using Tylenol. The first critical public relations decision, taken immediately and with total support from company management, was to cooperate fully with the news media. *The press was key to warning the public of the danger* [emphasis added].

A CREDO OF OPENNESS

Ethical guidance came from Johnson & Johnson's corporate credo that called for complete openness with media and public.

The company halted production of the product, recalled 22 million bottles from retailers nationwide, warned through the media against taking the capsules—and saw Tylenol begin a slide from its 37 percent of market share to 6 percent, which resulted in an after-tax loss of $50 million.

Foster pulled scores of public relations executives into headquarters from throughout the Johnson & Johnson system, installed extra telephone lines and began taking what turned out to be thousands of calls from reporters seeking information.

VIEWPOINT

Key to Success?

"Successful publicity, over the long pull, must be grounded in works that the public defines as good, motives that the public accepts as honest, and presentation that the public recognizes as credible."

Cutlip, Center, and Broom, *Effective Public Relations*

"During the crisis phase of the Tylenol tragedy," Foster says, "virtually every public relations decision was based on sound, socially responsible business principles, which is when public relations is most effective."

Within a week, answering the corporate imperative to get business back on track, Johnson & Johnson began a public relations effort to restore Tylenol's market position. The company's chief executive officer, James Burke, made himself available to reporters. A press conference was held for reporters in 30 cities linked by satellite.

Foster says surveys show that within one week, 90 percent of the public knew of the Tylenol crisis; after the second week, 90 percent knew Johnson & Johnson was not to blame, and that the cyanide that eventually killed seven persons had been inserted in capsules on the shelves of retail stores, not on the production line. Tylenol quickly regained more than 30 percent of the total market—and CEO Burke publicly thanked the media for fair, responsible coverage.

Says Foster: "The Tylenol tragedy proved once again . . . that the best public relations decisions are closely linked to sound business practices and a responsible corporate philosophy."[13]

Compare Johnson & Johnson's handling of its crisis with Washington's handling of the Libyan disinformation affair:

Lesson No. 1: Johnson & Johnson had an established corporate credo that, although it obviously could not anticipate an event such as the Tylenol crisis, did require frank, open, truthful, revelation of details to customers, media and the wider public. Media faith in Johnson & Johnson's handling grew and the public sensed the company was as much a victim as those who died. And Foster, by being so forthcoming, in effect controlled how the media developed the news story.

Lesson No. 2: Johnson & Johnson and Foster not only protected their corporate and personal credibility with media and public, but they also came away from the near-disaster with enhanced reputations and image. For Foster, the Tylenol affair was opportunity to serve as public relations adviser in a principled manner that not only protected his own personal sense of ethics and responsibility but also buttressed the business fortunes of his company.

Lesson No. 3: Johnson & Johnson avoided adversarial relationships with reporters and, indeed, employed open, principled tactics that in effect permitted

CASE STUDY

Pepsi and the Public

You are public relations director for a soft drink firm battling for market share against a major competitor.

Suddenly, a PR disaster: There are nationwide reports that hypodermic needles, bolts and even a bullet are being found in your firm's soft drink cans.

On the evening news, people are televised holding needles they say the found in cans. Some even claim the needles pricked their lips—a horrendous thought in this era of AIDS being spread through contaminated needles.

On front pages everywhere, Wall Street analysts are quoted as saying your company will lose market share to its major competitor (your company has about 32.4 percent of the nation's soft-drink sales; your competitor, Coca-Cola, 41 percent).

What will be your public response? Your options range from stonewalling to any number of manipulative strategies designed to limit damage to your company.

Those questions were faced by Pepsi-Cola Co. executives on June 10, 1993, when a Tacoma, Wash., couple reported finding a syringe in a can of Diet Pepsi. Within hours, other reports started coming in. Within days, consumers in virtually every state stepped forward to say they, too, had found foreign objects in Pepsi cans.

Now, *You* Make the Call

As Pepsi's PR director, you must advise management on how to respond. Questions:

- Will your proposed course of action be founded in societal values such as truth-telling and promise keeping? That is, will you proceed under the assumption that your company has a social responsibility—or that your company's only mission is to protect its profits? Should the values we discussed in Chapter 1 as applicable to journalists and media companies also be applied to soft drink companies? They are in fundamentally different businesses, after all, with entirely different missions and impact on society. Therefore, should Pepsi be judged on a different ethical yardstick than the one we use on, say, Washington Post Co. or Knight-Ridder?
- Will you, as PR director, be guided by the journalistic principles we discussed in Chapter 1? Will you act to serve the public? Will your loyalty be to self and conscience? To society? To the hand that feeds you?
- Will you stonewall? Or be open?

Pepsi chose an aggressive PR response featuring open dealings with public, press and government. The strategy had these components:

- *Use of media.* Pepsi's president, Craig Weatherup, went on TV talk shows and news programs virtually nonstop. He gave interviews to any reporters who asked and used satellite transmission to reach the media in cities distant from corporate headquarters in Somers, N.Y. The media were not stonewalled; indeed, they were used to spread company assurances. And, Pepsi's top executive, not a PR spokesperson, was out front.
- *Publication of specifics.* Pepsi produced photos of its production process, showing how each can was cleaned and, in 9/10ths of a second, filled and sealed. Graphics illustrating the process appeared on June 17 in a *USA Today* front-page cover story about Pepsi and on the front page of the *New York Times'* business section the same day. This was priceless exposure for Pepsi's claim of "99.999 percent certainty" that its process was tamper-proof.
- *Accessibility to the public.* Pepsi set up a 1-800 telephone line so company executives could respond directly to consumer calls. Pepsi sent faxes to its bottlers each morning so they could respond to local retailers.
- *Cooperation with government.* Pepsi dealt openly with the Food and Drug Administration whose investigators quickly reported arrests of persons on charges they attempted a hoax—or extortion of Pepsi—by claiming they found needles in cans.
- *Declaration of victory.* On June 21, just 11 days after the first report of trouble from Tacoma, Pepsi took out full-page newspaper ads nationwide that began, "Pepsi is pleased to announce . . . nothing. As America now knows, those stories about Diet Pepsi were a hoax. Plain and simple, not true. Hundreds of investigators have found no evidence to support a single claim . . ."

The long-term impact of the incident is hard to measure. However, four months after the hoax broke, Pepsi estimated the cost was about $35 million in lost sales and increased expenses for the company and its bottlers. Nevertheless, sales of Pepsi products—and the company's stock price—quickly regained ground lost at the height of the scare.[14]

Now, *You* Make the Call

Questions What is the media's responsibility when product tampering is reported?

Is the media's first loyalty to the reading, viewing and listening public and, therefore, should unsubstantiated claims of tampering be covered?

Or, should the media, recognizing the damage that could do to a company, withhold coverage until proof is in hand?

Without exception, the media put loyalty to public first and gave prominent coverage to even initial, unsubstantiated claims of product tampering in six major incidents between 1982 and the Pepsi affair. They involved the Tylenol case (discussed previously), poisoning of eyewashes and headache remedies, glass fragments in baby food and chemical adulteration of bottled water.

it to use the media to warn Tylenol users and even use newspapers and television to rebuild public confidence in the company and product. Contrast that with Washington's decision to launch a secret disinformation program that could only result in misleading the media, embarrassing them with their reading/viewing publics and creating a sense of betrayal that brought down on administration heads a storm of newspaper and television criticism.

When his crisis passed, Johnson & Johnson's CEO Burke thanked the media for fair and accurate handling; when the disinformation crisis broke, Secretary of State Shultz virtually taunted reporters by suggesting they easily could be set up to report any story as long as it carried a security classification.

Which approach was ethical—and, in a public relations sense, effective?

CAREER DRIVE VERSUS ETHICAL PRINCIPLES

It would be comforting to suggest corporate public relations is dominated by the ethics and social responsibility displayed by Johnson & Johnson. But, of course, it isn't. The Tylenol affair, in fact, must be put forward to illustrate what corporate public relations should be, not what it universally is.

Many public relations practitioners are strongly career-oriented, in hot pursuit of higher salaries and greater corporate prestige, and thus open to compromise over ethics. In their authoritative *Public Relations Practices,* Allen Center and Frank Walsh, both experienced practitioners, comment bluntly:

> Ethical standards have tended to be reflections of the employers and clients served. Putting it another way, the public relations voice has generally emerged publicly more as the echo of an employer's standards and interests than of a professional discipline applied to the employer's problems. The practitioner comes on as narrowly organizational rather than broadly professional.[15]

And, of course, employer standards and interests by definition are directed at influencing public opinion to more favorably regard a company, product, idea, individual or cause. Certainly, in the corporate world, where management's first obligation is to enhance shareholder return on investment—to increase profits—the basic mission of public relations is to help improve business fortunes.

Moral considerations often enter the equation only secondarily or, frankly, as important to higher profits.

Scott Cutlip notes that in his 40 years of research into the public relations function he finds top management too often "instinctively inclined to keep decisions secret, to work out of public view, to make only favorable news known."[16] And, too often, the public relations function stands indicted—"with some validity"—for cynically "loading our channels of communication with noise and clogging them with the clutter of manufactured stories."[17]

The very term *public relations* carries with some a heavy connotation of unethical practices, rather than constructive contributions to free flow of information with a legitimate role in the nation's decision-making process. Public perceptions of public relations often are negative and media attitudes sometimes poisonous.

Journalists often view public relations as a massively financed, slick effort to manipulate the news—in fact, create it—to penetrate news columns or airtime and thus obtain free advertising and the patina of respectability—the legitimacy—of appearing in a newspaper's news pages or on a broadcast news program.

Journalists sometimes feel chagrin and anger at being reliant on practitioners for so much information and repeatedly susceptible to their manipulation. For example, Washington correspondents are furious—but helpless—when herded away from the president by White House news managers who then stage photo opportunities and otherwise ensure a story of their choosing receives widespread coverage and that the president is linked only to favorable news. It is not happenstance that bad news often is released in other departments of government, whereas good news comes from the White House.

UNETHICAL DEVICES ARE USED

Unethical practitioners use many devices to suppress news or give it a spin favorable to a client.

For example, in corporate public relations, practitioners sometimes simply sit on bad news, release only part of it—or time its release for a day and hour when it likely will get little notice. Bad news released at 10 p.m. on Saturday is too late for many Sunday newspapers (which have earlier deadlines) and there won't be another newspaper on the streets before Monday morning. TV networks will only lightly touch the news on their Monday morning entertainment shows and won't get down to serious news coverage until Monday night—and by that time the world often will have gone on to other things.

Sometimes, bad news is held until front pages and broadcasts are dominated by a major news story, then quietly released in hopes it will be overlooked.

Conversely, good news timed for Sunday release is perfect for Monday morning newspapers, always short of hard news because relatively little news breaks on Sunday and, anyway, most reporters have that day off.

Many practitioners consider it standard—and not particularly unethical—procedure to use such devices and manipulate the media through intimate understanding of their mechanical limitations or to bar reporters from direct access to news or newsmakers.

But, of course, practitioners often have legitimate complaints about the media—that public relations brings into view valid news which reporters unfairly refuse to recognize as legitimate or that PR in fact assists the media in doing their own job. And, practitioners complain, too many journalists fail to realize times have changed—that not all practitioners are disreputable flacks, that not all information channeled through the public relations function is disguised propaganda.

Nevertheless, many reporters see themselves as targets of unprincipled, unethical attempts to manipulate the news.

Obviously, the public relations function can serve with social utility. If conducted with motives openly revealed, it can assist public debate by legitimately, ethically pleading a point of view in the marketplace of ideas; properly and ethically employed, it can inject clarifying fact and reliable information into a media and public dialogue burdened by misinformation and lack of true communication; and, importantly, a socially responsible public relations effort can influence conduct of the individual, company or group it serves by representing in executive policy-making circles the external public's attitudes and demands. Optimum business conditions often exist when corporate policy and public attitudes are consonant.

But, can these seemingly disparate goals—serving, say, corporate interest yet remaining true to a personal sense of ethics—be reached simultaneously? The public relations industry has tried to lay down guidelines for individual practitioners desiring to achieve both.

THE INDUSTRY AND ETHICAL STANDARDS

If you plan a PR career and seek guidance in ethics from current practices in the public relations industry you may be disappointed. The industry was late in coalescing as a recognized discipline with any coherent approach to questions of conscience and even today demonstrates uncertainty over how to treat such issues.

Individual practitioners still are responsible for developing and following their own personal code.

Public relations generally became identified as an organized calling only in the 1920s, after other business disciplines such as sales and advertising were solidly entrenched in American corporate design and public awareness.[18] Only in the mid-1930s did practitioners form major industry groups; not until 1948 did two of the largest, in New York City and San Francisco, form today's leading industry organization, the Public Relations Society of America (PRSA).

After PRSA was formed, ethics and matters of conscience were more widely discussed throughout the industry. PRSA adopted a code of standards in 1954, and subsequently revised it four times (the current version can be found in Appendix G); another industry group, International Association of Business Communicators (IABC), adopted in 1976 a code of standards; industry conferences featured seminars on public relations ethics; and universities taught the subject.

Yet, practitioners today are divided on even whether there should be codes, let alone what should be in them or how—indeed, if—they should be enforced.

Some say codes not only provide behavioral standards for individual practitioners in ethics but also create for employers and the general public an image of principled behavior distinct from the disreputable flackery of old.

For others, ethics is a subject far too personal, depending altogether too much on each situation, for comprehensive or meaningful treatment in any code.

For some, even voluntary codes are objectionable because there is danger of adherence to them one day becoming a condition of practice, which could lead to government control and licensing (which the society describes as offending the American tradition of free speech).

A code of ethics and social responsibility, subscribed to by practitioners, is among criteria necessary before public relations can achieve professionalism in the generally accepted sense of the word. That would include a requirement that practitioners adhere to industry standards—not to employer standards if they

VIEWPOINT

Ethical Codes: Another View

"Not needed: A namby-pamby code of ethics that will be given only lip service. People engaged in public relations need hard-headed morality that will make top management feel they are as devoted to the company's interests as any lawyer. At the same time, however, this morality must cause those engaged in public relations to be proud of what they do."

Alec Benn, "The 23 Most Common Mistakes in Public Relations," American Management Association, New York

contradict the code—in questions of ethics and conscience, as well as operational technique.

Clearly, neither public relations practitioners nor employers are ready for that. For many individual practitioners who are employees or who work for outside public relations firms that are retained by an employer, the secret to career success is adapting to, not bucking against, the employer's business thrust and ethical stance. For many individual practitioners, particularly those with home mortgages and children in expensive colleges, the penalty for nonconformance—being fired—is too stiff.

But even large, prosperous public relations firms, presumably somewhat insulated against financial punishment by a single client, rarely resign the account over ethical disputes.

Other characteristics generally regarded as essential to achieving professionalism are as follows:

- Subordination of private profit and interest to achieving social good and serving the public interest—or, at least, being strongly motivated in that direction and being recognized for it by the general public. Actually, none of the recognized true professions—medicine, law—can claim for all their members such selflessness. And, it would be a concept slow to take root in the public relations industry or public mind.
- A sense of independence and personal accountability by members. Individual practitioners tend to reflect employer attitudes and ethics, and there is no widespread notion, particularly among employers, that this should change.
- Special education and training or apprenticeship, followed by accreditation or licensing by an appropriate industry or government authority. Universities do offer public relations education and special training is available—but neither is required for entry into the field. Both PRSA and IABC offer accreditation to members but few seek it. Only 25 to 30 percent of PRSA's members are accredited with the organization's designation APR—Accredited Public Relations. To receive that, a member must have five years experience in practice or teaching

public relations, must pass written and oral examinations and have two sponsors who testify to the applicant's integrity. Few of IABC's members have gone through that group's accreditation procedure to win the designation of Accredited Business Communicator.

INDUSTRY DESIRE FOR PROFESSIONALISM

Public relations as practiced is far from professionalism in the classic sense. Yet, there is considerable desire within the industry to reach that goal. It is reflected notably in PRSA's efforts to maintain a code of ethics and behavioral standards that, in theory at least, takes precedence over standards established by an employer and that is enforced by colleagues within the industry.

The PRSA code, for example, requires members to "deal fairly with clients or employers, past and present, with fellow practitioners and the general public," and to "conduct his or her professional life in accord with the public interest." Members pledge "truth, accuracy, fairness and responsibility to the public."

However, some code language is wide open to liberal interpretation. For example, the code states, "A member shall adhere to truth and accuracy and to *generally accepted standards of good taste* [emphasis added]." That permits virtually any conduct if enough practitioners engage in it to make it "generally accepted."

And, PRSA enforces its code unevenly. Complaints about practitioner behavior go before six-member panels in each of nine PRSA regions, then to the board of directors serving as a national grievance board. The proceedings are confidential. The penalties are censure, suspension or expulsion from PRSA. Complaints are few and deal mostly not with matters affecting the public but, rather, quarrels between members.

Because PRSA procedures directly affect only members, most practitioners in the industry are untouched by either the code or its enforcement. And, even members can avoid action by resigning from the society. In 1986, that course was followed by none other than the society's own president. He resigned as the board of directors was meeting to consider whether he had violated the code. (The president shortly before had signed a consent decree with the Securities and Exchange Commission in a case involving allegations of insider trading based on information gained from a client.)[19]

There have been, then, steps backward as well as forward for practitioners striving for ethical professionalism in public relations. However, if we synthesize specific ethical principles raised in the PRSA and, to a lesser degree, IABC codes, as well as in current writing by leading practitioners and scholars, we note considerable progress toward at least defining exactly what is ethical behavior in PR practice.

PR'S THREE CONSTITUENCIES

The codes and leading textbooks counsel principled behavior toward three major constituencies—clients, the media/public and other practitioners.[20]

VIEWPOINT

PR's "Hot Button" Topics

Susan Fry Bovet, editor of *Public Relations Journal,* a leading PR trade publication, surveyed the industry and found these "burning ethical questions" practitioners must handle in the 1990s:

- Discrimination in human relations, including sexual harassment.
- The flow of misinformation or dissemination of misleading information.
- Propaganda versus the public's right to know.
- Profiting from inside information.
- Misuse of funds.
- Avoiding corporate responsibility for unsafe products or those that can harm consumers.
- Destruction of natural resources or pollution.[21]

With clients, the effort is to establish a professional relationship similar to that between physicians and patients or lawyers and their clients. The PRSA code requires members to "safeguard the confidences of present and former clients." (Societal acceptance of that principle has not yet reached the point where practitioners can refuse in court to divulge client confidences, as can physicians and lawyers.)

Practitioners are counseled to avoid conflict of interest with duty to clients, and generally disclose fully any circumstances that might disadvantage the clients. It's considered unethical to promise clients specific results from a public relations campaign—guaranteeing, for example, a news release will appear in a certain number of newspapers.

Much attention is paid ethical relationships between practitioners and the media/public. Consistent themes in codes and writings on the subject include: Don't conceal the client's identity, purpose or motive; openly identify your role as a public relations practitioner; be truthful, accurate and fair in what you say, write or do on behalf of the client; conduct your professional life, as the PRSA code puts it, "in accord with the public interest"; don't corrupt the integrity of communication (with, for example, false or misleading news releases); and don't corrupt the processes of government (by, for example, unethically lobbying or bribing officials).

Despite their dependence on each other—practitioners need the media to reach the public, the media need information from practitioners—the relationship between the two disciplines is sharply adversarial. Ethical codes and scholarly writings counsel practitioners to exercise principled professionalism in relations with the media by ensuring reporters never are lied to and news releases never falsified.

In addition to such ethical considerations, practitioners operate under legal constraints in dealing with both the media and public. The Securities and Exchange Commission, for example, requires publicly owned companies to fully and promptly disclose information—good or bad—on such things as earnings, dividends, mergers, new products or, that is, anything that might affect the company's stock price. The Fair Trade Commission patrols against deceptive promotion and advertising, fraudulent testimonials and unsubstantiated claims. The Food and Drug Administration regulates promotion of food and drugs.

In defining ethical relations between practitioners, codes and writings generally make two broad points:

First, do nothing to injure the business of another practitioner; don't pirate accounts, for example, or defame another's reputation.

Second, do all you can to enforce adherence by others to ethical standards. This is difficult to make stick. PRSA requires members to report to the society any "unethical, illegal or unfair practices" by other members and appear if summoned as a witness in society investigations of unethical conduct. Yet, PRSA is demonstrably uneasy about enforcing its own code, as we have seen, and many practitioners question the need or feasibility of codes.

THE BOTTOM LINE

Perhaps the public relations industry's fundamental ethical challenge can be stated this way:

Practitioners insert themselves into the information flow in America as champions of institutions, causes and ideas with a right to be heard. They demand access to the marketplace of ideas and claim a legitimacy equal to that of, say, print or broadcast media in influencing public attitudes. And, it must be said, many particularly adroit practitioners carve out influential—not to say operative—roles in how the nation makes its political, economic, social and cultural decisions.

Enormous responsibilities attend such claims for legitimacy and adoption of such influential roles—and surely those responsibilities include helping guarantee the integrity of the information system and its ethical, professional operation.

Should not those who live by influencing the nation's decision-making process undertake to conduct themselves in accord with the highest of principles?

Summary

No study of media ethics is complete without considering the multibillion dollar public relations industry and its enormous impact on news and information reaching the American reading/viewing publics. An estimated 40 percent of news is created, shaped, packaged or handled by public relations practitioners.

For individual practitioners, ethical conflict can arise in trying to vigorously represent a client, yet remain independent in matters of conscience and principle.

For media and society, an ethical question is how much of the public relations output is truthful, legitimate pleading in the marketplace of ideas on behalf of a client, employer, idea or cause, and how much is untruthful and unprincipled.

Bernard Kalb revealed a classic case of ethical conflict when he publicly resigned as U.S. State Department spokesman, rather than front for a secret disinformation campaign that enticed newspaper and broadcast journalists to write untrue stories about U.S.-Libya relations. A public relations disaster flowed from the Libyan affair, underscoring the fundamental weakness of any public relations effort structured on untruths.

By contrast, Johnson & Johnson, a worldwide distributor of pharmaceuticals, achieved a stunning public relations success by fully and openly explaining to the media and public exactly what happened when some of its Extra-Strength Tylenol capsules were poisoned in Chicago-area retail stores, resulting in seven deaths.

The public relations industry has made considerable progress in defining ethical standards for practitioners, notably through efforts of the Public Relations Society of America and International Association of Business Communicators. These groups and writers in public relations counsel standards for three main constituencies: Clients (practitioners should create a professional relationship similar to that between physicians and patients, safeguard client confidences and disclose to a client any possible conflict of interest); media/public (don't conceal the client's identity or motive; identity yourself as a practitioner; be truthful, accurate and fair; and conduct your professional life in accord with public interest); and other practitioners (do nothing to injure another's business or reputation; and do all you can to enforce adherence by others to ethical standards).

However, the public relations industry is far from achieving widespread adherence to such principles or true professionalism.

Notes

1. Scott M. Cutlip, Allen H. Center, Glen M. Broom, *Effective Public Relations,* 6th ed. (Englewood Cliffs, N.J.: Prentice Hall, 1985, p. 429).
2. Allen H. Center and Frank H. Walsh, *Public Relations Practices* (Englewood Cliffs, N.J.: Prentice Hall, 1985, p. 7).
3. Cutlip, Center, Broom, *Effective Public Relations,* op. cit.
4. James McAvoy, "Tactics for the Military in the Media War," *Wall Street Journal,* Feb. 7, 1991, p. A-14.
5. Scott M. Cutlip, interview with author, Athens, Ga., Dec. 7, 1986. For further discussion of ethical issues also see two books by Michael Schudson: *Discovering the News* (New York: Basic Books, 1978, particularly pp. 134–144) and *Advertising, The Uneasy Persuasion* (New York: Basic Books, 1984, pp. 99–128).
6. A *Columbia Journalism Review* study published in March 1981 and quoted by Dennis L. Wilcox, Phillip H. Ault and Warren K. Agee in *Public Relations Strategies and*

Tactics (New York: Harper & Row, 1986, p. 238). This text offers an excellent overview of the public relations industry.

7. For more details on the Kalb affair see David K. Shipler, "Spokesman Quits State Dept. Post on Deception Issue," *New York Times,* national edition, Oct. 9, 1986, p. 1; "Defining Disinformation Dispensers," an editorial, *Advertising Age,* Oct. 20, 1986, p. 17; "Editors Protest to White House," an AP dispatch for morning papers, published in *New York Times,* national edition, Oct. 13, 1986, p. 4; John Walcott, "U.S. Credibility on Libya Is Damaged by White House Campaign of Deception," *Wall Street Journal,* Oct. 6, 1986, p. 7.
8. "Lies Wound America, Not Libya," *New York Times,* national edition, Oct. 3, 1986, p. 22.
9. Associated Press dispatch for morning papers of Oct. 13, 1986, published that day in *New York Times,* p. 4.
10. Bernard Gwertzman, "Shultz Justifies Scaring Qaddafi by Use of Press," *New York Times,* national edition, Oct. 3, 1986, p. 1.
11. "A Most Exclusive Club: Others Who Quit," *New York Times,* national edition, Oct. 9, 1986, p. 8.
12. Foster describes the Tylenol affair in the March 1984 issue of *Public Relations Journal.*
13. Ibid.
14. See particularly Gary Strauss and Michael Clements, "Keeping the Top on a P.R. Disaster," *USA Today,* June 17, 1993, p. 1, and Michael Janofsky, "Under Siege, Pepsi Mounts a TV Counteroffensive," *New York Times,* June 17, 1993, p. C-1. Details of the $35 million cost and share-price recovery are in an Associated Press dispatch from New York for morning papers of Friday, Oct. 8, 1993, and published in the *Atlanta Constitution* under the headline, "Pepsi-Cola Says Syringes Hoax Costly, But Sales in Key Months Still Up 76%," on that date, p. F5.
15. Center and Walsh, *Public Relations Practices,* op. cit., p. 345.
16. Scott Cutlip, interview with author, op. cit.
17. Cutlip, Center, Broom, *Effective Public Relations,* op. cit., p. 452.
18. For early chronology see Ivan Hill, *The Ethical Basis of Economic Freedom* (Chapel Hill, N.C.: American Viewpoint, 1976) and broader background in David F. Linowes, *The Corporate Conscience* (New York: Hawthorne Books, 1974) and Thomas Donaldson, *Corporation and Morality* (Englewood Cliffs, N.J.: Prentice Hall, 1982).
19. The resignation is discussed in a letter dated Oct. 5, 1986, from PRSA's new president, John W. Felton, to society members and in a news release from PRSA of the same date. Further details are in Jack Bernstein, "The Franco Fiasco-The Wages of Sin," *Advertising Age,* Oct. 27, 1986, p. 28, and the weekly newsletter *pr reporter,* Sept. 1, 1986, p. 1.
20. Superb scholarly discussions are in Cutlip, Center, and Broom, *Effective Public Relations,* op. cit.; Center and Walsh, *Public Relations Practices,* op. cit.; writing of a more topical nature often appears in *pr reporter,* a weekly newsletter, PR Publishing Company, Inc., Dudley House, P.O. Box 600, Exeter, N.H., 03833-0600, and *PRSA News,* Public Relations Society of America, 845 Third Avenue, New York, N.Y., 10022.
21. Susan Fry Bovet, "The Burning Question of Ethics," *Public Relations Journal,* Nov. 1993, p. 24.

APPENDIX A

AMERICAN SOCIETY OF NEWSPAPER EDITORS STATEMENT OF PRINCIPLES

PREAMBLE

The First Amendment, protecting freedom of expression from abridgment by any law, guarantees to the people through their press a constitutional right, and thereby places on newspaper people a particular responsibility.

Thus journalism demands of its practitioners not only industry and knowledge but also the pursuit of a standard of integrity proportionate to the journalist's singular obligation.

To this end the American Society of Newspaper Editors sets forth this Statement of Principles as a standard encouraging the highest ethical and professional performance.

ARTICLE I: RESPONSIBILITY

The primary purpose of gathering and distributing news and opinion is to serve the general welfare by informing the people and enabling them to make judgments on the issues of the time. Newspaper men and women who abuse the power of their professional role for selfish motives or unworthy purposes are faithless to that public trust.

The American press was made free not just to inform or just to serve as a forum for debate but also to bring an independent scrutiny to bear on the forces of power in the society, including the conduct of official power at all levels of government.

ARTICLE II: FREEDOM OF THE PRESS

Freedom of the press belongs to the people. It must be defended against encroachment or assault from any quarter, public or private.

Journalists must be constantly alert to see that the public's business is conducted in public. They must be vigilant against all who would exploit the press for selfish purposes.

ARTICLE III: INDEPENDENCE

Journalists must avoid impropriety and the appearance of impropriety as well as any conflict of interest or the appearance of conflict. They should neither accept anything nor pursue any activity that might compromise or seem to compromise their integrity.

ARTICLE IV: TRUTH AND ACCURACY

Good faith with the reader is the foundation of good journalism. Every effort must be made to assure that the news content is accurate, free from bias and in context, and that all sides are presented fairly. Editorials, analytical articles and commentary should be held to the same standards of accuracy with respect to facts as news reports.

Significant errors of fact, as well as errors of omission, should be corrected promptly and prominently.

ARTICLE V: IMPARTIALITY

To be impartial does not require the press to be unquestioning or to refrain from editorial expression. Sound practice, however demands a clear distinction for the reader between news reports and opinion. Articles that contain opinion or personal interpretations should be clearly identified.

ARTICLE VI: FAIR PLAY

Journalists should respect the rights of people involved in the news, observe the common standards of decency and stand accountable to the public for the fairness and accuracy of their news report.

Persons publicly accused should be given the earliest opportunity to respond.

Pledges of confidentiality to news sources must be honored at all costs, and therefore should not be given lightly. Unless there is clear and pressing need to maintain confidences, sources of information should be identified.

These principles are intended to preserve, protect and strengthen the bond of trust and respect between American journalists and the American people, a bond that is essential to sustain the grant of freedom entrusted to both by the nation's founders.

This Statement of Principles was adopted by the ASNE Board of Directors on Oct. 23, 1975; it supplants the 1922 "Cannons of Journalism."

APPENDIX B

SOCIETY OF PROFESSIONAL JOURNALISTS CODE OF ETHICS

SOCIETY of Professional Journalists believes the duty of journalists is to serve the truth.

We BELIEVE the agencies of mass communication are carriers of public discussion and information, acting on their Constitutional mandate and freedom to learn and report the facts.

We BELIEVE in public enlightenment as the forerunner of justice, and in our Constitutional role to seek the truth as part of the public's right to know the truth.

We BELIEVE those responsibilities carry obligations that require journalists to perform with intelligence, objectivity, accuracy and fairness.

To these ends, we declare acceptance of the standards of practice here set forth:

I. RESPONSIBILITY:

The public's right to know of events of public importance and interest is the overriding mission of the mass media. The purpose of distributing news and enlightened opinion is to serve the general welfare. Journalists who use their professional status as representatives of the public for selfish or other unworthy motives violate a high trust.

II. FREEDOM OF THE PRESS:

Freedom of the press is to be guarded as an inalienable right of people in a free society. It carries with it the freedom and the responsibility to discuss, question and challenge actions and utterances of our government and our public and private institutions. Journalists uphold the right to speak unpopular opinions and the privilege to agree with the majority.

III. ETHICS:

Journalists must be free of obligation to any interest other than the public's right to know the truth.

1. Gifts, favors, free travel, special treatment or privileges can compromise the integrity of journalists and their employers. Nothing of value should be accepted.
2. Secondary employment, political involvement, holding public office and service in community organizations should be avoided if it compromises the integrity of journalists and their employers. Journalists and their employers should conduct their personal lives in a manner which protects them from conflict of interest, real or apparent. Their responsibilities to the public are paramount. That is the nature of their profession.
3. So-called news communications from private sources should not be published or broadcast without substantiation of their claims to news value.
4. Journalists will seek news that serves public interest, despite the obstacles. They will make constant efforts to assure that the public's business is conducted in public and that public records are open to public inspection.
5. Journalists acknowledge the newsman's ethic of protecting confidential sources of information.
6. Plagiarism is dishonest and unacceptable.

IV. ACCURACY AND OBJECTIVITY:

Good faith with the public is the foundation of all worthy journalism.

1. Truth is our ultimate goal.
2. Objectivity in reporting the news is another goal that serves as the mark of an experienced professional. It is a standard of performance toward which we strive. We honor those who achieve it.
3. There is no excuse for inaccuracies or lack of thoroughness.
4. Newspaper headlines should be fully warranted by the contents of the articles they accompany. Photographs and telecasts should give an accurate picture of an event and not highlight a minor incident out of context.

5. Sound practice makes clear distinction between news reports and expressions of opinion. News reports should be free of opinion or bias and represent all sides of an issue.
6. Partisanship in editorial comment which knowingly departs from truth violates the spirit of American journalism.
7. Journalists recognize their responsibility for offering informed analysis, comment and editorial opinion on public events and issues. They accept the obligation to present such material by individuals whose competence, experience and judgment qualify them for it.
8. Special articles or presentations devoted to advocacy or the writer's own conclusions and interpretations should be labeled as such.

V. FAIR PLAY:

Journalists at all times will show respect for the dignity, privacy, rights and well-being of people encountered in the course of gathering and presenting the news.

1. The news media should not communicate unofficial charges affecting reputation or moral character without giving the accused a chance to reply.
2. The news media must guard against invading a person's right to privacy.
3. The media should not pander to morbid curiosity about details of vice and crime.
4. It is the duty of the news media to make prompt and complete correction of their errors.
5. Journalists should be accountable to the public for their efforts and the public should be encouraged to voice its grievances against the media. Open dialogue with our readers, viewers or listeners should be fostered.

VI. MUTUAL TRUST:

Adherence to this code is intended to preserve and strengthen the bond of mutual trust and respect between American journalists and the American people.

The Society shall—by programs of education and other means—encourage individual journalists to adhere to these tenets, and shall encourage journalistic publications and broadcasters to recognize their responsibility to frame codes of ethics in concert with their employees to serve as guidelines in furthering these goals.

Adopted 1926, revised 1973, 1984, 1987

APPENDIX C

Radio/Television News Directors Association Code of Broadcast News Ethics

The members of the Radio/Television News Directors Association agree that their prime responsibility as journalists—and that of the broadcasting industry as the collective sponsor of news broadcasting—is to provide to the public they serve a news service as accurate, full and prompt as human integrity and devotion can devise. To that end, they declare their acceptance of the standards of practice here set forth, and their solemn intent to honor them to the limits of their ability.

ARTICLE ONE

The primary purpose of broadcast journalism—to inform the public of events of importance and appropriate interest in a manner that is accurate and comprehensive—shall override all other purposes.

ARTICLE TWO

Broadcast news presentations shall be designed not only to offer timely and accurate information, but also to present it in light of relevant circumstances that give it meaning and perspective.

This standard means that news reports, when clarity demands it, will be laid against pertinent factual background; that factors such as race, creed, nationality or prior status will be reported only when they are relevant; that comment or subjective content will be properly identified; and that errors in fact will be promptly acknowledged and corrected.

ARTICLE THREE

Broadcast journalists shall seek to select material for newscast solely on their evaluation of its merit as news.

This standard means that news will be selected on the criteria of significance, community and regional relevance, appropriate human interest, service to defined audiences. It excludes sensationalism or misleading emphasis in any form; subservience to external or "interested" efforts to influence news selection and presentation, whether from within the broadcasting industry or from without. It requires that such terms as "bulletin" and "flash" be used only when the character of the news justifies them; that bombastic or misleading descriptions of newsroom facilities and personnel be rejected, along with undue use of sound and visual effects; and that promotional or publicity material be sharply scrutinized before use and identified by source or otherwise when broadcast.

ARTICLE FOUR

Broadcast journalists shall at times display humane respect for the dignity, privacy and the well-being of persons with whom the news deals.

ARTICLE FIVE

Broadcast journalists shall govern their personal lives and such nonprofessional associations as many impinge on their professional activities in a manner that will protect them from conflict of interest, real or apparent.

ARTICLE SIX

Broadcast journalists shall seek actively to present all news the knowledge of which will serve the public interest, no matter what selfish, uninformed or corrupt efforts attempt to color it, withhold it or prevent its presentation. They shall make constant effort to open doors closed to the reporting of public proceedings with tools appropriate to broadcasting (including cameras and recorders), consistent with the public interest. They acknowledge the journalist's ethic of protection of confidential information and sources, and urge unswerving observation of it except in instances in which it would clearly and unmistakably defy the public interest.

ARTICLE SEVEN

Broadcast journalists recognize the responsibility borne by broadcasting for informed analysis, comment and editorial opinion on public events and issues. They accept the obligation of broadcasters, for the presentation of such matters by individuals whose competence, experience and judgment qualify them for it.

ARTICLE EIGHT

In court, broadcast journalists shall conduct themselves with dignity, whether the court is in or out of session. They shall keep broadcast equipment as unobtrusive and silent as possible. Where court facilities are inadequate, pool broadcasts should be arranged.

ARTICLE NINE

In reporting matters that are or may be litigated, the journalist shall avoid practices which would tend to interfere with the right of an individual to a fair trial.

ARTICLE TEN

Broadcast journalists shall not misrepresent the source of any broadcast news material.

ARTICLE ELEVEN

Broadcast journalists shall actively censure and seek to prevent violations of these standards, and shall actively encourage their observance by all journalists, whether of the Radio/Television News Directors Association or not.

APPENDIX D

Associated Press Managing Editors Code of Ethics

This code is a model against which newspaper men and women can measure their performance. It is meant to apply to news and editorial staff members, and others who are involved in, or who influence news coverage and editorial policy. It has been formulated in the belief that newspapers and the people who produce them should adhere to the highest standards of ethical and professional conduct.

RESPONSIBILITY

A good newspaper is fair, accurate, honest, responsible, independent and decent. Truth is its guiding principle.

It avoids practices that would conflict with the ability to report and present news in a fair and unbiased manner.

The newspaper should serve as a constructive critic of all segments of society. Editorially, it should advocate needed reform or innovations in the public interest. It should vigorously expose wrongdoing or misuse of power, public or private.

News sources should be disclosed unless there is clear reason not to do so. When it is necessary to protect the confidentiality of a source, the reason should be explained.

The newspaper should background, with the facts, public statements that it knows to be inaccurate or misleading. It should uphold the right of free speech and freedom of the press and should respect the individual's right to privacy.

The public's right to know about matters of importance is paramount, and the newspaper should fight vigorously for public access to news of government through open meetings and open records.

ACCURACY

The newspaper should guard against inaccuracies, carelessness, bias or distortion through either emphasis or omission.

It should admit all substantive errors and correct them promptly and prominently.

INTEGRITY

The newspaper should strive for impartial treatment of issues and dispassionate handling of controversial subjects. It should provide a forum for the exchange of comment and criticism, especially when such comment is opposed to its editorial positions. Editorials and other expressions of opinion by reporters and editors should be clearly labeled.

The newspaper should report the news without regard for its own interests. It should not give favored news treatment to advertisers or special interest groups. It should report matters regarding itself or its personnel with the same vigor and candor as it would other institutions or individuals.

Concern for community, business or personal interests should not cause a newspaper to distort or misrepresent the facts.

CONFLICTS OF INTEREST

The newspaper and its staff should be free of obligations to news sources and special interests. Even the appearance of obligation or conflict of interest should be avoided.

Newspapers should accept nothing of value from news sources or others outside the profession. Gifts and free or reduced-rate travel, entertainment, products and lodging should not be accepted. Expenses in connection with news reporting should be paid by the newspaper. Special favors and special treatment for members of the press should be avoided.

Involvement in such things as politics, community affairs, demonstrations and social causes that could cause a conflict of interest, or the appearance of such conflict, should be avoided.

Stories should not be written or edited primarily for the purpose of winning awards and prizes. Blatantly commercial journalism contests, or others that reflect unfavorably on the newspaper or the profession, should be avoided.

No code of ethics can prejudge every situation. Common sense and good judgment are required in applying ethical principles to newspaper realities. Individual newspapers are encouraged to augment these guidelines with locally produced codes that apply more specifically to their own situations.

Adopted 1975

APPENDIX E

Dow Jones & Company Conflicts of Interest Policy

Growth of business and financial reporting by newspapers and television forces editors to consider more carefully ethical implications in handling that type news, and, particularly, possible conflicts of interest. Dow Jones & Company, Inc., publisher of the *Wall Street Journal* and other newspapers, has a detailed policy each employee must adhere to as a condition of employment. Pertinent excerpts:

CONFLICTS OF INTEREST POLICY

This policy statement is designed to provide all employees with guidelines which will enable them to avoid conflicts of interest that might be construed to be detrimental to the best interests of Dow Jones. It is important for all employees to keep in mind the tremendous embarrassment and damage to the Company's reputation and that of fellow employees that could come about through a lapse in judgment by one person, or someone closely associated with that person, no matter how well-intended that person may be. Because we think it is so essential that every employee be above suspicion, we consider any slip in judgment in the areas covered in this policy statement to be serious enough to warrant dismissal.

CONFIDENTIAL INFORMATION

1. Employees should not use, directly or indirectly, for their own or any other person's financial gain, any information about Dow Jones which the

employee obtained in connection with Dow Jones employment. Further, employees should not disclose to anyone confidential information obtained in connection with Dow Jones employment until such information has been made available to the public . . .

SECURITY TRANSACTIONS

6. Dow Jones has always had a strict policy on security transactions by employees who have access to inside information regarding unpublished stories or advertising schedules. It also has had a strict related policy on the conduct of news and advertising staff members dealing with corporations we cover or whose advertising we carry. Each employee is expected to bend over backwards to avoid any action, no matter how well-intentioned, that could provide grounds for suspicion:

   a. that an employee, his family or other close to the employee made financial gains by acting on the basis of inside information gained through a position on our staff, before it was available to the general public. Such information includes hold-for-release material, our plans for running stories, items that may affect price movements, or projected advertising campaigns;
   b. that the writing of a news story or item or scheduling of advertising was influenced by a desire to affect the stock's prices;
   c. that an employee is financially committed in the market so deeply or in such other way to create a temptation to biased writing or scheduling of advertising;
   d. that an employee is beholden to brokers or any other group we cover or advertisers. Such indebtedness could arise through acceptance of favors, gifts or payments for performing writing assignments or other services for them;
   e. that an employee is beholden for any tips, allocations or underwritten new issues or in any other way to anyone in the financial community.

We do not want to penalize our staff members by suggesting that they not buy stocks or make other investments. We do, however, want employees to avoid speculation or the appearance of speculation. Members of the Management Committee, national department heads, and members of the news and advertising departments must not engage in short-term trading; they must hold securities a minimum of six (6) months, unless they get approval from the Vice President/Legal or his designee to meet some special need. They must not buy or sell basically speculative instruments such as futures or options. No employee of the Company should engage in short selling of securities.

We reiterate that it is not enough to be incorruptible and act with honest motives. It is equally important to use good judgment and conduct one's outside activities so that no one—management, our editors, an SEC investigator, or a political critic of the Company—has any grounds for even raising the suspicion that an employee misused a position with the Company.

With these general propositions in mind, here are some further specific guidelines:

i. First and foremost, all material gleaned by you in the course of your work for Dow Jones is deemed to be strictly the Company's property. This includes not only the fruits of your own and your colleague's work, but also information on plans for running items and articles on particular companies and industries and advertising schedules in future issues. Such material must never be disclosed to anyone outside the Company, including friends and relatives. Viewing information as the Company's property should avoid a great many of the obvious pitfalls.

ii. No employee regularly assigned to a specific industry should invest, nor should his family, in any company engaged in whole or significant part in that industry.

iii. No employee with knowledge of a forthcoming article, item or advertisement concerning a company or industry should, prior to the publication of such article, item or advertisement, invest or in any way encourage or assist any other person in selling a security in that company prior to publication without the approval of the appropriate Management Committee member.

iv. Further, any employee having prior knowledge of a forthcoming article, item or advertisement, should delay buying or selling the securities of the company involved, as should his family, until the general public has an opportunity to read and digest the information contained in any Dow Jones publication or news service. Employees should wait two full trading days after an article or advertisement first appears in a Dow Jones publication or news service.

v. If an employee thinks there is a possibility he or a family member may have inadvertently violated any of the above guidelines, or if an employee should buy a security prior to publication, and then acquire knowledge of a proposed article, item or advertisement, the employee should notify his or her department head as soon as practical. In the case of a purchase, the employee or family member should hold the security for six months.

SERVING ON THE BOARDS OF DIRECTORS OF OTHER COMPANIES

7. Dow Jones' employees are prohibited except with written approval of the chief executive officer from serving as directors or officers of any other company devoted to profit-making. This prohibition, of course, does not apply to

employees appointed to serve as directors or officers of companies in which Dow Jones has a significant equity interest. If an employee is involved in a family-owned profit-making business, clearance should be obtained from the appropriate member of the Management Committee . . .

Should any question ever arise in your mind as to propriety of your activity, you are urged to consult in confidence with your national department head or any Dow Jones officer.

We would like to emphasize that we have complete confidence in all our employees. It is essential, however, that all of us maintain the highest standards of ethics in the conduct of Dow Jones' business in actuality and also in appearances by acting within the framework of these guidelines. Please retain this policy statement in your files.

APPENDIX F

THE ADVERTISING CODE OF AMERICAN BUSINESS

1. Truth. Advertising shall tell the truth, and reveal significant facts, the concealment of which would mislead the public.
2. Responsibility. Advertising agencies and advertisers shall be willing to provide substantiation of claims made.
3. Taste and Decency. Advertising shall be free of statements, illustrations or implications which are offensive to good taste or public decency.
4. Disparagement. Advertising shall offer merchandise or service on its merits and refrain from attacking competitors unfairly or disparaging their products, services or methods of doing business.
5. Bait Advertising. Advertising shall offer only merchandise or services which are readily available for purchase at the advertised price.
6. Guarantees and Warranties. Advertising of guarantees and warranties shall be explicit. Advertising of any guarantee or warranty shall clearly and conspicuously disclose its nature and extent, the manner in which the guarantor or warrantor will perform and the identity of the guarantor or warrantor.
7. Price Claims. Advertising shall avoid price or savings claims which are false or misleading, or which do not offer provable bargains or savings.
8. Unprovable Claims. Advertising shall avoid the use of exaggerated or unprovable claims.
9. Testimonials. Advertising shall be limited to those of competent witnesses who are reflecting a real and honest choice.

This code was developed by the American Advertising Federation and Association of Better Business International. It has been endorsed by many newspaper, broadcast and other trade groups.

APPENDIX G

PUBLIC RELATIONS SOCIETY OF AMERICA CODE OF PROFESSIONAL STANDARDS FOR THE PRACTICE OF PUBLIC RELATIONS

Members of the Public Relations Society of America base their professional principles on the fundamental value and dignity of the individual, holding that the free exercise of human rights, especially freedom of speech, freedom of assembly and freedom of the press, is essential to the practice of public relations.

In serving the interests of the clients and employers, we dedicate ourselves to the goals of better communication, understanding and cooperation among the diverse individuals, groups and institutions of society, and of equal opportunity of employment in the public relations profession.

We pledge:

To conduct ourselves professionally, with truth, accuracy, fairness and responsibility to the public;

To improve our individual competence and advance the knowledge and proficiency of the profession through continuing research and education;

And to adhere to the articles of the Code of Professional Standards for the Practice of Public Relations as adopted by the governing Assembly of the Society.

ARTICLES OF THE CODE

These articles have been adopted by the Public Relations Society of America to promote and maintain high standards of public service and ethical conduct among its members.

1. A member shall deal fairly with clients or employers, past or present, or potential, with fellow practitioners and the general public.
2. A member shall conduct his or her professional life in accord with the public interest.
3. A member shall adhere to truth and accuracy and to generally accepted standards of good taste.
4. A member shall not represent conflicting or competing interests without the express consent of those involved, given after a full disclosure of the facts; nor place himself or herself in a position where the member's interest is or may be in conflict with a duty to a client, or others, without a full disclosure of such interests to all involved.
5. A member shall safeguard the confidences of present and former clients, as well as those of persons or entities who have disclosed confidences to a member in the context of communications relating to an anticipated professional relationship with such member, and shall not accept retainers or employment that may involve disclosing using or offering to use such confidences to the disadvantage or prejudice of such present, former or potential clients or employers.
6. A member shall not engage in any practice which tends to corrupt the integrity of channels of communication or the processes of government.
7. A member shall not intentionally communicate false or misleading information and is obliged to use care to avoid communication of false or misleading information.
8. A member shall be prepared to identify publicly the name of the client or employer on whose behalf any public communication is made.
9. A member shall not make use of any individual or organization purporting to serve or represent an announced cause, or purporting to be independent or unbiased, but actually serving an undisclosed special or private interest of a member, client, or employer.
10. A member shall not intentionally injure the professional reputation or practice of another practitioner. However, if a member has evidence that another member has been guilty of unethical, illegal or unfair practices, including those in violation of this Code, the member shall present the information promptly to the proper authorities of the Society for action in accordance with the procedure set forth in Article XIII of the By-laws.
11. A member called as a witness in a proceeding for the enforcement of this Code shall be bound to appear, unless excused for sufficient reason by the Judicial Panel.

12. A member, in performing services for a client or employer, shall not accept fees, commissions or any other valuable consideration from anyone other than the client or employer in connection with those services without the express consent of the client or employer, given after a full disclosure of the facts.
13. A member shall not guarantee the achievement of specified results beyond the member's direct control.
14. A member shall, as soon as possible, sever relations with any organization or individual if such relationship requires conduct contrary to the articles of this Code.

Adopted 1954; Revised 1959, 1963, 1977, 1983

APPENDIX H

FREEDOM OF INFORMATION SERVICE CENTER SAMPLE LETTER

The following letter is recommended by the Freedom of Information Service Center, Washington, D.C., for requesting documents under the Freedom of Information Act.

Business telephone number
Return address
Date

Name of Public Body
Address

To the FOI Officer:

This request is made under the federal Freedom of Information Act, 5 U.S.C. 552.

Please send me copies of *(Here, clearly describe what you want. Include identifying material, such as names, places, and the period of time about which you are inquiring. If you wish, attach news clips, reports, and other documents describing the subject of your research.)*_______.

As you know, the FOI Act provides that if portions of a document are exempt from release, the remainder must be segregated and disclosed. Therefore, I will expect you to send me all nonexempt portions of the records I have requested, and ask that you justify any deletions by reference to specific exemptions of the FOI Act. I reserve the right to appeal your decision to withhold any materials.

I promise to pay reasonable search and duplication fees in connection with this request. However, if you estimate that the total fees will exceed $_______, please notify me so that I may authorize expenditure of a greater amount.

(Optional) I am prepared to pay reasonable search and duplication fees in connection with this request. However, the FOI Act provides for waiver or reduction of fees if disclosure could not be considered as "primarily benefiting the general public." I am a journalist *(author or scholar)* employed by *(name of news organization, book publishers, etc.)*, and intend to use the information I am requesting as the basis for a planned article *(broadcast or book). (Add arguments here in support of fee waiver.)* Therefore, I ask that you waive all search and application fees. If you deny this request, however, and the fees will exceed $_______, please notify me of the charges before you fill my request so that I may decide whether to pay the fees or appeal your denial of my request for a waiver.

As I am making this request in the capacity of a journalist *(author or scholar)* and this information is of timely value, I will appreciate your communicating with me by telephone, rather than by mail, if you have any questions regarding this request. Thank you for your assistance, and I will look forward to receiving your reply within ten business days, as required by law.

Sincerely,
(Signature)

APPENDIX I

ASSOCIATED PRESS SPORTS EDITORS ETHICS GUIDELINES

1. The newspaper pays its staffer's way for travel, accommodations, food and drink.

   (a) If a staffer travels on a chartered team plane, the newspaper should insist on being billed. If the team cannot issue a bill, the amount can be calculated by estimating the cost of a similar flight on a commercial airline.

   (b) When services are provided to a newspaper by a pro or college team, those teams should be reimbursed by the newspaper. This includes providing telephone, typewriter or fax service.

2. Editors and reporters should avoid taking part in outside activities or employment that might create conflict of interest or even appearance of a conflict.

   (a) They should not serve as an official scorer at baseball games.

   (b) They should not write for team or league media guides or other team or league publications. This has the potential of compromising a reporter's disinterested observations.

   (c) Staffers who appear on radio or television should understand that their first loyalty is to the paper.

3. Writers and writers' groups should adhere to Associated Press Managing Editors and APSE standards: No deals, discounts or gifts except those of insignificant value or those available to the public.

   (a) If a gift is impossible or impractical to return, donate the gift to charity.
   (b) Do not accept free memberships or reduced fees for membership. Do not accept gratis use of facilities, such as golf courses or tennis courts, unless it is used as part of doing a story for the newspaper.
   (c) Sports editors should be aware of standards of conduct of groups and professional associations to which their writers belong and the ethical standards to which those groups adhere, including areas such as corporate sponsorship from news sources it covers.

4. A newspaper should not accept free tickets, although press credentials needed for coverage and coordination are acceptable.
5. A newspaper should carefully consider the implications of voting for all awards and all-star teams and decide if such voting creates a conflict of interest.
6. A newspaper's own ethical guidelines should be followed, and editors and reporters should be aware of standards acceptable for use of unnamed sources and verification of information obtained other than from primary news sources.

   (a) Sharing and pooling of notes and quotes should be discouraged. If a reporter uses quotes gained secondhand, that should be made known to the readers. A quote could be attributed to a newspaper or to another reporter.

7. Assignments should be made on merit, without regard for race or gender.

Guidelines can't cover everything. Use common sense and good judgment in applying these guidelines in adopting local codes.

Adopted June 22, 1991

APPENDIX J

National Victim Center's Suggested Media Code of Ethics

I shall:

- Provide the public with factual, objective information about crime stories concerning:

  the type of crime that has occurred;

  the community where the crime occurred;

  the name or description of the alleged offender if appropriate under existing state law; and

  significant facts that may prevent other crimes.

- Present a balanced view of crime by ensuring that the victim and the criminal perspective are given equal coverage when possible;
- Advise victim and survivors that they may be interviewed "off the record" or "on the record" if they desire such an interview, and advise them that they have a right not to be interviewed at all;
- Quote victims, families and friends fairly and in context;

  Avoid photographing or filming crime scene details or follow-up activities such as remains of bodies or brutality, instruments of torture, disposal of bodies, etc.; and

- Notify and ask permission from victims and their families before using pictures or photographs for documentaries or other news features.

I shall not:

- Photograph, film or print for publication photographs of victims, graphic crime scenes or victims in the courtroom without permission;
- Print or broadcast unverified or ambiguous facts about the victim, his or her demeanor, background or relationship to the offender;
- Print facts about the crime, the victim or the criminal act that might embarrass, humiliate, hurt or upset the victim unless there is a need to publish such details for public safety reasons;
- Print, broadcast, photograph or film lurid or graphic details of the crime; and
- Promote sensationalism in reporting crime or criminal court cases in any way.

This code was developed in a 1985 symposium co-sponsored by *Women in News* of Seattle and Seattle University and is strongly endorsed by the National Victim Center for journalists in contact with crime victims.

APPENDIX K

AMERICAN SOCIETY OF MAGAZINE EDITORS GUIDELINES FOR ADVERTISING

GUIDELINES FOR ADVERTISING PAGES

1. Any page of advertising that contains text or design elements that have an editorial appearance must be clearly and conspicuously identified with the words *advertising* or *advertisement* horizontally at or near the center of the top of the page in type at least equal in size and weight to the publication's normal editorial body type face.
2. The layout, design and type face of advertising pages should be distinctly different from the publication's normal layout, design and type faces.
3. No advertisement or advertising section may be promoted on the cover of the magazine or included in the editorial table of contents. The publication's name or logo should not appear on any advertising pages except that normal footlines may be used at the bottom of each page in the magazine's usual way.
4. Advertising pages should not be placed adjacent to editorial material in a manner that implies editorial endorsement of the advertised products or services.
5. In order for the publication's chief editor to have the opportunity to monitor compliance with the guidelines, advertising pages should be made available to the editor in ample time for review and to recommend any necessary changes.

GUIDELINES FOR SPECIAL ADVERTISING SECTIONS

A special advertising section is a set of advertising pages unified by a theme, accompanied by editorial-like text that supports the theme, consisting of two or more pages, often including a cover, that is supplied or printed by the publication and paid for by one or more advertisers.

1. Each text page of special advertising must be clearly and conspicuously identified as a message paid for by advertisers.
2. In order to identify special advertising sections clearly and conspicuously:

   (a) The words *advertising, advertisement, special advertising section,* or *special advertising supplement* should appear horizontally at or near the top of every page of such sections containing text, in type at least equal in size and weight to the publication's normal editorial body type face. (The word *advertorial* should not be used.)

   (b) The layout, design and type of such sections should be distinctly different from the publication's normal layout, design and typefaces.

   (c) Special advertising sections should not be slugged on the publication's cover or included in the editorial table of contents.

   (d) If the sponsor or organizer of the section is not the publisher, the sponsor should be clearly identified.

3. The editors' names and titles should not appear on, or be associated with, special advertising sections, nor should the names and titles of any other editorial staff members of the publication or regular contributors to it appear or be associated with special advertising sections. The publication's name or logo should not appear as any part of the headlines or text of such sections.
4. Editors and other editorial staff members should not prepare advertising sections for their own publication, for other publications in their field, or advertisers in the fields they cover.
5. In order for the publication's chief editor to have the opportunity to monitor compliance with these guidelines, material for special advertising sections should be made available to the editor in ample time for review and to recommend necessary changes. Monitoring would include reading the text of special advertising sections before publication for problems of fact, interpretation and taste, and for compliance with any relevant laws.
6. In order to avoid potential conflicts or overlaps with editorial content, publishers should notify editors well in advance of their plans to run special advertising sections.
7. The size and number of special advertising sections within a single issue should not be out of balance with the size and nature of the magazine.

Name Index

Subject Index